THE DEMOCRATIC PARTY

Reprints in Government and Political Science

Editor-in-Chief: Richard H. Leach

DUKE UNIVERSITY

THE DEMOCRATIC PARTY
A History

By

FRANK R. KENT

With a New Introduction by
ARTHUR KROCK
The New York Times (ret.)

Reprinted with the permission of
Appleton-Century, an affiliate of Meredith Press

JOHNSON REPRINT CORPORATION
New York and London
1968

71444

INTRODUCTION

This is the second reprint of a book in which Frank Richardson Kent of the *Baltimore Sun* analyzed the political process of the United States with the first-hand knowledge, native skill, and high journalistic integrity that made the book a classic in its field.

The first reprint, which, like this one, appeared years after the original publication, was "The Great Game of Politics" (Doubleday, Doran, 1930). The quality of permanence which lent to that book the abiding freshness of its text will be found in this new edition of "The Democratic Party."

It is an astonishing quality, especially so to other political writers who have cast their experience and observations in book form while maintaining the flow of their newspaper columns. Such books are coming off the presses in steadily increasing numbers. But I venture to doubt that many will survive the test of time as durably as I believe this one will, or impress a new generation of readers of political commentary as greatly as it did those who read the book when it first appeared.

There is an inexorably transient character in daily newspaper and periodical commentary that usually drifts into books by the same authors. Rarely can a journalist, necessarily being a short-range observer, write "for the ages."

His diaries and other forms of reporting the events he saw, and his impressions of the principals in these events, are often valuable, sometimes essential, footnotes to the solid history of an era. A historian, however, he basically is not, by the nature of his calling. Nor is he likely to produce a work on the subjects with which he is directly concerned that will not soon be overtaken and rendered obsolete.

But, though the Democratic Party sharply changed its course after the original of this reprint was published, Kent's anatomy of the party remains scientifically sound as well as enormously readable.

Not since Sydenham analyzed the causes and treatment of gout, and Harvey presented the facts of the circulation of the blood, has medical science improved on these findings of the seventeenth century. Of the party period which Kent covered in his history, I believe the same judgment can be made. That is because it reflects the same intuition, and extraordinary perceptiveness of the subject, that the great English physicians brought to their research.

The comparison seems apt to me because Kent's treatment of politics and politicians was definitely therapeutic. He was an editorial vivisector of what he adjudged to be the shams of both. For a number of years after he began writing the columns—then appearing only in the *Sun*—he adhered to the primarily reportorial form in his notable journalism. After it became a syndicated product in 1932, subscribed to and published regularly by more than 200 newspapers, the column took on the chief aspect of critical, editorial analysis, which could be and often was devastating.

But, though the articles became more and more editorial, Kent continued to seek out original sources for first-hand information on the facts before he evaluated them for his readers. For this and other reasons his career deserves to live in the memory of the American people, who benefited by his labor, and to serve as a model for all who are or hope to become political reporters and commentators.

He preserved the highest journalistic standard in not presenting as "fact" what was only "opinion," and it was plainly marked as such. In his wholly reportorial activity, Kent could not count the important news disclosures he was the first to make.

As aforesaid, he was diligent as a vivisector of the shams of politics and politicians. But simultaneously he attacked the attitude that politics is a low calling, conducted by the unsavory. "Political organizations," he wrote, "are absolutely essential to the conduct of government—city, state, or nation. . . . Without organizations there would be no parties. Without parties there would be no government."

Politics for him had an abiding fascination. Probably he was the first American reporter to write, on a fixed and continuing schedule of publication, articles of news analysis and comment that dealt entirely with politics and politicans and were nationally distributed. Yet when, in the nineteen-twenties, he was offered support for the Democratic nomination for United States Senator from Maryland that virtually assured it, and his election as well, he declined to stand as a matter of principle.

His answer was that, being unable to finance his own campaign, he would not enter into office beholden to any group or individual. This same determination to preserve his independence from any blandishment carried over into his own professional sphere.

He dined one evening in Washington at a time when he was writing very critical comments on several Democratic Senators with whom he had most agreeable private relations. "You are grieving your friends in the Senate," said one of them. "Who said I want any 'friends in the Senate'?" was the tart reply.

This acerbity, sometimes visible in private exchanges, was part of Kent's makeup. Also, he had strong prejudices for and against persons in public life, and these were unmistakably to be discerned in his simple, clear-cut prose. But he marked his targets plainly as personal estimates, scrupulously presenting the facts from which he drew the unfavorable conclusions. And throughout his career he wrote as he behaved—like a gentleman.

Typical of this was his return to President Truman of a hand-written personal disclosure so intimate that Kent felt he had no right to receive or retain the letter. He did keep a second hand-written letter in which the President thanked him for his rare and delicate act of consideration.

In private association, Kent charmed those he chose to; and they were not everyone—far from it! His humor was deep-seated, his wit sparkling, his speech eloquent and cultivated. A man small in stature, his presence could fill a room and become the focus of attention.

He drank and ate sparingly, but he was a gourmet whom the exquisite cuisine of the Maryland Club had nourished. I learned this one morning in Indianapolis.

He and I used to travel around the country appraising

political situations and prospects (this was before the time of the more or less clairvoyant Gallup & Company pre-election polls), and that morning he ordered deviled lamb kidneys for breakfast at the Claypool Hotel.

He might as well have asked for toasted hummingbird tongues: the incredulity of waiter, head-waiter, and chef could not have been more profound. Whereupon Kent rose from the table, saying: "I will not abide in this culinary desert. I'm taking the next train to Chicago, where you can join me after wrapping up the story."

And *he* did and *I* did.

Two years before Kent's death in 1958, at the age of 81, James M. Cain, the distinguished novelist and an old Baltimore newspaper colleague, wrote an impression of Kent whom he had not seen for many years. I append it in the hope that, as the new reader begins "The Democratic Party," something of the personality of its author will enrich the pages as it enriched my life and the lives of all who had the privilege of his companionship.

- - - - - -

"Mentally, or whatever you would call it, life has done marvelous things to him, for not only does he have his old geniality, but in some strange way, an increased warmth that was most affecting to feel. . . . The only chance I really had to say anything was in his limousine, when he hauled Hamilton Owens, Alfred Knopf, and me to Marconi's for the lunch we were going to have, but it was a sort of gumbo-yaya, with everyone talking at once, and I got cut off each time I tried. He got talking about [Herbert Bayard] Swope, whom he had seen, remarking the red was all gone from his hair, which he seemed to think most astonishing, and that [Swope] didn't asseverate all over the conversation the way he used to; and when I said 'this is the most perfect characterization in five words I ever heard,' he said: 'Well Jim, he did, you've got to admit it'—laughing very gaily, and suddenly it was Frank Kent, as always, quite indescribably delightful."

Arthur Krock

THOMAS JEFFERSON
The founder of the Democratic party

The Democratic Party

A HISTORY

Frank R. Kent

AUTHOR OF

"THE GREAT GAME OF POLITICS," "THE STORY OF MARYLAND POLITICS"

The Century Co.

NEW YORK   LONDON

FOREWORD

THE idea of this book is to tell the story of the Democratic party as a reporter rather than as a historian. There is no attempt here to compile a Democratic textbook, or to assume that those who read it are so ignorant of political history that all the fundamental facts must be fully stated as if they were entirely new. Complete political statistics, election and convention figures are to be easily found in almanacs and numerous other publications and it seemed unnecessary to give them here save as they were essential to the continuity of the account. So far as the author knows, however, there has not been any effort made to present in a single book a connected narrative of the Democratic party from its beginning—136 years ago—a narrative that would accurately describe its birth, picture the five great figures around whom its history has been largely draped, tell in consecutive form of its great victories and its equally great defeats, its undeniable merits and national service and its equally undeniable faults and frequent futility. It seemed that the age, the character, the successes, the failures, the past, the present, and the future of the Democratic party made such a book worth while. While recognizing the impossibility of analyzing public men or discussing

political causes and results without creating controversy, the effort in this book is at least to keep such
analysis and discussion free from partisan bias. The
purpose is not to glorify the Democratic party but to
tell the truth about it.

F. R. K.

Contents

Contents

Illustrations

ix

Illustrations

Illustrations

The Democratic Party

A History

The Democratic Party

A History

Chapter I

THE DEMOCRATIC PARTY IS INDESTRUCTIBLE

To attempt a complete history of the Democratic party, the oldest continuously existing political instrumentality in America, would be an appalling job. Volumes could be and have been written about its particular periods and around its outstanding personalities. To expect adequately to give the whole story in a single book is not reasonable. That might be done with the party now in power, and easily enough with those that lived awhile and passed away, but not with the Democratic party—not with a party whose unbroken life-line is one hundred and thirty years long; not with a party that through five generations has produced more interesting and influential figures than all the others combined; not with a party which, for good or bad, even in defeat has played a potent part in every national crisis and political development since the end of the eighteenth century.

3

The Democratic Party: A History

To such an extent is the history of this party also the history of the country that in writing even an outline sketch with the purpose of presenting merely the vital facts and figures in connected and coherent form, there is danger of being lost in the overwhelming mass of material. The real difficulty is to keep a view sufficiently clear and detached to enable the whole picture to be adequately seen and not to permit the genuine and indisputable greatness of the basic Democratic principles, the vast national value and essential soundness of the historic Democratic doctrines, and the inspiring fineness of intermittent Democratic achievement to obscure the almost incredible record of stupidity and failure, the frequency and violence with which its performances have clashed with its professions; the wreck it has time and again made of its own prospects, and the relative state of impotency to which it has apparently been reduced in the last four years through the poison of religious bigotry which has saturated its system. Least of all should the greatness of Democratic principles be obscured by an unprecedented prosperity, for which the Republicans are not responsible, but which none the less absorbs all criticism and which has plunged the people generally into an extraordinary state of political inertia and indifference. A final contributing cause of the existing situation has been of course the failure of the party to apply its fundamental tenet of States' rights to the single vibrant issue of the period,

4

prohibition—which failure is a completely typical proceeding.

On the other hand, it seems just as vital that the present abject state of the party, its obvious handicaps and divisions, should neither blot out understanding and appreciation of the really noble political and philosophical conceptions on which it was founded, nor lend reality to the false idea that it is to-day on its last legs, able to stand exactly one more crash in a Presidential election—that it is doomed to defeat, destruction, and disappearance. To forget the grandeur of the first is unthinkable; to believe the second is silly. It is the half-baked notion current among those who know as little of the practical politics of the present as they do of the real significance of the past, and it is calculatingly promoted by the propaganda and publicity agencies of the Republicans whose interest it obviously is to create, continue, and deepen such an impression. Actually no clear-headed and posted person takes the least stock in this stuff nor in the accompanying talk of the rise of a third party that will edge the Democrats out of second place. If there were not ample and convincing evidence of the ability of the Democratic party to survive an infinite number of national defeats without lowering its vitality in the individual States or appreciably diminishing its party representation in the national Congress, there are still any number of concrete facts past and present to make that notion untenable. One of these is the plain absurdity, on the basis of two Presidential defeats and a discouraging prospect, of wiping out of existence not only the oldest but the only really national party in the country—and one which happens to be the only party with a functioning organization in every one of the forty-eight States. It becomes particularly absurd when is recalled the frightful wreck of the party on the terrible rock of slavery, and the pregnant fact that after six consecutive national defeats following that great disaster it not only survived but in 1884 actually elected a Democratic President —Grover Cleveland; lost with him in 1888, regained the White House with him in 1892, and then proceeded stupidly, stubbornly, and everlastingly hard to again smash up on the treacherous Free Silver shoals in 1896.

For sixteen miserable years it then sloshed around without unity, wisdom, or strength, broken, beaten, futile, foolish, unable to shake off its incubus, straighten out the kinks in the party spine, get back to fundamentals. It may be recalled that at that time too there was considerable talk, after its third Presidential reverse, of the "death blow" dealt the Democracy, and a good deal was written and said about a new party to rise from the ashes of the old. But all that was completely buried and forgotten in 1912—four years later—when the Democracy, carrying forty of the forty-eight States, emerged from the campaign with the triumphant election of a Democratic President—Woodrow Wilson—in whose first administration concededly more constructive and important legislation was enacted than in any that had preceded it, and in whose second administration the nation participated in the greatest war of all history, on a scale unprecedented and undreamed of and with an ultimate success well beyond just criticism.

From the political standpoint the thing about that war that will in the eyes of all fair-minded men redound to the eternal credit of the Democratic party and its President is that from start to finish it was conducted without the taint of graft or the smell of scandal. There is plenty of room to question the wisdom of the Wilson administration before, during, and after the war. It is possible to point out flaws in judgment, gross misconceptions and blunders, grave errors of omission and commission, but it is not possible to sustain an attack on its honesty of purpose and conduct. Waste there was, of course, because all war is waste—and this was the greatest of all wars—but no wholesale stealings, no great governmental frauds, no War Department thievery. No greater tribute to any political party was ever paid by its opponents than that rendered the Democrats by the result of the "investigation into the conduct of the war" instituted by the Republican administration which followed its close and which went in proclaiming its purpose to "expose and punish the war-time thieves." After the expenditure of more than a million in money and nearly two years of painstaking probes, they found exactly nothing beyond two or three instances so amusingly petty that it was the Democrats who desired and sought publicity for them and the Republicans who did not. The net result was a reluctant and involuntary certificate of character from one political party as to the cleanness with which the other political party had conducted a great war—a thing without parallel, so far as can be recalled, in this or any other country, and a thing to which there have been some striking contrasts in this and other nations.

In another generation or so perhaps the unique character of this record and its full significance in face of the unstinted billions poured out in our two years of war participation, will be more clearly grasped. There are two reasons why it now lacks general appreciation or even general knowledge. One is because it is still too close to the war for all bitterness to have disappeared or to permit a calm view unclouded by political hate and prejudice. Another is because the Republican party has naturally not been interested in proclaiming Democratic honesty and achievement, particularly when, in advance of its exhaustive and determined investigatoin, it had sweepingly denied both.

The Democrats themselves failed to impress upon the public mind the real meaning of what must seem to a clear and balanced judgment one of the most if not the most creditable performance in its entire career—and for a number of reasons. For one thing, the Republicans came into power so quickly following the end of the war that they had no real chance. They not only came in but they have stayed in, which means that the Democrats, besides losing in prestige and position, were forced to relinquish to the enemy the immense publicity advantages that go with control of the Government and occupancy of the White House. They had lost the megaphone and could not make themselves nationally heard. For another thing, the people generally were terribly bored with the war and wanted to forget it. For still another, the Republican charges of thievery before their investigation made the initial impression, and the wave of prosperity upon which we still ride, arising about the time the investigation came to a fruitless end, absorbed all political emotion save that of soggy contentment. Finally, having lost their leader, the Democrats themselves were—most of them—too inert, inane, and discouraged either to drive home or make full use of what should have become, and under the right leadership with a little luck would have become, a priceless political asset.

All this is not stressed here at the beginning of this book with any purpose of glorifying the Democratic party. That is not, as I hope will be seen clearly enough before long, the idea of this work at all. There could be no surer way to rob it of all value. It is dwelt on here for two reasons—first, because it happens to be an incontrovertible truth which has been largely overlooked by contemporary writers and speakers, but is much too big to be ignored by any save the extreme partisan even in an outline history such as this; second, to further show the silliness of suggesting that a party that was capable of rallying after the slavery smash-up and presenting the two Cleveland administrations, and that, after the three Bryan and the Parker defeats, came sweeping back into power with the two Wilson administrations, could disappear after four, eight, twelve, or twenty years of "wandering in the wilderness." In addition to these reasons, so long as the "solid South," comprising one third of all the States, is unshakably wedded to the Democratic party nationally as well as locally, the opposition to the Republicans in other States will continue to call itself Democratic, regardless of issues and defeats. That is essential to the mechanics of the modern political state and city organization. Every man who knows precinct politics, which is the basis of all politics—at least in the United States—recognizes that. The point here sought to be made is that the Democratic party has a future as well as a past, no matter how things may look, what the flavor of the current propaganda, or what the result of the next election: that this outline is written not as an obituary but in the belief, shared, I think, by most men versed in practical politics and capable of a detached judgment, that soon or late it will come again into power. Further, that it really is a fool-proof party whose indestructibility is a most fortunate thing for the country. It is true that at this time it is issueless and leaderless, torn by doubt and divisions, and without prestige in the country. Also, it is up against a period of industrial prosperity—beginning to ebb a little now but still literally the wonder of the world, unapproached in any country at any time—though the farmer and the cotton-grower have not as yet had their share. In addition, the Democratic party is as usual financially embarrassed, without adequate journalistic support and depressed by the apparently overpowering physical strength of the other side, which, through the industrial development of the past forty years has become normally the most numerous party and which has not yet had a long enough tenure of unchecked power to begin to crack. But the issue will evolve, the leader arise, and the crack come. It may happen in the 1928 campaign. There is no reason why it should not; some very cogent ones why it should. Or it may not happen for four or even eight years. It is, however, impossible to doubt that it will happen. Democratic history supports that conviction.

In the meantime, it is certainly true that so interwoven are the two that no real understanding of the history of the country is possible without a clear knowledge of the history of the Democratic party. Although since 1860 it has elected but two Presidents, it has elected each of those twice, and no unprejudiced and posted person is likely to dispute

11

that those four administrations have been the most eventful, effective, far reaching of any since the close of the Civil War. The facts prove it. When in addition it is realized that in the one hundred and forty years that have elapsed since the first President was chosen and this Government of ours began to function, the Democrats have directed its destinies for considerably more than half that time— eighty years, to be exact—the reasons why it seems worth while to present in concrete and consecutive form the story of this party can be understood.

Chapter II

Jefferson's Letter to Washington Giving It a Name in
1792—Not Founded on the Anti-Federalists, Though
It Had Anti-Federalist Support

THE established and generally accepted facts about
the birth of the Democratic party are these:

Time—May 13, 1792.

Place—Virginia.

First official name—Republican.

Parent—Thomas Jefferson.

Whatever else may be vague about those distant
days, there is small dispute about these four things.
The date is fixed because it was on that day in a
letter to Washington, then beginning his second
term, that Jefferson, then secretary of state, wrote
making the first authoritative claim of a name for
the party of which he had become the recognized
leader. The high-tempered, sensitive, querulous
Adams was Vice-President, and Alexander Hamilton had already launched his plan for the payment
of the public debt and the creation of a great
national bank. Just as the handsome, brilliant, and
youthful secretary of the treasury was the practical

13

political boss of the dominant Federalists, so Jefferson—then forty-five years old—headed the opposition, which, while in a small and nameless minority in Congress, was neither futile nor inactive. In his Washington letter he wrote: "The Republican party who wish to preserve the government in its present form, are fewer in number than the monarchical Federalists. They are fewer even when joined by the two or three or half dozen anti-federalists, who though they dare not avow it, are still opposed to any general government: but being less so to a republican than to a monarchical one, they naturally join those whom they think pursuing the lesser evil." That letter is important chiefly because it contains the first mention of the name by which the party was known for about twenty-eight years and because of the fact that Jefferson gave it that name. It was not until 1810 that the word "democrat" was accepted as meaning the same thing as "republican," and not until the Jackson period that the designation of the Jeffersonian party became definitely "Democratic."

While the birth date was fixed by the Jefferson letter of 1792, because a party cannot be said to be in existence without a name, actually it was in existence as well defined opposition a year or so before that. Actually the seeds were sown in the constitutional convention of 1787, when the first battles were fought between those who wanted a strong centralized, energetic Federal government and those who wanted the least possible Federal government consistent with national security and convenience. There is no doubt that in those convention debates can be located the Democratic germ plasm, the ultimate outcome of which under the Jefferson genius was the establishment of a party whose theory aimed at "the increase in direct popular control over the government, the widening of the right of suffrage, the limitation of the power of the Federal Government and the conservation of the powers reserved to the States by the Constitution."

It is, however, a mistake to assert, as some do, that this Democratic party was really built on the anti-Federalist party. That is completely untrue. The anti-Federalists in the convention opposed any general government, and with that fight neither Jefferson nor Madison had the least sympathy. The compromises by which the Constitution had been made acceptable to the planters of the South, particularly Virginia, swung both these men and those who looked to them for leadership strongly behind it, and they aided in riding roughshod over the anti-Federalists in its ratification. After the Government had been organized in the First Congress, the convenience of the Federal scheme was so completely demonstrated that the bottom dropped from under the anti-Federalists, and most of them were anxious to drop the discredited name and allow their opposition to ratification to be forgotten. It is interesting to note in that 1792 letter of Jefferson's the adroit way in which he makes plain that while his new Republican party had certain support from the handful of surviving anti-Federalists in Congress, it had no sympathy with them; that they attached themselves to the new party not because it in the least represented their views or was in harmony with their aims but because it seemed to them more bearable than the Federalists. In a word, Jefferson accounted for his anti-Federalist support by proclaiming the division to be between republicanism on the one side and monarchy or aristocracy on the other; between government by the people and government of the people, the Republicans representing the former, the Federalists the latter creed.

The founder of the new party did not propose to have the anti-Federalist stigma attached to it— and rightly so. It really is amazing how much Jefferson managed to say in those two sentences extracted from this relatively little-known letter to Washington. He not only named his party, and swung it beautifully clear of the anti-Federalist taint, which was a danger, but he also drew sharply the distinction between the Federalists and the Republicans. As a matter of fact, the distinction at the time was much more theoretical than real. It was quite true, as he charged, that the Federalist feeling was that the Government should be run for the people by the aristocracy, whereas the Jeffersonian conception on which his party was founded was of a government for the people run by the people.

The Birth of the Party

Actually it was a good many years after the Democrats took over the Government that the people had very much to say about it. The new party, like the Federalist party, was in the hands of men like Jefferson and Madison, who by birth, breeding, and education were entitled to be regarded as aristocrats, and who assumed a direct initiative in party and governmental affairs that would be unthinkable if attempted now. It is true that Jefferson's party from the start was far more in tune with the public will than the other, more in unison with the popular aspirations and desires; but its course was not then nor for more than a quarter of a century later directed by "the people."

It was molded by its able leaders, most of whom were gentlemen, and "the people" followed. The fact is "the people," as we to-day understand that phrase, were not a genuine power in American politics until after 1820. Partly this was due to the long distances that separated the masses of the population, and the slow means of travel and communication; partly to the fact that suffrage was largely restricted to the property-owning and tax-paying class; partly to the lack of a strong national feeling in the country and of any form of nominating primary or convention; partly to the fact that it took the new party, after it obtained power, a long time to bring the people to the point of political efficiency where they could and would intelligently exercise the power Democratic doctrine insisted was properly lodged in their hands. In spite of the fact that no party could live to-day that disputed that idea, and that every party that came after the Democratic party has adopted the basic Democratic principle—with a good many others—as its own, there are those who maintain that the idea is ridiculous, that the people never have and never will reach the point where they intelligently exercise their power; and they point to the popular blunders all along the political road to sustain their belief. There is no intention here to digress into a discussion of the merits and demerits of a republican form of government, except to point out that it seems a fairly complete answer to say that, conceding the terrific blunders, political inertia, stupidity, and generally inept ways of the people in the exercise of their power over their own government, brought to them by the Democratic party, these do not seem too high a price to pay. It may not, as is urged, last forever, but it has lasted longer now than any other conceivable political system would have lasted in this country—and its end is certainly not in sight.

To return, however, to the fact that after the party that stood for government by the people came into existence it was at least thirty years before "the people" really took hold of their own government. Up to the Jackson administration it was "held in trust" for them by the party leaders, who, however strong their faith in the capacity of the people to rule, were not themselves "of the people" but of the landed aristocracy, and did not wait for popular inspiration before taking the initiative in matters of party and public policy. They could not do it now, but they did then. It is of course true that while the Jefferson effort was to lead rather than reflect, there was scarcely a time during the entire period of his leadership in which he was not supported by a majority of the American people. He led in the direction they instinctively wanted to go, but it was he who took them with him, not they who took him.

The truth is that in the first thirty years of its existence the Democratic party was Thomas Jefferson and Thomas Jefferson was the Democratic party. Not only in the years between its birth, in 1792, and its first national victory in 1800; and not only during his own administration but through those of Madison and Monroe, both of whom became President through his influence and choice, the personality of Jefferson dominated his party clear up to the day of his death on July 4, 1826. His mind molded its policies, directed its activities, selected its candidates just as completely after it got started as the great principles upon which it was founded came from him at the time of its birth. It is true that the part played by James Madison, whose clear-headed vision, wisdom, and ability unquestionably entitle him to recognition not only as one of the really great men produced by the Democratic party but one of the greatest of our Presidents, has been to a considerable extent overshadowed by the towering figure of Jefferson. It was none the less vital for that. Next to Jefferson, there is no doubt his impress on the party principles and policies and his force in its early battles were the most potent. And there were others—lieutenants, advisers, aids —all of whom helped put the party on its feet, and contributed to its first victory and to the popular strength and political skill that kept it in power without a break—and for most of the period without serious opposition—for nearly forty years. But none of this detracts from the fact that the story of the party's first quarter of a century is the story of the man who founded it—and who was its first President.

There is such a vast and exhaustive literature on Jefferson that in an outline sketch such as this it is almost impossible to write of him at all without repeating a story so well known that repetition should be avoided. When to the numerous biographies are added that last great book of Claude M. Bowers, "Jefferson and Hamilton," it seems ridiculously superfluous to attempt any portrayal of the personality, character, and achievements of the man. And none will be made here other than to say that the partisan Republican who would question the greatness and ability of Thomas Jefferson is comparable only to the partisan Democrat who would withhold unstinted admiration from Abraham Lincoln. For the rest, the effort will be confined to reporting as simply and clearly as possible the practical political activity of Jefferson as the Democratic leader in bringing his party into power and continuing it in complete control of the Government as long as he lived.

It is not meant to convey the idea that through all these years Jefferson's word was absolute law in all party matters, or that there were not turbulent elements and recalcitrant leaders and a lot of trouble; that he did not have to compromise and make practical political alliances with an unsavory crowd, or that everything about the Democratic party in those days was high-minded and pure. Not by a long shot. Politics then was pretty much as is politics now—a mixture of good and evil, with often the evil predominating and compromise an essential and inevitable part of the game—even in those days when there was no such thing as universal suffrage, and the popular whims and prejudices were far less politically potent than now. But whatever political corners Jefferson found it necessary to cut—and there is no doubt he did cut some—few will question that the political ends he sought were high and patriotic and that his politics was largely free from sordidness or selfishness.

By the end of 1792 he had his new "Republican" party fairly formed. There were in House and Senate a fairly formidable minority who acknowledged allegiance to its broad general principles (which will be fully presented in the proper place), to its concrete and specific attitude on pending legislative proposals from the Federalist Government, and to the leadership of Jefferson, still serving as secretary of state under Washington. In these days the Jefferson attitude would be regarded as patently disloyal to his chief, who was a Federalist, and to his party. In those days it was not so regarded. For one thing, it was not then a party Government; Washington had not been elected as a party man. The division between parties was just beginning, and Washington placidly watched the bitter political feud in his cabinet, between Hamilton and Jefferson, with interest but without resentment, though his feelings were Federalistic. The fundamental doctrine which Jefferson and Madison labored to lay down as the most reliable basis for a permanent party was that of strict construction of the Constitution. They strongly opposed any effort broadly and liberally to interpret its provisions, insisting that all power not expressly granted the National Government adhered to the "sovereign and indestructible states." In particular, the Republicans opposed the Hamilton measures of a national bank, a protective tariff, a national excise tax, a funding system for the debt, and in general all measures tending specially to favor the commercial or creditor class over the agriculturists, who were then in the majority, but because they were widely scattered and separated by great distances were not nearly as politically potent as the industrial minority centralized in the cities.

The Birth of the Party

About this time the sympathetic reaction in America to the French Revolution for a while obscured all local issues and broad political policies, but undoubtedly helped promote the Republican cause. Washington, who was supposed to be acting under Federalist influence, issued his proclamation of neutrality, which lent color to the Republican claim that the Federalists were at heart really monarchistic and they the only genuine friends of the republic. The proclamation also brought to the surface a class of small politicians who attempted to capitalize the popular prejudice favoring the new French Republic. They were mostly of low type and are, perhaps, the earliest demagogues of whom our political history contains record. Calling themselves Democrats, they modeled their organizations on the Jacobin clubs of Paris, and denounced the unexcited political bystanders as well as their opponents as "enemies of the people," violently appealing to the passions of the unthinking in the name of "liberty." To the Federalists these men and their followers appeared literally horrible. To the Republican leaders they were almost equally contemptible, and in accepting their support the Republicans were painstakingly careful to make it plain, as Jefferson did with the anti-Federalists, that they opposed Hamilton and the Federalists upon vastly different grounds, that they had no sympathy with the denunciations of Washington indulged in by these "democrats," that they deplored their violence of word and deed.

None the less, it is undoubtedly true that these men served with the Republican cause—performed a service it greatly needed. Jefferson and Madison did the thinking and theorizing for their party, promulgated the noble principles, wrote and spoke with eloquence, logic, and force; but it was these demagogic so-called "democrats"—men like Bache, Collender, and Freneau—who cared nothing at all about the Constitution one way or the other, but who could and did translate the fine theories of Jefferson and Madison into popular language. They possessed a personal touch with the common people, a power to stir up their prejudices, an enthusiastic disregard for where, how, or whom they hit so long as it was the other side, utterly lacking in the far finer Republican leaders. By some of the best authorities—Dr. Alexander Johnston for one—it is held, and with reason, that it was these small, utterly insincere, and mainly unscrupulous fellows who supplied the lowness lacking in the others and really made the Republican theory the basis of a great and successful party.

From that time on, all the "breaks" were with the Republicans, against the Federalists. When the Third Congress met in 1793 they elected the speaker of the House by a majority of ten votes, and the alliance between the Democrats and Republicans was so tightly welded that they took the name of "Democratic-Republican" party. This name did not last long, though for years the Federalists persisted in

24

applying the term "Democrat" as an expression of contempt to every Republican. In the Fourth Congress, the Republicans, under outside guidance of Jefferson and Madison, sharply drew the line between themselves and the "Democrats" in their treatment of Washington. By the latter he was violently abused and denounced. By the former he was spoken of only with affection and respect, which, however, did not disguise their regret that they could not strike directly at the Federalists without reaching around him, nor altogether hide their impatience for his retirement from politics, which would make possible a head-on clash with the Federalist party.

The opportunity came in 1796 with Washington's retirement, known to his intimate friends early in the year. From that moment the battle was on, the Federalists, directed by Hamilton, fighting brilliantly and desperately to check the Republican onslaught and keep Jefferson, who as the recognized Republican leader was their inevitable candidate, out of the Presidency. The thrilling political duel between these leaders—Hamilton the Federalist, and Jefferson the Republican—the most dramatic, eventful, and far-reaching that has occurred in American politics, dating back to their personal clash as members of Washington's first cabinet and really ending only with the tragic death of Hamilton at the hands of Burr, has been too graphically pictured by Mr. Bowers to need more than general reference here. But it was the 1796 and the 1800 campaigns that furnished the climax for this head-on clash, which was one not only of immense personalities but of diametrically opposed basic principles of government. It had been preparing for eight years, gathering force and fury, piling up bitterness and hate with a curious mingling of personal feuds, grudges, and ambitions, practical and at times sordid politics, with deep convictions and the loftiest patriotism. They were—these 1796 and 1800 fights—the first contests over the Presidency. In both 1788 and 1792 Washington had been chosen without opposition and not as a party man.

It is interesting that the party lines were drawn under this first and only non-partisan President, that each party was organized and led by one of his secretaries and friends, that throughout the years of his incumbency they strained like dogs on leash, but were unable to come to grips so long as he remained a factor in politics. His sympathies were more Hamiltonian than Jeffersonian, more Federalist than Republican, but not to the point of declared partisanship. And so potent were his name and popularity that with him as President it was impossible for a real test of strength to be had. There could be no real fight for the Presidency so long as Washington stayed in politics. Once he stepped out, the struggle was inevitable.

Chapter III

THE DEMOCRATIC CREED

The Bitter Fight That Preceded the First Victory in
1800—The Struggle between Jefferson and Hamilton
—Part Played by Kentucky and Virginia Resolutions

PERHAPS of the thirty-four Presidential elections
that have occurred in the country since the ratification of the Constitution, these first two contests—
1796-1800—were filled with more bitterness, the
struggle was more vital and prolonged, the closeness and uncertainty of the result more nerve rack-
ing, the political deals more devious, the intrigues
more difficult to follow, the final drama as tense as
any that have followed. Neither was a popular election in the sense we now have them. Of the sixteen
States that then constituted the Union—New Hampshire, Vermont, Massachusetts, Rhode Island, Connecticut, New York, New Jersey, Pennsylvania, Delaware, Maryland, Virginia, North Carolina, South
Carolina, Georgia, Kentucky, Tennessee—in only
six were the electors chosen by popular vote; in ten
they were selected either by the state legislatures or
by more or less informal caucuses. It is worth mentioning that in the 1796 election occurred the only

27

case on record of an elector who betrayed the trust of the State that had chosen him. Samuel Miles, a Federalist elector from Pennsylvania, voted for Jefferson, and though Jefferson lost the Presidency, Miles was most violently denounced at home.

It was early in 1796 that Washington let his purpose to retire not only from the Presidency but from politics become known to a few of his friends. Immediately the clear-headed Hamilton saw the inevitability of Jefferson's Presidential candidacy, and —quite as plainly—that if Jefferson won, the Federal party was doomed. Clearly, the Federalists had to put forth the strongest possible candidate if the disaster of a Republican triumph was to be averted. The logical thing and the thrilling thing would have been for Hamilton himself to run against Jefferson —the two giants in the two parties pitted personally one against the other for the great prize of the Presidency. In his "History of the Presidency," Dr. Edward Stanwood asserts that while Hamilton was eligible he had many enemies, and his candidacy would have aroused violent antagonisms. Besides, he says, there was a stain upon his private character, and threats were made that if he came forward as a candidate certain papers damaging to his integrity would be published. By his admirers the idea that his integrity was ever seriously questioned is deeply resented.

Whatever the reasons, he did not regard his own candidacy as feasible; but it is true that he finally came to the support of Mr. Adams reluctantly. He did not admire Mr. Adams; considered—and had said—that he lacked discretion and good temper; but his course as Vice-President with Washington had been entirely pleasing to the Federalists, his character was unimpeachable, and he was the logical candidate. Hamilton paired him with Thomas Pinckney of South Carolina as the Federalist candidate for Vice-President. In the other camp, Jefferson made an alliance with Aaron Burr, who had displaced George Clinton as leader of the Republicans in New York, it being understood that Burr was the candidate for Vice-President and Jefferson for President.

The campaign started off merrily enough after Washington's farewell address in September, but in a few weeks attained a violence and heat unprecedented at the time and not often approached since. The Federalists were confident, but knew they were fighting for their lives. The Republicans were jubilant at this, the first chance for a real trial with the enemy. Neither side left much undone. Both were guilty—not the candidates, of course, but their journalistic and oratorical supporters—of the grossest misrepresentation and unfairness. The charges and counter-charges on both sides grew grotesque before the finish, and feeling was intense. The country was relatively small, the voting population restricted, the election machinery primitive, and the campaign methods crude; but the fight was big and

vital. In the end the Federalists won by the narrow
margin of two votes in the Electoral College—
Adams got 71, Jefferson 68. The Hamilton candidate
for Vice-President, Pinckney, whom at the last moment Hamilton would have preferred to Adams, and
for whom he tried to swing the same number of
votes, failed, and Jefferson, the next highest, was
chosen Vice-President.

They won—the Federalists—but at a cost and
with a margin that frightened them. They won—
the Hamiltonians—with a Presidential candidate
not of the inner circle; not one to their liking, not
one—high as were his qualities and character—who
inspired either personal devotion or political cooperation, not one who would take advice. He was
personally disliked by Hamilton and his lieutenants
because of what they considered his vanity, pride,
and testy disposition. His really fine qualities of
mind and heart were obscured by his small defects,
and his administration was neither happy nor successful. Unquestionably he was badly treated by
members of his cabinet, who recognized Hamilton
and not the President as their political chief, and
rendered to Hamilton the loyalty they owed to
Adams. Under the circumstances a successful administration was impossible. When to these handicaps was added the fact that the presiding officer of
the Senate was Jefferson, leader of the opposition
party, astute, watchful, alert to take full advantage
of the mistakes of the administration and to improve

his position for the second fight, in 1800—when this, too, is taken into consideration, it is easy to understand why historians of the period seem to agree that the administration of John Adams witnessed the total wreck of the Federalist party, due chiefly to "divided leadership."

During the whole of that four years Jefferson, as Vice-President, was a candidate for President, writing, advising, consulting, planning for the 1800 battle, as a result of which the Federalist party was not only defeated but destroyed, and the Republicans triumphantly and for the first time secured control of the Government. There are differences of opinion among the authorities as to the main contributory reasons for the final Federalist defeat. One view is that the hostile relations between President Adams and the prominent leaders of his party, from Hamilton down, were the sole reason for the political overturn; that Adams was fairly popular with the people but not with the politicians, that he should have and could have won had there been back of him an enthusiastic, cordial party support—which there certainly was not. So reluctant were the Hamiltonians to make the fight again with Adams that a tremendous effort was made to call Washington from his retirement and induce him to stand for the Presidency. Washington was told that if he would run, there would be no opposition and the country and the party would both be saved. He absolutely refused, though the efforts did not cease until within a week or so of his death. On December 9, 1799, Gouverneur Morris wrote him at Mount Vernon, urging him to run and saying, "During a late visit to New York I learnt that the leading characters over in Massachusetts consider Mr. Adams as unfit for the office he now holds." Washington, ill, probably never read the letter; but it is cited here to show the state of mind with which the Federalist leaders went in for their final battle behind Adams. Reluctance is a mild name for their feeling.

The other view of why the Federalists were overwhelmed in the election is wholly different. It holds that the passage by the Federalist Congress of the Alien and Sedition acts created so strong a public sentiment against the administration, and the Kentucky and Virginia resolutions contributed so much to strengthen the Republican party with the people, that the combination was irresistible. These Kentucky and Virginia resolutions, prepared by Jefferson and Madison, were passed by the legislatures of those States and set forth more clearly and strongly and extremely the States' rights doctrine than had been done before. Their theme was that the state governments are the foundation of the American political system, that their powers are unlimited except by state constitutions and the Constitution of the United States; that the Federal Government, on the contrary, has no powers except those granted by the Constitution; that, therefore, whenever a doubt of power arises between State and Federal Govern-

WASHINGTON CITY, DEC. 8.

THIS DAY

At twelve o'clock, the following MESSAGE was
delivered to each House by Mr. LEWIS, Secretary
to the PRESIDENT.

MESSAGE

OF THE PRESIDENT OF THE UNITED STATES,
TO BOTH HOUSES OF CONGRESS.

DECEMBER 8, 1801.

SIR,

THE circumstances under which we find ourselves at this place rendering inconvenient the mode
heretofore practised, of making by personal address
the first communications between the Legislative
and Executive branches, I have adopted that by
Message, as used on all subsequent occasions thro'
the session. In doing this, I have had principal regard to the convenience of the legislature, to the
economy of their time, to their relief from the em-
barressment of immediate answers, on subjects not
yet fully before them, and to the benefits thence resulting to the public affairs.—Trusting that a procedure, founded in these motives, will meet their ap-
probation, I beg leave, through you, Sir, to communicate the inclosed message with the documents accompanying it, to the honorable the House of Representatives, and pray you to accept, for yourself and
them, the homage of my high respect and consideration.

TH: JEFFERSON.

The Honorable the Speaker of the
House of Representatives.

INTRODUCTORY PARAGRAPH OF A
JEFFERSON MESSAGE TO CONGRESS

Jefferson departed from precedent by sending his message to congress instead of
delivering it personally

(A clipping from "The New York Evening
Post," December 12, 1801).

ment, the presumption must be that it is with the State. It is interesting to note, too, that the plan urged in resolutions of "frequent conventions of the States" as the surest means of preventing the encroachments of the Federal Government, was recalled and renewed for exactly the same purpose in the summer of 1927—one hundred and thirty-one years later—at the conference of governors held at Mackinaw Island, Michigan. While the party in its platforms and its performances has often departed from the principle laid down in these resolutions; while Jefferson himself did not at all times wholly live up to this strict constitutional creed, none the less the spirit of these resolutions has since been the theoretical basis of the party's existence.

As to the Alien and Sedition acts, they were the outgrowth of the relations with France, which in 1797 had induced considerable hysteria in this country. The Alien Act authorized the President to deport such aliens as he judged dangerous to the peace and safety of the United States or whom he suspected of being engaged in treasonable machinations against the Government. The Sedition Act made it a crime to "conspire" against the Government, to "intimidate" an officer of the Government; to publish "false and misleading writings" against the Government. There is no doubt that these acts created a sentiment as unfavorable to the Federalist party as the Kentucky and Virginia resolutions aroused a favorable feeling for the Republicans.

Notwithstanding these undoubted facts, however, it is perhaps true that if the Federalist leaders had been united behind Adams he could not have been defeated. It was again a bitter and a violent campaign. Again Jefferson was allied with Burr, it being perfectly understood that the latter was the candidate for Vice-President. Burr would not have been at any time seriously considered by the Republicans for the Presidency, but was acceptable for Vice-President largely because of his political strength in New York, which State then, as now, seemed essential to success in electing a President.

The fight was filled with misrepresentations and "campaign lies." Both Jefferson and Adams personally kept on a high plane, but this was certainly not true of their friends and followers, and there was as much mud thrown in the course of that three-months battle as in any campaign of this generation. It was really a life and death struggle. Jefferson had been wholly sincere in his retirement in 1794, and was a reluctant candidate in 1796, but in 1800 there was nothing reluctant about him. He had again assumed active direction of the party, regarded himself as its inevitable candidate, believed the fight had to be made and had to be won. That was the spirit in which he went into it and the spirit with which his party supported him. The Federalists started out with considerable confidence, lost it all before the end, became panicky and desperate. It was New York that settled their business. It had saved them with its twelve votes in 1796; by swinging again to the other side in 1800 it destroyed them. Jefferson and Burr each received 73 votes, Adams 65, C. C. Pinckney, Federalist Vice-Presidential candidate, 64.

To understand what followed as a result of the equal vote of Jefferson and Burr, for which Jefferson's supporters had striven, it must be understood that at that time the votes for President and Vice-President were not separately cast as now. All the candidates were voted for as Presidential candidates. The one receiving the highest number of votes became President; the next highest Vice-President. Following realization of their defeat, the Federalist leaders seized the opportunity offered in the equal vote of Jefferson and Burr to initiate a movement that did more ultimately to bury their party even than the defeat. There being no choice in the electoral college, it became the duty of the House of Representatives to elect the President. With Burr lending himself treacherously to the scheme, the Federalist strength was thrown behind him in an effort to keep Jefferson out of the Presidency. It was a desperate and a despicable plan and it pretty nearly succeeded. Almost the limit was reached in intrigue, and thirty-six ballots were taken in the House before Jefferson finally won with 55 votes to Burr's 49. It was a tremendous struggle, and the defeated Federalists, regarding Jefferson as they did the devil, felt that any means were justifiable to prevent his triumph. It is to the everlasting credit of Hamilton that he did not lend himself to the effort to elect Burr, but opposed it as strongly as he could. To a friend he wrote: "I trust the Federalists will not finally be so mad as to vote for Burr. I speak with an intimate and accurate knowledge of character. His elevation can only promote the purposes of the desperate and profligate. If there be a man in the world I ought to hate it is Jefferson. With Burr I have always been personally well. But the public good must be paramount to every private consideration." Nothing in his whole career shows Hamilton in a finer light as a patriotic and high-minded man than his unequivocal stand on this issue.

Before continuing the story, it ought to be mentioned here that this device, adopted by the convention of 1787, of having the electors vote for two persons without designating who was to be President, and which in 1800 so nearly resulted in putting into the Presidency an utterly unfit man, was not changed until nearly four years after. It is interesting, too, to note that one of the arguments against the present method was that the effect would be that "the office of Vice-President will be carried to market to purchase the vote of particular States." That this prophecy has been many times fulfilled is too obvious to argue. It has, upon the death of the President, opened the door of the White House to several men who would never have been seriously thought of in connection with the Presidency and who were not even approximately Presidential size. Theodore Roosevelt is the one notable exception.

With Jefferson's election the party he founded eight years before assumed full control of the Government for the first time. With its leader in the Presidency and a clear majority in both House and Senate, it was in complete command, and a new political era began. For the forty following years the party remained in uninterrupted power—most of that time without really formidable opposition. In the next twenty years it was defeated only twice, and its opponents were in real control of the Government for only a single Presidential term.

What this means is that for sixty years following the election of Jefferson in 1800 the destinies of the country were directed by the Democrats, with the exception of the four years of the Zachary Taylor administration, between 1848 and 1852. It is true that in 1840 the party lost its candidate for the Presidency—Lewis Cass—but the early death of President Harrison thrust Vice-President Tyler into the White House. He, deserting the Whigs, cooperated with the Democrats to such an extent that they were in practical control of the situation, and it was in effect a Democratic administration. Altogether it is a remarkable record, not approached by any other political party in this or any other democratic country—and not likely to be. It is true, of course, that in the sixty-eight years since 1860 the Democrats have elected their Presidential candidate but four times and been in power a total of sixteen years. It would, however, be fallacious to argue from this that the party that so magnificently held ascendancy for more than half a century was on its way to dissolution—fallacious not only for the reasons given in the first chapter of this book, but because, regardless of its departure from principles, its blunderings, stumblings, wanderings, and stupidities, its apparent feebleness and frequent futility, the place for the Democratic party in our political system is so obviously essential, the thought upon which it was built is so basicly human, its need as a corrective and checking force in a great government so clear, that there need be no fear it will lapse wholly into innocuous desuetude.

There is a vital spark in the Democratic party that cannot be extinguished, an unquenchable vitality which even at its lowest ebb renders victory always possible. Its leaders may fail it, its followers falter and fall by the wayside, but ultimately the reaction comes, strength, solidity, and success are achieved. If the four victories of the party since the Civil War do not prove that, they do not prove anything. The reason this is true and the reason the Democratic party promises to be as permanent as the Government is because it is one of the two great natural divisions into which people in every self-governing country must inevitably fall. It was so intended to be by its founder. The Jefferson purpose was to create a party that was far more than a "strict construction" States' rights party. The Jefferson purpose was to create a party that would be really democratic in personnel, purpose, and method —a party that would represent one of the great natural views of government. It was to be the party of the people. While it is true that in its early days, between 1792 and 1800, it was mainly a party of opposition, back of the opposition to the concrete Federalist proposals was antagonism to the inherent Federalist attitude; and the thing that gave the new party strength, that tied men to it all over this new country, and that finally brought it into full power, was the strong appeal to the people made by the great conception of government which Jefferson had in mind and which he laid down as the basis of his party in its earliest struggles, and announced as its guiding principles and policy after it achieved its initial success.

In one of his letters he expressed it as follows:

Men by their constitutions are naturally divided into two parties: 1—those who fear and distrust the people and wish to draw all powers from them into the hands of the higher classes; 2—those who identify themselves with the people, have confidence in them, cherish and consider them as the most wise depository of the public interests. In every country these two parties exist and in every one where they are free to think, speak and write, they will declare themselves. Call them therefore liberals and serviles, Jacobins and ultras, Whigs and Tories, Republicans and Federalists, aristocrats and Democrats, or by whatever name you please, they are the same parties still and pursue the same object. The last appellation of aristocrats and Democrats is the true one expressing the essence of all.

The Democratic Party: A History

That gives about as well as can be given the main thought back of the Democratic party and the reason for belief in its permanency as a party, no matter how often defeated nor to what state depressed. What has been called by various historians "the creed" of the Democratic party as generally accepted during the first quarter of the nineteenth century is contained in Jefferson's first inaugural address. In fact, it is still claimed as the creed of the party, and no element or faction wanting to maintain influence in the party can even now admit any essential departure therefrom. Here it is:

About to enter, fellow citizens, on the exercise of duties which comprehend everything dear and valuable to you, it is proper you should understand what I deem the essential principles of our government and consequently those which ought to shape its administration. I will compress them within the narrowest compass they will bear, stating the general principle but not all its limitations. Equal and exact justice to all men, of whatever state or persuasion, religious or political; peace, commerce and honest friendship with all nations, entangling alliances with none; the support of the State governments in all their rights, as the most competent administrations for our domestic concerns and the surest bulwark against anti-Republican tendencies; the preservation of the general government in its whole Constitutional figure as the sheet anchor of our peace at home and safety abroad; a jealous care of the right of election by the people—a mild and safe corrective of abuses which are lopped by the sword of revolution where peaceable remedies are unprovided; absolute acquiescence in the decisions of the majority, the vital principle of Republics from which is no appeal but to force, the vital principle and immediate parent of despotism; a well disciplined militia, our best reliance in peace and for the first moment of war until regulars may relieve them; the supremacy of the Civil over the Military authority; economy in the public expense that labor may be lightly burdened; the honest payments of our debts and sacred preservation of the public faith; encouragement of agriculture and of commerce as its handmaid; the diffusion of information and arraignment of all abuse at the bar of the public reason; freedom of religion, freedom of the press, and freedom of person under the protection of the habeas corpus and trial by juries impartially selected. These principles form the bright constellation which has gone before us and guided our step through an age of revolution and reformation. The wisdom of our sages and blood of our heroes have been devoted to their attainment. They should be the creed of our political faith, the text of civic instruction, the touchstone by which to try the services of those we trust; and should we wander from them in moments of error or of alarm, let us hasten to retrace our step and to regain the road which alone leads to peace, liberty and safety.

To this must be added the great slogan given the party by Jefferson—"Equal Rights for All, Special Privileges for None," which has been repeated in almost every Democratic platform, which sums up so much of the Democratic doctrine, and without ringing the changes on which few Democratic candidates for any office have ever gone through a campaign.

That Jefferson was a great party leader and a profound political thinker there is no room for doubt. As to the sort of President he made, opinions differ. It has been repeatedly said that after his election he really killed the Federalist party by adopting its principles, which of course is not true. What, however, undoubtedly is true is the fact that in power and with responsibility Jefferson found it impossible to be in action the strict constructionist he was in theory. For example, the outstanding act of his first administration was the acquisition of Louisiana—a step that required a far broader construction of the Constitution than Hamilton had placed on it; a step for which, in fact, there seemed at the time no constitutional warrant at all. It was, however, a step tremendously popular in the South and almost as much so in the North. It required boldness and decision, but of its wisdom there was no question and the popular approval was almost unanimous. But it pretty nearly drove the bruised and defeated Federalists wild. They were by this time sunk into a pitiable state, resorting to all sorts of futile intrigues in the vain effort to regain power, and when oppressed by their futility actually consulting and conspiring in secret to break up the Union. In this, as in the Burr business, they had neither sympathy nor support from Hamilton. "Tell them," he wrote to a friend just a week before Burr killed him, "from me as my request for God's sake to cease these conversations and threatenings about a separation from the Union."

A good many critical things are said of Jefferson as President by hostile historians. He is accused of niggardly neglect of the navy, of an outrageous attack on the judiciary, of using the offices to reward his party friends, of various things to all of which

his admirers have offered answers. But from whatever angle he is viewed, there is no dispute concerning the fact that as President the people were with
him, and, as the time passed, his administration grew
stronger. He would almost certainly have been re-
elected anyhow, but the Louisiana purchase practically removed all real opposition. The Federalists
had candidates, but they made not even a show of
fighting except in Connecticut and one or two other
places where they were still fairly strong. Jefferson,
with George Clinton as Vice-President, received 162
of the 176 electoral votes. Immediately after his second inauguration Jefferson announced he would not
be a candidate for a third term.

In his second administration the lack of a virile
party of opposition bred feuds and factionalism in
the party in power. There was no split on principles,
and Jefferson had little trouble in getting what he
wanted through Congress, but the inevitable aspirations and ambitions of the politicians made considerable trouble and at one time threatened its success in
the 1808 campaign. John Randolph of Virginia
turned against the administration, and the plain
preference of Jefferson for James Madison, his secretary of state and devoted personal friend, not only
wounded his other warm friend and disciple, James
Monroe, but soured George Clinton, who, as Vice-
President, felt that he was entitled to the promotion,
just as Adams had under Washington, and Jefferson under Adams. Restiveness against the "Virginia

dynasty" manifested itself in South Carolina and Maryland as well as in New York. In other words, Democrats began then to exercise their constitutional right to differ among themselves, and some bitter feuds developed. The protest against Madison was pronounced, but the Jefferson influence was sufficient to nominate him. Outwardly Jefferson preserved an appearance of neutrality between Madison and Monroe, but there was never any real secret of his support of the former nor of his influence inducing the latter to withdraw from the field in Virginia.

In the end peace was patched up within the party. The Federalists were unable to revive as a fighting force, and John Quincy Adams, in Massachusetts, went bodily over to the party of Jefferson, supporting Madison, who received 122 of the 175 electoral votes. The result was largely due to the skilful political deals made by the Democrats in the important States, notably Pennsylvania. There was little or no discussion of issues or of men. It was a pure case of politics from beginning to end, and at no time were the people deeply stirred. There were neither men nor issues to arouse them. Jefferson, still in the Presidency, had the strength with the party and with the people to secure ratification of his choice—and he secured it.

That was all there was to it. Having succeeded in that, he for the second time retired to Monticello, from which lovely spot he continued to exert a tremendously potent influence in party affairs, to be the party oracle, consulted by its Presidents and leaders, advising, directing, dominating through the power of his personality and recognition of his wisdom and strength. Throughout his two terms Madison was in constant communication with him, and in most vital matters sought and acted upon his advice. When Madison finally retired, the Jefferson power was still strong enough to continue the "Virginia dynasty" for eight more years through the election of his friend James Monroe for two terms. He lived then just long enough to see elected another President of the party he had founded—John Quincy Adams of Massachusetts, whose candidacy he favored over that of Andrew Jackson—and then beautifully died in his eighty-fourth year.

Chapter IV

The Jefferson Influence Still Dominant—The Remarkable Scope of His Political Power—The Party
Begins to Depart from Its Principles

IN writing this outline of the Democratic party the
main thought was to tell a clear, connected story,
following the trend without a single break from its
beginning in 1792 up to the present time. This, of
course, is the essential thing, but it is none the less
apparent that the real story of the Democratic party
is the story of the five or six genuinely great men
who stand out in its history, who gave the party its
principles, molded its policies, shaped its destiny, led
it in the critical conflicts, were responsible alike for
its most glorious achievements and its monumental
failures, who lent it color and character, vibrancy,
and vitality. Plainly the picture would be all out of
drawing if the same emphasis and space were here
given to each Democratic President and each Democratic administration.

Therefore, the obvious and sensible thing to do,
not only in order to retain the proper perspective
and the right proportions but to keep the book from

being needlessly dull, is to drape the party history largely around these towering party personalities where it belongs and treat the more or less mediocre party Presidents and party leaders who came in between with only sufficient fullness to preserve the continuity of the account, and at the same time refrain from omitting essential facts of real party significance and importance. It is the easier to do this because this work does not pretend to be a record of each Democratic administration nor a history of the country, but merely the story of the Democratic party. It is therefore possible to leave in the hands of the historians the details of many developments under Democratic Presidents, and in this effort touching upon such things, for example, as the War of 1812, which so completely shadowed the second Madison administration, only as they affect the party story.

Of these great party personalities Jefferson was, of course, the first and Andrew Jackson the second. In the twenty years that separate them there were three Democratic Presidents and five Democratic administrations, but, as has been pointed out, during four of these—the two of Madison and the two of Monroe—Thomas Jefferson, though in retirement at Monticello, was still the party's guiding influence. Factions and feuds developed, as they were bound to do within a party that had no organized outside opposition to face. To these Jefferson was serenely indifferent, concerning himself in his retirement only with questions of broad public policy, remote and aloof from the sordid squabblers and schemers but none the less the mightiest power in his party clear to the end of his days—an amazing man, an utterly unparalleled record. No other since the American Republic was founded has equaled the political influence, power, and prestige of this man. Few other men in any other country at any other time have equaled the Jefferson record in either the continuity of his party leadership or the potency of his party influence, not only during the eight years in which he personally held the reins, the whip, and the brake, but for an equal number of years while he and his party were in a futile minority completely outside the breastworks—and, most remarkable of all, for the eighteen long years after he had retired from office, relinquished his power, and had neither patronage to dispense, favors to confer, nor a future upon which to speculate.

As a rule our ex-Presidents are among our most pathetic political exhibits. The strong ones have while still in the White House, through the use of the patronage power and the weight of the Federal machine, been able to nominate their successors, but in most cases the moment they left the White House their power fell from them like a cloak. All the glamour that surrounds the President of the United States and makes it impossible to see him clearly, save at extremely close range, vanished, and they became the most ordinary of mortals. Some were hard put

A CLIPPING FROM "THE NEW YORK EVENING POST," NOVEMBER 1, 1812, SHOWING THE ELECTORS VOTED FOR IN NEW YORK STATE IN MADISON'S SECOND ELECTION

to it to make a living after they had left Washington, and extremely few figured in the councils of their party, retained a following, or remained a political factor after their term ended. As a rule the politicians leave the passing President like rats leave a sinking ship. There is as a rule no more lonely political figure, than an ex-President. The exceptions that can now be recalled have been Wilson, Cleveland, Roosevelt. Each of these clear to his death was a force within his party, a factor to be reckoned with, a figure whose support was sought and whose words had weight. But compare the record of any of them as a party leader to Jefferson and it sinks into insignificance.

Here was a man who founded a great party that maintained unbroken ascendancy for nearly half a century, who was its acknowledged leader in office and out for more than thirty years, who was three times nominated and twice elected President, who served as secretary of state and as Vice-President, who not only nominated his successor in the Presidency—Madison—but his successor's successor—Monroe—and even, as intimated in Francis Hirst's "Life and Letters of Thomas Jefferson," influenced the selection of his successor's successor's successor —John Quincy Adams, whom, Mr. Hirst declares, he very greatly preferred over Jackson and let that fact be known to his friends in an effective and not to be misunderstood way. At the time he was seventy-five years old and had been out of the Presidency and active politics for sixteen years. It is literally an amazing record. In character and extent the political power wielded by Jefferson was incomparably greater than that of any predecessor or successors. It completely permeated four full administrations. It is true that the sixteen years that followed his retirement and during the first half of which one devoted friend and disciple sat at the head of the Government, giving way to the other devoted friend and disciple for the second half, were not marked by any particular strides in party progress. On the other hand, they were extremely eventful years—and productive of at least one Democratic policy so strong and sound and great that it has come ringing down through the generations intact and unchallenged, now accepted by all parties and all factions. No public man who to-day differed with the Monroe Doctrine or was suspected of weakness in its support could hope to be President.

But before coming to that and in order not to lose the thread it is best to dwell briefly on the character of party government and party leadership under the "Father of the Constitution," as Jefferson's successor is so often called in the histories. Various writers have contended—Dr. Stanwood among them —that during the first part of Madison's administration the Government of the United States was never weaker in all its departments. The truth seems to be that Madison, a scholar and a gentleman, a profound political and philosophical thinker, cultured, informed, with a beautiful mind and a fine character, was a poor executive and an ineffective leader. It is interesting to note that according to one of his biographers—Sydney Howard Gay—he was the original prohibitionist—not in fact but in theory, the first public man who thought deeply on that subject. He believed the country would be vastly better off economically and the people happier if the sale and manufacture of liquor could be abolished and it is stated that but for his doubt of the ability of the Government to enforce prohibitory laws he would have proposed them.

It is difficult to believe he could have had in mind Federal legislation on the subject, because a clearer violation of the Democratic creed of States' rights could hardly be imagined. It is also interesting to know—also on the authority of Dr. Gay—that Madison favored woman suffrage, and that with Jefferson he felt that slavery was inherently wrong and should be abolished; that it menaced the existence of the party if a solution were not found. These things unquestionably show Mr. Madison to have possessed not only extraordinary originality in political thought but to have had a political vision singularly clear and far sighted. But none of this made him a great executive, and his handling of our foreign relations with both France and England cannot be fairly said to have been characterized by skill or ability. In 1811 he appointed Monroe as secretary of state in place of Robert Smith of Maryland, characterized by Dr. Stanwood in his "History of the Presidency" as "the weakest incumbent of the office in the history of the country," which is certainly saying an awful lot. The Monroe appointment must have been pleasing to Jefferson. It placed Monroe directly in line to succeed to the Presidency and put both the Jefferson disciples where he wanted them at the time. Once Jefferson wrote to Monroe, "I have always regarded you and Madison as the two pillars of my happiness."

But the Monroe appointment as secretary of state did not appear immediately to lessen the indecision of the President whether to fight England or continue through ineffective embargo and other equally futile measures to submit to treatment little short of intolerable. In the Twelfth Congress, which met in 1811, there were in the House a group of new and virile young Republicans—John C. Calhoun, William Lowndes, Langdon Cheeves of South Carolina, and Henry Clay of Kentucky. Clay, then thirty-four, was chosen speaker of the House. Cheeves, the oldest of the group, was only thirty-five. They formed the House machine and ran the party so far as that body was concerned. From the first their weight had been thrown on the side of war, and there is little doubt that they forced a change in the Madison policy and at least hastened the war message which he finally sent to Congress in 1812. His renomination came with comparatively little trouble, though there was no party enthusiasm and no party unanimity about the caucus that named him, nor among the people. He had none of the qualities to stir the popular heart.

The feature of the campaign was the unexpected opposition in New York. De Witt Clinton, nephew of George Clinton, who had been Madison's Vice-President and died in office, had made himself the boss of the party in that State. He *was* the boss, too —there is no doubt of that. His control of the organization was complete, and when he declared himself a candidate against Madison, everybody with even a surface knowledge of politics knew it meant the loss of New York and involved some danger. It was not a question of principle with Clinton. He had no issue, no grievance, no cause. He just wanted to be President, and thought that with his control of New York it might be possible to make deals with leaders in other States not enamored with Madison, and sick of the "Virginia dynasty," by which he could win. A coalition was formed between the Clintonians and the Federalists, each side despising the other but willing to join hands for the purpose of changing the government and getting their feet in the trough. The combination came after a Federalist convention held in New York had indorsed Clinton and Jared Ingersoll of Pennsylvania. It was a mean fight and completely unsuccessful. Clinton carried New York of course; also Massachusetts, New Hampshire, Delaware, New Jersey, and got five votes from Maryland, but his total was only 89. Madison carried the other eleven States, totaling 128 electoral votes. With him was elected Elbridge Gerry of Massachusetts, as Vice-President. The "solid South" voted for Madison, most of the North for Clinton. Aside from the disgracefulness of the coalition between the New York Democrats and the Federalists, the noteworthy and most interesting thing about the fight was the fact that the Clinton campaign was managed by Martin Van Buren, then thirty years old. It is an illustration of the strange turns of the political wheel that Van Buren's entrance into national politics should have been as the manager of an unsavory conspiracy to defeat the candidate of the party that afterward elevated him to the Presidency.

It was said in the first chapter of this book that part of the record of the Democratic party was built on the frequency with which its performance clashed with its professions—in other words, a repudiation of its own principles. It began to do exactly that in the first Jefferson administration—the Louisiana Purchase being the very sort of thing the Democrats had contended could not be constitutionally done—and off and on they have been doing it ever since. Sometimes this departure from "basic Democratic principles" has had a strengthening and beneficial party effect, as in the Louisiana instance, but very often it has had disastrous, not to say calamitous, effects. Three times since 1800 such departures have split the organization wide open, left it helpless and stunned. Any one of them would have killed a party less deeply rooted. It is a dreadful habit and apparently there is no cure for it.

Of course it was impossible once it achieved power and responsibility for the Democratic party to live up to the rigid construction of the Constitution which, while out of power and unhampered by executive responsibility, it so eloquently urged. No one to-day, in the Democratic or any other party, believes in the very strict construction of the Constitution as Jefferson understood it. No one places, as did he, the State above the nation, or denies the right of the Supreme Court to act as the interpreter of the Constitution, as did he. Everybody agrees it is the one, final, and proper interpreter. In the early days, of course, the National Government was more or less an experiment and there was not the feeling for it there is to-day. That explains the impossibly rigid construction attitude taken at the time. But conceding that, and conceding that no Democratic or any other administration could make the Government function if, as the early Democrats insisted, every constitutional word was to be literally construed, still, almost no one denies that the menace that Jefferson saw of the encroachment of the Federal Government on the rights of the States was a real one, and that there exist to-day innumerable evidences of the soundness of that great Democratic principle and every reason why the party should swing back to its support.

To return to this departure from principle, it is possible to find an instance of it, of one sort or another, in most Democratic administrations—not all, but most. In the main, it is not the Presidential acts that have hurt the party. They have mostly been necessary and departures of a particular, not a general, nature. The departures that have hurt are those recorded in the party platforms, in the campaigns and in the candidates. The Presidential departures, as has been said, have frequently been politically helpful and have not altered the party direction. Jefferson's Louisiana Purchase certainly was popular, and the various acts of Madison in the course of the war, in the making of peace, it has been claimed were so nearly in accord with the former Federalist views that they left no issue between the parties. The assertion is made that "the Federalist party was destroyed by the success of its own principles in the hands of its opponents," and a list, too long to give here, of instances during the Madison and Monroe administrations is cited to substantiate the fact. Perhaps when the tremendous opposition of the Democrats to the establishment of a United States Bank in Washington's time is recalled, the most striking is the incorporation of the second United States Bank by a Congress overwhelmingly Democratic and approved by Mr. Madison, a rigid constructionist.

Actually the Federalist party literally disintegrated in the second Madison administration. The famous Hartford convention in which Federalists seriously proposed separation from the Union and the formation of a Northern Confederacy, and in which radical action was prevented only by the sober and more substantial leaders of the George Cabot type, removed the last possibility of the return of the Federalists to power. Although Mr. Madison and the Jefferson influence were strongly behind Mr. Monroe for the nomination, there was a considerable revolt within the party. No principles and no issues were involved but outside of Virginia the leaders were certainly getting tired of the complete domination exercised by that State. In the end the Democratic caucus nominated Mr. Monroe by a margin of eleven votes and with him as Vice-Presidential candidate Governor Daniel D. Tompkins of New York. They were not popular selections and there was open resentment against the congressional caucus custom of making nominations that had been smoldering for a long while.

A great many meetings of protest were held and the friends of Senator W. H. Crawford of Georgia, whom Henry Clay and other party leaders had backed against Monroe, made considerable trouble. But it was all ineffective. The Federalist party had broken up. No real opposition existed. The nomination was equivalent to an election. Actually no nominations were made against Monroe and Tompkins. In no State was there a real contest. The Democrats had no one to fight except themselves. There was no danger from the outside. They could only be hurt from within. It was a wonderful situation—but not without its danger.

Chapter V

THE MONROE DOCTRINE AND ITS JEFFERSONIAN
INSPIRATION

The "Era of Good Feeling" and the Bad Feeling Underneath—Complete Disappearance of an Organized
Opposition—Monroe a Jefferson Choice

In the period at which this story has now arrived—
the Monroe administrations—there was neither
"outstanding personality" in the Presidency, nor
startling strength in party leadership, no sensational
political development or particular party excitement.
On the contrary, there was, on the surface at least,
so much peace and harmony, such freedom from
what seemed vital public problems, such general
prosperity and relief from war restrictions, that
the last four years in which Monroe was President
have gone down into history as the "era of good
feeling." There was not even left a remnant of the
opposition party by this time. Its former members
came over bodily to the dominant party, calling
themselves Federal Republicans, claiming to be
in accord with the Washington-Monroe policies,
proclaiming the "era of good feeling," and declining to make any nomination against Monroe for a
second term. In 1816 only three States—Delaware,

Connecticut, Massachusetts—voted against him. In 1820 these came over, and if it had not been for one elector who, whimsically or stubbornly, voted for John Quincy Adams, Monroe would have had a unanimous reelection.

It is true, of course, that with the end of the war the issues that divided the parties largely disappeared, and that on the new domestic questions that rose neither Madison in his last term nor Monroe left much room for the Federalists to stand. Following up the establishment of the United States Bank, largely along Hamiltonian lines, which they had so bitterly opposed, the Democrats enacted in 1816 the first positive Tariff Law—on cotton and woolens. It was slight protection it is true but none the less a clash with the Democratic strict construction principle which maintained that Congress has power to lay tariffs only to "pay the debts" of the United States and to provide for "the common defense and general welfare." It had been a fundamental party theory that "general" welfare did not mean "particular" welfare, and that under the Constitution no special industry could be granted protection.

Yet they departed from that principle and gave that protection in 1816, because the situation demanded it for one thing, and because the increase in power of manufactures and manufacturers was too pronounced to be ignored. They had grown up under the Republican system and they turned to that party for protection when they needed it. Though of course the great industrial growth of the country had not then begun and the city industries were small in comparison with agricultural strength, still, the manufacturers were in position to make their political strength felt, and did. When, in addition, the demand came also from the Southern cotton planters the anti-protection tariff principle of the party went overboard as it and others have since. In 1819-20 the House passed a Tariff Law increasing the protection. This was rejected in the Senate but in 1824 a still more pronouncedly protective measure was proposed, went through and was signed. More than anything else, this amelioration of its stand on the tariff issue, following the establishment of the bank and certain modifications in the matter of "internal improvements," lends substance to the contention before mentioned that the destruction of the Federalist party was due to "the success of its principles in the hands of its opponents." It also is the first concrete—if not the best— evidence of the truth of the statement made early in this book that the history of the Democratic party is full of instances in which its performances and platforms sharply diverged from its principles, sometimes wisely and reasonably, at others stupidly and with dire party results. The truth is, of course, that once weighed down with administrative power and responsibility no party can—or at least ever did—live wholly up to its platforms or principles.

The party policies that carry campaigns are almost inevitably tempered and toned down by expediency and fact, sometimes wholly forgot.

Nothing is more natural. In the first both sides are forced to extremes before election which are found impossible after election. Always too the minority party in Congress, unhampered by responsibility, goes much farther than it could or would if it and not the enemy had to shoulder the administrative job. It is further true that the dominant party in other periods has aided in the continuation of its ascendancy by the adoption of policies forced on it by the active opposition, or at least has so modified its own policies as to blunt the edge of the attack and avoid reaction. If the Democrats under Madison and Monroe did that to the Federalists, Roosevelt and the Republicans certainly did the same thing to the Democrats nearly a hundred years later. It may not be high minded but it is certainly good politics for the winner to bend forward instead of backward if he wants to continue winning. Also, it is not necessarily discreditable, indicative of instability or lack of character. It may be fair-minded recognition that all the right is not on one side and a sober reaction from the lengths to which the winning side was forced during the fight. In any event, it is certainly what the Democrats did to the Federalists to a small extent under Madison and to a very much greater extent under Monroe. It was the thing that brought the Federal Republicans over, wiped out all organized opposition in any State, and created the "era of good feeling."

As a matter of fact, the "era of good feeling" was more or less a sham. Differences in human nature, which are the root of party differences, are not so easily abolished, and during the "era of good feeling" there was some tremendous seething underneath, various party feuds and factions, considerable bitterness and squabbling. The outside opposition had vanished, it is true, but the good feeling was on the surface and it soon developed that the all-powerful Republican party, or, as it was now beginning to call itself, the Democratic party, contained the elements of a new party which was to be broader constructionist than the Federal party itself. It is true too that, unexciting as seemed the political situation, bright and beautiful as appeared the party prospects in the Monroe administration, it was in this era that the first crack in the party over the issue of slavery occurred, the fundamental error of failing to consistently apply its basic States' rights principle was made, the first sign that the party was really not a homogeneous party was given. Ultimately this question, which first raised its head under Monroe, so nearly destroyed the party in 1860 that it makes it easy to believe that, having survived that smash, it is as indestructible as the Government itself.

So far as Mr. Monroe is concerned, the facts seem to be that he was neither a great party leader nor a great President. He was a good man, not a great one. Jefferson once said of him that he was "a man whose soul could be turned inside out without disclosing a single blemish." It is difficult to think of a finer tribute than that to a man's character, and it may have been a hundred per cent. true without necessarily making him either a first-class executive or an effective political manager. As a matter of fact, the delusion about the "era of good feeling" simply broke to pieces about the close of his second administration. The internal party situation was less harmonious than when he took hold, evidences of a new organized opposition were beginning to appear, and he retired from office without pronounced regret or joy. The fact is that, despite his stainless soul and peaceful administration, Monroe was a mild and moderate man, with no talent for initiative or aggressive leadership. Before his elevation to the Presidency he had been secretary of state, an aspirant for the highest office, and had represented his country abroad on various vital missions. In some of these he had succeeded, in some he had rather dismally failed. Clearly he had rendered no conspicuous party or public service before his election, and clearly he would not have been nominated in the first place but for the determined support of the Madison administration and the tremendous political effectiveness of the close personal friendship of the old party founder at Monticello.

Yet, notwithstanding these things, the truth is

that there have been few Democratic administrations as pregnant from the party standpoint as those of Monroe. Not only did they mark the initial party mistake on the slavery question, from which it was impossible afterward to retreat, but in them was formulated and promulgated a great national foreign policy, the unchangeableness of which through more than a hundred years, and its complete acceptance by all parties since, make it stand out as one of the great constructive things the Democratic party has given to the nation. Called the Monroe Doctrine, it has become one of the three fundamental foreign policies to which every secretary of state and every President since Monroe has unwaveringly adhered. It is one political principle from which not only the Democratic party has never deviated, but which has been so completely adopted by the other parties that it has long since ceased to have the slightest partisan stamp—if it ever did. The fact remains, however, that it was a policy laid down by the Democratic party, promulgated by a Democratic President, inspired by the Democratic founder.

No history of the Democratic party, however outlinish would be complete without presenting this policy in full. Revolt in the Spanish possession of Cuba and the prospect of a seizure of that island by Great Britain were the immediate reason for its evolution. It is contained in a message written and sent to Congress by President Monroe on December 2, 1823, but its inspiration came from Thomas Jefferson, then seventy-six years old and in what was supposed to be complete retirement at Monticello. The fact is that he was in communication with Monroe and with other party leaders, consulted there on all important policies. On this issue Monroe had written him several times, and on receiving evidence of England's sincerity and the absence of any sinister purpose behind her policy, had forwarded the letters to Jefferson and asked his opinion and advice. The text of the reply cannot be omitted, because it not only shows with extreme clarity the inspiration of the Monroe message but marks the culminating success of the great conception of American foreign policy which Jefferson had always in his mind and heart and which less than two months later took shape in the Monroe Doctrine.

His letter to Monroe follows:

The question presented by the letters you have sent me, is the most momentous which has ever been offered to my contemplation since that of Independence. That made us a nation. This sets our compass and points the course which we are to steer through the ocean of time opening on us. And never could we embark on it under circumstances more auspicious. Our first and fundamental maxim should be, never to entangle ourselves in the broils of Europe. Our second, never to suffer Europe to intermeddle with cis-Atlantic affairs. America, North and South, has a set of interests distinct from those of Europe, and peculiarly her own. She should therefore have a system of her own, separate and apart from that of Europe. While the last is laboring to become the domicile of despotism, our endeavor should surely be, to make our hemisphere that of freedom. One nation, most of all, could disturb us in this pursuit; she now offers to lead, aid, and accompany us in it. By acceding to her proposition, we detach her from the bands, bring her mighty weight into the scale of free government, and emancipate a continent at one stroke, which might otherwise linger long in doubt and difficulty. Great Britain is the nation which can do us the most harm of any one, or all on earth; and with her on our side we need not fear the whole world. With her then, we should most sedulously cherish a cordial friendship and nothing would tend more to knit our affections than to be fighting once more side by side in the same cause. Not that I would purchase even her amity at the price of taking part in her wars. But the war in which the present proposition might engage us, should that be its consequence, is not her war but ours. Its object is to introduce and establish the American system of keeping out of our land all foreign powers, of never permitting those of Europe to intermeddle with the affairs of our nations. It is to maintain our own principle, not to depart from it. And if to facilitate this we can effect a division in the body of the European powers and draw over to our side its most powerful member surely we should do it. But I am clearly of Mr. Canning's opinion, that it will prevent instead of provoking war. With Great Britain withdrawn from their scale and shifted into that of our two continents all Europe combined would not undertake such a war. For how would they propose to get at either enemy without superior fleets? Nor is the occasion to be slighted which this proposition offers of declaring our protest against the atrocious violations of the rights of nations, by the interference of any one in the internal affairs of another so flagitiously begun by Bonaparte and now continued by the equally lawless Alliance calling itself Holy.

But we have first to ask ourselves a question. Do we wish to acquire to our own confederacy any one or more of the Spanish provinces? I candidly confess that I have ever looked on Cuba as the most interesting addition which could ever be made to our system of States. The control which, with

Florida Point, this island would give us over the Gulf of Mexico and the countries and isthmus bordering on it as well as all those whose waters flow into it, would fill up the measure of our political well-being. Yet, as I am sensible that this can never be obtained, even with her own consent, but by war and its independence, which is our second interest, (and especially its independence of England,) can be secured without it, I have no hesitation in abandoning my first wish to future chances and accepting its independence, with peace and the friendship of England, rather than its association, at the expense of war and her enmity.

I could honestly therefore join in the declaration proposed, that we aim not at the acquisition of any of those possessions, that we will not stand in the way of any amicable arrangement between them and the Mother country but that we will oppose with all our means the forcible interposition of any power, as auxiliary, stipendiary, or under any other form or pretext, and most especially, their transfer to any power by conquest, cession, or acquisition in any other way.

It was less than six weeks later that Monroe sent his message to Congress laying down the Monroe Doctrine. Here it is:

. . . In the wars of European powers in matters relating to themselves we have never taken any part, nor does it comport with our policy so to do. It is only when our rights are invaded or seriously menaced that we resent injuries or make preparations for our defense.

With the movements in this hemisphere we are, of necessity, more immediately connected, and by causes which must be obvious to all enlightened and impartial observers. The political system of the allied powers [the Holy Alliance] is essentially different in this respect from that of America. This difference proceeds from that which exists in their respective Governments. And to the defense of our own, which has been achieved by the loss of so much blood and treasure, and matured by the wisdom of their most enlightened citizens, and under which we have enjoyed unexampled felicity, this whole nation is devoted.

We owe it, therefore, to candor and to the amicable relations existing between the United States and those powers, to declare that we should consider any attempt on their part to extend their system to any portion of this hemisphere as dangerous to our peace and safety. With the existing colonies or dependencies of any European power we have not interfered and shall not interfere. But with the Governments who have declared their independence, and maintained it, and whose independence we have, on great consideration and on just principles, acknowledged, we could not view any interposition for the purpose of oppressing them, or controlling in any other manner their destiny, by any European power, in any other light than as the manifestation of an unfriendly disposition towards the United States.

Our policy in regard to Europe, which was adopted at an early stage of the wars which have so long agitated that quarter of the globe, nevertheless remains the same, which is, not to interfere in the internal concerns of any of its powers; to consider the Government de facto as the legitimate Government for us; to cultivate friendly relations with it, and to preserve those relations by a frank, firm, and manly policy, meeting, in all instances, the just claims of every power; submitting to injuries from none.

But in regard to these continents, circumstances are eminently and conspicuously different. It is impossible that the allied powers should extend their political system to any portion of either continent without endangering our peace and happiness; nor can any one believe that our Southern brethren, if left to themselves, would adopt it of their own accord. It is equally impossible, therefore, that we should behold such interposition, in any form, with indifference.

Chapter VI

End of the Virginia Dynasty—The Missouri Compromise of 1820—Jefferson's Position on Slavery and His Apprehensions—The Scramble for the Nomination of 1824

I

IT was in 1819, the year before the Presidential election, that slavery first reared its head as a great political issue within the party. It broke then with all the unexpectedness and violence of a tornado. Nothing since the Government had really got steady on its feet had so deeply stirred the passions of the people. It immediately proved the "era of good feeling" to be the veriest sham. The question arose over admitting Missouri to the Union as a slave State and the intensity of the conflict can hardly be exaggerated. Some idea of the depth of feeling aroused can be gained by the description given by Carl Schurz, who in writing of the struggle said:

The dissolution of the Union, Civil War and streams of blood were freely threatened by Southern men, while some anti-slavery men declared themselves ready to accept all these calamities rather than the spread of slavery over the territories yet free from it. Neither was the excitement confined to Congress. As the reports of the speeches made there went over the land people were profoundly astonished and alarmed. The presence of a great danger, and a danger too springing from an inherent antagonism in the institutions of the country suddenly flashed upon their minds.

That does not sound just like the sort of thing possible in an "era of good feeling." It makes one think that that soothing phrase must have become a sort of general joke among politicians before the era ended. The fact is that the fight over Missouri's admission revealed in the country and in the party the most menacing of all political conditions— the coincidence of a great moral principle with a geographical line. Literally there is no possible party division as dangerous as that. It can—and in this case did—lead to war. When you look back and realize that most of the early leaders of the Democratic party, the really thoughtful and effective men, not only foresaw this danger to the party and to the country, but were personally opposed to slavery as a moral wrong utterly unthinkable in a free republic, it is amazing that some way out was not found. The ultimate smash was clearly seen by many. For example, Jefferson. In 1784 he was chairman of a committee appointed by Congress to devise a plan of government for the Western Territories embracing the domain which was afterward converted into the States of Alabama, Mississippi, Tennessee, and Kentucky. The report drafted by him and presented on March 1, 1774, provided that "after the year 1800 of the Christian Era there should be neither slavery nor involuntary servitude in any of the United States." Unquestionably this would have checked the growth of the slave power. In all probability it would have averted the Civil War. Almost certainly it would have steered the Democratic party away from that rock which it hit with such force in 1860 that it took twenty-odd years to gather up the pieces. It is one of the great tragedies not only of the Democratic party but of the country that it was lost by a single vote. Writing of it later, Jefferson is quoted by Francis Hirst as saying: "The voice of a single individual would have prevented this abominable crime from spreading itself over the new country. Thus we see the fate of millions hanging on the tongue of one man, and Heaven was silent in that awful moment. But it is to be hoped it will not always be silent and that the friends of the rights of human nature will in the end prevail."

In 1808 the foreign slave trade was prohibited, and it was the Jefferson conviction that with this the value of slaves would diminish and in the end the owners in the South could be induced to abandon them. His calculation was all wrong. Instead of diminishing, the value of the slaves, with the invention of the cotton gin and the great growth of the cotton industry, was trebled. As their value rose, the South became far less inclined to surrender to the philanthropy of the North, particularly as there was at no time in that section any disposition to follow the British example in the West Indies of equitable compensation. In the South it seemed not only a question of right but one of both economic and political life to hold on to the slaves. The political aspect was due chiefly to the fact that the free States of the North were rapidly outdistancing the South in wealth, power, and population. In 1790 the representation in Congress of the two sections was about the same. In 1820 the North had a majority of some thirty votes in the House of Representatives, and it became vital to the South to hold its own in the Senate. Hence, when a new State knocked on the Union door, it seemed enormously important morally, economically, and politically in the South that it be a slave State which could be counted upon to line up politically with the other slave States, even then on the defensive in the battle for their rights. In the view of Mr. Schurz this was the real significance of the Missouri question.

The close of the fight was a compromise—the famous Missouri Compromise—which in the end turned out to be an almost fatal one for the Democratic party. It not only compromised the concrete question at stake by ceding slavery in Missouri while prohibiting slavery in the rest of the territory bought from France north of "36 degrees and thirty minutes," but it hopelessly compromised the basic principle of the Democratic party. For a long time after the Missouri Compromise it seemed as if the question, so far as the party was concerned, had been satisfactorily settled; but that was a delusion. When the crisis came again, it was found that the party was entrapped by its half-way application of its doctrine of strict construction to the subject of slavery—trapped and unable to extricate itself. As a Territory, it had insisted upon the loosest possible construction of the Constitution—which of course nowhere even remotely suggests a sanction of slavery under Federal auspices where it did not exist at the formation of the Constitution—in order to localize slavery in Missouri Territory. After this had been done the party applied the strictest possible construction of the Constitution to keep Congress from interfering with slavery in Missouri as a State.

The success which met this method of heading in both directions to gain their ends encouraged the application of the same reversible policy to the Territories of Arkansas and Florida and to the State of Texas. What it meant was that having finally after a tempestuous battle accepted the Missouri Compromise on the question, the northern members of the strict construction party were committed to the policy of ignoring the discussion of slavery, while the South was left free to spread slavery in the new Territories by the loosest possible construction and to insist upon non-interference in the States by the strictest possible construction. It was a curious, utterly illogical, wholly indefensible party position, filled with high explosives bound in the end to burst in pieces.

It lasted, however—getting worse all the time—for forty years, and that fact is one of the best examples in history of the power of party cement to hold together factions as completely separated on a great moral issue as the southern and the northern wings of the Democracy. It required no special gift of prophecy in those days to know the thing could not last—that the issue of slavery was the sort of issue that in the end could not be compromised but had to be fought to the finish. A good many party leaders—Jefferson among them, and Madison too, Clay and Calhoun, Van Buren and others—saw this clearly enough, but the bulk of the party people shut their eyes, told themselves that the question had been settled, and went blindly and blithely ahead without thought.

It is interesting to note that in 1928 there exists again in the Democratic party that menacing coincidence of a moral issue and a geographical line. Prohibition has divided the dry Democrats in South and West from the wet Democrats of the North and East with singular similarity to the way in which slavery divided the North and the South. It is also a striking coincidence that the split among Democrats on prohibition is largely due to their failure again to consistently apply their basic States' rights principle. The idea of Federal

75

prohibition is in every way abhorrent to that principle. It cannot in any way be reconciled with it or with traditional Democratic interpretation of the Constitution. Yet, the solid South, where lies the bulk of the Democratic strength, is just as solidly in favor of prohibition as the Democratic leaders and organizations in Maryland, New York, New Jersey, Massachusetts, Illinois, and other States of the East are violently opposed to it.

Once again the party is in an inconceivably illogical position. The chief way in which the present differs from that other historic division lies in the fact that there is to-day not only a party of opposition but a dominant party, and that the prohibition issue has split the ranks of the other party too—the wet East and the dry West seeming just as incongruous, though a bit better behaved and less bellicose, under the big Republican tent as in the Democratic camp. The difference is this: the Republican party has no basic and historic principle upon which its party was founded that clashes with prohibition, and the Democratic party has. If the Democrats had from the start consistently applied that principle to this issue, and let Federal prohibition be a Republican policy, they would to-day be in an infinitely sounder position. The split would be all on the other side.

But to return to 1820 and the Missouri Compromise: it seems to be established that in this, the most exciting, far-reaching, and politically pregnant controversy of his entire service as President, Mr. Monroe took no active part. He did not supply the leadership on either side. Personally, it is believed, he shared the slavery views of his friends Jefferson and Madison, that the whole issue filled him with alarm. But if he took any real part in this fight it is not so recorded. As a matter of fact, he held himself as aloof from the battle as he could—but he had to sign the act. Perhaps this neutrality upon the part of the President was good politics. He could hardly have been defeated had he taken an active part, because the time was too short to organize an opposition party. His non-participation, however, undoubtedly did avoid enemies, and he had less trouble succeeding himself than any President except Washington. He did not have to fight—and the popular excitement over the Missouri question died down almost immediately, the people supposing the compromise had ended the controversy.

It did not figure in the campaign at all. For one reason there was no campaign. For another, everybody on both sides wanted to forget it. It is, however, somewhat astonishing that Mr. Monroe should have been so remote from the one great and politically important battle of his two terms. It throws a rather illuminating light on the man.

II

Following Monroe's retirement in 1824 came a period of really remarkable party chaos and turmoil.

In the first place, there was the wildest sort of scramble for the Presidential nomination. Issues there were really none. Of personal ambitions there was an oversupply. The struggle started as early as 1822, and there were at one time sixteen active candidates in the field. By the end of that year, through a process of elimination, the number had been reduced to six, three of whom were in the Monroe cabinet and one the speaker of the House of Representatives—Henry Clay. The cabinet members were John Quincy Adams, secretary of state; William H. Crawford, secretary of the treasury; John C. Calhoun, secretary of war.

Then there was that same De Witt Clinton, boss of the party in New York, who had made such a discreditable attempt to defeat Madison, and finally Andrew Jackson, who had been a senator for Tennessee in the first Adams administration, but who was known chiefly as a soldier and was the great popular hero of the battle of New Orleans. There was no secret that the preference of President Monroe was for Mr. Crawford. He was officially committed to him, and while his support was given in decorous fashion without any aggressiveness calculated to offend other candidates still, it was quite clear that if the usual method of nomination that had prevailed up to this time—namely, by a caucus of House and Senate party members— the success of Mr. Crawford was assured. Quite naturally the other candidates were in accord in

opposing the caucus, denouncing it as an undemocratic, utterly unjustifiable way of selecting party
candidates, insisting that they would not accept or
acquiesce in caucus selections, that the time had come
to kill this obnoxious system of selection for all time.

It was a hot, violent fight, and if there had been
any real opposition party it might easily have proved
fatal in the general election. As it was, the bitterness of the internal dissensions was harmless, though
the developments created deep political excitement.
One definite result was to end the "Virginia dynasty"
that had begun to go stale, and it checked the custom
of each administration selecting its own successor.
While the legislatures and mass meetings in various
States put the other candidates in the field, the Crawford forces held hard to the caucus, fully aware that
outside of it their chances were extremely poor.
Only sixty-six of the 261 senators and representatives attended the call, but the Crawford-Gallatin
ticket was put out none the less as the regular party
selection. From the other aspirants this "regularity"
was denounced with the utmost energy and eloquence. By this time the anti-caucus, anti-administration candidates had been cut down to three—
Adams, Jackson, Clay. Calhoun had withdrawn as a
Presidential aspirant, and all the anti-caucus elements united on him for Vice-President.

Early in the campaign it became clear that each
of the four in the field had sufficient strength to
make a choice of President by the electors impos-

sible, and that for the second—and until now the last
—time in the country's history the election would
be thrown into the House of Representatives. That
is exactly what happened. Twenty-four States took
part and no candidate received a majority of electoral votes. This is the first election in which any
effort was made to tabulate the popular vote, and it
is conceded that the tabulations made are both inac-
curate and misleading, due to the entire lack of con-
formity in the way the elections were conducted by
the several States. The best calculation—in Stanwood's "History of the Presidency"—gives Jackson
152,901, Adams 114,023, Crawford 46,979, Clay
47,217.

There is doubt as to the exactness of these figures,
but there is no doubt at all that Andrew Jackson
received both more popular votes and more electoral
votes than his rivals. That record was Jackson 99,
Adams 84, Crawford 41, Clay 37. Yet, on the first
ballot in the House of Representatives John Quincy
Adams was elected through the support of the
Clay forces.

Immediately there was, from journalistic and
political supporters of Jackson the charge of a "corrupt bargain" between Adams and Clay, echoes of
which were heard for years afterward in Democratic politics, the stigma clinging to Clay clear to
the end of his days. The truth is that there was not
the least substantial evidence of any such corrupt
bargain, that the charge was a great injustice to

both Clay and Adams, and no historian of standing has regarded it as credible. However, it must be admitted that Jackson himself appeared to believe in it, and in his next fight revived the scandal in a letter which was made public and in which he maintained that James Buchanan, then a member of Congress, had approached him on behalf of the Clay people with a "proposition." Mr. Buchanan denied that he had done any such thing, insisting that General Jackson had completely misunderstood him. But the story never died. Clay could not live it down. It embittered his life, made him the relentless foe of Jackson, threw him into the Whig movement, and unquestionably had an effect in the following campaign of 1828, as a result of which Andrew Jackson was overwhelmingly elected amid vast popular enthusiasm, and another era in the history of the Democratic party that colored the politics of the country for a hundred years began.

Chapter VII

The Party Changes Its Name to Democratic—The Nullification Fight and the Jackson Proclamation—The Absence of Issues in 1828—The Jacksonian Doctrine and Leadership

IT is hard to select the right starting point to tell the party story of the Jackson period. It marked a change so momentous and far-reaching, there was such a swing backward in one way and such a swing forward in another, so profound a disturbance of the old political standards and such ruthless uprooting of the men and methods that had had control of the party, that that first popular wave by which the old hero was swept into the Presidency partook more of the nature of a revolution than an election. One historian has well described it by saying that in 1829 the people first assumed control of the governmental machinery which had been held in trust for them since 1789, and that the party and administration which then came into power were the first in our history which really represented the people without restriction and with all the faults of the people.

For one thing, it was with the election of Jackson that the party changed its name from "Republican," as it was christened by Jefferson, to "Democratic." Before the election both the Adams wing and the Jackson wing had claimed the name Republican, the Adams supporters being "administration Republicans," the Jackson element "opposition Republicans," or merely "Jackson men." Many of the administration papers formed the habit of attaching the word "national" to the title of the Adams wing, and after the election the victorious Jackson forces began calling themselves "Democrats." In less than a year the other name had passed altogether, and the word "Democrat," which had originally been used by the Federalists toward the Jeffersonian Republicans to express their unbounded contempt, was pridefully adopted—and by it the adherents of the party have been known ever since.

Up to the Jackson election this party, which was based on belief in the capacity of the people to rule, had not been run by the people at all. The people had had singularly little to do with their Government or with the choice of the men who ran it. Largely, the party had been in the hands of the Jefferson-Madison-Monroe type of men, statesmen or politicians, as you choose, but almost without exception men of substance, education, breeding, background, and social station, who, no matter how deep their devotion to the people nor how firm their faith in the masses, were not themselves of the masses and were personally far removed from "the people" as the phrase is now understood. The selection of Presidents had largely been in the hands of the congressional caucus of politicians at Washington. A system of promotion to the Presidency from the cabinet had been followed, and it had been easy enough up to 1820 for each President to hand on the reins of government to the successor of his choice.

The first break in this custom came in 1820 when the Monroe administration failed to put through the man of its choice—Mr. Crawford—and Adams was elected. That, however, was not a real break—as Adams was himself in the cabinet, and the fight was largely among the politicians, not with the people. The only popular side of the battle was represented by the Jackson candidacy, the first failure of which marked a real perversion of the popular desire. But in 1828 the dam broke and the Democratic current swept everything before it. There was nothing sudden about this. Some few who looked ahead saw it coming. The facts and figures of the 1824 election, it would seem, ought to have made it plain to every one in politics at the time. Actually the Jackson election was the culmination of a change in political conditions that had been under way for a long time but which had developed most rapidly after 1810.

In all the older States the voters prior to that time had been limited to those who owned some sort of property or paid some sort of taxes; but as the new States were added the party, one of whose basic policies was the widest possible extension of the suffrage, provided that every white male over

Photograph by Brown Brothers

ANDREW JACKSON

Under whom the Democratic party became really democratic

twenty-one years old should be entitled to vote. Naturally this reacted on the older States, and in one after another the property qualification, either by amendment to state constitutions or adoption of new constitutions, was wiped out—Maryland in 1810, Connecticut in 1818, New York in 1821, Massachusetts in 1822—until by 1828 there was only one of the twenty-eight States in which the choice of electors had not been taken away from the legislatures and put in the hands of the people.

Once this had been done, real political power was transferred from the politicians to the voters. It became possible to create a public sentiment and capitalize it as a candidate. It became possible for the people to put in a man of their choice—and that is what they did. With the election of Jackson we became a democracy in reality rather than in theory, and with Jackson the character not only of the Democratic party underwent a change but the whole method of playing the political game was altered. Not that Jackson gave to the party any new principles or policies. On the contrary, he swung it back to its legitimate political position and reverted to the strict construction basis from which its leaders —he among them—had strayed. He did not depart from the Jeffersonian creed; rather he reverted to it. But with the recent enfranchisement of so many thousands of the poorer classes throughout the country, and the realization that with the voter rested the real power, the whole political picture changed. Party discipline and party propaganda alike became essential. Organization to cover the country was plainly necessary. Machinery for reaching the individual voter as he had not been reached before had to be created, and the Jackson period marked the beginning of party government and party politics as we now understand it.

It was more or less an unorganized but enthusiastic mass that swept Jackson into office, and one of the first things he had to do was to inject order and discipline in the ranks. Prior to the Jackson *régime* there had not been in the country real party government in the sense those words are now understood. The lines had been loosely drawn; the noble art of distributing the patronage among the party leaders and workers had not been developed; real party organization did not exist. There were politicians, of course, but in the main they made themselves count either through influence and personality, natural character and ability, or deals and intrigues among themselves. With Jackson's election all that changed. With the extension of the franchise, the active participation of the common people in politics, the realization among them that they had themselves the power to pick a President, it became necessary, if political power was to be maintained by the party, to establish close and constant contact with the voters.

Jackson, aided by as astute a set of politicians as have surrounded any President—constituting his "kitchen cabinet"—went about this business with a precision, skill, and determination characteristic of his military career. Under him modern party methods originated. Under him the so-called "spoils system" made its appearance. Under him for the first time the Federal jobs were deliberately, calculatingly used by the wholesale as rewards for party service. Under him a real party organization was built clear down to the precincts; the card-index system, or something remarkably like it, was put into effect, and the political game began to be played along lines new at the time, but which are now one hundred years old.

It is amazing how little the political rules have altered in that period. It was in the Jackson administration not only that the pleasing custom of using the Federal patronage to build and strengthen the Federal machine first flowered, but it was then too that there began to develop a purely party press of intense and unshakable partisanship. It was in the Jackson administration, too, that the delivery of congressional speeches for "home consumption" began, and out of the Jackson administration sprang the national convention, the party platforms, and the keynote speech, all still regarded as indispensable features of American political life and likely to continue to be so regarded for another hundred years. The story of the change is graphically told in Bowers's "Party Battles of the Jackson Period." In addition to the party developments above noted as originating then, he writes: "With the appearance of Democracy in action came evils that have persisted through the succeeding years—the penalties of the rule of the people. Demagogy then reared its head and licked its tongue. Class consciousness and hatreds were awakened. And on the part of the great corporations intimidation, coercion and the corrupt use of money to control elections were contributed."

That might with very slight modifications be written of present-day politics, and forces the reflection that since the Jackson day there has been extremely little change at bottom in either politics or politicians. They may look different now at first glance but actually they are the same, operating in the same way, for the same purposes, with the same ideals and standards. No Democratic President ever had more influence on his party than Jackson, and it is no exaggeration to say that, though founded by Jefferson, who gave it its principles and creed, it was made into a party as the word is to-day understood by Andrew Jackson, whose entrance into the Presidency brought to the front a swarm of new leaders and workers, driving into political oblivion those who had before guided the party ship and who hailed with horror Jackson's election as "the triumph of the mob," characterizing his administration as the "millennium of the minnows."

All of this sounds as if Jackson were a queer mixture of demagogic popular hero and practical political boss. Actually, of course, he was the second great outstanding personality of the Democratic party, a figure that in some ways towers high above all the others, save only Jefferson—a man of rugged character, tremendous courage, force, and vigor, with an iron will, rigid honesty, complete sincerity. There was not a demagogic bone in his body. He had not the thought power of Jefferson or Madison. He was not a great political philosopher. He did not promulgate profound principles that have come down through the generations. He was full of faults, bitter, unforgiving, even vindictive; but of the utter sincerity of his devotion to the masses, whose choice he was, and his belief in them, there is not the least doubt.

Of the people himself and neither an aristocrat nor a scholar, in many ways crude and without culture, he possessed qualities of heart and mind that tied his friends to him with bonds of steel and kept the unwavering confidence and affection of his countrymen as long as he lived. He was a born leader, a real leader, a fighter whom men unflinchingly followed. There will always be differences of opinion as to his fitness for the Presidency, as to the bigness of the man, as to his influence on the political morals of his country. Undoubtedly he was as relentless and ruthless toward his foes as he was unshakably loyal to his friends. Undoubtedly, too, he was swayed in his administrative and political policies by the violence of his prejudices on the one hand and the strength of his predilections on the other. But even superficial study of the man and his career carries conviction that deep down in his heart there was an intense devotion to the interests of the masses and a genuine desire to serve them. In that first message of his, in 1828, he expressed this feeling in words that have been taken generally as the Jacksonian political creed. They present his views of the sphere of government and came from the Jackson heart.

Distinctions in society [he wrote] will always exist under every just government. Equality of talents, of education, or of wealth, cannot be produced by human institutions. In the full enjoyment of the gifts of heaven and the fruits of superior industry, economy and virtue, every man is equally entitled to protection by law. But when the laws undertake to add to those natural and just advantages artificial distinctions—to grant titles, gratuities and exclusive privileges—to make the rich richer and the potent more powerful—the humbler members of society—the farmers, mechanics and the laborers—who have neither the time nor the means of securing like favors for themselves, have a right to complain of the injustice of their government.

This, of course, is fundamental Democratic doctrine. It logically arrays the party against the protective tariff, against all forms of governmental subsidies, against the concentration of power in the hands of wealth, against the latter-day Republican faith that if the rich are protected in their prosperity and allowed unchecked to grow more prosperous, automatically the poorer classes and the country generally will benefit most. In the past two years the Democratic party's representatives in Congress abandoned completely this Jacksonian Democratic

creed and joined with the Republicans in enacting
a bill by which the taxes on the very rich were reduced first and most, on the theory that this would
best promote general prosperity. That was not the
Jackson idea and it was not the Democratic idea.
It is in fact directly opposed to both the Jeffersonian
and the Jacksonian principles upon which the party
was first founded and then organized.

The curious thing about the first Jackson election
was the complete absence of issues. The one controlling aim was the election of Jackson, the defeat
of Adams. The one cry—to redress "the wrong" of
1824. To this all political principles were not only
subordinated but forgotten. In the ranks back of
the General were protectionists, internal improvement advocates, supporters of the Bank of the
United States, men of every shade and variety of
political opinion. As has been said, neither as a
congressman nor a senator from Tennessee before
he became President had Jackson been in any sense
opposed to protection, to internal improvements, even
to the bank. His policies on all these subjects crystal-
lized after he got in, and his drift toward strict
construction was unquestionably accelerated by the
fact that the "National Republicans," the Adams
men and particularly Henry Clay, were broad con-
structionists, favoring the tariff, the bank, and various projects for governmental aid, all of which
clashed with the inherited and natural tendencies of
the strong Jackson support in the South.

The Democratic Party: A History

In all our political history there have been no such turbulent administrations as those of Jackson. No other of the eleven Presidents of the party ever engaged in fights approaching those of Jackson in sheer ferocity and violence. Beside them the League of Nations fight of Woodrow Wilson and the great tariff struggle of Grover Cleveland were relatively tame affairs. From the beginning of his first term to the end of his second the story of the Jackson administrations is a story of furious and continuous political conflict. Sometimes the fights were over great and vital issues and the results far-reaching and tremendously important; sometimes they were over trivial things not really worth fighting about.

No attempt will here be made to detail or even outline these historic and brilliant battles. Nor will there be any effort either to write the full history of the Jackson administrations or to more deeply portray the fascinating personality and character of this remarkable man, whose popularity lasted not only all his life but long afterward, who was literally worshiped by thousands of his fellow-countrymen, who has been, along with Jefferson, enshrined as one of the two great Democratic saints of its early history, whose influence upon his party has been perhaps more indelibly impressed than that of any leader since. This is one of those periods in the party history around which not only volumes could be but have been written, and the difficulty here is to treat it adequately for the purposes of this outline without

BORN TO COMMAND.

KING ANDREW THE FIRST.

THIS CARTOON OF ANDREW JACKSON IS ONE OF THE BEST OF
THE EARLY POLITICAL CARTOONS IN AMERICAN
HISTORY

being dragged off the path by its drama and interest.

It is not possible, however, to pass along without mention of the two greatest of the Jackson battles, in both of which he was overwhelmingly victorious, though at terrific cost—first the fight to put the Bank of the United States out of existence; second the struggle with the South Carolina nullificationists. Each of these is worth a book by itself. Whatever may be said of General Jackson, however much opinion may diverge as to the greatness of the man, even his severest critics concede his conduct in the South Carolina crisis was fearless to the limit, patriotic, of infinite service to the country, genuinely great.

Actually, these two great clashes of the Jackson period were to a large extent personal duels between Jackson and two remarkable men—John C. Calhoun of South Carolina in the one, Nicholas Biddle, president of the United States Bank, in the other. The desperate nature of these fights has no parallel in the whole history of American politics; certainly none in Democratic politics. Neither the Roosevelt-Foraker, the Cleveland-Gorman, nor the Wilson-Lodge conflict approaches them in fire and ferocity. Literally they were to the death, and echoes of the clash were heard in many a following campaign.

Calhoun was the head, the front, the center of the nullification movement, just as later he became, in the words of his biographers, the "personification of the slavery cause." He had entered Congress a young man during the Madison administration, and by his

93

fire, force, eloquence, audacity, and actual genius as a statesman contributed largely toward forcing the peace-loving Madison into the declaration of war against England, which the latter had been trying in every way to avoid. An aspirant for the Presidency almost from the start, he entered the Monroe cabinet, and was one of those who scrambled for the nomination at the expiration of the "era of good feeling." Pulling out of the race before it reached a climax, he succeeded in uniting all elements on him for second place and was elected Vice-President with Adams.

Almost immediately he began to intrigue against Adams and was part of the Jackson movement in 1828, again succeeding to the Vice-Presidency. Counting on Jackson, who was over sixty years old when first elected, being satisfied, as he had indicated, with a single term, Calhoun was from the start an active Presidential candidate to succeed him. The original cause of the break between Calhoun and Jackson is asserted by some students of the period to have been due to the discovery by the latter that Calhoun in the Monroe cabinet had been active in a movement to discredit General Jackson. The moment he learned of the deceitful part played by Calhoun the Jackson resentment flamed and personal relations were almost completely severed. But the open breach came over the nullification issue, the whole soul of the old hero of The Hermitage revolting against the seditious South Carolina efforts to break

94

up the Union by defying the Federal Government.

Intensely resentful of the tariff laws from the beginning, each succeeding one had been an added provocation in South Carolina, and that of 1828— enacted before Jackson went in and while the broad construction Adams still held the reins—was the last straw. The spirit of sedition broke out all over the State, and Calhoun, then about to enter on his second term as Vice-President, wrote his famous "Exposition," later presented to the legislature by a committee, in which the principles of nullification were set out. There is no space here to follow through the nullification story, to tell of that conspirators' dinner at which Jackson threw dismay into the nullificationists who had staged things so as to commit him by his famous toast, "The Federal Union—it must and shall be preserved"; of the way in which the fire was fanned in South Carolina until the whole State was ablaze; of the dramatic features of the Calhoun leadership in the Senate, to which he had promptly been elected after he resigned the Vice-Presidency; of the stern preparations of Jackson to crush out the rebellion with the armed forces of the nation, and of the final crumbling of the movement under the iron will and unflinching determination of the President.

The story is one of the most dramatic and tragic in all American politics, but it has been too fully set forth by others to need repetition here. However, it does seem as if no story of the Democratic party would be complete without presenting that part of the proclamation which has caused it to be placed by some alongside the Emancipation Proclamation as one of the greatest documents in American history. It swept aside party lines, rang through the country, and rallied to the Jackson banner Unionists all over the land. Though Jackson was over sixty when he wrote it, the passion, fire, and feeling of the paper reveal the tremendous force and vigor of this amazing old man, frail in body but with a lion's heart. There is no dispute concerning the fact that this nullification issue presented one of the great crises in the country's history, and that Jackson met it as a patriot and a man. Conceding every fault and failing with which he has been charged, if there had been nothing else in all his career save this, it would be enough to make Democrats proud that their party produced that sort of President.

That proclamation had a ring and a fervor about it that no other defense of the Union has contained. It is one of the country's imperishable documents. It is one of the things the Democratic party treasures as having been given to the nation by a Democratic President. It is too long to give in full here, but the heart and fire of his appeal are to be found in the following extracts:

. . . I consider, then, the power to annul a law of the United States, assumed by one State, *incompatible with the existence of the Union, contradicted expressly by the letter of the Constitution, unauthorized by its spirit, inconsistent with every principle on which it was founded, and destructive of the great object for which it was formed. . . .*

The wisdom of man never yet contrived a system of taxation that would operate with perfect equality. If the unequal operation of a law makes it unconstitutional, and if all laws of that description may be abrogated by any State for that cause, then, indeed, is the Federal Constitution unworthy of the slightest effort for its preservation. We have hitherto relied on it as the perpetual bond of our Union; we have received it as the work of the assembled wisdom of the nation; we have trusted to it as to the sheet anchor of our safety in the stormy times of conflict with a foreign or domestic foe; we have looked to it with sacred awe as the palladium of our liberties, and with all the solemnities of religion have pledged to each other our lives and fortunes here and our hopes of happiness hereafter in its defense and support. Were we mistaken, my countrymen, in attaching this importance to the Constitution of our country? Was our devotion paid to the wretched, inefficient, clumsy contrivance which this new doctrine would make it? Did we pledge ourselves to the support of an airy nothing—a bubble that must be blown away by the first breath of disaffection? Was this self-destroying, visionary theory the work of the profound statesman, the exalted patriot, to whom the task of constitutional reform was intrusted? Did the name of Washington sanction, did the States deliberately ratify, such an anomaly in the history of fundamental legislation? No; we were not mistaken. The letter of this great instrument is free from this radical fault. Its language directly contradicts the imputation; its spirit, its evident intent, contradicts it. . . . To say that any State may at pleasure secede from the Union is to say that the United States are not a nation. . . . Fellow-citizens of my native State, let me not only admonish you, as the First Magistrate of our common country, not to incur the penalty of its laws, but use the influence that a father would over his children whom he saw rushing to certain ruin. In that paternal language, with that paternal

97

feeling, let me tell you, my countrymen, that you are deluded by men who are either deceived themselves or wish to deceive you. . . . Contemplate the condition of that country of which you still form an important part. Consider its government, uniting in one bond of common interest and general protection so many different States, giving to all their inhabitants the proud title of *American citizen,* protecting their commerce, securing their literature and their arts, facilitating their inter-communication, defending their frontiers, and making their name respected in the remotest parts of the earth. Consider the extent of its territory, its increasing and happy popula-tion, its advance in arts that render life agreeable, and the sciences which elevate the mind! See education spreading the lights of religion, morality, and general information into every cottage in this wide extent of our Territories and States. Behold it as the asylum where the wretched and oppressed find a refuge and support. Look on this picture of happiness and honor and say, *"We two are citizens of America."* Carolina is one of these proud States; her arms have defended, her best blood has cemented, this happy Union. And then add, if you can, without horror and remorse, This happy Union we will dissolve; this picture of peace and prosperity we will deface; this free intercourse we will in-terrupt; these fertile fields we will deluge with blood; the protection of that glorious flag we renounce; the very name of Americans we discard. And for what, mistaken men? For what do you throw away these inestimable blessings? For what would you exchange your share in the advantages and honor of the Union? For the dream of a separate inde-pendence—a dream interrupted by bloody conflicts with your neighbors and a vile dependence on a foreign power.

Chapter VIII

THE FIRST PARTY CONVENTION

Origin of the Two Thirds Rule—Jackson Renominated
and Van Buren Becomes Vice-President and Heir
Apparent—The Great Bank Fight

THE tragic figure of Calhoun will reappear in this
story, but for the time being the crushing of the
nullification movement dropped the curtain on him.
His break with Jackson was of far-reaching political
effect. It not only smashed Calhoun's chances for
the Presidency, but it made Martin Van Buren first
Vice-President and then President. It paved the
way for Jackson to promote his friend and threw the
South Carolina statesman wholly over into the Clay
camp. Clay, embittered toward Jackson largely because of his belief of the "corrupt bargain" story,
was the real power of the Whigs, who had become
organized as a party under his leadership, and was
as completely consumed by the fever to be President as ever Calhoun had been.

The Bank fight extended over both the Jackson
terms, and while for a time it threatened his own
prestige and power and very badly scared the ambitious among his close political friends—chiefly

Mr. Van Buren—in the end it turned out to be the most popular of all acts of his administration, the one that strengthened him more than any other with the people. This is no place to discuss the merits of the Bank business, or to consider the propriety or legality of his withdrawal of deposits from it, or the political morality of his fighting methods. As to this last, there certainly seemed to be a complete absence of such on both sides. The battle was so hot and so long, the political consequences so great, and the financial stakes so big, that scruples and fairness alike were thrown overboard and both sides hit below the belt as often as above. Henry Clay, Daniel Webster, and John C. Calhoun were all arrayed against the President in this famous struggle, with Mr. Biddle, the Bank president, really the directing head of the fight. He supplied a considerable part of the brains as well as the money. The charge was made, and seems to have been true, that the funds of the Bank were freely spent for propaganda and campaigning, that money was "loaned" to editors without interest or security, that a large section of the press was owned or controlled by Bank interests, that Daniel Webster while in the Senate personally solicited and obtained a retainer from the Bank, that it was in politics clear up to the neck. Mr. Biddle made a terrific fight. He had the disadvantage of being on the defensive and the disfavor that comes from being attacked as the "monster," and assailed as the "money power." But he had the money and back of him to a large extent the financial forces of the country.

At times they seemed to have the old man at the head of the Government, who was appealing over the heads of the Congress to the people, down and out. The Senate passed a resolution of censure; the House rejected his plans and refused to follow him back to the original Democratic policy of opposition to a great central bank. When, over the protest of cabinet officials and against the advice of friends, he forced the radical step of withdrawing the deposits, Mr. Biddle brought on a panic for which Jackson was generally blamed. He had, however, in his fight the aid of some of the most astute politicians who ever supported a President, and in the end not only put through the withdrawal but prevented the re-chartering of the Bank, which effectually put it out of business. It was, of course, predicted that he had ruined the country, and it is likely that he was not altogether sure whether he had or not—but it did not turn out that way. There was immense dislocation for a while and a bad period of readjustment followed, but the readjustments were eventually made, though not in Jackson's administration. Whatever the cost short of disaster—and there was no disaster—it was certainly worth it to put the Bank out of politics, where it had no business to be. It was a stirring and historic fight, won and lost many times, and full of far-reaching influence on the party as well as the country.

But to pick up the thread of the story again: the year 1832, when Jackson was reelected, is notable in party history as the one in which the first Democratic national convention was held. It was at this first convention that the famous rule requiring a two thirds vote to nominate, over which there has been so much bitter controversy and so many heart-breaking and unsuccessful efforts to repeal, was adopted. Its singular inconsistency in a party that first and always has advocated the rule of the majority, and which under the unit rule allows in its conventions a majority of the state delegations to vote the whole delegation, is obvious and without defense. It has not, however, been possible to date to alter it, even though it is a recognized danger, putting it always in the power of a minority to break up the convention and prevent a nomination by the majority—which is exactly what happened in 1860, and nearly happened once much more recently.

Prior to 1832, Presidential and Vice-Presidential nominations had been made either by the state legislatures or by the congressional caucus, loosely, without order or system and with mighty little formality. Yet those methods worked more or less satisfactorily until the franchise was extended in all the States, real party organization became established, and politics developed to the point where recognition was general of the right of the people in a democratic form of government to participate in the selection of their candidates as well as in a choice between them. That notion did not take real hold until after the 1828 Jackson tidal wave and the reorganization of the party on a permanent basis. The suggestion of a national convention it is believed originated in the fertile political heads of the Jackson "kitchen cabinet," the most influential members of which were Major Lewis, second auditor of the Treasury; Amos Kendall, fourth auditor of the Treasury, and the well-known and extremely shrewd Isaac Hill. These three men were closer to Jackson than any others, and wholly loyal to him. They played the really practical politics of the administration, made the necessary deals and dickers, manipulated the machinery of his campaigns and carried out the strategy of his congressional fights. They were extremely influential, thoroughly practical in their politics, and without reflecting on their personal integrity it can be fairly said they did "the dirty work."

There was not the least doubt in 1831 of Jackson's renomination. He had, it is true, said in 1828 he thought one term enough for a President, but he evidently meant for the Presidents who followed him. Within the party there was no one who could make a formidable fight against him. Clay was the inevitable and logical candidate of the new Whig party and took with him, of course, Calhoun and the other enemies of the General, who had by the fury of their onslaught on the administration, and the equal fury of the administration's onslaught on them, been completely driven out of the Democratic camp. Jackson was not only the leader of the party but he was the party. Added to his vibrant personality, great prestige, and popularity was the weight of the Federal machine he had built up.

It was irresistible then in his hands and has been irresistible in the hands of most Presidents who have followed him who chose to use it in the effort for renomination. In recent years its growth has been so great that it has come to be recognized as completely futile to oppose the renomination of a President able and willing to manipulate it. In spite of this, it is occasionally tried, but never so far with success. The best illustration of its futility was the failure of Roosevelt to prevent the renomination of Taft in 1912. Since that time the addition of the prohibition enforcement unit, with its thousands of Federal officials, the extension of the Internal Revenue Department, and the increase in Federal bureaus, boards, and positions generally, have so vastly increased the weight of the machine that in the selection of delegates to national conventions it is hopeless to oppose it. Since the Jackson day the foundation of all party organization has been the Federal patronage. It is an enormous political asset, and one of the reasons for the present-day weakness of the Democratic party nationally is the length of time it has been "outside the breastworks," without Federal jobs with which to reward the party workers, promote unity in the ranks, and offer as an incentive for party activity. With the exception of

sixteen years, since 1860 the Democrats have had
to rely exclusively upon patronage in the States
where they happened to be dominant to cement the
local machines. It has been so great a handicap
that the chances of party success since the Civil War
have been largely dependent either upon a popular
revolt against or a wide split within the party in
power. What the vast Federal patronage and the
Federal power to distribute favors other than
patronage means to-day is that the administration is
able not only to control its party convention but enter
the campaign after the convention with weapons
and ammunition utterly lacked by the opposition. It is
an enormous advantage.

Though he had it, Jackson did not perhaps need
the Federal machine to secure his own renomination,
but he did need it and he did use it to secure the
nomination of Martin Van Buren for Vice-President. Soon after his first election, the old hero had
picked Van Buren as his successor, was determined
he should first be Vice-President, then President.
There was no secret about it. One of the many reasons given for his break with Calhoun was because
that statesman had, as Vice-President, cast in the
Senate the deciding vote that rejected the Jackson
nomination of Van Buren for ambassador to Great
Britain, an act that threw Jackson in a rage, and
which he resented as a direct reflection on himself.
More than ever he was set on Van Buren as his successor, and when he came back Van Buren entered

the Jackson cabinet as the recognized heir apparent.

But there was opposition of a very real sort to the "Red Fox." He had been too long in politics, had participated in too many fights, and made too many deals not to have accumulated a good many enemies. Naturally these, as well as every other aspirant for the Presidency, open or under cover, were arrayed against him. Some of the strongest Jackson men in the country were extremely antagonistic to Van Buren, and the utmost personal and political pressure was exerted to swing them into line. It was early in 1831 that Major Lewis wrote to Amos Kendall from Washington urging the desirability of having a convention to nominate the Vice-Presidential candidate, and suggesting that it would be a good thing to have the New Hampshire legislature propose such convention. The first public notification came in June, 1831, when the "Globe," published in Washington and recognized as the President's organ, printed the following:

The Republican members of the New Hampshire Legislature to the number of about 169 met last evening. An address and resolutions approving of the principles and measures of the present administration, the veto of the President on the Mayville Road bill, disavowing the doctrine of Nullification, disapproving Clay's American system, but recommending a judicious reduction of the duties, disapproving of the United States Bank, passed the convention unanimously. The convention also recommended a general convention of Republicans friendly to the election of General Jackson to consist of delegates equal to the number of electors of President in each State, to be holden at Baltimore on the third

The First Party Convention

Monday of May, 1832, to nominate a candidate for Vice-President and take such other measures in support of the re-election of Andrew Jackson as may be deemed expedient.

That was in effect the call for the first national convention. There was at the time no national committee, no national headquarters. As has been said, the Democratic party was Jackson and Jackson was the party. The initiative as well as the idea for the convention came from the men around him, and the reason undoubtedly was to facilitate the nomination of Van Buren, who would have had hard sledding in the state legislatures that renominated Jackson with a whoop. Appearing first in the paper regarded as the mouthpiece of the administration, the convention suggestion was at once taken up by the party organs in every State and the delegates were chosen.

The official account of the convention is contained in a little bound pamphlet in the Library of Congress, whose title page reads, "Proceedings of a Convention of Republican Delegates from the several States in the Union, for the Purpose of Nominating a Candidate for the Office of Vice-President of the United States. Baltimore. Printed by Samuel Harker. Republican office. Gay Street opposite the Exchange." Contrary to a rather widespread impression, the convention did not nominate Jackson, nor was he a candidate before it, though it did by resolution indorse his nomination, which had already been made by legislative caucuses and conventions and accepted by Democrats everywhere. The convention met on the third Monday in May in the saloon of the old Baltimore Athenæum, and General Robert Lucas of Ohio, previously and privately slated by the ubiquitous gentlemen of the "kitchen cabinet," presided.

It is extremely interesting that this first convention should have originated both the two thirds rule and the unit rule, which have remained unchanged for nearly a hundred years in spite of the fact that one recognizes the principle of majority and the other rejects it. Yet such is the fact. After the convention had organized, selected its chairman, and appointed a committee of one from each State to report the number of delegates in attendance, it got down to work. There was almost no oratory and there was an almost complete lack of friction and fight. As a matter of fact, the convention was to a considerable extent an organized protest against the "Senate coalition" headed by Calhoun in refusing confirmation of Van Buren, and it was skilfully managed by the Jackson leaders. Beyond doubt it was the "kitchen cabinet" experts who framed the two resolutions which were offered and adopted on the second day. The first of these in effect appears to be the unit rule. At least, the unit rule under which most States in national conventions now vote is the outgrowth of this resolution. It follows:

Resolved that in taking the vote for the Vice President, a majority of the delegation from each State shall designate the member or members who shall vote for that State.

The First Party Convention

There are two versions of the two thirds rule resolution. In the Harker account it reads as follows:

Resolved That the delegation from each State in this convention be entitled to as many votes in selecting a suitable person for the office of Vice President as each State will be entitled to in the Electoral College for the choice of this office, equally to the apportionment bill recently framed by the Congress of the United States, and that two-thirds of the whole number of votes given be required for a nomination and on all questions connected therewith.

While newspaper accounts of the time followed the official report closely, the last phrase, "and on all questions connected therewith," does not appear in several examined, and in histories and magazine articles the two thirds rule of the 1832 convention is often stated without it.

In Stanwood's "History of the Presidency" the wording of the resolution is slightly different. It is there given as follows:

Resolved that each State be entitled in the nomination to be made of a candidate for the Vice Presidency to a number of votes equal to the number to which they will be entitled in the Electoral Colleges under the new apportionment, in voting for President and Vice-President; and that two-thirds of the whole number of the votes in the convention shall be necessary to constitute a choice.

Whichever is the correct version, the sense and effect are the same. The interesting question is why it was done. It has been contended by some that the purpose of the rule was to prevent the nomination of Calhoun and insure the selection of Van Buren. But the facts do not bear that theory out. The convention was completely dominated by Jackson's friends, and on the first ballot Van Buren got 208 of the 283 votes, considerably more than the two thirds. There simply isn't any logic in the contention that the two thirds rule was used to put Van Buren over. It is certainly easier to secure a majority than it is two thirds. Why then should the Van Buren backers have evolved a rule that put it in the power of one third of the convention to block his nomination? The idea does not click, and it is far easier to believe the reason given at the time on the floor of the convention by William R. King, a delegate from Alabama and a member of the Committee on Methods and Procedure. In supporting the resolution he said:

And as a nomination made by two-thirds of the whole body would show a more general concurrence of sentiment in favor of a particular individual, would carry with it a greater moral weight and be more favorably received than one made by a smaller number, I sincerely hope the resolution will be adopted.

In reply to Mr. King, "The Baltimore Republican" says that Mr. Pollard, a delegate from Virginia, "objected to the proposition for two-thirds as inconsistent with the fundamental principles upon which our government is founded, which provide that the rule of majority shall prevail and because it might possibly be found to be impracticable to unite the voices of so large a proportion in favor of any one individual; and moved, accordingly, that a majority should be substituted for two-thirds. The amendment was, however, rejected and the original resolution carried."

The more it is contended that this rule was conceived in order to nominate Van Buren, and that without it he could not have been nominated, the sillier it seems. It would have been logical enough for the weaker candidates or the friends of Calhoun, who were conspicuously absent, to have proposed such a rule. For the Van Buren people to propose it, without being sure of the nomination anyhow, would have been absurd. The only reasonable explanation is the desire to make the Van Buren nomination as convincing and impressive as possible. If the opposing candidates in the convention had combined their votes they would not have had one third, much less a majority. The only ballot taken resulted as follows:

Martin Van Buren of New York.....................208
Philip P. Barbour of Virginia....................... 49
Richard M. Johnson of Kentucky................... 26

    Total 283
Necessary for nomination, 188.

Virginia and South Carolina voted solidly for Barbour, who also got fifteen votes from Maryland, Alabama, and North Carolina. Johnson got Kentucky and Indiana and two votes from Illinois. Van Buren had all the rest.

The convention adopted no platform, largely, it is supposed, because of the difficulty of saying anything on the Bank question that would not alienate the support of Pennsylvania, a strongly pro-Bank State. However, the following resolution was adopted amid real enthusiasm and which in effect was the only platform the politics of the situation really called for:

> Resolved, that the convention repose the highest confidence in the purity, patriotism and talents of Andrew Jackson and that we most cordially concur in the repeated nominations which he has received in various parts of the Union as a candidate for re-election to the office he now fills with so much honor to himself and usefulness to his country.

Just before adjournment a resolution offered by Mr. Archer of Virginia was adopted "that a general corresponding committee from each State be appointed by the President of this Convention." In pursuance of this, General Lucas named the committee at once, the names having been previously obtained from the leaders of the delegations. This was the forerunner of the Democratic National Committee, which, however, did not come into formal and official existence under that name until the convention of 1848. Only one other resolution of note seems to have been adopted at the 1832 convention and that was one offered at the outset, prohibiting all nomination speeches. It does seem rather a pity that that rule which would have saved an infinity of time and much mental and physical suffering could not have been preserved, and the two thirds rule from which nothing but trouble has flowed cast into the discard. Instead, the nomination speeches began not in the next but in the third convention, and the two thirds rule, which originally applied only to the Vice-Presidential nomination, was extended to cover the Presidency as well in the second. Space has been taken here to present the details of the 1832 Democratic national convention rather fully not only because it is the first of its kind but because it is important to know definitely the origin of various party customs, agencies, and instruments that are still in force within the party to-day.

Chapter IX

More About the Two Thirds Rule—Jackson's Fight to
Nominate His Friend—The Election Closer Than
Was Comfortable—Shrinkage in Popular Vote—Van
Buren as a Leader and a President

THE final triumph of the "old hero" came in the election of Van Buren as his successor. Ill and in pain but indomitable always, it must have been an immense satisfaction to him to witness, as he did, Van Buren, the man of his choice, once rejected by the "factious Senate," sworn into office by his friend Chief Justice Taney, also rejected for the Jackson cabinet by that same "factious Senate," the moving spirit in both rejections being his flaming South Carolina foe John C. Calhoun. The grim enthusiasm over the Van Buren election and the whole character of the man make it easy to believe that he really did say, not long before he died, those words so often quoted, "My one regret is, I did not hang Calhoun." That was like him. But "putting over" Van Buren for President was an even harder job than making him Vice-President. It took the full weight of the office-holding machine, all the prestige and power of General Jackson, and all the political skill of Van Buren himself. It was a stiff fight and a long one.

Fearing that his failing health might interfere with his plans, anxious to forestall opposition, it was at Jackson's suggestion that the second Democratic national convention was held—again in Baltimore —on May 20, 1835, more than eighteen months in advance of the election. There was little trouble in the convention. That was an administration affair and the extreme Southern wing of the party held aloof, counting upon the candidacy of Senator Hugh L. White of Tennessee to split the ranks and help the Whigs and the scattered opposition to throw the election again into the House of Representatives. That was the game of the opposition, and it was to block it that the second national convention was called with the idea that it would present an appearance of harmony and unity behind the administration candidates—Van Buren for President and Richard M. Johnson of Kentucky for Vice-President.

Besides Senator White, who had been a devoted friend of Jackson but had had a violent and foolish old men's quarrel with him, there were in the field as Presidential candidates, nominated by various legislative caucuses and state conventions, William Henry Harrison of Ohio, Daniel Webster of Massachusetts, and Willis P. Mangum of North Carolina, all aiming to take enough electoral votes away from Van Buren to void the election. In the House the opposition by combining could probably have defeated the Jackson choice. The plainness of this Whig strategy brought about the second convention so long in advance, and though its action was not particularly important, and neither speeches were made nor platform adopted, it again is worth giving space to, because it was here that the two thirds rule was first applied to the selection of a Presidential candidate—not, however, before it was first rescinded and then reconsidered. It was a curious convention—more a mass-meeting without oratory than anything else, and in these days would be absurd. Even then it was denounced by the opposition as an office-holders' assemblage, and the idea that the delegates were "fresh from the people," as the President had proclaimed, was greeted with derision. Altogether there were 626 names on the list of delegates, but 422 of these came from Maryland, Virginia, New Jersey, and Pennsylvania, Maryland alone contributing 181. Twenty-two States, two Territories—Michigan and Alabama—and the District of Columbia were represented, but there was no one present from Illinois, South Carolina, or Alabama. When it was found that Tennessee had sent no delegates, it being the home of both Jackson and White, the embarrassment was so great to the President that an obscure Tennessee man—Edward Rucker—who happened to be in Baltimore, was drafted as a delegate from that State, which act gave rise to the word "ruckerize" used to describe similar proceedings in politics but now long forgotten. It was a loose and not really representative assemblage, but under the direction of the administration managers, with Van Buren himself in the background skilfully supplying the real political generalship, and the gaunt, powerful figure of Jackson solidly behind him, it did the business. Andrew Stevenson of Virginia, formerly speaker of the House, presided and made a speech which illuminates the situation that confronted the party. In part he said:

As the period for this important election approaches, efforts will no doubt be made to divide and distract the Republican [Democratic] Party, and put in jeopardy, and possibly defeat the election of a President by the people, in their primary colleges—a result deeply to be deprecated by all who love their country, its repose and union. Under such circumstances we must all be sensible that the union of our friends, and an election by the people, can only be secured by harmony, and concert, and by an adherence to the good old usages of our Republican fathers. The amendments to the Constitution, secured to the people this important election, so often and zealously impressed upon Congress and the nation by our venerable President, having failed, the democracy of the nation have been forced to look to a national convention as the best means of concentrating the popular will, and giving it effect in the approaching election. It is, in fact, the only defense against a minority President, one which prudence recommends, precedent sanctions and experience has proved to be effectual.

That was the real purpose of the convention—to make an impressive showing of party unity back of Van Buren—and again the two thirds rule was

invoked in order to add to that impression. The idea
that it was needed to nominate Van Buren is rendered ridiculous by the fact that he was unanimously
nominated on the first ballot, and his running-mate,
Mr. Johnson, got 178—more than two thirds—for
Vice-President. Virginia refused to accept Johnson
and kicked up considerable rumpus, but his selection
went through just the same. The excuse for not
allowing speeches was given by the chairman, who
said they might be "productive of much evil and the
rule against them is intended to prevent any violent,
angry and unnecessary discussion that might otherwise arise." Imagine a presiding officer getting away
with that in a national convention now! The resolutions embodying both the unit and the two thirds rule
were presented by Mr. Saunders of North Carolina
and were worded a little differently from those of
1832, but not much. Here they are:

> Resolved That in taking the vote for the nomination of
> President and Vice President, a majority of the delegation
> from each State shall designate the member or members who
> shall give the vote of the state.
> Resolved That the delegates from each state in this Con-
> vention be entitled to as many votes in selecting suitable per-
> sons for the offices of President and Vice President, as such
> state is entitled to in the Electoral College for the choice of
> the officers by law and that two-thirds of the whole number
> of votes given be required for a nomination, and all ques-
> tions connected therewith.

A strong opposition to the two thirds rule was
voiced by Mr. Allen of Massachusetts, and his mo-

tion to substitute the word "majority" was carried by a vote of 231 to 210. The next day this vote was reconsidered and the two thirds rule adopted. A running report of the debate from old Baltimore newspapers includes the following:

Mr. Saunders, chairman of the rules committee, supported the two-thirds because it would have a more imposing effect, but Mr. Allen of Massachusetts, declared in favor of a majority as being according to democratic principles.

Mr. Daniel of Virginia made a few remarks in favor of the original resolution, and Mr. Allen briefly rejoined. Mr. Allen said it might be three weeks before a majority of two-thirds could be fixed on one man.

Mr. Saunders begged leave to add a word or two further in explanation in reply to the gentleman's motion about being governed by the usages of the Republican party, that in the Convention which assembled at Baltimore three years ago, and which nominated a distinguished individual for the office of Vice-President, a resolution was adopted not only in the form but he believed in the precise words of the one under consideration. Still, if the difficulty contemplated by the gentleman from Massachusetts should arise, it would be competent at any time for a majority of the Convention to reconsider their votes and change the resolution. Mr. Saunders hoped, therefore, that the resolution as reported from the committee would be at once adopted.

It was to be presumed that no one had the most remote desire to frustrate the proceedings, and provided a majority should on the first or second ballot fix upon an individual, it was reasonably to be expected that the minority would be disposed to yield and unite with the majority so as to produce the effect contemplated by the foregoing resolution.

"The Baltimore Chronicle," not friendly to the Jacksonians, said of Mr. Strange of North Carolina, a convention vice-president who moved to reconsider the vote requiring only a majority to nominate: "He made a very good speech in favor of it, which he might have saved himself the trouble of delivering—the matter having already been determined by the 'fuglemen.'"

From the "Niles Register," which was hostile to Jackson, the following comment is worth reprinting:

The two-thirds principle was probably intended to affect the nomination of Vice President and to keep out R. M. Johnson, many being willing, as we understand, to make no nomination, rather than accept of him.

Obviously, it was not with the idea of putting through its slate that the rule was supported by the Van Buren forces. It made it harder, not easier, for them, and the only advantage from their standpoint that seems reasonable is the one they gave—it made the convention selections more impressive. It will be noted here that though "Democratic" had been used as a descriptive term for the party for nearly eight years, "Republican" was still used in the convention as the formal designation. It was not until the 1840 convention that the word "Republican" was finally dropped from the official title.

In the election a year and a half following the convention the party won, but not without losing a lot of its tail feathers. It was not a popular ticket, and though Jackson did everything short of taking the stump—and he did that in Tennessee—the result contained some painfully humiliating features. There was an enormous slump over the Democratic vote of 1832. While Van Buren got 170 electoral votes—23 more than a majority—the shrinkage in the popular vote was extremely significant. In 1832 Jackson's plurality was 157,293; in 1836 Van Buren's was 24,893 out of a total of 1,498,205 in twenty-six States. A change of 2500 votes in Pennsylvania would have lost that State and thrown the election into the House.

Apparently the slump was due not only to the fact that though a master politician and a really fine man, Van Buren was no idol of the masses as Jackson had been, but also because of the inevitable reaction against the party following eight years of administration by as strong, dominant, violent, fighting a President as Andrew Jackson. When the whole situation is reviewed, it really is amazing that Van Buren pulled through at all. It was not only the let down and swing back that followed the passing from power of such a personality as Jackson, but the outbreak of factions which Jackson's strength had kept subdued, with which he had to contend. There were other things, and one that ought to be noted was the embarrassment caused him by the appearance of the slavery issue during the campaign, developed by the violent tactics and extreme propaganda of the Abolitionists in New York and elsewhere. Calhoun and Clay in Congress out did their best to have this issue cut Van Buren both North and South. It required a great deal of adroitness upon the part of the "Red Fox" not to be caught in the trap. There was also the resentment which the "crown prince" idea always arouses in this country, plus the fundamental fact that the Democratic party had been in unbroken power in the Government for thirty-six years—an almost incredibly long time.

Take it all together, it is not to be wondered that this able, astute, and exceedingly adroit politician should have had difficulty in winning his fight, nor that, considering the problems that confronted him later and the panic that came to the country through no fault of his, he should have lost the next one. It was the only close shave the party had had since the first Jefferson election in 1800. Though the Adams election in 1824 went into the House, that was not a party crisis. The fight then was among Democrats. If Adams had not won, some other Democrat would, as there was no opposition party. In the Van Buren fight, however, the Whigs were a real party, organized, militant, and well led, though without principles, patronage, or platform. It was solely an opposition party, cemented together at the time largely by hatred of Jackson and all his works, and by an overwhelming desire on the part of its leaders for Presidential power.

All that has been written here so far about Mr. Van Buren seems likely to leave the impression that there was not a great deal to him besides being a friend and *protégé* of the iron-willed

Jackson, and a very skilful and exceedingly practical politician. It would be a great mistake not to erase that impression. It is perfectly true he was both the *protégé* and the politician, but he was in addition a man of parts, extraordinarily able, clear headed, pure minded, and patriotic. It is true that he is not one of the great "outstanding personalities" of the party—he does not rank with Jefferson and Jackson, Cleveland or Wilson, but he was so high above the average President, so far removed from mediocrity as an executive and a man, so potent, effective, and far sighted a party leader, that it is not possible to pass him by in this sort of running history in the way some of his successors can—and will—be passed by without spoiling the accuracy, adequacy, and proportions of the story.

Not one of its towering figures, neither was he one of its accidents or mediocrities, and a considerable part of the Democratic story is draped around him. Van Buren was a man grown when Thomas Jefferson was elected. He lived to the very eve of Lincoln's election and the great smash-up of the Democratic party on the slavery rock. In most of that time he was an influential party factor and for a considerable period its leader. There has been a more or less general disposition to overlook his virtues and dwell upon his faults, to send him down in history as the "Red Fox," conveying the idea of a crafty, cunning, scheming politician, who

played the game in devious ways and lacked direct-
ness, courage, and character. It is a false picture.
It is true that in New York he had mixed in and
developed from the unsavory politics of that State.
It is true that he was neither a political purist nor
an apostle of reform. He knew the rough and practical side of politics and had a long and varied experience in political intrigues, but none of this prevented him from being a gentleman, a statesman,
a man of honor and integrity. That he was all these
will be conceded by most fair-minded men who give
more than superficial study to his record—as senator, secretary of state, ambassador to England,
Vice-President, President. It was really a remarkable career, equaled by few in the history of the
country, and the whole political story of the man
is as fascinating as it is important.

Van Buren had the support of Jackson, but he
did not get that support or reach the place where
such support could be effectively used for him
merely because of his cunning as a master political
strategist or his engaging personality, or because of
the Jackson fondness for him. Besides Jackson, he
had back of him a great record of political ability
extending over many years, of public services of
the first order, recognition by party leaders as the
most distinguished active member of his party, and
a general popular appreciation for a long while
before his promotion that he was among the three
or four Americans from whom a President would

naturally be chosen. The brightest period of his whole public career was his single term of the Presidency, and this is so in spite of the fact that there occurred under his administration one of the worst panics in our history, and notwithstanding the contention that his effort to establish an independent treasury conflicted with all sound views of private and public finance then and since.

For the panic of 1837, which began two months after his inauguration, he was in no way responsible. It was his hard luck to have the storm, that had gathered all through the last violent Jackson days, burst almost as soon as he took office. But in the face of as trying a time as any President, save Lincoln, has faced, there was no shrinking or timidity upon the part of this President. Clear headed, courteous, unwavering, he met the crisis with courage, capacity, and dignity. In spite of the panic, the suspension of specie payments, and a cry for governmental relief on all sides, he maintained his party's policies and principles with a steadiness that even his severest critics concede. After a three-year struggle he secured the complete "divorce of state and bank," made the Federal Government the custodian of its own funds, obviated the necessity of direct intercourse with any bank, and took from the banks the power to issue national paper money. What this meant was the placing of the country on a "hard money" basis, making gold and silver the only money recognized by the Federal Government.

It is possible to dispute the soundness of the Van Buren fiscal policy, but not the manner or method by which it was executed, the conduct of the President in office, or the direct and explicit way in which he dealt with living and legitimate issues. The complete absence of extravagance and invective in his messages, speeches, and papers—and the quite unnecessary length of some of them—go a long way to obscure his real ability and hide the vital character of his action. The idea that he was not popular with his party or that it deserted him is wholly unfounded. Color to it is lent by the reverses he suffered in the fight to "separate the state from the bank." The fact was that the off-year election went against the Democrats and there was no party control over the House in 1839. So close was the fight that when that body assembled in December there were 119 Democrats, 118 opposition—mostly Whigs—and five members from New Jersey whose seats were contested. The House was unable to organize, and chaos was only averted by former President John Quincy Adams, who had returned to the House from Massachusetts, calling the members to order and appealing to them to elect a temporary chairman, the response to which appeal was the selection of Mr. Adams himself.

In the end Van Buren succeeded not only in his financial program but in swinging his party back to a strict construction basis on every mooted political question of the day. His popularity within the party and his leadership are attested by the complete absence of party opposition to his renomination, to the fact that in the 1840 convention the Democrats for the first time in their history found themselves in position to formulate their party principles, and that those principles were in complete accord with Van Buren's policies and ideas. Not many Presidents have had a steadier loyalty to their political principles than Van Buren, nor have shown more quiet resolution and efficiency in the performance of executive duties.

Before telling the story of the 1840 convention it is worth while to quote here the picture drawn by his best biographer—Edward M. Shepard—of this man who so vitally affected party history.

He did not [Mr. Shepard writes] have the strong and vivid personality of Jackson. Jackson stands in a rank by himself. But useful as he was to the creation of a powerful sentiment for union and of a hostility to the schemes of a paternal government, it is clear that in those questions of steady wisdom, foresight and patience which of right belong to the chief magistrate of a republic he was far inferior to his less picturesque and less forceful successor. Van Buren did not have the massive and forcible eloquence of Webster or the more captivating though fleeting speech of Clay, or the delightful warmth of the latter's leadership, or the strength and glory which their very persons and careers gave to American nationality. But in the persistent and fruitful adherence to a political creed fitted to the time and to the genius of the American people, in that noble art that gathers and binds one to another and to a creed the elements of a political party, the art which disciplines and guides the party, when formed, to clear and definite purpose, without wavering and

127

without weakness or demagoguery, Van Buren was a greater master than either of these men, in many things more interesting as they were. In this exalted art of the politician, this consummate art of the statesman, Van Buren was close to the greatest of the American party leaders, close to Jefferson and Hamilton.

Chapter X

PARTY PRINCIPLES PROMULGATED

The First Defeat in 1840—The Slavery Issue Arises—
The Whig Campaign One of "Noise, Numbers and
Nonsense," but Successful—Van Buren Hurt in 1844
by His Attitude on Texas Annexation

UNDER Van Buren the party swung into the 1840
campaign, notwithstanding the panic and notwithstanding the narrow margin in 1836, strongly confident of victory. The basis of this confidence was
largely the character of the opposition. The Whigs
were a curious party. Whether you thought the
Democratic principles right or wrong, they at least
had them. The Whigs had neither. They united in
condemning everything Democratic; but if they
had a program, policy, or principle in their whole
party, they certainly did not avow it. And there is
no record of one. It was wholly a party of opposition, but with the aged General William Henry
Harrison and Mr. Tyler as candidates it conducted
an amazing hullabaloo campaign, without issues,
logic, or coherence, but with tremendous fire, furious denunciation, vast parades, songs, slogans,
noise, and confusion.

It was an extraordinary campaign, and filled the Democrats with disgust and loathing. It was incredible to them that the country would not revolt against the character of the Whig appeal, would not see through its humbuggery and pretense, would be swept by any such wild and disordered demonstrations. They went into their convention with that feeling, jeering and deriding the Whig bombast and bluster, contemptuous of the Whig candidates and certain of their ability to defeat them. There was still no such thing as a national committee, no central authoritative party agency to issue a convention call. The first two conventions had been called on the initiative taken by members of the New Hampshire legislature, and once more the call came from that source. Also once more the place designated was Baltimore and the day May 4. Again it was a loosely organized convention, but not so loose as the other two. There were twenty-one States represented, and four—Delaware, Virginia, South Carolina, and Illinois—absent. It was called to order by Governor Isaac Hill of New Hampshire and presided over by Governor William Carroll of Tennessee.

The platform was adopted on the second day in advance of the nominations, which has been the rather illogical custom of all parties since. It is notable as the first formal Democratic platform, and is particularly interesting as a comparison with Democratic platforms of recent years, in which no trace of the original Democratic strict construction principles can be found. It is further interesting to compare its crisp brevity with the windy, wordy ones that have followed it. It is here given in full:

Resolved, That the Federal Government is one of limited powers derived solely from the Constitution and the grants of power shown therein ought to be strictly construed by all the departments and agents of the government, and that it is inexpedient and dangerous to exercise doubtful constitutional powers.

2. Resolved, That the Constitution does not confer upon the general government the power to commence and carry on a general system of internal improvement.

3. Resolved, That the Constitution does not confer authority upon the federal government, directly or indirectly, to assume the debts of the several States, contracted for local internal improvements, or other State purposes; nor would such assumption be just or expedient.

4. Resolved, That justice and sound policy forbid the federal government to foster one branch of industry to the detriment of another, or to cherish the interest of one portion to the injury of another portion of our common country; that every citizen and every section of the country has a right to demand and insist upon an equality of rights and privileges, and to complete and ample protection of person and property from domestic violence or foreign aggression.

5. Resolved, That it is the duty of every branch of the government to enforce and practice the most rigid economy in conducting our public affairs, and that no more revenue ought to be raised than is required to defray the necessary expenses of the government.

6. Resolved, That Congress has no power to charter a United States Bank; that we believe such an institution one of deadly hostility to the best interests of the country, dangerous to our republican institutions and the liberties of the

people, and calculated to place the business of the country within the control of a concentrated money power, and above the laws and the will of the people.

7. Resolved, That Congress has no power, under the Constitution, to interfere with or control the domestic institutions of the several States, and that such States are sole and proper judges of everything appertaining to their own affairs not prohibited by the Constitution; that all efforts of the Abolitionists or others, made to induce Congress to interfere with questions of slavery, or to take incipient steps in relation thereto, are calculated to lead to the most alarming and dangerous consequences, and that all such efforts have an inevitable tendency to diminish the happiness of the people, and endanger the stability and permanency of the Union, and ought not to be countenanced by any friend to our political institutions.

8. Resolved, That the separation of the moneys of the government from banking institutions is indispensable for the safety of the funds of the government and the rights of the people.

9. Resolved, That the liberal principles embodied by Jefferson in the Declaration of Independence, and sanctioned in the Constitution, which makes ours the land of liberty and the asylum of the oppressed of every nation, have ever been cardinal principles in the Democratic faith; and every attempt to abridge the present privilege of becoming citizens and the owners of soil among us ought to be resisted with the same spirit which swept the Alien and Sedition laws from our statute-book.

The adoption of this was followed by the unanimous renomination of Van Buren, but no Vice-Presidential candidate was named, largely, it is held, because of the opposition to R. M. Johnson. Quite a fight was put up by Johnson's friends, who felt that he was entitled to indorsement, but when it appeared that the opposition was apparently strong enough to prevent a two thirds vote, they yielded, acquiescing in a resolution leaving the nomination for the second place to the several States, the hope being that the selection would eventually be thrown into the Democratic Senate, out of which Johnson, with administration support, could emerge.

Clear to the finish the Whig campaign was a whirlwind. "Noise, nonsense and numbers" was the way Democratic orators characterized it and that is what it was, with nothing real in it save the military prestige of General Harrison and the accumulated opposition to the Democrats. But it won—won by a smashing popular majority—1,275,016 to 1,129,102, and by an even greater electoral vote—234 for Harrison, 60 for Van Buren. The Democrats carried New Hampshire, Virginia, South Carolina, Alabama, Missouri, Arkansas, Illinois—and that was all. It was a crushing defeat, the first in forty years, and it left the party stunned, bruised, angry, bedeviled, and bewildered. All sorts of reasons were given for the result—fraud, the lavish use of money, the stupidity of the people. For a while there was the utmost confusion and despair; but before long the fighting spirit was recovered, and party leaders generally formed the determination to reelect Van Buren in 1844. It is unnecessary to say that Van Buren himself was the brains and inspiration of the movement, and that from the moment he left Washington he employed all of his political astuteness and strength to the promotion of his candidacy.

The sudden death of General Harrison and the succession of John Tyler to the Presidency robbed the Whigs of the fruits of victory, and in a little while the President was cooperating far more with the Democrats in Congress than with the party that had elected him. Naturally, the whole Whig outfit burned and seethed with indignation, and the complete break between Tyler and his party redounded to the benefit of the Democrats, who made just as much out of the situation as they could. The Tyler administration, in fact, is one of the most unusual periods in the history of the Democratic party. Beaten at the polls in 1840, it yet shaped to its liking all important legislation for the next two years. The Democrats really ran the Government, not only through the backing of the President they had not elected but because in the off-year election they had captured the House of Representatives. The Whig President had turned Democrat, the House was Democratic by a clear working majority; only the Senate was against them by a slender margin. It was a remarkable situation that has not been duplicated since.

As for Van Buren, he took his 1840 defeat with dignity and composure, greeted his successor with characteristic graciousness and courtesy, and went unhurriedly back to New York, where he was given a tumultuously enthusiastic reception by the Democrats of his home State. He was almost as much the recognized leader of his party out of office as he had been in. Jackson was still living, but in retirement out in Tennessee. He cherished his friendship for Van Buren up to his death, and there was no one with either the political prestige, power, or skill to compete with him. This is not to say that there was not party opposition to renaming Van Buren. There was, and it was bitter enough too, and determined, but in the main the party was behind him. He had vastly more strength than any other aspirant and was the logical choice as well as the logical leader. The tragic, solemn, saturnine Calhoun in his "high hat" way was a candidate; so was the late Vice-President, Colonel Johnson, whose unconcealed eagerness contrasted with the careful propriety of the Calhoun candidacy. Pennsylvania brought forth James Buchanan—who later was to become President—as a "favorite son," and General Lewis Cass was pushed forward by his friends.

One party element thought it would be suicidal to name Van Buren again following his rejection by the people at the polls. The other was thoroughly convinced that the only way to win was to make the fight with Van Buren. The latter were by far the stronger. They were, in fact, a clear majority, and up to the early part of 1844—within one month of the convention, in fact—there was little doubt in the minds of posted persons that he would be nominated. In fact, when the convention met he got thirteen more than an actual majority on the first ballot, but, curiously enough, was beaten by the very two thirds rule which he had had so much to do with establishing as a Democratic convention custom in the first convention of 1832. He was the first Democratic Presidential candidate to secure a majority vote in the convention and then fail to get the necessary two thirds. The only other was Champ Clark, who had exactly the same experience in the 1912 convention at which Woodrow Wilson was first nominated.

What really knocked Van Buren out was the question of the annexation of Texas which suddenly loomed up, just when his road to the nomination seemed smoothest and at a time when his success in the convention was conceded. Back of the annexation question, which was raised by President Tyler, who submitted to the Senate a treaty with Texas looking to annexation, was the devastating issue of slavery. In the South the sentiment was overwhelmingly, even wildly, favorable to annexation, the extension of slavery into the vast Texan territory fitting in with Southern political and economic policies. This was the first time the issue had been really injected into politics since the days of the Missouri Compromise under the Monroe administration. Recognizing its explosive nature, sensing the party danger that lurked in it, both Northern and Southern Democratic leaders had for the most part joined in avoiding discussion, regarding it, or pretending to regard it, as a settled subject. Those with clearest vision knew better, knew the inevitability of the finish fight on the issue, but were naturally anxious to cooperate in postponing it as long as possible. The Texas annexation question literally reeked with slavery and anti-slavery poison. The real thing at stake was whether slavery should be extended into new territory or not.

It must be conceded that Van Buren's courage in meeting this issue was fine. No one with his knowledge of politics could fail to have known the effect on his candidacy of opposing annexation. Yet that is exactly what he did and he did it without equivocation, straddling, or hedging. It was on April 22 that Tyler sent the treaty to the Senate, and it was on April 27 that Van Buren, unable of course to ignore the matter which had tremendously stirred the people, made public a letter pointing out that annexation meant war with Mexico, that annexation without the consent of Mexico was not honorable, that he was completely opposed to the treaty. He did not in this letter mention slavery, but beyond question back of his opposition to the treaty was opposition to the further extension of slavery— and the South quickly and accurately sensed it.

That they were right was abundantly proved by Van Buren's course four years later when he left his party on that issue and actually accepted the Free Soil party nomination for the Presidency as a protest against the pro-slavery slant of the Democrats.

137

As soon as his letter on Texas was published, though his views were almost identical with those of his real rival, Henry Clay, looked upon as sure to make the fight against him as the Whig candidate, it at once ditched the Van Buren chances. From that moment he was sunk. More than a majority of the delegates to the convention had been instructed for him—but it made no difference. In some States the instructions were rescinded but he still had his majority when the gathering was called to order. The support given the motion to adopt the two thirds rule, again by supposedly Van Buren delegations, was the thing that killed him.

Nothing in the Van Buren career seems more creditable to him than this Texas letter. He deeply desired the nomination and had it in his hand. Jackson, his friend and supporter, had before he knew the political consequences written a letter strongly indorsing annexation. A Southern delegate to the convention asked Van Buren for his views and he gave them in no uncertain words. This Texas annexation fight was the first of the great pro-slavery movements that ultimately broke the party's back. It is a mistake to assume, as has been done, that slavery was a continual issue in American politics after the Missouri Compromise. It was a continual and consistent issue after Texas annexation raised it up in 1844, but not prior to that time. Occasionally the Abolitionists flared up and created resentment in the South and embarrassment to candidates, as in 1836, but it was not permitted to become an issue. In 1836 and 1840 there was upon the subject of slavery no real difference between the utterances of the candidates and other leaders, whether they were Whig or Democrat, Northern or Southern.

The one notable exception was John C. Calhoun, who had as early as 1830, according to the Van Holst biography, become the "personification of the slavery cause." But Calhoun, though always flaming in his advocacy of the cause and frequently its defender on the floor of the Senate, had found no opportunity to make it a political issue before 1840. That he was the real force back of the annexation movement there is no doubt. Close personally to Tyler, the enemy of Van Buren, an aspirant for the Presidency, an overwhelmingly earnest believer in the necessity of protecting slavery in the States where it existed against interference by the Federal Government, and in extending it under the Federal Government as new territory was acquired, the whole question fitted equally well with his political purposes and personal desires. Its rise in 1844 definitely marks the beginning of the great split in the party.

Before that year it had been kept out of politics. After that year it was not only never out but grew stronger, more menacing, more impossible to avoid with every campaign. After that year it was clear the fight had to go to the finish. Before that year, through Southern sentiment, focused, led, manipulated by Calhoun, who more than any other individual was responsible for the failure of his party to apply its basic principle consistently on this question, and for the ultimate smash-up that so nearly destroyed it for all time—before that year there were three distinct elements in the Democratic party. There was the Northern agricultural element, which was generally unfriendly to slavery; there was the Northern commercial and city element, largely indifferent on the subject, and there was the Southern element, for the most part agricultural, which was flamingly pro-slavery. These three elements, had been united into a great national party because they were in complete harmony on every other question with the exception of slavery, and that question by common, tacit consent they had barred from discussion as not a proper political subject. This understanding was smashed in 1844—perhaps it would have come anyhow—by the insistence of the Southern wing upon bringing in a vast new territory whose status as to slavery was sure to involve a political and sectional struggle between North and South. As has been said once before in this book, there is no more deadly division in a political party than one formed by the coincidence of a moral issue with a geographical line.

Chapter XI

Van Buren, Though He Had a Majority of Delegates,
Beaten by Two Thirds Rule in 1844 Convention—
Silas Wright, Nominated for Vice-President, De-
clines to Accept

WHEN the convention met, the feeling over the
Texas question was deep and the delegates were in
a considerable state of excitement. It was in fact a
political situation singularly acute and without
parallel. Van Buren, the leader of the party, its most
distinguished active member and logical choice, with
a clear majority of the delegates instructed for him,
had taken the side of the only vibrant issue in sight
so unpopular that his nomination seemed out of the
question if success in the election were hoped. As
has been explained, the real Van Buren friends
strongly opposed the two thirds rule. His false
friends, those instructed for him but anxious to
break away, joined with his foes in supporting it.
It was adopted, and his chance of that nomination
was over. The convention passed a beautiful resolution eulogizing his record and personality, full of
fine phrases and high tributes but they refused to
accept him again as the candidate.

His is really the only case in the whole party history in which the candidate, with a majority of the convention instructed for him and receiving a majority on the first ballot, was rejected. Champ Clark, in 1912, got a majority but only after days of balloting, and he had no instructed majority. The Van Buren case is so isolated and singular that it seems worth giving here the convention vote for the first seven ballots, for the purpose of showing two things—first, the extraordinary way in which his majority shrank after the first ballot; and second, the fact that the man who eventually got the nomination—James K. Polk of Tennessee—was not even voted on at all until the eighth ballot. He was nominated on the ninth and goes down in party history as the first "dark horse" candidate. Here is the vote:

	1st	2d	3d	4th	5th	6th	7th
Whole number of votes	266	266	266	265	265	265	265
Necessary for choice	178	178	178	177	177	177	177
Martin Van Buren, New York	146	127	121	111	103	101	99
Lewis Cass, Michigan	83	94	92	105	107	116	123
Richard M. Johnson, Kentucky	24	33	38	32	29	23	21
James Buchanan, Pennsylvania	4	9	11	17	26	25	22
Levi Woodbury, New Hampshire	2	1	2				
Com'dore Stewart, Pennsylvania	1	1					
John C. Calhoun, South Carolina	6	1	2				

The biographers of Polk make an effort to show that General Jackson, in retirement at The Hermitage, after Van Buren's anti-annexation letter, ceased advocating him and really wanted Polk, but the facts do not substantiate that idea, and the letters of Mr. Polk to his friends suggesting it and reporting the Jackson preference for himself are not convincing in themselves. Nor was such a course in the least like General Jackson. He loved his friends and hated his enemies, and it is not at all likely that Van Buren's views on annexation caused him to change his desire to see him nominated. It is true he thought he had made a political blunder, but he was still with him and gave concrete evidence of that fact later.

So far as Mr. Polk was concerned, compared to Van Buren and Calhoun he was a relatively obscure and certainly inferior man. He was an aspirant for the Vice-Presidency and not for the Presidency. No thought of the first place entered his or any one else's mind seriously until after the Van Buren letter. Then Mr. Polk, with his friends Donaldson and Pillow, began to make tentative movements toward the prize. They did—Polk and Donaldson—go to see Jackson at The Hermitage, and found him feeling that Van Buren had endangered his nomination and possibly his election. It is probable, too, the old man expressed himself as feeling kindly toward Polk, but not at all probable he went as far as Polk's desire led him to indicate to some of his friends.

When the convention met, the Polk movement was still under cover, and it was not brought out until Van Buren's strength had shrunk below that of Lewis Cass of Michigan. The faithful Pillow, custodian of the Polk boom, was convinced that if Polk were to be an acceptable compromise candidate the suggestion of his name had to come from the North, not the South. He had been working steadily along those lines from the start, had convinced George Bancroft, head of the Massachusetts delegation, and finally, after a night of conferences, New Hampshire agreed to lead off for Polk. They did on the eighth ballot—seven from Massachusetts, all from Alabama and Tennessee, and a few others followed. The vote was announced: Van Buren, 104; Cass, 114; Polk, 44.

Between the eighth and ninth ballots some sort of deal was made with the Virginia delegation, and the appeal for Polk as a compromise candidate was urged on all sides. Polk was, his friends pointed out, a "pure, whole hogged Democrat," and the thing to do was to take him for the sake of "harmony and unity." It was plain to the Van Buren leaders their man could not go over. The Calhoun people infinitely preferred Polk to Cass. Butler of New York read a letter from Jackson strongly urging Van Buren's nomination, but also a letter from Van Buren authorizing him to withdraw his name if it seemed in the interests of "harmony" so to do. Polk had no particular enemies, he was for the annexation of Texas, he was an ideal compromise man, with few rough edges and not big enough to excite animosity. On the ninth ballot New York cast its block of thirty-five votes for him and the "stampede" was on. When the smoke cleared he had been unanimously nominated. Word of his selection was sent to Washington over the first Morse telegraph line, that had just begun operation, and there it was received with emotions largely composed of disgust. "Polk! Great God, what a nomination!" the Whig governor of Kentucky wrote to Buchanan.

He was indeed a different type nominee from any the Democrats had heretofore presented. It had been the unbroken party custom to put forward for the Presidency its leading men, statesmen of the first rank, men whose party and public services made them natural selections. Polk was not one of these. He was not a party leader in any sense; he was a subordinate, and neither his public nor his political career marked him as Presidential timber. He had, as related, been speaker of the House and governor of his State, but he had also been twice defeated in Tennessee for governor and was unquestionably the most obscure man up to that time who had been proposed for the Presidency. He was not a particularly strong man and he did not make a particularly strong campaign, but he won. Vastly inferior to Henry Clay, the Whig candidate, he defeated Clay by carrying New York, largely because Van Buren loyally and heartily supported the ticket. However, the Polk majority was only 5000 in the State, and he could not have won had not James G. Birney, the Abolitionists' candidate for President, polled nearly 16,000 votes, the bulk of which Clay would surely have got had Birney not been in the field.

It is, of course, impossible to tell now exactly what the convention combination was that swung things to Polk, but the best information is that the two men who had most to do with it were Pillow and Bancroft. Before putting the convention behind us it should be noted that, following the nomination of Polk, Silas Wright was nominated for Vice-President and peremptorily declined to accept, on the ground that he was a friend of Van Buren and it savored of disloyalty to him to take second place with any other man. No man in the history of the country has ever declined a Presidential nomination. Silas Wright remained the only one who ever declined a Vice-Presidential nomination until 1924, when Frank O. Lowden of Illinois declined the nomination of the Republican National Convention of that year. George M. Dallas of Pennsylvania was named after Mr. Wright refused to run. A platform was adopted, in large measure modeled on that of 1832, but the heart of it was a resolution favoring the Texas annexation, in these words:

Resolved, that our title to the whole of the territory of Oregon is clear and unquestionable; that no portion of the same ought to be ceded to England or any other power; and that the re-occupation of Oregon and the re-annexation of Texas at the earliest practical period are great American measures which this convention recommends to the cordial support of the Democracy of the Union.

Polk the First Dark Horse

The Whig platform did not mention Texas, and Mr. Clay having expressed himself early on the subject also avoided mention of it. It is interesting to note that the Abolitionists, by refusing to support Clay, helped elect Polk and thereby contributed to the annexation of Texas as a slave State, to which they were violently opposed. It is one of the clearest of the many instances of popular political stupidity with which American history is plentifully sprinkled. After the election the current for annexation was too strong to stop, and a resolution passed both branches of Congress authorizing the admission of Texas as a State. It provided for the formation of four additional States out of the Texas territory. In States thus formed north of the Missouri Compromise line slavery was to be prohibited, but in those south of that line slavery was to be permitted or prohibited as the inhabitants might choose.

Slavery was now clearly before the conscience of the country and could no longer by tacit agreements or understandings be sidetracked and shelved in campaigns. From this point on the stream widened and the party ship tossed about in the rapids headed for the rocks. It was sixteen years before it finally struck, but every campaign accelerated its speed and brought it closer. With Polk's accession and the Mexican War the schism in the ranks became deeper and plainer. After the passage of the Texas resolution came the struggle over the Wilmot Proviso, which is exceedingly important in political history. It embodied the opposition to the extension of slavery in the Territories, and while it failed to pass, it was upon this proviso that the modern Republican party was really formed eight years later, that fourteen years later Lincoln was elected President, and the war for the preservation of the Union began.

David Wilmot was a Pennsylvania Congressman, and it was in 1846 that he proposed his amendment to the pending bill appropriating $2,100,000 to purchase territory from Mexico as part of the peace. All it did was to provide that slavery should be excluded from such territory. The Democratic legislature in New York twice approved it, the House of Representatives twice passed it, and the Senate twice rejected it. It was beaten, but each time feeling between North and South increased, the sectional breach widened, bitterness was bred. It is pretty generally agreed that the Wilmot Proviso did as much as anything else to precipitate the "irrepressible conflict."

There is no reason here to dwell longer on Mr. Polk or Mr. Polk's administration. His chief biographer—Dr. Eugene Irving McCormac—earnestly contends that far from being a mediocrity and weakling, a conspirator, and a "tool of the slave power," Polk was a constructive statesman, an able executive, a sound patriot; that his tariff policy produced prosperity, and his expansion policy added five hundred thousand square miles of territory and gave the United States free access to the Pacific. Dr. McCormac also pictures him as Jackson's *protégé* and insists Jackson wanted him for President. It may all be true, but it is hard to conceive of Mr. Polk, even after reading the 700 pages of this biographer, as either a great man, a great President, or a great party leader. The truth is he was none of these, and that no President has been so quickly and completely forgotten as Polk after he finished his single term.

The contrast between him and Van Buren in this respect is singularly great. When Polk left the Presidency and was at once swallowed up in oblivion, Van Buren had been out eight years, had been defeated once as a Presidential candidate, and again defeated for the nomination. Yet he was still, despite the eulogistic convention resolutions on his "retirement" in 1844, a potent party force, a factor to be reckoned with, infinitely the more virile and interesting man, with vastly more friends and enemies. Accepting his disappointment in the 1844 convention with outward complacency, Van Buren did not altogether accept that sentence to "honorable retirement" pronounced on him there. Between him and the Southern leaders of the Democratic party had opened a deep division over the greatest single issue in American politics since the election of Thomas Jefferson. As a result of his convictions on this issue he was forced out or bolted—whichever way you choose to put it—the Democratic

149

party, in whose progress and development he had
for so many years played a conspicuous and effective part. There is no doubt that he helped in the
1848 defeat to the extent of his ability and added
enormously to the bitterness and number of his
enemies. It was easy then, and is easy now, to
charge him with party ingratitude and "soreness"
over his defeat; with "delusions of grandeur" and
a lot of other things; but the Van Buren record and
personality make it more reasonable to regard his
really deep antagonism to slavery and its spread over
the country as the thing that carried him out of his
party. Credit him with that and there is no occasion
for hunting another motive.

Chapter XII

He Blazes the Way for the Republican Party—His Attitude on Slavery Extension Identical with Republican
Attitude of 1856—His Free Soil Party the Forerunner of Republicanism

THE story of the Van Buren bolt is not only interesting but of such real importance in party history
that it must be told more or less fully. Early in the
Polk administration the New York Democrats began to split up into "Barnburners" and "Old
Hunkers." The Barnburners were the strong Van
Buren men, the anti-Texas element. The Hunkers
were the supporters of annexation and the respect-
ably dull and indifferent. Leading the Barnburners
were men of high party and private standing—
men like Silas Wright, who had refused the Vice-
Presidential nomination and was now governor;
Benjamin F. Butler, John A. Dix, who was in the
Senate; Azariah C. Flagg; and John Van Buren,
son of the ex-President, attorney-general of the
State and a picturesque political figure familiarly
called "Prince John." The chief leaders of the
Hunkers were William L. Marcy and Daniel C.
Dickinson. Among the younger followers and ad-

mirers of Van Buren and one of the active leaders
of the Barnburners was Samuel J. Tilden.

The Barnburners gained control over the legislature and approved the Wilmot Proviso; and Mr.
Polk, angered at the opposition to the pro-slavery
slant of the administration in the matters of Mexico
and Texas, cut the Van Buren wing off from all
recognition in the way of Federal patronage. The
jobs were given to the Hunkers. This, with administration support, enabled them to control—after a
fierce fight over contested seats—the state Democratic convention at Syracuse in September, 1847.
For the Barnburners, David Dudley Field—an an-
cestor of Dudley Field Malone, the New York lawyer—offered a resolution which said in effect that
while the New York Democracy would faithfully
adhere to the compromise of the Constitution and
maintain the reserved rights of the States, they
would still declare, since the crisis had come, "their
uncompromising hostility to the extension of slavery
into territory now free."

What followed is of particular interest when a
look ahead is taken to the 1860 national convention
and the secessions and splits in that body over this
question—and their results. As soon as the resolution was defeated, the Barnburners seceded—or
bolted, as it is called in later-day political parlance.
They asserted that the anti-slavery resolution had
been defeated by fraudulent organization of the
convention, and proceeded to call a mass-meeting on

Van Buren Bolts

October 6 at Herkimer "to avow our principles and consult as to future action." It has been held by some of the deepest students of American politics that this Herkimer convention was a really important preliminary to the formation of the present-day Republican party, and it is certainly interesting that Van Buren, one of the strong men of the Democratic party, one of its notable Presidents, a Democratic force for nearly half a century, should have been back of this convention. It was, in fact, a gathering of Van Buren's friends, and it was Van Buren's son who reported the resolutions and acted for his father. David Wilmot addressed the meeting, the "fraud" at Syracuse was denounced, and a convention called to choose Barnburner delegates to the national convention to contest the seats of the Hunkers. It was further declared in the resolutions that the New York Democracy, replying to the threat of the South that it would support no candidate for President who did not assent to the extension of slavery, would not vote for any candidate who did so assent.

Clearly the elder Van Buren was in accord with all this, though he did not personally appear. His old hostility to slavery, indicated by his vote twenty-eight years before against admitting Missouri other than free, strongly revived, and he was angered, too, at the proscription of his friends by Mr. Polk. There must also have been in his system considerable pent-up soreness—and quite naturally so, in spite of his outward composure—over the manner in which he had been treated in the 1844 convention. These things, added to his anti-slavery convictions, probably contributed to putting this most regular of regular Democrats, this out-and-out organization man, this party leader and manager, this stickler for political discipline and party loyalty, into a frame of mind where he let himself be persuaded to run as an independent candidate for the Presidency as a protest against his party's stand on the slavery question.

Reflection on this phase of the Van Buren career, beginning with his vote against the Missouri admission, his anti-Texas letter that cost him the 1844 nomination, the organization of the Barnburners as the anti-slavery wing of the party, the Herkimer convention managed by his son and brother, and his own nomination for President in 1848 by the Free Soil party on an anti-slavery platform—when all these things are considered, it does seem that if Calhoun were the "personification of the slavery cause," Van Buren was the personification of the anti-slavery cause; that as much as any other man Van Buren stimulated the sentiment that led to the formation of the modern Republican party and resulted in the great Democratic disaster of 1860. It is a curious and interesting story, pregnant with political significance, this story of the final political play of Martin Van Buren, who was elected President once, defeated twice, and deprived of the nomination by the most courageous act of his whole career. In 1847 the Barnburners, or Van Buren men, outnumbered the Hunkers in the legislature and began to call themselves and be called "Free Soilers." They met in 1848 at Utica, chose delegates to the national convention, and issued an address, which had been prepared by Van Buren, his son John, and Samuel J. Tilden. It demonstrated at length that Democratic principles were in direct conflict with the institution of slavery, and that the Democratic party was untrue to itself, to the Constitution, and the country in countenancing the extension of slavery in new territory.

It was in May, 1848, that, again in Baltimore, the national convention assembled. It offered to admit both the Hunker and the Barnburner delegations from New York, but this the Barnburners or Free Soilers would not permit, on the ground that it was simply a nullification of the vote of the State, which was of course true. Lewis Cass of Michigan was nominated for President and William O. Butler of Kentucky for Vice-President. The platform eulogized the Polk administration, praised Polk and Dallas, indorsed the Mexican War, thanked the soldiers, greeted the French Republic, spoke disparagingly of monarchs—contained in all some 1500 meaningless words. Mr. Polk, who was highly praised, got not a single vote in the convention, the entire party taking him at his word that he was not a candidate. The platform made no mention of the slavery issue, but the nomination of Cass was a sufficient condemnation of the Wilmot Proviso; and the Barnburners, returning to New York, held a huge mass-meeting in the City Hall square at which the ticket, the party, and the platform were all denounced. An address written by Mr. Tilden, "calling independent Democrats to action," was read, and a Barnburner or Free Soil convention followed at Utica. It was presided over by Samuel Young, who said that "if the convention does its duty a clap of thunder in November will make the propagandists of slavery shake like Belshazzar." A long letter from Mr. Van Buren was read, explicitly declaring against the Democratic candidates. He discussed the question whether the surrender of the power of Congress over the Territories and the refusal to use that power to exclude slavery were in accord with Democratic principles. He cited Washington, Adams, Jefferson, Madison, Monroe, Jackson, and himself on the subject. He was convinced, as they had been, that "slavery is the one subject that can endanger our blessed Union." In departing from its principles on this issue the Democratic party could not carry him with it. As the national convention had rejected the old Democratic doctrine, he would not vote for its candidate, Lewis Cass; if there were no other candidate but General Taylor (the Whig nominee) he would not vote at all.

This was the first blast in the open from Van Buren. It created a profound impression. It was unquestionably a great political sensation. Here was the most distinguished living Democrat publicly repudiating the Democratic Presidential ticket. The Utica convention promptly nominated Van Buren as the Free Soil candidate for President, much against his will and in spite of his protest. A national convention was called in Buffalo and there he was again nominated, with Charles Francis Adams, son of John Quincy Adams, one of his oldest and bitterest political and personal foes. It was an exceedingly curious combination but one not to be ignored, one also of real political significance, indicative of the enormous power of the slavery issue.

So clearly was this Free Soil convention and the whole Barnburner-Van Buren movement the foundation upon which the present Republican party was built, that, strange as it seems, it is almost possible to call Van Buren the real founder of that party. Anyhow, he sowed the seeds, showed the way, and the tone of his Free Soil platform on the real issue that led to the formation of the Republican party was almost identical with the first platform of that party in 1856 and with the one on which it came into power with Lincoln in 1860. It is too long, as all Van Buren's compositions were, to give here in full, but from start to finish anti-slavery was the keynote. The heart of the platform is contained in the following section:

Resolved, therefore, that we, the people here assembled, remembering the example of our fathers in the days of the first Declaration of Independence, putting our trust in God for the triumph of our cause, and invoking his guidance in our endeavors to advance it, do now plant ourselves upon the national platform of freedom in opposition to the sectional platform of slavery.

It ought to be noted here that neither Mr. Van Buren and his Free Soil party nor the Republican party which in 1856 succeeded it was in complete accord with the Abolitionists. Neither went that far. Both were anti-slavery. Both recognized and denounced the existence of slavery as an evil, but neither proposed to uproot it in the original States where it had always existed. The common bond between them was their opposition to the extension of slavery into free territory. Neither the Free Soilers in 1848 or 1852, nor the first Republican platform in 1856, went the full length of the Abolitionists. This was one instance in which the extremists were right. They and they only took the view that the Union could not survive half slave and half free. In neither its 1856 nor its 1860 platform did the Republican party take an unequivocal stand against the existence of slavery; only against its extension, which was exactly the attitude of the Free Soilers and Van Buren.

It is impossible to believe that any one as clear headed and experienced in politics as he could have thought there was any chance of success in the election of 1848 for his party. Probably, as he was intensely human, he was inspired by some personal resentment and feeling, but it cannot be doubted, in the light of the consistency of his record on the slavery question, that in the main his course was dictated by principle and by a grasp on the greatness of the issue and its dire possibilities not only for the party but for the country. No man had a cooler political judgment than he. No one knew better than he how strong was party discipline in the Democratic ranks, because no one had done more to build up that strength. He knew too the intense feeling against him among the Whigs. It is, however, possible that he believed the strength of this moral issue might swing to him the great States of New York and Ohio, where the anti-slavery sentiment was strongest, and the election be thrown into the House. That is the hope of every third party movement. It did not materialize in this the last Presidential effort of Van Buren. He got no electoral votes, but he got in New York a bigger vote than the Democratic candidate. His vote gave that State to the Whigs and defeated Cass and Butler. There is no doubt about the fact that he did it. Not only in New York, which with its thirty-six votes decided the election, but the Van Buren candidacy in other States encouraged the opposition and lost them to the Democrats. It marked the close of Van Buren's career. This time he went really into retirement—and he went with the curses of the Democrats ringing in his ears. But it was a great fight and its effects were far-reaching and vital. It would have been better for Van Buren's ultimate reputation if he had not lived to dim the fineness of this battle by joining the compromisers of 1850 on the question of the admission of California later on. His support of neither Pierce nor Buchanan was consistent. The excuse made for him then is that he was an old man, that he, as Mr. Shepard says in his biography, "yielded through mistaken patriotism to the soporific which Clay in his old age administered to the American people." But the part Van Buren played later was a minor one, and it is fair to regard his political life as closing with the 1848 fight.

Chapter XIII

Party Blindness on the Slavery Issue—The Fatal Compromise of 1850—The Rise of Douglas and the Return of Van Buren to the Fold—Pierce an Unexciting President, a Weak Party Leader

FROM 1848—when for the second time in forty-eight years it suffered defeat—until 1860, when the great smash-up occurred from which it all but died, the story of the Democratic party is the story of a terribly torn party desperately trying to conceal its unhealable and widening wound. For eight of those twelve years it was in full power at Washington, and for a considerable part of that time its leaders persuaded themselves that unity had been restored and the great issue which had split their ranks and the country into sections successfully smothered. But they lived in a fool's paradise. The attempt to blind their eyes to the basic facts was wholly futile. The slavery situation had too far advanced to permit again of any such tacit agreement not to discuss it as had held for so many years following the Missouri Compromise, though the effort was made, and though this time the opposition party as well as the

Democrats, being equally rent by the question, was equally anxious to get it out of politics. But the very idea was absurd. From the inauguration of General Taylor until the outbreak of the Civil War the slavery question not only dominated the country but it overshadowed every other topic in the minds of the people. Its discussion could no more be averted than breathing could be avoided. Obviously it is impossible here to give a complete account of the events of this twelve-year period that so profoundly affected the history of the Democratic party. To do so would be to write the history of the country for those years. All it is possible to do is to sift from the mass of material the time afforded the salient facts necessary to a consecutive narrative of party history.

At the very outset of the Taylor administration the slavery question came up. It became necessary to organize a government over the vast area obtained from Mexico in which there was no slavery but in which the South was determined to extend slavery. It was in January that Henry Clay, the great leader of the Whigs, and then an old man three times disappointed as a Presidential candidate, presented in the Senate eight resolutions bearing on this subject. Stanwood's "History of the Presidency" gives the gist of these resolutions as follows—

The admission of California as a free State;
The new Territories to be organized without restriction as to slavery;

The boundary to be established between Texas and New
Mexico;
The United States to pay the public debt of Texas;
Slavery not to be abolished in the District of Columbia;
The slave trade to be abolished in the District;
A fugitive slave law to be passed;
Congress to declare it had no power to interfere with the
slave trade between the States.

There was a tremendous and exciting debate on
these resolutions. The three great intellectual giants
of the Senate—Clay, Webster, and Calhoun—all
now advanced in years, were making their last appearance in that body. Clay introduced the resolutions, Webster supported them, Calhoun opposed
them. In the midst of the battle President Taylor,
who had opposed them, died, and Vice-President
Millard Fillmore, who favored the compromise, succeeded to the Presidency. The whole series of resolutions passed and were signed. They are known in
history as the compromise of 1850, and curiously
enough were acquiesced in by both elements of the
Democratic party. They had, in fact, a much more
unifying effect on the Democrats than on the
Whigs, who lost the unswerving Abolitionist vote
without gaining Southern support. The Democrats,
out of power, were extremely anxious to elect a
President in 1852, and the tendency both North and
South among party people was to seize any chance
to sidetrack slavery discussion for the purpose of
securing a candidate behind whom all could unite.

Consequently, the compromise of 1850 was generally accepted as a satisfactory solution of the problem, and it was regarded as unpatriotic to reopen the question. As has been pointed out, one of those who joined in this general view was Van Buren, and while he took no prominent part in the fight, his support greatly contributed to the necessary harmony. Probably there were clear-visioned leaders who knew the slavery issue was still vibrant and horribly explosive, but if there were they do not appear in the records. Both Democrats and Whigs joined in the general delusion. Both parties avoided a controversial slavery plank in their platforms. Both indorsed the compromise of 1850. Only the Abolitionists and the weakened remnant of the Free Soilers, now deserted by the Van Burens, remained militantly consistent in parading the slavery issue as the great, unsettled, live question of the day. For the rest, the politicians of all factions and in both parties vied in deluding themselves.

But to pick up the party thread again: the campaign for the 1852 Presidential nomination began as early as the spring of 1851. The most active, energetic, pushing aspirant was Stephen A. Douglas of Illinois, who had established his supremacy in that State, was its senator, and had by his eloquence and force, his personal charm, and engaging physical qualities won a nation-wide reputation in Congress. He was only thirty-eight years old and was hailed as the leader of the "Young Democracy." The West was still wedded to Lewis Cass as its candidate, and there were vast obstacles in the Douglas way. But he went after the nomination tooth and toenail, traveling about the country, New York, New England, Virginia, here, there, everywhere, making speeches, making deals, making friends. He was the "Little Giant" to drive the elder statesmen out of party power they had held too long. He was inducted into Tammany Hall, had banquets given for him, gave money contributions to educational institutions, pledged himself anew to the compromise measures, which he had helped frame. Brilliant, shrewd, ambitious, for a time he had an alliance with the renowned General Gideon J. Pillow of Tennessee, who had had most to do with the nomination of Mr. Polk in 1844. The Cass and Buchanan forces became alarmed, but needlessly so. In spite of the rushing around, Douglas made comparatively little progress, and General Pillow shifted his allegiance rather early in the game. It was charged that the lobbyists at Washington and all the corrupt elements of the party were Douglas's friends, that he lavishly promised every office in the President's gift in return for support, and had attempted deals with every other candidate in the field. In his study of "The Democratic Machine—1850-1854," published by Columbia University, Dr. Roy Franklin Nichols sums up his candidacy by quoting from a terrible letter written by an unfriendly leader at Washington:

Douglas the candidate of the cormorants of our party is now considered a dead cock in the pit, unless some throe in the agony of political death should enable him to kill off his opponents which is not likely to occur. He is a mere hotbed production a precocious politician warmed into and kept in existence by a set of interested plunderers that would in the event of success disembowel the treasury, disgrace the country and damn the party to all eternity that brought them into power. Those arms thrown about his neck along the street—reading pieces to him in the oyster cellar of a complimentary character which are to be sent off to some subsidized press for publication, then a drink, next a haugh, haugh, then some claim to be discussed by which they expect to practice some swindle upon the government. If you were here where you could see some of the persons engaged and the appliances brought to bear for the purpose of securing his election you would involuntarily denounce the whole concern a poor miserable, vile Bandetti and much fitter to occupy cells in the penitentiary than places of state.

The leaders, however, were linked against him, and by the opening of 1852 he had ceased to be regarded as a formidable candidate, though this fact did not discourage Douglas himself, either then or later. It was early in the year that the idea of nominating Franklin Pierce of New Hampshire, not for first place but for second, took hold in New England. Handsome, engaging, a good speaker, and semibrilliant, Pierce had been a member of the legislature of his State and had later represented it in the House and Senate at Washington. Dr. Nichols asserts that his chief weakness was an inherent taste for alcohol, and that the uncontrollable nature of this taste had made him resign his seat in the Senate in 1842 and return to the practice of law in Concord. When the suggestion of the Vice-Presidency was first made to him he shrank from it. Mrs. Pierce was violently opposed to returning to Washington; Pierce was afraid of himself. He let it be known he did not want the nomination and discouraged his friends.

It was Edmund Burke, conspicuous for years as a New Hampshire politician, an office-holder under Polk, and an exceedingly shrewd manipulator, who first conceived the notion that, as the situation was developing, Pierce could be made the candidate for President in the way Polk had been. He interested Caleb Cushing of Massachusetts and later the astute General Pillow. Among them they got Pierce to consent to let his name go before the convention when chances for other candidates had been exhausted. There is no question that he hoped he would not be nominated—and believed he would not be. Pillow, Cushing, and Burke did an enormous amount of effective and quiet missionary work in his behalf. Pierce did nothing for himself. Further, he was determined not to let his name be put up except as a last resort. Actually, that attitude fitted in better with the plans of the men pushing him than any other.

The convention again met in Baltimore in May. The city was crowded, excited, in a turmoil of intrigue, speculation, conspiracies. All the political hangers-on of the party, all the job hunters, all the party hacks and scavengers were on hand. Everywhere the Douglas men were the most active and the most noisy. Cass, Marcy, Buchanan, and he were considered the leading candidates, and to the reasonably detached observers it was plain they were so evenly matched that the opening for another "dark horse" was wide. Burke and his allies were busy spreading the Pierce propaganda, and the bitterness of the struggle was intense. In the midst of the turbulency, when the adherents of the rival candidates were ready to fly at each other's throats, a Baltimore clergyman at the opening session petitioned the Almighty that "plenteous streams of mercy and love may descend upon this convention." In the five days that followed, threats, cajolery, pleadings, promises, money, and liquor were all used in the effort to gain advantage. The two thirds rule at this, as at all Democratic conventions, was in force, and 197 of the 288 votes in the convention were necessary to a choice. John W. Davis of Indiana presided, and the only departure from customary procedure was the adoption of the platform after the selection of the candidates instead of before. Forty-nine ballots were required before the deadlock on the Presidential nomination was broken. The first ballot was as follows:

```
Lewis Cass ..............................116
James Buchanan .......................... 93
William L. Marcy ........................ 27
Stephen A. Douglas ...................... 20
Joseph Lane ............................. 13
Samuel Houston .......................... 8
Scattering .............................. 4
```

Pierce Another Dark Horse

At one time Douglas reached ninety-two and Buchanan 104. Candidates slid up and down the scale in bewildering fashion. It was not until the twenty-ninth ballot that Pierce's name was put forward. On that ballot he got fifteen votes from Virginia. On the thirty-sixth ballot he had thirty, on the forty-eighth, fifty-five—and then the "stampede" came. The thing was fixed between the forty-eighth and forty-ninth. On the final roll-call Pierce was named with 282 votes. When the news of his nomination was taken to Pierce by messenger he at first refused to believe it. Mrs. Pierce fainted. William R. King of Alabama was nominated for Vice-President on the second ballot, and the platform was in complete accord with the policy of acquiescence in the compromise of 1850 and the determination to regard the slavery issue—for the time being at least—as settled business. Its first part was composed of the usual glittering generalities—reaffirmation of the Jeffersonian doctrines, opposition to a national bank, and strong advocacy of economy in government. The vital parts were the following:

Resolved, That Congress has no power under the Constitution to interfere with, or control, the domestic institutions of the several states, and that such states are the sole and proper judges of everything appertaining to their own affairs, not prohibited by the Constitution; that all efforts of the Abolitionists or others, made to induce Congress to interfere with questions of slavery, or to take incipient steps in relation thereto, are calculated to lead to the most alarming and dangerous consequences; and that all such efforts have an inevitable tendency to diminish the happiness of the people, and endanger the stability and permanency of the Union, and ought not to be countenanced by any friend of our political institutions.

Resolved, That the foregoing proposition covers, and is intended to embrace, the whole subject of slavery agitation in Congress; and therefore the Democratic party of the Union, standing on this national platform, will abide by, and adhere to, a faithful execution of the acts known as the Compromise measures settled by the last Congress, "the act for reclaiming fugitives from service labor" included; which act, being designed to carry out an express provision of the constitution, cannot, with fidelity thereto, be repealed, nor so changed as to destroy or impair its efficiency.

Resolved, That the Democratic party will resist all attempts at renewing in Congress, or out of it, the agitation of the slavery question, under whatever shape or color the attempt may be made.

Resolved, That the Democratic party will faithfully abide by and uphold the principles laid down in the Kentucky and Virginia resolutions of 1798, and in the report of Mr. Madison to the Virginia legislature in 1799; that it adopts those principles as constituting one of the main foundations of its political creed, and is resolved to carry them out in their obvious meaning and import.

Resolved, That the war with Mexico, upon all the principles of patriotism and the law of nations, was a just and necessary war on our part, in which no American citizen should have shown himself opposed to his country, and neither morally nor physically, by word or deed, given aid and comfort to the enemy.

The above extracts are given to show the extent of the party delusion that the slavery issue had been put out of politics. As to the campaign, it was without particular feature or particular excitement. Pierce remained at home, received visitors, made three or four speeches, wrote some letters. His fight was in the hands of the Democratic National Committee, which had been officially and formally established in the convention of 1848, and of which Benjamin F. Hallett of Massachusetts was the first chairman. General Winfield Scott was the Whig nominee, and there was no burning question, no sharp line between the parties. There was as little to choose between the candidates as there was between the parties, and the country was much too prosperous to get heated up over a battle without living issues. Since the time of Jackson it had been normally Democratic. Consequently, with the Democrats united, the normal result followed—they won. The desire for Federal patronage, from which they had been debarred for four years, had a unifying effect upon the political workers. They wanted to win in order to have something to fight about. Pierce got 254 electoral votes to forty-two for his rival. His popular majority was over 214,000. He carried twenty-seven States—all save Kentucky, Massachusetts, Tennessee, Vermont. It was the death-blow to the Whig party. By 1856 it had decayed and disintegrated to such an extent that it was no longer a factor and its convention was futile and foolish. The new Republican party, the logical successor of that 1848 Free Soil movement of Van Buren's, rose out of its ashes and a new era began.

The Pierce administration was not much more exciting than his campaign. He was the second mediocrity nominated by the party—a dark horse or compromise candidate is almost certain to be one. If it were otherwise, if he were an outstanding figure, with positive views, it would be impossible to compromise on him. Pierce had a kind heart. He hated to say "no." His desire for harmony led him to promise in the way of patronage more than he could fulfil. His greeting to those who sought favors from him was so cordial that, though he did not promise, they felt he had. Further, his habit of avoiding disputatious argument led a lot of those who discussed issues and patronage with him to consider him in agreement with them. The result was that when he finally made his decision there was disappointment and resentment. The tragic death of his young son, the ill-health of his wife, her dislike of Washington, the impossible task of satisfying all factions by treating them all fairly, combined to make Mr. Pierce a more or less miserable man while he was President, and Dr. Nichols is authority for the statement that while President he lapsed into his old habit of intemperance. His distribution of the patronage, from cabinet offices on down, was with the idea of strengthening the party machine, but he made some grave mistakes of judgment and was not particularly fortunate in his selection of advisers. He did not realize how accidental a nomination his was and how devoid of real following in the country he was.

The name of Franklin Pierce meant nothing outside his State without the title of President attached. It would therefore have been wise had he selected for his cabinet outstanding party men who could have supplied the real prestige and leadership he lacked. Instead he chose Dobbin, McClelland, Campbell, Guthrie, Cushing—all fairly efficient fellows and of good character, but unknown beyond their States and without real party or public position. All in all, his administration is not one of which the party need be particularly ashamed, but it most certainly was not one to arouse especial pride. Throughout the administration of Mr. Pierce the party was controlled by its Southern contingent. While the Calhoun extremists in the South had opposed the compromise slavery measures in 1850, after the election they seemed to assume that the compromise had been a concession of their contentions, and from its inception they began to urge measures that would make the introduction of slavery into the Territories easy and its exclusion hard. They held that no power was vested in a Territory, or could be given to it, to exclude slavery, but that any American citizen moving into such Territory with his slaves or other property was entitled to protection under the laws and was within his rights, and that only when the people came together to form a state constitution could the power originate as to whether slavery was to be allowed or permitted. Stephen Douglas, as senator from Illinois, denied this doctrine and held that the people of any Territory had the right to exclude slavery. The utter impossibility of keeping the slavery issue down was apparent.

At the start Mr. Pierce congratulated the country that the agitation had ceased and both parties were pledged to treat a revival of the controversy as an unpatriotic act. But it was revived with greater bitterness and violence than before when the proposition to organize the Territories of Kansas and Nebraska came up. It was at once declared in the South that the compromise of 1850 had superseded the Missouri Compromise, and there ensued a dreadful struggle between the pro-slavery and anti-slavery forces over these two Territories—particularly Kansas. Within and without the fight was a violent one, and in the midst of it—early in 1854—the new Republican party originated in the West—at Ripon, Wisconsin. From the start it had a remarkable growth, because the Whig party had, through fear of losing its Southern support, insisted upon deluding itself and trying to delude the country with the notion that the slavery issue had been decided. With the Whigs holding blindly to that idea, with the Democratic party controlled by the Southern element, the field was wide open for the party that definitely and without equivocation made the foundation stone of its existence opposition to the extension of slavery anywhere, anyhow, any time.

Chapter XIV

The Futile Effort to Ignore the Issue in 1856—Buchanan
and His Troubles—No First-Class Leadership in the
Party—Disappearance of the Whigs—The First Republican National Campaign

As the 1856 convention approached, Mr. Pierce was
strong with the Southern people, but the Northern
and more moderate wing of the party favored James
Buchanan of Pennsylvania, a candidate for President four years before and a factor for years in
Pennsylvania party politics. Douglas had increased
his popular hold, had taken a conspicuous part in the
Kansas-Nebraska debates, gained in prestige and
power, and was looked upon as likely to fall heir to
Pierce's strength should Pierce fail to get the nomination. The convention was held in Cincinnati, and
for days before it met feeling was high. Particularly were the Northern delegates agitated over the
prospect of their favorite, Buchanan, being sidetracked and another "dark horse" candidate developed. There was considerable talk of a bolt on their
part if that happened. It didn't. The convention met
on June 2. Buchanan, whose campaign had been
quietly but effectively in progress for four years, and

who was at all stages of the game acceptable to the effective Southern party leaders who knew him well, led the field from the start. On the first ballot the vote was: Buchanan, 135; Pierce, 122; Douglas, 33; Cass, 5.

Buchanan went steadily up, Pierce steadily down. On the tenth ballot Buchanan had a majority and Pierce had faded completely out of the picture. On the seventeenth the slump came, and Buchanan was nominated with 296 votes. There were ten candidates voted for Vice-President, but John C. Breckinridge of Kentucky was nominated on the second ballot. The platform reiterated the preamble of 1844, and again took the stand on the compromise of 1850 taken in 1852, in effect insisting that the slavery issue was settled by it. In view of the extraordinary way in which the religious issue was raised in the Democratic convention of 1924, the offensive political activity of the Ku-Klux Klan in recent years, and the fact that in this year (1928) the most conspicuous candidate for the Democratic nomination, Governor Alfred E. Smith of New York, happens to be a Catholic, there should be particular interest in the section of this 1856 platform dealing with the religious issue. The so-called "American party," also known as the "Know Nothings," had been organized, held a national convention, raised the religious issue, and was conducting an anti-Catholic crusade, mostly "under cover" but none the less virulent.

INAUGURATION OF JAMES BUCHANAN MARCH 4, 1857

The Approach of the Crisis

On this subject the convention said:

And whereas, Since the foregoing declaration was uniformly adopted by our predecessors in national convention, an adverse political and religious test has been secretly organized by a party claiming to be exclusively American, and it is proper that the American Democracy should clearly define its relations thereto, and declare its determined opposition to all secret political societies, by whatever name they may be called,

Resolved, That the foundation of this Union of States having been laid in, and its prosperity, expansion and preeminent example of free government built upon, entire freedom in matters of religious concernment, and no respect of persons in regard to rank, or place, or birth, no party can be justly deemed national, constitutional, or in accordance with American principles which bases its exclusive organization upon religious opinions and accidental birthplace. And hence a political crusade in the nineteenth century, and in the United States of America, against Catholics and foreign born, is neither justified by the past history or future prospects of the country, nor in unison with the spirit of toleration and enlightened freedom which peculiarly distinguishes the American system of popular government.

It is also essential to the story to quote the platform sections touching the subject of slavery, for two reasons—first, because it is important to make clear the attitude of the party in the convention just ahead of the great smash when the menace of approaching sectional conflict terrifyingly lit up the political skies; and second, to show the utter foolishness and futility of attempting by party fiat to ignore a vital issue, of trying to solve a moral question in which one way or another the bulk of the people are obviously and openly concerned, and which is widely agitated, by pretending either that it does not exist or that it has been solved.

That is what the Democratic party did in its platforms of 1852 and 1856 in regard to the slavery issue, and that, in effect, is what both Democratic and Republican parties have done in their platforms with the prohibition issue since 1920. It is due, of course, to the inherent timidity of politicians generally and the natural desire of candidates for office and the job-hunting and job-holding hordes to avoid flat-footed declarations on dangerously controversial questions that involve risk of party defeat. In the end, however, such questions have to be faced. It is as impossible for the present-day parties to continue indefinitely dry and wet as it was for the pre-war Democratic party to continue, as it did for nearly a generation, pro-slavery and anti-slavery. That sort of "pussy-footing" on a great and vital issue can be done for some time but not all the time. That kind of issue does not disappear because not dwelt on in platforms. In 1856 the Democrats tried to dismiss the slavery issue, with which the whole country was seething, in the following resolutions:

That the Democratic party will resist all attempts at renewing in Congress or out of it, the agitation of the slavery question, under whatever shape or color the attempt may be made.

The Democratic party will faithfully abide by and uphold the principles laid down in the Kentucky and Virginia resolutions of 1798 and in the report of Mr. Madison to the Virginia legislature in 1799; that it adopts these principles as constituting one of the main foundations of its political creed and is resolved to carry them out in their obvious meaning and import.

And that we may more distinctly meet the issue on which a sectional party, subsisting exclusively on slavery agitation, now relies to test the fidelity of the people, North and South, to the Constitution and the Union,—

Resolved that, claiming fellowship with and desiring the cooperation of all who regard the preservation of the Union under the Constitution as the paramount issue, and repudiating all sectional issues and platforms concerning domestic slavery which seek to embroil the States and incite to treason and armed resistance to law in the Territories, and whose avowed purpose, if consummated, must end in civil war and disunion, the American Democracy recognize and adopt the principles contained in the organic laws establishing the Territories of Nebraska and Kansas as embodying the only sound and safe solution of the slavery question, upon which the great national idea of the people of this whole country can repose in its determined conservation of the Union, and non-interference of Congress with slavery in the Territories or in the District of Columbia.

2. That this was the basis of the compromise of 1850, confirmed by both the Democratic and Whig parties in national conventions, ratified by the people in the election of 1852, and rightly applied to the organization of the Territories in 1854.

3. That by the uniform application of the Democratic principle to the organization of Territories, and the admission of new States with or without domestic slavery, as they may elect, the equal rights of all the States will be preserved intact, the original compacts of the Constitution maintained inviolate, and the perpetuity and expansion of the Union insured to its utmost capacity of embracing, in peace and harmony, every future American State that may be constituted or annexed with a republican form of government.

Resolved, That we recognize the right of the people of

179

all the Territories, including Kansas and Nebraska, acting through the legally and fairly expressed will of the majority of the actual residents, and whenever the number of their inhabitants justifies it, to form a constitution, with or without domestic slavery, and be admitted into the Union upon terms of perfect equality with the other States.

Resolved, Finally, that in view of the condition of popular institutions in the Old World (and the dangerous tendencies of sectional agitation, combined with the attempt to enforce civil and religious disabilities against the rights of acquiring and enjoying citizenship in our own land), a high and sacred duty is devolved, with increased responsibility, upon the Democratic party of this country, as the party of the Union, to uphold and maintain the rights of every State, and thereby the Union of the States; and to sustain and advance among us constitutional liberty, by continuing to resist all monopolies and exclusive legislation for the benefit of the few at the expense of the many; and by a vigilant and constant adherence to those principles and compromises of the Constitution which are broad enough and strong enough to embrace and uphold the Union as it was, the Union as it is, and the Union as it shall be, in the full expansion of the energies and capacity of this great and progressive people.

By this sort of treatment the party kept together for the purposes of the campaign, retained the melancholy, reluctant, and apprehensive support of anti-slavery Democrats in the North of the Van Buren type, and postponed the fatal day. It is perhaps true that by now things had gone too far to turn around and that there was nothing that could have been done in that convention to avoid the conflict and preserve the party health. Perhaps if there had been at this period another Andrew Jackson, some great Democratic leader loved by the people, fol-

lowed by the politicians, wise, fearless, magnetic, far
seeing, to speak to the party in the clarion tones of
the anti-nullification proclamation—perhaps if there
had been such a man in 1856, the Civil War might
have been averted, the party switched, deep as were
the slavery roots, from the wrong side of this moral
issue, and the great problem ultimately worked out
without complete wreckage.

At this critical moment the South was not called
upon to give up its slaves—only the Abolitionists demanded that—but merely to cease fighting for the
extension of slavery in new territory. That was the
sole basis of the new Republican party. At the time
of its formation, and in 1860 when it elected Lincoln, there was a sharp line between it and the
Abolitionists, who, however, saw in it the ultimate
instrument for their ends. But at the time it was not
an abolition party; and, while it was wide, it was not
an utterly unbridgable gulf the Democrats would
have had to cross in 1856 to reach a basis where the
new Republican party would have had no reason for
existence and certainly no chance of success. It is
conceivable that under a great leader it could have
been done, notwithstanding that the South felt with
a fervor hard to exaggerate that not only its political power but its material prosperity and its social
system were involved in maintaining the right to
hold slaves in the new territories as well as in the
slave States.

Perhaps even a great man could not have saved

the situation, but the truth is there was no great man at the time in the party, either North, South, West, or in the border States. No tall oak towered in the party forest. The outstanding figures were dead and none had arisen to take their place. There not only was not a really great man in sight on the Democratic side, but there does not seem to have been any particularly near-great man. Polk, Pierce, and Buchanan did not qualify as great Presidents or great party leaders. The best that can be said of them is that they were first-rate second-rate men, not cast for the rôle of commander, not capable of inspiring a party or charting its course away from the rocks. They were—these three Presidents—party subordinates, not party chiefs. Two of them became Presidents by accidental convention compromises; the third was nominated because both elements in the party thought him "safe."

Of the three, Buchanan was probably the weakest. The campaign preceding his election was a curious one. In the South it was sluggish enough, the only candidate against Buchanan being Mr. Fillmore, nominated by the decaying Whigs. In the North and West, however, the new Republican party, with its ticket of Frémont and Dayton, waged a fight in which there was plenty of enthusiasm and fire. With a clearly understood purpose and the right side of a moral issue, they took the aggressive, and while their campaign ended in defeat, it left the Democrats shaken and alarmed. They lost New York, Massachusetts, Connecticut, Iowa, New Hampshire, Ohio, Vermont, Wisconsin, Maine, Michigan, Rhode Island, to the Republicans, and Maryland to the Whigs. Their ticket—Buchanan and Breckinridge —got 174 electoral votes and a popular plurality of approximately 500,000. The new party polled 1,341,264 popular votes and got 114 electoral votes —in this its first nation-wide fight.

What happened to the poor old Whigs is perhaps the best of all illustrations of the futility of ignoring a vital issue. Since 1850 the Whigs had avoided squarely facing the slavery question, superficially acquiescing in the compromises of 1850, insisting that the subject was not in politics, trying desperately to hold slave support in the South and at the same time retain anti-slave strength in the North. The net result was a loss of both. The Republican party elbowed it out of existence, and its Presidential candiate in 1856—Millard Fillmore, the ex-President—carried exactly one State, Maryland. The Whig ticket polled only 875,000 votes in the whole country, and its candidate got but eight electoral votes. That was the last ever heard of the Whigs as a national party. It sank without a trace and a great new party, vibrating with moral wrath, took its place as the opposition to the battle-scarred Democratic party, with its long line of fine Presidents, its great history and splendid traditions, its services to the country, and its imperishable principles, now hopelessly split on an issue it had for ten years been desperately but vainly trying to shelve by declaring it "not a political question."

For practically the whole of Mr. Buchanan's administration the drift of the country was steadily toward war, and thoughtful men of all parties and in all sections looked on helpless and aghast. Slavery was the sole absorbing question. Men talked and thought about nothing else. All other issues were obscured, and the feeling between the sections grew more tense and bitter every day. Since the election the sectional line had been drawn more sharply than before, Pennsylvania and New Jersey being practically the only Northern States left in the Democratic party, now almost completely a Southern party, wholly dominated by that section. It had been hoped by his Northern supporters before his inauguration that Mr. Buchanan would, after he took hold, stand firmly against the aggressive attack of the South to extend the slave power; but he completely disappointed these expectations, was dominated by that element, and yielded all along the line.

Buchanan was a bachelor, conservative, conciliatory, but not constructive. He could not have been elected but for the free States—Pennsylvania, New Jersey, Indiana, Illinois, California. He was at heart opposed to slavery, but he had opposed the Wilmot Proviso and supported the 1850 Clay compromise. In public life for nearly forty years, his best work was done in Russia during the Jackson administration and as Ambassador to England under Pierce.

As President, his handling of foreign affairs was fine. He not only knew conditions but had a fine conception of the way in which the dignity of the country should be upheld and its interests guarded in dealing with other nations. It is conceded that on this side he was a good President, sound, sure, safe. But on the domestic side he was unable to function successfully. He wanted to but lacked the strength. In dealing with the great slavery and secession problems he was on the defensive. He tried to conciliate both sides when conciliation was out of the question. He thought the North should not agitate and the South should not push, but he did not resist the push when it came and he utterly lacked initiative. He opposed secession and denied in his 1860 message the right of any State to secede. Yet they did secede under him and he was unable to do anything to stop it. His appeals to Congress for men and means, for power and authority, were discarded and he was reduced to a state of helplessness where all he could do was to refuse to receive the commissioners of the seceding State of South Carolina when they asked for an audience.

The questions are asked about Buchanan: Why did he allow State after State to go out of the Union, and why did he not crush the rebellion in its first stages? The only answer given by his biographical defenders is that Congress would not give him the power, that not only his own party refused to vote him what he asked, but the Republicans in Congress, to their shame, likewise failed to support administration measures that would have made it possible for the President to quell the outbreak and to have brought the seceding States into line. The real answer seems to be that Buchanan was Buchanan and not Andrew Jackson. It was a time for a great man, and he was not that. When he went out of office, seven States had already seceded: the catastrophe had occurred.

To return to the details: the Dred Scott decision of the Supreme Court, which came early in his administration, completely sustained the Southern contention as to their right of property—when the property was in the form of slaves. It gave their struggle to maintain political power and uphold their social and economic system full support from the highest judicial authority in the land. They had an obvious legal and technical justification for the extraordinarily violent fight to extend slavery into Kansas, and were convinced to their souls of the moral justification. In the South the fight seemed not only righteous, sanctioned by all the laws of God and man, but vital to the salvation of white civilization. In the North there was complete inability to see or to sympathize with the Southern viewpoint. All they saw there was an outrageous effort upon the part of the slave-holders in the South to force on an unwilling people an abhorrent and inhuman custom.

It was over Kansas that the great struggle occurred. It began in the first year of the Pierce administration, extended clear through the four years of Buchanan, and ended only in 1861 after the war began, when it was admitted as a free State. In those seven years Kansas as a Territory went through a terrible time. She bled as she has never bled since. The story of the contest over the State is a dark chapter in American political history—a contest that stirred both slavery and anti-slavery forces to white heat. Kansas was pulled almost to pieces between them, had seven Governors in five years, and was the scene of many violent incidents and disorders. The picture drawn in that first Republican platform—1856—is, of course, a partisan and extravagant one. Nevertheless and allowing for this extravagance, it will serve here, where the full story cannot be told, to give an idea of the feeling as well as the facts.

On this subject the new party said:

Resolved, That while the Constitution of the United States was ordained and established by the people in order to form a more perfect Union, establish justice, ensure domestic tranquillity, provide for the common defense, and secure the blessings of liberty, and contains ample provision for the protection of life, liberty and property of every citizen, the dearest constitutional rights of the people of Kansas have been fraudulently and violently taken from them; their territory has been invaded by an armed force, spurious and pretended legislation, judicial and executive officers have been set over them, by whose usurped authority, sustained by the military power of the government, tyrannical and unconstitutional laws have been enacted and enforced; the rights of the people to keep and bear arms have been infringed; test oaths of an extraordinary and entangling nature have been imposed as a condition of exercising the right of suffrage and holding office; the right of an accused person to a speedy and public trial by an impartial jury has been denied; the right of the people to be secure in their persons, houses, papers and effects against unreasonable searches and seizures has been violated; they have been deprived of life, liberty and property without due process of law; the freedom of speech and of the press has been abridged; the right to choose their representatives has been made of no effect; murders, robberies and arsons have been instigated and encouraged, and the offenders have been allowed to go unpunished;— that all these things have been done with the knowledge, sanction, and procurement of the present administration; and that for this high crime against the Constitution, the Union, and humanity, we arraign the administration, the President, his advisers, agents, supporters, apologists, and accessories, either before or after the fact, before the country and before the world, and that it is our fixed purpose to bring the actual perpetrators of these atrocious outrages, and their accomplices, to a sure and condign punishment hereafter.

All the Whigs had to say about this in 1856 was this:

Resolved, That we regard with the deepest interest and anxiety the present disorderly condition of our national affairs,—a portion of the country ravaged by civil war, large sections of our population embittered by mutual recriminations; and we distinctly trace these calamities to the culpable neglect of duty by the present national administration.

There is no better illustration of why the Whigs carried but one State in the election. That in the face of this sort of situation Buchanan displayed neither character nor courage there is not much room for doubt. There was probably no possible way for him at this stage to avert the "irrepressible conflict," but it does seem reasonable to think that his lack of strength to resist the extremists on both sides hastened the war, in that it encouraged the one side to press its advantage and goaded the other to fight more furiously.

Chapter XV

THE GREAT SLAVERY SMASH-UP

Douglas's Candidacy and the Bolt of the Southern Delegates from the Charleston Convention—The Breckinridge Nomination and the Excitement in the South —Wrecked on the Wrong Side of a Great Moral Issue

BUT the great party smash-up would have come anyhow. Back in 1850, those with clear heads saw its inevitability, appealed for action to avoid the clash, knowing full well that there was no leader and no program that could restore the equilibrium between the sections. In his last speech in the Senate in 1850 Calhoun, then a sick man not far from death, said, "I have, Senators, believed from the first that the agitation of the subject of slavery would, if not prevented by some timely and effective measure, end in disunion." No "timely and effective measure" had been found, no "timely and effective" man had arisen, and when the time came for the various political parties to nominate candidates in 1860, there were few who did not recognize that the crash was close at hand.

The whole political sky was full of lightning. During the Buchanan administration a great many events, which cannot be reviewed here, calculated to increase popular excitement had occurred, of which the John Brown raid at Harper's Ferry was the most sensational and stirring. When the delegates to the Democratic convention of 1860 began to assemble in Charleston, South Carolina, on April 23, they were in a highly emotional and explosive state. The feeling of the smash-up was in the air; its signs were all about. Men were far more tense and deeply stirred than they had been at any previous convention. There was general recognition that a party crisis existed; that one way or the other a bolt threatened; that the breach in the party could not be healed; that a "harmony" convention with the Polk-Pierce-Buchanan type of compromise candidate was not again possible. The Whig party had practically disappeared and the new born Republican party, militant, vigorous, vibrating with a great moral purpose, on the right side of a great moral issue, was in the field. Its great leader—Abraham Lincoln—had forged to the front and the feel of victory unified and thrilled the rank and file. An indication of the sort of President and party leader Buchanan was is that his name did not go before the Democratic convention at all—and he did not receive even the sort of complimentary vote that Pierce did in 1856.

The real candidate was Stephen A. Douglas, who had opposed in the Senate the administration's program in Kansas and promulgated his "popular sovereignty" doctrine, which appealed to the Northern and Western Democrats but was not opposed to slavery or its extension under that doctrine. His debate with Lincoln in 1858 had added to his fame, and he came to the convention with more delegates than any one else. Moreover, his friends were in control of the National Committee, which enabled them to organize the convention and to recognize Douglas delegations in contests, one of which was from his own State of Illinois. Caleb Cushing of Massachusetts presided, and again it was decided to adopt the platform first, name the ticket last. They never got that far. Before a nomination could be made the split came.

What happened was this. The Committee on Resolutions brought in a majority report and two minority reports. The first set forth the South's point of view, the others ignored that view and took refuge behind the Supreme Court. There was a fierce debate, violent and excited, lasting two days. All the reports were recommitted to the committee, which promptly reported back the majority report, to which the Southern delegates were pledged. But the convention, led by Douglas's friends, substituted the minority report, presented by Mr. Samuels of Iowa, for the majority report by a vote of 165 to 138. This action stood the party on this platform:

1. Resolved, That we, the Democracy of the Union, in convention assembled, hereby declare our affirmance of the

Courtesy of Harper & Brothers

THE NATIONAL DEMOCRATIC CONVENTION AT CHARLESTON, SOUTH CAROLINA,
APRIL, 1860. HERE THE PARTY WAS WRECKED ON THE DAVEY ROCK

resolutions unanimously adopted and declared as a platform of principles by the Democratic convention at Cincinnati in the year 1856, believing that Democratic principles are unchangeable in their nature when applied to the same subject-matters; and we recommend as the only further resolutions the following:—

Inasmuch as differences of opinion exist in the Democratic party as to the nature and extent of the powers of a territorial legislature and as to the powers and duties of Congress, under the Constitution of the United States, over the institution of slavery within the Territories,—

2. Resolved, That the Democratic party will abide by the decisions of the Supreme Court of the United States on the questions of constitutional law.

3. Resolved, That it is the duty of the United States to afford ample and complete protection to all its citizens, whether at home or abroad, and whether native or foreign.

4. Resolved, That one of the necessities of the age, in a military, commercial, and postal point of view, is speedy communication between the Atlantic and Pacific States; and the Democratic party pledge such constitutional government aid as will insure the construction of a railroad to the Pacific coast at the earliest practicable period.

5. Resolved, That the Democratic party is in favor of the acquisition of the island of Cuba, on such terms as shall be honorable to ourselves and just to Spain.

6. Resolved, That the enactments of state legislatures to defeat the faithful execution of the fugitive slave law are hostile in character, subversive of the Constitution, and revolutionary in their effects.

Contrast this with the majority report supported by the slave-holding States, and adopted by them later in their rump convention:

Resolved, That the platform adopted by the Democratic party at Cincinnati be affirmed, with the following explanatory resolutions:—

1. That the government of a Territory organized by an act of Congress is provisional and temporary; and during its existence, all citizens of the United States have an equal right to settle with their property in the Territory, without their rights, either of person or of property, being destroyed or impaired by congressional legislation.

2. That it is the duty of the federal government, in all its departments, to protect, when necessary, the rights of persons and property in the Territories, and wherever else its constitutional authority extends.

3. That when the settlers in a Territory, having an adequate population, form a state constitution, the right of sovereignty commences, and, being consummated by admission into the Union, they stand on an equal footing with the people of other States; and the State thus organized ought to be admitted into the Federal Union, whether its Constitution prohibits or recognizes the institution of slavery.

4. That the Democratic party is in favor of the acquisition of the Island of Cuba, on such terms as shall be honorable to ourselves and just to Spain, at the earliest practicable moment.

5. That the enactment of state legislatures to defeat the faithful execution of the fugitive slave law is hostile in character, subversive to the Constitution, and revolutionary in their effect.

6. That the Democracy of the United States recognize it as the imperative duty of this government to protect the naturalized citizen in all his rights, whether at home or in foreign lands, to the same extent as its native-born citizens.

Whereas, One of the greatest necessities of the age, in a political, commercial, postal, and military point of view, is a speedy communication between the Pacific and Atlantic coasts,—

Therefore be it resolved, That the Democratic party do hereby pledge themselves to use every means in their power to secure the passage of some bill, to the extent of the constitutional authority of Congress, for the construction of a Pacific railroad from the Mississippi River to the Pacific Ocean, at the earliest practicable moment.

It was the second, third, fourth, and fifth sections of these resolutions that were important—not only important to the Southern delegates, but vital. They had come there to get that sort of declaration from their party on this subject, because the whole South flamed with a demand for it. When the convention rejected their demand, ignored their position, refused to listen to their impassioned pleas, overrode the committee's majority report with votes from Northern and Western States which the Democratic ticket stood no chance whatever of carrying in the election—when these things happened, the South, where the bulk of the Democratic electoral votes were lodged, felt that it could not be borne, and amid a scene of the wildest excitement and confusion half of the Southern delegates bolted the convention of the party the South had been running for so many years.

Alabama, Mississippi, Florida, Texas, Louisiana, South Carolina, Arkansas—it was a wild rush to get out. When it was over, what was left of the convention, shaken by the explosion and uncertain of its ground, endeavored to do business. A ballot was taken to select a Presidential candidate, resulting as follows:

Stephen A. Douglas, Illinois.............. 145½
R. M. T. Hunter, Virginia................ 42
James Guthrie, Kentucky................ 35
Andrew Johnson, Tennessee............. 12
Daniel S. Dickerson, New York........... 7
Joseph Lane, Oregon................... 6

Isaac Toucey, Connecticut................ 2½
Jefferson Davis, Mississippi............... 1½
James Alfred Pearce, Maryland........... 1

Douglas was far in the lead. He had a majority of the full convention, but he did not have and could not get two thirds. Fifty-seven ballots were taken. His highest vote was 151½, the next highest man, Guthrie, 65½. After ten days of fruitless sweating, swearing, hoping, and hating, an adjournment was taken to meet in Baltimore on June 18. There were at this time only about sixty-one votes from the South left in the convention. The balance—the bolters—representing perhaps a dozen States, had hired another hall in Charleston, pressed James A. Bayard of Delaware into service as presiding officer, and adopted unanimously and with cheers the series of resolutions above given, and which the South held as vital to its existence.

It remained in session four days, adjourned to meet in Richmond on June 11, met there, did nothing, adjourned to reassemble on June 21. What they were doing was playing for time in order to see the ultimate outcome of the regular convention. When the "regulars" assembled in Baltimore on the eighteenth there was a hope that perhaps a modification of the platform might be effected that would reunite the convention, and Mr. Cushing rather intimated that the resolutions were open to change. But it never got to that. When the Committee on Credentials began to seat other Douglas delegations to take

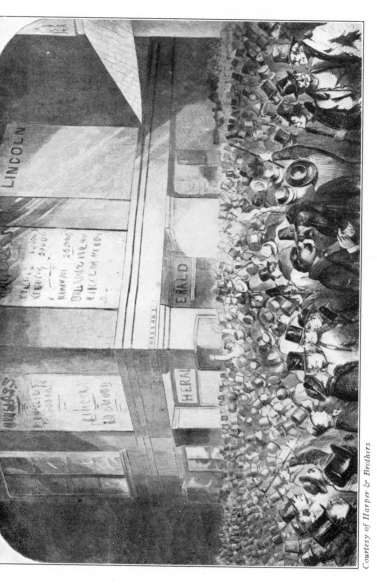

WATCHING THE ELECTION RETURNS IN FRONT OF "THE NEW YORK HERALD"
OFFICE, NOVEMBER 6, 1860

the place of the Southern secessionists, another bolt, this time led by Virginia, occurred, and when that was over, there were about thirty-six Southern delegates left, including the contesting delegations just admitted. A ballot was taken: Douglas, 173½; Guthrie, 10; John C. Breckinridge, 5; scattering, 3.

Still, Douglas did not have two thirds of the full convention required by Democratic procedure. At last a resolution was adopted amending the rule so as to regard two thirds of the vote present as two thirds of the convention. Douglas was then declared nominated and Herschel V. Johnson of Georgia named for Vice-President after Benjamin Fitzpatrick of Alabama had declined.

The bolters at Baltimore adopted the Southern resolutions and nominated John C. Breckinridge of Kentucky and Joseph Lane of Oregon by unanimous vote. At once the bolters at Richmond reassembled and ratified the nominations of Breckinridge and Lane. Thus stood the party—wrecked, ruined, and exhausted by internal struggle before the battle with the real enemy opened, foredoomed to defeat and facing a future as bleak as well could be. The "regular" convention had been left to the States from which no electoral votes could be expected. The "irregulars" represented the section where lay the real party strength. Neither ticket had been regularly nominated in accord with the regular two thirds rule Democratic custom. Between them on the real issue of the day lay a chasm too deep to bridge. Without hope of unity or reconciliation, they went into the campaign as hopeless and helpless as it was possible to be.

There was not a chance from the start. No wonder the Republicans rejoiced. Small idea from this sparse outline of this 1860 series of Democratic conventions, regular and irregular, can be had of the tremendous excitement of the time. There has not—very fortunately has not—been any issue capable of so deeply stirring men since that time. There was no blinking the fact that the country was on the verge of civil war; that the melancholy prophecy of Calhoun in 1850, the fear of the great Democrats of the early days—of Jefferson, Madison, Monroe, and others—that in the great problem of slavery lay the only real menace to national unity and to the party, were all about to be realized. The first steps toward secession were being taken; South Carolina and her sister States were straining at the leash. There was no strong voice in Washington to thunder again the noble sentiments of the anti-nullification proclamation, no iron will determined that secession was unthinkable and intolerable. Divided and desperate though the party was in the South, there were still some not very clear headed leaders in the South who thought victory might be achieved.

They entered the campaign grimly determined to win if possible but almost openly set against submitting to a defeat that they felt meant an ultimate breakdown of the whole civilization of their section, an uprooting of their social system, a destruction of their happiness, prosperity, and safety. While, as has been explained, the new Republican party was not at this time an abolition party, while there was no platform declaration on the subject of emancipation, no suggestion of conferring suffrage on the negro, yet the Southern Democrats saw and sensed all that coming—as it did—and were revolted, outraged, dismayed, desperate at the prospect. The defeat was even more overwhelming than seemed possible. The two Democratic tickets—Douglas and Johnson, Breckinridge and Lane—between them only carried twelve of the thirty-one participating States, had combined only eighty-four of the total electoral vote of 303. Of the two, the Douglas ticket got by far the greater number of popular votes— 1,376,957 as compared to 849,781 for Breckinridge —but received only twelve electoral votes as compared to seventy-two for the Southern ticket. The only State carried by Douglas was Missouri, but he only got nine of its sixteen electoral votes. Added to this he got three from New Jersey. The Breckinridge-Lane ticket carried the following States:

Alabama	9	Missouri	7
Arkansas	4	North Carolina	10
Delaware	3	South Carolina	8
Florida	3	Texas	4
Georgia	10		
Louisiana	6	Total	72
Maryland	8		

Virginia, Tennessee, and Kentucky went for the candidates of the Constitutional party—Bell and Everett—which made in that campaign its first and last appearance, polled 588,879 popular votes, and got thirty-nine electoral votes from the above mentioned three States. In ten of the Southern States the Republican candidates—Lincoln and Hamlin—did not run at all. Yet in the twenty-one others they polled 1,866,452 popular votes and garnered 180 electoral votes, more than the other three tickets combined. An analysis of the vote, however, shows that Lincoln, despite his great electoral majority, was a minority President. He got a popular plurality, but was half a million and more short of a popular majority. The combined vote of the two Democratic tickets, not counting in the Constitutionalists, who were mainly Democrats, was far in excess of the total Republican vote. Clearly the Democrats beat themselves and were not beaten by the Republicans. They divided and were defeated, but in 1860 they were still the majority party. It has been contended that even without the Charleston disruption the Democrats could not have carried the 1860 election, in that, except for three in New Jersey, no Northern State gave either Democratic ticket an electoral vote, and that together they did not poll nearly a majority. That is true; but it is also true that if the party had not split its vote three ways and been able again to soft-pedal and ignore the burning issue, it could easily have carried a number of

Northern States—and the election. But that could not be done—and they not only beat themselves but pretty nearly killed their party. It was the first great party split—the 1848 Van Buren Free Soil movement was a splinter, not a split—the first time Democrats had deliberately thrown overboard all chance of success in order to fight among themselves over the vital issue of the day instead of fighting the enemy; the first time but not the last.

Chapter XVI

THE BLACK DAYS AFTER THE SPLIT

The War and the Elimination of the South Turn the
Democrats Into a Minority Party—Republican De-
pendency on the Negro Vote—Democrats Without
Issues or Unity—Astonishing Size of the McClellan
Vote

I

SINCE 1860 the Democratic party most of the time
has had a terrible row to hoe, a rocky road to travel.
It had the history, the traditions, a grand record, an
inspiring creed, noble principles—when it remem-
bered them—but it did not have the votes. With the
war it changed from the majority party into the
minority party, and in the sixty-eight years that
have elapsed since the Buchanan administration it
has been defeated thirteen times in Presidential contests, successful in four. It should be said here—and
will be developed in detail later—that one of these
thirteen defeats was not really a defeat but a victory, though the party was, with outrageous injustice, deprived of its fruits. It should also be said
that during these sixty-eight years the Democrats
have several times controlled the House of Repre-

sentatives under Republican Presidents, and, except in those dreadful years immediately following the secession of the South, almost invariably have had a Congressional representation sufficiently large to make itself felt as an opposition party even when its chances in the Electoral College were at their lowest ebb.

It is also true that its representatives in Congress, even in the blackest period, were usually animated by the idea that the true function of an opposition party is to oppose. It has only been since 1924 that the party leaders in Senate and House appear to have discarded that conception of politics. Under great business and journalistic pressure they have actively or passively cooperated in the Republican taxation theory of benefiting the poor by cutting the taxes of the rich first and most, apparently forgetting that basic Democratic doctrine goes in the other direction; and unequal in a period of political inertia and general prosperity to the task of vitalizing Democratic principles or formulating a Democratic program in either foreign or domestic field.

The fact is that the Civil War left the Democratic party, so long dominant in the nation, in a position where its only real hope of victory lay in a division within the Republican party or a revolt against Republican administration. It is still in that position, kept there, it would seem, by three outstanding factors—first, the negro vote in the pivotal States with the big electoral vote, which gives the Republicans a running start in every race, and without which, disguise it as they will, ignore it as much as they please, resent it as strongly as they do, they would be utterly unable to maintain their ascendancy in either House or Senate and could never in the world have scored any such succession of unbroken victories as they have.

It is not possible to find any point about their party on which Republicans are as sensitive as this, one which they are less willing to discuss candidly, or are more vehement in openly denying. Yet it is true. Most of the better class and more intelligent Republican leaders of this day in their hearts know and privately concede it was a great mistake to have given the negro the unrestricted right of suffrage, and hate to have to deal with him on a footing of equality, which the exigencies of practical politics make social equality, at least during campaigns. But so completely are they dependent for success on the solidarity of negro support that they would publicly deny these views and feelings with their last breath. The only exception to this is Senator William E. Borah, who, living in a State where the negro vote is almost non-existent, and not being an aspirant for President, could afford to speak the truth—and has—on the Senate floor, denouncing his Republican colleagues as hypocritical, deceitful, cowardly, and contemptible on this subject, afraid to look it in the face except behind closed doors.

For proof of the truth of the above assertions one

TAMMANY HALL.
REGISTER!

NEW REGISTRY FOR VOTING REQUIRED.

Go Tuesday, the 13, and Register!

REMEMBER

That SEYMOUR is the first Democratic candidate for President of the United States that the State of New York has had in thirty-two years; and that HOFFMAN is the only candidate for Governor the City has had in forty years.

BOUNDARIES OF ELECTION DISTRICTS, REGISTRY AND POLLS.

FIRST WARD

Dist.

1. North river, Morris and Greenwich sts., Battery place, Bowling Green, Whitehall st. and East river, including Governor's, Ellis, and Bedloe's Islands. Registry and Polling-place, 22 Greenwich st.

2. North river, Rector st., Broadway, Battery place, Greenwich and Morris sts. Registry and Polling-place, 53 Greenwich st.

3. North river, Liberty place, Broadway, and Rector st. Registry and Polling place, 127 Washington st.

4. Greenwich and Liberty sts., Broadway, and Rector st. Registry and Polling-place, 95 Greenwich st.

SIXTH WARD

Dist.

1. Broadway, Chatham, and Chambers sts. Registry and Polling-place, 4 Tryon Row.

2. Broadway, Chambers, Centre, and Pearl sts. Registry and Polling-place, 379 Pearl st.

3. Chatham, Chambers, Centre, and Pearl st. Registry and Polling-place, 36 Centre st.

4. Broadway, Franklin, Centre, and Pearl sts. Registry and Polling-place, 138 Leonard st.

5. Centre, Franklin, Baxter, Pearl and Chatham sts. Registry and Polling-place, 43 Hudson st.

6. Bayard, Mott, Park, Mulberry, Chatham, and Baxter sts.

NINTH WARD

Dist.

1. West Houston, Varick, Charlton, Hudson, Leroy, and West sts. Registry and Polling-place, 400 Hudson st.

2. West Houston st., Cottage place, Bleecker, Leroy, Hudson, Charlton, and Varick sts. Registry and Polling-place, 36½ Carmine st.

3. Leroy, Hudson, Christopher, and West sts. Registry and Polling-place, 438 Hudson st.

4. Leroy, Bleecker, Barrow, Bedford, Christopher, and Hudson sts. Registry and Polling-place, cor. Morton and Bleecker sts.

ELEVENTH WARD.—Continued.

Dist.

7. Houston st., Av's B and D, and 3d st. Registry and Polling-place, 7 Av. C.

8. Second st., Av's B and D, and 3d st. Registry and Polling-place, 27 Av. B.

9. 3d st., Av's B and C, and 5th st. Registry and Polling-place, 55 Av. C.

10. 5th st., Av's B and C, and 7th st. Registry and Polling-place, 95 Av. C.

11. 7th st., Av's B and C, and 9th st. Registry and Polling-place, 358 9th st.

12. 8th and 9th sts., Av's B and C . . . . . .

PART OF A TAMMANY HALL POSTER, 1868

need go no farther than the figures in Presidential and off-year Congressional elections in States such as Ohio, Indiana, Illinois, Maryland, Missouri, New York, Connecticut, Massachusetts, Pennsylvania, New Jersey. In these States the negro vote ranges from 60,000 in Maryland to approximately 600,000 in Pennsylvania. The Republicans have that much in the ballot box in every election before the Democrats start to count. Subtract the negro vote in their districts and States from the majority of the Republican senators and representatives now serving from these States, or who have served in the last fifty years, and see how many would have been elected. The answer is very few, even in the strong Republican tides. Subtract the total negro vote in those States from the majority by which successful Republican Presidential candidates have carried them, and see how many since—say 1872—would have been President. The answer is not half. There is not space here to present an analysis of the figures, but those are the facts.

The Republican reply to all this is that while it may be true that few Republican Presidents could have been elected and most Republican senators and representatives—east of the Mississippi at least— would not make the grade without the negro vote, it is also true that it is the negro vote that keeps the South Democratic; that if it were not for it, the Democratic white solidarity there would be broken, and the Republicans might carry such States as Virginia and North Carolina. There is a flavor of plausibility to that but no real substance. In the first place, it is a mere guess, while the charge to which it is an answer is disproved by incontrovertible facts and figures. In the second place, if there were no negro vote there would probably be more white Republicans in the South but not, it is reasonable to think, enough to make them any more likely to carry those States than for the Democrats to carry Vermont and Maine, or Idaho, where the negro vote is too small to count. The South was a strongly Democratic section long before the negro had a vote. It would likely stay that way if he had no vote. With most voters—far more than is generally grasped—the party to which they adhere is fixed for them by their inherent and inherited prejudices and predilections. In the South these are all Democratic and were long before the Fourteenth and Fifteenth amendments were conceived.

The second thing that since the Civil War—and particularly in the last forty years—has helped keep the Democrats a minority party has been the extraordinary industrial growth of the country, a growth undreamed of and without precedent, a growth that has gradually undermined the once dominant political position of the rural and agricultural elements, to which the Democratic party originally owed its success, and with which it had always been strong. This amazing development, due not to political policies but to great, inexorable economic laws and physical facts, gave to the great financial, business, banking, and railroad interests, to which the Republican party has always turned for financial supplies —and never in vain—and which it has in return treated with especial tenderness, afforded particular protection, granted unusual favors, an enormous weight and power in the molding of public opinion and in influencing elections.

With a few notable exceptions, every ounce of this weight has since 1860 been uniformly thrown in the scales on the Republican side. The natural tendency of Big Business is toward the Republican party. It is there it feels safer and less restricted, more naturally at home and in better odor, freer to cut corners and make its own laws. But it must be admitted this attachment has been increased and riveted by the various occasions since 1892 that the Democratic party has run up economic blind alleys chasing unsound financial theories. As a net result, there has grown up a pretty general belief in business circles, big and little, that the Republican party is the "party of prosperity," that business does better under Republican than under Democratic rule, that Republicans are more capable of running the country.

Besides these two facts just cited—the natural Republican leanings of Big Business and Democratic mistakes—this idea has been nursed and strengthened by the newspapers of the country, which a generation or so ago were fairly evenly divided between the parties, but which by a process of elimination, mergers, consolidations, and syndicate ownership have to-day reached a point where four fifths of the daily and weekly press outside the "solid South," are wholly in Republican hands, as are the other channels of modern publicity—to wit, the radio and the moving pictures.

This popular belief about being the party that most surely promotes prosperity which, in one way or another, they have inculcated has been an incalculably valuable asset to the Republicans and a corresponding liability to the Democrats. It has led to the formation of a comparatively incurable habit among many business men, unshakably Democratic in State and other elections, of voting the Republican ticket in Presidential years. These exist numerously in every State and explain better than anything else why the Republicans can elect a President by a huge majority and then, in an off year, lose effective control of Congress and find themselves in the minority in the matter of State governors and legislatures.

It is a curious and illogical situation and strikingly illustrates the power of propaganda and the mighty influence of the great business and banking forces. They seem sufficient to wholly obscure the fact that it was during a Democratic administration, under a Democratic President—Woodrow Wilson—that a law was enacted—the Federal Reserve Act—which has meant more to the prosperity of the people and the protection of the business interests than any other in the history of the country; a measure that

Courtesy of Harper & Brothers

A CARTOON BY THOMAS NAST IN THE RICHARD CROKER DAYS

Mr. Nast not only was the first to use the tiger as the symbol for Tammany but it was he in his

has literally made impossible such panics as used to occur periodically; a measure that made it possible for the allied cause to win the World War—because without it the allied cause could not have been financed; a measure that in vague, unsatisfactory, half-baked shape had been kicked about by various preceding Republican administrations, unable successfully to cope with the problem.

The third thing that has kept the Democrats from regaining their position as the majority party or even achieving approximate numerical equality with their opponents is their failure to find a unifying issue in accord with traditional Democratic principles, and their habit of fighting more violently among themselves over the vibrant question of the day than with the Republicans. About this last, however, there is this to be said: it may be and is extremely silly from the viewpoint of practical politics. It is destructive of party prospects in the general election, and seems particularly absurd in the minority party, to which unity is the indispensable essential but it shows at least a capacity for political feeling and thought, a willingness to tackle the explosive subject, a character and independence, a lack of subserviency and smugness that may be looked for in vain in the Republican party since the death of Abraham Lincoln.

Founded on a great moral issue—slavery—since the settlement of that issue and its accession to power the Republican party has not had, so far as can be gleaned from its record, a single moral impulse; has not furnished the nation with an idea or an ideal, in either the foreign or the domestic field; has been a cold, complacent, wholly materialistic party, dominated by its big business bosses and its practical politicians; controlled and disciplined to regard success at the polls as more important than any principle; a party that has established without evidencing shame the high record for corruption and crookedness in governmental offices; a party that since Lincoln has given the nation exactly one first-class, high-grade, flamingly righteous, vibrant, virile President and party leader—Theodore Roosevelt.

Perhaps, in the long run, the Democratic party, regularly wrecking its hopes on the moral issue, pulling two ways on the vital questions, splitting into sections over economic principles and policies, performs a national service out of power as great as the party in power, which consistently avoids controversial questions, minimizes, excuses, and defends corruption in its administration. preserves its unity by walking around instead of through such issues as religious intolerance, governmental crookedness, and personal liberty.

It has not, it is true, got the Democratic party far. It has not improved its health very much, nor increased its prospects, to split up over these questions; but they exist, and somebody has to tackle them if progress is to be made in settling them. It ought of course to be the job of the majority party—but the Republican is not that kind of a majority party. It may be that there is less practical sense in the Democratic party, but there is more human emotion. It may be that it has less gumption, but it certainly has more soul. It may not since the Civil War be as strong a political organization as the Republicans, but it is less easily controlled by corporate wealth and power, more responsive to the popular wish, more truly a party of "the people," notwithstanding its lack of leadership and the absence of unity, clarity, and issues. Its sinister machine bosses and sordid financial influences often gain control of its conventions, but never without a battle, and frequently they are completely and gloriously routed, which never happens in the Republican conventions. There has been but one instance in the history of the Republican party since Lincoln in which the party bosses, backed by the secret business interests, have not organized and controlled its conventions, molded its platforms, picked its candidates. Since 1880 there have been at least five Democratic candidates put up not desired by those influences, and two of them—Cleveland and Wilson—were elected. The other three were Bryan.

II

The immediately foregoing shows how easy it is to be diverted from the consecutive telling of this Democratic story, how hard it is to keep on the track. It is high time to get back and pick up the thread again. With the 1860 defeat and the secession of the Southern States that followed—seven of them seceding before Buchanan went out and the rest almost immediately after the Lincoln inauguration—the South was completely eliminated from the politics of the nation. The border States remained, but the whole South was gone. It was a long time, too, before any of the seceding States regained their political feet. Even after the war when, one by one, they came straggling back into the Union, with new state constitutions forced down their throats and the carpet-bagger sitting about their necks, they were unable to function freely in any election—much less a Presidential election. The Federal Government kept its clutch on their collars for years, and it was not until 1880 that all of them were enabled to throw it wholly off and the entire South safely reverted to its Democratic moorings.

When the extra session of Congress convened in 1861 the party position was really dreadful. The marvel is that it survived at all. Based on a strict construction of the Constitution and yet called upon to face a war in which the Constitution and laws were sure to be strained to the extreme limit, there was no direction in which it could really turn. Thousands of Democrats in the North and border States took the Douglas view that "there can be no neutrals in this war—only patriots and traitors." Many of these became merged in the Republican party; others retained their party label but supported administration war measures and furnished their share of men and officers to the Union army. There were many others who strongly sympathized with the South, opposed the war, criticized its conduct.

However, the intolerance of the North, the arbitrary arrest of citizens, the suspension of the writ of habeas corpus, drove into opposition many whose loyalty was above question. To steer the party successfully under such circumstances was literally impossible. In the midst of an enormous revolution of thought and feeling it was absurd to try to stem the tide by applying to 1861 the precedents and principles of 1850. Yet that is what it did try to do. In the measures the Republicans held essential to the conduct of the war, patriotic and necessary, such as the issues of paper money, the draft, the confiscation of rebel property and slaves, Democratic politicians saw merely partisan motives and efforts to increase party votes by gratifying party leaders.

Throughout the rebellion, therefore, it is perfectly true that the bulk of the party was arrayed against the methods by which the war was conducted. It was not as a party, of course, in sympathy with the South. It was even avowedly in favor of the Union, wholly against secession. To have taken any other stand would have been unthinkable, but this did not prevent the remnant of the party from severely criticizing the administration for its course, nor did it prevent the existence of a strong underlying sentiment in the party that the war itself was unnecessary and that the troubles of the country could be settled by a convention of the States. There was, of course, an active minority in the border States openly anxious for Southern success. This, together with the opposition of the great mass of Democrats to the more violent war measures, plus the ugly temper of the North, led to the epithet of "Copperheads" applied by the Republicans at this time to the whole Democratic party. Naturally, this did not add to the pleasantness of politics and undoubtedly made the lot of the Democrats who were loyal in every way but wanted to stay in their party because of belief in it, and knowledge that the war would not last forever, particularly hard.

In the first Congress of the war the Democrats had but ten of the fifty members of the Senate, forty-two out of one hundred and seventy-eight in the House; in the second war Congress—1863-1865 —they had nine out of fifty senators, seventy-five out of one hundred and eighty-six representatives. The extraordinary political folly of secession can be grasped when it is pointed out that the absence of the twenty-two senators and sixty-six members of the House to which the seceding States were previously entitled—and all of whom would have been Democrats—was the only thing that gave the Republicans a majority in either branch of Congress during any session of the war. It is a curious and interesting fact, of which there seems a paucity of clear explanation, that during the war the Democrats made considerable gains in the House, elected governors in New York, New Jersey, and Ohio, and maintained in the North for the four years from 1860 to 1864 about its proportionate vote. The best explanation presented in the histories is that the continued Democratic loss of voters who went into the Republican party through desire for a vigorous prosecution of the war was offset by Democratic gains of Republicans who were offended by the gradual adoption of anti-slavery measures, who were opposed to abolition, and who looked with horror upon political equality for the negro.

In any event, though all chance of success in electing a President had been taken away from the Democrats by the elimination from politics of the section where was lodged their largest electoral vote, the war had not appreciably weakened them in other sections, though it had left them hopelessly at sea for a platform or an issue—other than that of criticism of the war conduct. They seemed to be helped by the feeling against President Lincoln in his own party and the nominations made in 1864 by a group of radical anti-administration Republicans who met in Cleveland. These nominated General Frémont and General Cochrane. Actually, this movement amounted to little, and the candidates did not get on the ballot in the general election. The Lincoln nomination was a foregone conclusion, unanimously made, and his reelection almost as unanimous so far as electoral votes are concerned, although the popular majority was less than half a million—1,802,237 votes being cast for the

Democratic candidates, McClellan and Pendleton.

They, however, carried but three States—Delaware, Kentucky, New Jersey. The Democratic candidates got a total of twenty-one electoral votes as compared to 212 for Lincoln and Johnson. This seems like a crushing defeat—looks as if there was nothing left of the party save a thin shell, a mere pretense. But the facts prove this not so. In the first place, eleven seceding States—all Democratic—are out of the Union, and therefore out of the election. In the second place, the popular vote of the party in the other States is amazingly strong under the circumstances, convincing évidence that there is a strength there not to be accounted for either by the personality of its candidates, the character of its platform, or the conduct of its representatives in Congress. For example, a change of 3500 would have given McClellan New York; the Republicans carried Connecticut by a little more than 2000; Illinois by 30,000; Indiana by 20,000; Maryland by 7000; New Hampshire by 3000; lost New Jersey by 8000, and carried Pennsylvania by only 20,000. The total Republican vote was 2,213,665; the total Democratic vote 1,802,237. The fact is the election was a lot closer than the electoral vote indicates; but the Democratic party was in such a fix that there was not a chance of its electing its candidates in this or in any subsequent Presidential contest for the next twelve years. Republican nominations were equivalent to elections not only in 1864 but even more so in those following contests after the seceding States came back, because of the grip the Federal Government kept on the election machinery.

It is worth while here to give the Democratic platform of 1864, adopted at its convention held in Chicago on August 29, and presided over by Governor Horatio Seymour of New York, in order to show its attitude during this period of its worst humiliation and defeat. Here it is:

Resolved, That in the future, as in the past, we will adhere with unswerving fidelity to the Union under the Constitution as the only solid foundation of our strength, security, and happiness as a people, and as a framework of government equally conducive to the welfare and prosperity of all the States, both Northern and Southern.

Resolved, That this convention does explicitly declare, as the sense of the American people, that after four years of failure to restore the Union by the experiment of war, during which, under the pretense of a military necessity, or war power higher than the Constitution, the Constitution itself has been disregarded in every part, and public liberty and private right alike trodden down, and the material prosperity of the country essentially impaired, justice, humanity, liberty, and the public welfare demand that immediate efforts be made for a cessation of hostilities, with a view to an ultimate convention of the States, or other peaceable means, to the end that, at the earliest practicable moment, peace may be restored on the basis of the federal Union of the States.

Resolved, That the direct interference of the military authorities of the United States in the recent elections held in Kentucky, Maryland, Missouri, and Delaware was a shameful violation of the Constitution; and a repetition of such acts in the approaching election will be held as revolutionary, and resisted with all the means and power under our control.

Resolved, That the aim and object of the Democratic party is to preserve the federal Union and the rights of the States unimpaired; and they hereby declare that they consider that the administrative usurpation of extraordinary and dangerous powers not granted by the Constitution; the subversion of the civil by military law in States not in insurrection; the arbitrary military arrest, imprisonment, trial and sentence of American citizens in States where civil law exists in full force; the suppression of freedom of speech and of the press; the denial of the right of asylum; the open and avowed disregard of state rights; the employment of unusual test oaths; and the interference with and denial of the right of the people to bear arms in defense,—are calculated to prevent a restoration of the Union and the perpetuation of a government deriving its just powers from the consent of the governed.

Resolved, That the shameful disregard of the administration of its duty in respect to our fellow-citizens who are now, and long have been, prisoners of war and in a suffering condition, deserves the severest reprobation, on the score alike of public policy and common humanity.

Resolved, That the sympathy of the Democratic party is heartily and earnestly extended to the soldiery of our army and the sailors of our navy, who are and have been, in the field and on the sea, under the flag of our country; and, in the event of its attaining power, they will receive all the care, protection, and regard that the brave soldiers and sailors of the republic have so nobly earned.

It was an unpopular platform from the start, was openly repudiated by General McClellan at the opening of his campaign, and certainly attracted few votes. With neither candidate nor platform of real appeal, with no issue or program, with no money and no hope, it really at this distance seems amazing the party could poll as large a popular vote as it did. For reasons that have been given, the electoral vote was not really significant of its strength. It should be noted here that the platform of 1840, the basis of the party's legitimate existence, was completely dropped, and in 1864 there is not the slightest mention of any economic principle on which the party proposed to manage the government if intrusted with power. What the platform did was to make every issue on which it had ever succeeded, or on which it ought to succeed, subordinate to an issue on which it had no hope of success, a mistake which it has more than once repeated since. That, under such conditions, the party should still poll 45 per cent. of the total popular vote in the twenty-five States participating in the election is under the circumstances astonishing.

Chapter XVII

Seymour and Greeley as Candidates—Effect of the Negro
on Both Parties—Democrats Fighting Without Hope
but Holding Together in Spite of Mistake After
Mistake

BUT the revulsion came very swiftly after the assassination of Lincoln, and from July, 1865, to July, 1866, the Democratic party passed through the very blackest part of its valley of humiliation, the most desperate period of its long, varied, and exciting existence. Neither before nor since has it been so close to extinction. It is hardly possible to go any lower and live. In every Northern State it was beaten by increased majorities, and outside of the South only little Delaware had a Democratic governor. When Congress met in December, 1865, there were only ten Democrats out of fifty-two senators, only forty out of one hundred and eighty-five representatives. All of the excluded members from all the seceded States could not now have given the party even an approximate majority in either branch. The open and violent breach between President Andrew Johnson, who succeeded after Lincoln's death, and the Republicans, ought to have afforded a reasonable Democratic opportunity. It was very similar to the break between Tyler and the Whigs in 1841, of which the Democratic leaders took such skilful and full advantage.

But they were either too stupid or too listless, or still too full of passion from the recent conflict, to utilize the chance this time. Further, there were no big men in the party ranks, no outstanding leaders. Still further, the party had so long been dealing with questions not basic to it that it was not now up to following a course of neutrality and pursuing with steadiness its own economic objectives. Unquestionably its strict construction principles would have compelled it to oppose reconstruction in the South by Congress, even if its sense of justice and fairness had not been revolted over the awful dose which the Republican leaders were determined to—and did —force the seceding States to swallow before returning to the Union. Still, it was not good politics to permit reconstruction to overshadow everything else and become the single note in Democratic platforms and campaigns eight years after the war.

Yet, that is what happened. Clear to the end of the Johnson term they fought violently and vainly against the reconstruction program. In view of what was done in and to the South in the name of reconstruction it is difficult to blame them. Yet, it was futile. By enfranchising the negroes and disfranchising those who had borne arms against the

Union, which meant nearly all the whites; by setting up military state governments and by other measures, some constitutional, others plainly not, the former ruling classes in the South were completely deprived of their privileges. By the simple expedient of excluding the Democrats, who had taken part in the war against the Union, from exercise of the franchise, every Southern State was at once made Republican. It was enough to justify flaming indignation and there was just ground for the strongest denunciation. Still, it does seem as if, three years after hostilities had ceased, the Democrats in their second post-war national convention would have found it feasible and wise to return to one or more of the party's fundamental economic principles and straighten itself out once more as a constructive party.

The reconstruction program making the Southern States Republican under force, of course, rendered the Democratic chances of gaining a majority of the Electoral College in 1868 even more remote than in 1864. There simply was no way it could be done. Reconstruction, with negro suffrage fully protected by the Federal Government and coupled with the disfranchisement of the whites, made the South safe for Republicanism. In Texas and Virginia no election was held at all. General Grant carried all the other Southern States save Georgia and Louisiana, got 214 out of 294 electoral votes, and a popular majority of approximately 300,000. Throughout the South the election was, of course, a farce. The most interesting feature in the North was that for the first time since 1856 the Democrats carried New York. The Democratic candidates were Governor Horatio Seymour of New York for President, and General Francis P. Blair of Missouri for Vice-President. The convention was held in Tammany Hall, New York, on July 4, and it is a curious though somewhat characteristic thing that in this convention, preceding a campaign in which no clear-headed person could possibly have thought there was a chance for Democratic victory, there should have been an exciting fight over the nomination.

The leading aspirant was General George H. Pendleton of Ohio. It was a case of the field against Pendleton, though other aspirants had strong support—President Johnson, for example. The Democratic platform had indorsed his course and thanked him for his "patriotic efforts in resisting the aggressions of Congress upon the Constitutional rights of the States and the people." Many Democrats wanted to see this man, elected in 1864 as a Republican Vice-President, made the Democratic candidate for the Presidency. The Southern delegations were, outwardly at least, in favor of Mr. Johnson, but there was a strong sentiment for General Winfield S. Hancock among those who had favored the war and admired the fairness of his conduct as military commander at New Orleans during the Johnson administration. The Pendleton people had the fire and the noise and the enthusiasm, but they were unable to effect the combination to swing the votes. The struggle for the nomination in the convention was one of the most interesting and curious in the whole history of national conventions. No darker horse than Governor Seymour has ever been known. For twenty-one ballots his name was not mentioned in the convention. As presiding officer, he was apparently far removed from the fight altogether. Early in the balloting it became plain that the Eastern delegations, particularly New York and Pennsylvania, would not accept Pendleton, and gradually the contest narrowed down to Thomas A. Hendricks of Indiana and Winfield S. Hancock of Pennsylvania. Neither seemed acceptable to New York, and that delegation switched from one candidate to the other as the ballots were held in order to prevent any nomination. Some who were voted for besides Pendleton, Johnson, Hancock, and Hendricks, the four leaders, were Sanford E. Church of New York; Asa Packer, Pennsylvania; Joel Parker, New Jersey; James E. English, Connecticut; James R. Doolittle, Wisconsin; Salmon P. Chase, Ohio.

It was on the twenty-second ballot the Seymour sensation was sprung. General Seymour promptly refused to sanction his candidacy, but conferences were held, the vote for him persisted, he withdrew from the chair, and within twenty minutes it was all over—Seymour became the unanimous nominee

Courtesy of Harper & Brothers

THE TENT IN WHICH THE DEMOCRATIC CONVENTION WAS HELD IN CHICAGO, AUGUST, 1864

with 317 votes, amid a scene of great enthusiasm and excitement, though why the enthusiasm is hard to understand. The Republicans, holding the Southern States seemingly by the throat, had nominated the popular idol of the North, General Ulysses S. Grant, a natural and almost an inevitable choice. The tide of public sentiment was overwhelmingly for him and swept aside the protests of the politicians who feared his "views" were not soundly Republican, and held a party risk to be involved in naming him. There was no opposition to General Grant's selection in the convention, and from the start his election was assured. Governor Seymour was about as strong a man as the Democrats could have put up, but with no hope of electoral votes from the South, plus the Grant popularity in the North, the campaign was more or less one-sided.

The platform upon which Seymour and Blair ran in 1868 was largely devoted to reconstruction criticism of the Republicans. The so-called acts of reconstruction by a Republican Congress were called "an usurpation, unconstitutional, revolutionary and void," and in a letter prior to his nomination for Vice-President, and which probably caused his selection, General Blair had written that the President-elect must "declare these acts null and void, compel the army to undo the usurpations at the South, disperse the carpet-bag governments and allow the white people to reorganize their own governments. Until this is done it is idle to talk about bonds, greenbacks, gold, the public faith and the public credit." In other words, in 1868 the plight of the South, held under the Federal heel, politically dominated by negroes and "carpet-baggers," was too conspicuous to permit any other issue to be more than incidental. Yet it was not an issue upon which a successful appeal could be made in the North, to which section the fighting field was limited.

By critics of the Democratic party the stand against negro suffrage taken in this 1868 platform, and the action of the Southern States in later years in passing amendments and laws designed to disfranchise the enfranchised negroes, are held to be the most flagrant examples of the repudiation by the party of its fundamental principles. One of these unquestionably was the broadest possible extension of the suffrage. It is held that the negro slaves in 1868, having become legally persons instead of property, the Democratic party, to be consistent with its creed and its record, should have indorsed the Fourteenth and Fifteenth amendments instead of opposing them, should have adopted the "universal suffrage" resolutions prepared by Chief Justice Salmon P. Chase. Such a course, it is argued, would have preserved the homogeneity of the party, prevented its policy from being "dwarfed to the care of a single section, thus checking again the national growth which had fairly begun."

It is further argued that failure to consistently adhere to its suffrage extension principle when con-

fronted with the problem of the freed and enfranchised slaves forced the negroes of the South to
hold to the Republican party, and left the Southern
whites no choice save to take the name of Democrat,
regardless of what their personal political views
might be. The result was that there was not then,
and is not now, any unifying belief among Southern Democrats save on the single issue of the right
of each State to self-government. "If," Dr. Alexander Johnston asserts, "the Chase platform of universal suffrage had been adopted in 1868 and
adhered to, it would probably not have affected the
negro vote in that year or, perhaps, in 1872, but the
party in 1874 with but a fair half of the Southern
vote would have been in far better position to take
the crest of the wave of opportunity and develop
again into a true national party. Here as always
since 1844, the party felt the want of those leaders
who, until 1844, strenuously and successfully opposed the acceptance of any issue whatever which
would narrow the party action to the care of a
section."

That is one view of it, but a cold view and not
entirely a sound one. It is, of course, impossible to
maintain that Democratic opposition to negro suffrage was, or is, consistent with the original Democratic theory of the unrestricted right of the people
to participate equally in the selection of their government. It may as well be admitted now that the
charge of inconsistency and lack of logic is theo-

retically and technically true. The attitude of the party in 1868, and since, on this subject cannot be reconciled with this basic principle. All that can be said in defense is this: in the first place, the founders of the Democratic party when they spoke and wrote of "people" meant white people. Even those who, like Jefferson and Madison, were opposed to slavery as an anomaly in a free country, did not remotely conceive of conferring the right to vote upon the negroes, nor regard them as either fit or entitled under the Democratic theory to such right.

In the second place, the Republican party itself, prior to the war, did not contemplate conferring suffrage on the negro, had no such program or idea, did not plan in 1860 to even free the slaves, much less make voters of them. In the third place, Mr. Lincoln himself gravely doubted the wisdom of the policy which later resulted in the Fourteenth and Fifteenth amendments, realized the utter unfitness of the negro to vote, was doubtful that he could be made fit, but was forced into it by the military and political necessities of the situation. In the fourth place, the chief and only result of negro suffrage at the time was to swing the naturally Democratic States of the South, under governmental force, into the Republican column and impose upon the white people of this section an outrageous and intolerable condition. In the fifth place, it is to-day difficult to find in any party many intelligent and candid men who believe that unrestricted negro suffrage was justi-

Photograph by Brown Brothers

THE OLD TAMMANY HALL BUILDING ON FOURTEENTH STREET

fied at the time, that it has worked for the benefit of either race, or that it ever will be beneficial to the country of the people as a whole. In the sixth place, and finally, the net effect of negro suffrage has been to give the Republican party an unshakable support, utterly impervious to the merits of any public question or political issue, a support without which its representation in Congress would be greatly reduced and its chances of electing Presidents much diminished.

As to the probable effect of technical "consistency" on this subject by the Democrats in 1868, there seems no good reason for believing that it would have split the negro vote away from the Republicans or in the least altered the political situation in the South. On the contrary, had the party indorsed the suffrage amendments and approved giving the right to vote to the negro now that he was free, there is every reason to believe he would still have clung to the party that gave him his freedom. Also, there is every reason to believe that any such action upon the part of the Democratic party would not in the least have altered the determination of the whites in the South not to submit to negro political domination. In any event, the Democrats did not indorse negro suffrage in 1868, and so far as the party is concerned, those amendments are still unindorsed. They were acquiesced in by the party in the North, pushed aside in the South through "amendments" to the state constitutions, "grandfather" clauses, and other discriminating legislation of doubtful constitutionality. To-day these have either been set aside by the courts or expired by limitation, and in no Southern State is there any general election law imposing restrictions on the negro that are not also imposed on the white voter. In various States, it is true, the primaries are by law limited to the whites, but in the general election there is now no legal discrimination. The South has found constitutional ways of relieving itself of negro suffrage, and cannot now be accused of any sort of nullification. It is, as admitted by Republican Senators in 1928, wholly within its right.

The real weapon however by which the vote has been taken from the negro in the South is the fixed determination of the great bulk of the whites that he shall not vote and the general acceptance by the negro that, one way or another, he would not be permitted to vote. It has been done by constitutional means, but if that had not been possible, the negro is convinced it would have been done anyhow. The result is that he has in the South largely gotten out of the habit of voting and has in the main lost his political interest. The result leaves the Republican party in most of those States a mere shell held together solely for the purpose of having these States represented in the national convention and for the distribution of Federal patronage. The Republican national committeemen in the South are mostly all negroes, the delegates to the national conventions are almost exclusively negroes, and the patronage is largely distributed by Republican administrations in Washington through negro leaders, whose venality and corruption have been frequently exposed and whose outrageously open sale of the Federal offices has been the subject of Congressional investigation and attack, without, however, producing any change in the facts.

If there were no Democratic inheritance to do it, the character and color of the Republican party leaders in the South would unquestionably be enough to keep the South solidly Democratic. Whether it would stay Democratic with the same solidity if that condition were changed is a matter of uncertainty. It might not—in the end probably would not.

The Republican trouble is that there is no way to change the situation. They may deeply deplore— as they do—the necessity of parceling out offices and dealing for delegates through corrupt and venal negroes, but the necessities of Republican national politics as they have developed leave no alternative. It is dirty work, but there seems no way out. Various administrations have made tentative efforts to break away but have been forced to abandon them. The best a Republican President can do is to leave this sort of thing in the hands of practical, hardboiled, not oversqueamish white politicians, of whom there are always plenty, and not let any one even tell him what goes on down there.

The Democratic Party: A History

It isn't a nice situation in which the negro vote has put the two parties in the South. For the Democrats, it has compelled the most radical and illogical departure from their fundamental principle of unrestricted suffrage. For the Republicans it has created a disgraceful and scandalous situation which involves humiliating experiences for every Republican President, renders ridiculous any Republican pretensions of purity in politics, and makes every Republican chairman apprehensive of an exposure. It is seldom that the real truth is told about this situation in the South. The facts are easily available and they are thoroughly shameful. Yet there is a sort of tacit connivance between Democratic and Republican politicians to keep them from being brought wholly out in the open, where the smell would be so bad that something would have to be done. The Republican motive, of course, is to hide their party dirt, and is at that more admirable than the Democratic motive privately avowed some years ago by a Democratic senator, who said: "Everybody in my State knows the Federal offices are bought and sold through the negro committeeman there, but if the Republican party can stand that, I can. So long as that condition is an open scandal in the State there can be no decent or respectable Republican party there. Why should I want to break it up and give them a chance to build up in my State?"

During the Sixty-ninth Congress an investigation conducted by Senator George Norris, independent

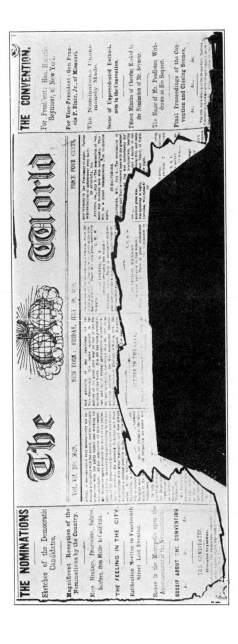

FIRST PAGE OF "THE NEW YORK WORLD" THE DAY FOLLOWING THE SEYMOUR-
BLAIR NOMINATIONS—JULY 19, 1868

Republican of Nebraska, disclosed in committee
some amazing facts concerning the corrupt dealing
in Federal offices in several Southern States, but the
Democratic senators from those States could not be
got to take any very active interest in the matter.
They took it as a matter of course. Once in a while
there will be a senatorial speech on the subject, but it
never means much. Whether the politics of both
parties in the South as affected by the negro will
alter in the future is a matter for speculation, but it
is certainly true there are no signs of a change at
this time.

But to return to the story: though the popularity
of General Grant and the forcible Republicanization
of the South made Democratic success in the Electoral College out of the question, and though the platform of 1868 was disappointing to those who insist
upon party consistency—no party ever yet having
been consistent—still, the Democratic total popular
vote rose from 45 per cent. in 1864 to 47½ per cent.
There was no sign of a change in the electoral vote
in the North. The only votes from that section gained
by the Democrats were in New York, New Jersey,
and Oregon. The Republicans charged that New
York State had been carried by frauds practised
in New York city by the Tammany Hall organization. It was probably true, as the Tammany of that
day makes the Tammany of the present day seem
angelically pure. In any event, when Congress met
in December, 1869, there were fifteen Democratic

senators out of seventy-two, and ninety-six out of 227 members of the House. The 1870 congressional elections increased this to seventeen Democratic senators and 105 representatives.

The first term of General Grant developed a strong feeling among the more liberal element of the Republicans, the element of which Horace Greeley was chief spokesman, that the national police power had been exercised far beyond legal limits in the Southern States since reconstruction, which of course was the fact. The work of "reconstruction" in the South had practically been completed before Grant's first term began. Only three States then remained unadmitted to the Union, but this did not prevent the keeping of military forces in most of them throughout, nor did it mean quiet and order in the readmitted States. The obvious mistakes of Grant from both the public and the political point of view aroused keen opposition to him, and the Liberal Republicans, revolting, called a convention at Cincinnati on May 1, 1872.

A coalition with the Democrats was early in the air, and it was believed that the defeat of Grant as the regular Republican candidate could be achieved if a union were effected. The Liberal Republicans nominated Horace Greeley of New York for President and B. Gratz Brown of Missouri for Vice-President. Its platform denounced Grant personally and politically, arraigned his administration for a disregard of law, for the retention of corrupt men in office, and for general inefficiency and mismanagement. It accepted but did not indorse the Thirteenth, Fourteenth, and Fifteenth amendments, urged reform of the civil service, demanded immediate and absolute removal of all disabilities imposed on account of the rebellion. It demanded for the individual "the largest liberty consistent with public order, for the State self government, for the nation a return to the methods of peace and the Constitutional limitations of power."

All this happened on May 1, in Cincinnati. On July 9, in Baltimore, the Democrats met, nominated as their own Greeley and Brown, the Liberal Republican candidates, and adopted in toto the Liberal Republican platform. Actually, the platform came closer to former Democratic platforms than either of those they had themselves adopted in 1864 and 1868, but it did not seem so to a lot of Democrats at the time, whose opposition to the Greeley movement led to a call for a "straight" Democratic convention at Louisville, on September 3. There the "betrayal" at Baltimore was denounced, the "false creed" and "false leadership" repudiated, and a ticket nominated, after some difficulty in getting the candidates to accept—Charles O'Conor for President, Charles Francis Adams for Vice-President.

At no time was there any doubt as to the result of the fight. To start with, the Greeley nomination was a mistake. It is conceded Charles Francis Adams would have been a stronger man, and that the New

York editor did not appeal strongly either to conservatives in his own party or in the other. Adams and an acceptable Democrat might have changed the result, though that is doubtful. The number of Democrats who refused to vote at all was very large, and the net result of the coalition was a defeat worse than those of either 1864 or 1868. The total vote polled sank from 47½ to 42 per cent., and the number of Democratic members in the House was reduced to eighty-eight out of 290. The "straight" Democratic ticket of O'Conor and Adams did not in any State affect the result, polling all told less than 30,000 votes. Altogether, it was a most completely unsuccessful coalition. Greeley got almost no electoral votes at all, and the Grant plurality was larger than any previously given a President—close to 800,000. One interesting thing about the campaign is that it was in this year—1872—that the Prohibitionists first made their appearance as a national party. James Black of Pennsylvania was its candidate for President, John Russell of Michigan for Vice-President, and its platform was long and denunciatory of the liquor traffic, which it sought to abolish.

THE DEMOCRATIC CONVENTION HELD IN TAMMANY HALL, 1868, WHEN
SEYMOUR AND BLAIR WERE NOMINATED

Chapter XVIII

THE GREAT TILDEN-HAYES CONTEST

The Democratic Revival After 1872—Recapturing the
House in 1874—Enthusiasm in Convention—Confidence in Campaign—W. E. Chandler Directed Fight
to Deprive Democrats of Victory

THOUGH worse beaten in 1872 than ever before,
the Democratic prospects for national success, amazing as it may seem, really date from that year. For
twelve years it had been in about as hopeless a condition as a political party well could be, with a representation in Congress too discouraged to be an
effective minority, and the Electoral College vote so
rigged against it that it could not make a Presidential fight even close, in spite of the fact that its popular vote never got below 42 per cent. It does seem
reasonable to believe that if the Democratic party
could survive those terrible twelve years and then
achieve victory, it is really an indestructible party,
notwithstanding the inconsistencies of its platforms,
the frequent repudiations of its principles, and the
conceded stupidity of its internal conflicts. It is certainly a tough old party. Unlike the Federalists, the
Whigs, the Free Soilers, the American Constitu-

tionalists, the Populists, and the Progressives, a defeat or two is not a knockout for the Democratic party. It has taken six in succession and then won a battle.

One reason given for the increase in Democratic prospects right after its worst defeat is that it had in the 1872 platform sloughed off most of its anti-slavery and reconstruction memories and swung more or less back to its economic principles, with the exception of the tariff. Another reason unquestionably was the character of the Grant administration and the increased resentment against some of his more conspicuous and influential political friends and advisers. But perhaps the greatest reason was the general financial distress that began to be felt in 1873, and the business depression which always reacts disastrously upon the party in power, just as prosperity strengthens its grip.

A very real financial panic occurred in 1873. Coupled with the corruption and abuses of power in the Government, and the character of the Republican party in the South, it was enough to create a very genuine public distaste for a continuation of its control. By this time, too, the Southern States were beginning to get out from under the Federal heel, and the Republican administration was unable by coercive methods to hold them longer in the Republican column. They were swinging back fast. Probably there were other reasons besides those here given, but in 1874, just fourteen years after it smashed up, the Democratic party carried the country in the off-year congressional elections, and when the House met in 1875 it had control of that body by a vote of 198 to 94.

It was an amazing reversal of figures and left the Republican leaders stunned and bewildered. Even Massachusetts had a Democratic governor. It was in effect a tidal wave and seemed a sure indication of victory, barring some accident, in the next Presidential election; and though the Democrats had only one third of the Senate, it at once put the party in a stronger position than it had been since 1856. With the war really behind it, escaped from the reconstruction problems, which had dominated everything else, with the South for the first time since 1860 in a position to deliver its electoral vote in accord with the will of the white people, with the Republicans weakened and on the defensive, the whole political stage seemed set for ·a return of the Democratic party to power. Every Democratic leader believed it, and when the national convention met in St. Louis, June 28, 1876, there was more real enthusiasm and a better fighting spirit in the party ranks and among the delegates than there had been since the war. They knew that victory was possible this time. They felt it in the air. The platform was unduly lengthy, but it was at least in almost complete harmony with the hereditary economic principles of the party, and for the first time it returned to a clear-cut Democratic position on the tariff. The tariff plank and one other plank are here presented as the important features of that platform. On the tariff these words were used:

We denounce the present tariff, levied upon nearly four thousand articles, as a masterpiece of injustice, inequality, and false pretense. It yields a dwindling, not a yearly rising revenue. It has impoverished many industries to subsidize a few. It prohibits imports that might purchase the products of American labor. It has degraded American commerce from the first to an inferior rank on the high seas. It has cut down the sales of American manufactures at home and abroad and depleted the returns of American agriculture,— an industry followed by half our people. It costs the people five times more than it produces to the treasury, obstructs the processes of production, and wastes the fruits of labor. It promotes fraud, fosters smuggling, enriches dishonest officials, and bankrupts honest merchants. We demand that all custom-house taxation shall be only for revenue.

The other plank is the one detailing the corruption and crookedness in the Grant administration. It seems worth giving for two reasons: first, because it is so similar in tone to the plank in the Democratic convention of 1924, which followed another Republican administration conspicuous for its corruption, and second, because in a story of the Democratic party it certainly ought to be emphasized that in the whole history of the country there have been but two administrations publicly indicted by the opposition as crooked, openly charged with cabinet corruption and wholesale venality—and all without denial or defense. Neither of these administrations has been of the Democratic party. Both were of the Republican party—one that of Grant, the other that of Harding. The Democratic party has been accused of stupidity, inefficiency, ineptitude, extravagance, waste, incapacity, weakness, offensive and extreme partisanship—and it has at times in its long life been guilty of all these things, and some others. It has not, however, been successfully charged with wholesale thievery in high places while in control of the Government. That distinction exclusively belongs to the Republicans.

Here is the 1876 plank on corruption under Grant:

Reform is necessary even more in the higher grades of the public service. President, Vice-President, judges, senators, representatives, cabinet officers,—these and all others in authority are the people's servants. Their offices are not a private perquisite; they are a public trust.

When the annals of this republic show the disgrace and censure of a Vice-President; a late Speaker of the House of Representatives marketing his rulings as a presiding officer; three senators profiting secretly by their votes as law makers; five chairmen of the leading committees of the House of Representatives exposed in jobbery; a late secretary of the treasury forcing balances in the public accounts; a late attorney general misappropriating public funds; a secretary of the navy enriched or enriching friends by percentages levied off the profits of contractors with his department; an ambassador to England censured in a dishonorable speculation; the President's private secretary barely escaping conviction upon trial for guilty complicity in frauds upon the revenue; a secretary of war impeached for high crimes and misdemeanors,—the demonstration is complete that the first step in reform must be the people's choice of honest men from another party, lest the disease of one political organization infect the body politic, and lest, by making no change of

241

men or parties, we get no change of measures and no real reform.

All these abuses, wrongs and crimes, the product of sixteen years ascendancy of the Republican party, create a necessity for reform confessed by Republicans themselves; but their reformers are voted down in convention and displaced from the cabinet. The party's mass of honest voters is powerless to resist the eighty thousand office holders, its leaders and guides.

Reform can only be had by a peaceful civic revolution. We demand a change of system, a change of administration, a change of parties, that we may have change of measures and of men.

Certainly, that is sufficiently definite, direct, and specific. It was on this platform that Samuel J. Tilden of New York was nominated for President and Thomas A. Hendricks of Indiana for Vice-President, and the Democrats went into the campaign full of real confidence. The convention had been unusually harmonious. There were besides Governor Tilden six other aspirants for the Presidential nomination—Winfield S. Hancock, Pennsylvania; William Allen, Ohio; Thomas F. Bayard, Delaware; Joel Parker, New Jersey; Allen G. Thurman, Ohio, and Mr. Hendricks—but only two ballots were required for the Tilden nomination. The Democratic prospects were also brightened by the scramble over the Republican nomination. In the first place, there was General Grant's unsuccessful effort for a third term. As early as 1875 it was reported that he wanted a renomination. In a letter to General Harry White of Pennsylvania, who had presided over a state convention that had passed an anti-third term resolution, General Grant said: "Now for the third term, I do not want it any more than I did the first." He then proceeded to point out, however, that the people are not restricted to two terms by the Constitution and that the time might come when it would be unfortunate to make a change at the end of eight years. He then added that he "would not accept a nomination if it were tendered unless it should come under such circumstances as to make it an imperative duty—circumstances not likely to arise."

That was the Grant way of expressing himself. More than fifty years later another Republican President—Mr. Coolidge—dealing with the same subject, said: "I do not choose to run." Grant's friends then (as Coolidge's friends for months in 1927) took his words to mean that if nominated he would accept, and that being "drafted" would be pleasant. That that was the Grant idea there is no doubt, but it made little headway except among the immediate administration wheel-horses and patronage-dispensers. The knockout blow to the third term business came in December. Just after Congress convened, a Democrat from Illinois presented a resolution which declared "that in the opinion of this House the precedent established by Washington and other Presidents of the United States in retiring from the Presidential office after their second term has become by universal concurrence a part of our republican system of government, and that any departure

243

from this time honored custom would be unwise, unpatriotic and fraught with peril to our free institutions."

This resolution passed the House by the extraordinary vote of 234 to 18. Seventy of the eighty-eight Republicans voted for it. In the face of this the third term movement for Grant collapsed and the field was thrown wide open. Senator Conkling of New York, Senator Morton of Indiana, and James G. Blaine of Maine were the foremost candidates. Secretary of the Treasury Benjamin H. Bristow also had strong support, as did several others. Rutherford B. Hayes, then governor of Ohio, was put in the field by his State, but on the early ballots received few votes. Blaine led the lot from the start and came within twenty-eight votes of a majority. It was after the sixth ballot that the combination against him was formed—Morton, Bristow, and Conkling all swinging in behind the Ohio governor, a rather obscure man who had not figured in the national arena and had therefore aroused no animosities. He was nominated on the seventh ballot and the nomination made unanimous, though Blaine's friends were bitterly disappointed. William A. Wheeler of New York was selected for Vice-President and a platform which once more "waved the bloody shirt," denounced the Democrats as a "treasonable party," declared for tariff sufficient to pay current expenditures and care for the public debt, and dismissed the charges of corruption with the same casualness and lack of indignation similar charges were dismissed forty-eight years later by the 1920 Republican convention. They said: "We rejoice in the quickened conscience of the people concerning political affairs and will hold all public officials to a rigid responsibility and engage that the prosecution and punishment of all who betray official trusts shall be swift, thorough and unsparing"—a pledge which, like others of the same sort since, was completely forgotten after the election.

This story now comes to what was undoubtedly the most extraordinary contest that ever took place over the Presidency. It is the great disputed Tilden-Hayes election. There had been nothing like it before nor has there been since. It will always be the Democratic contention that Mr. Tilden, clearly elected, was cheated out of the Presidency. To Democrats it will always remain the "crime of '76." The Republican stand is that their candidate, Mr. Hayes, was fairly chosen by the margin of one electoral vote and that the amazing measures taken later by the Republican party and the Republican administration were necessary to hold that majority and retain the Presidency. The contest was incredibly close in a number of States and it is clearly not possible to tell —certainly not fifty years after the fact—whether a complete and fair recount of all the ballots would have elected Mr. Hayes or Mr. Tilden.

The presumption, however, based on the figures and facts and on the past election record is certainly in Mr. Tilden's favor. Practically every Republican organ, the Republican national headquarters and the Republican candidate himself on the night of the election conceded defeat. It was not until the next day that the blind, and certainly at the time untruthful, claim that Hayes had 185 electoral votes was put out, and the movement to make that claim good in three disordered and army-ridden Southern States—Louisiana, Florida, and South Carolina—started. It will be conceded by every fair-minded man capable of a detached view that once the idea of claiming the Hayes election had been advanced, every ounce of weight in the party and every power of the administration was used to back it up; that in the effort both the law and the Constitution were disregarded; that limits of partisanship not heretofore known were reached; that no stone was left unturned to keep Tilden out of office; that all pretense of fairness passed, the sole idea being that the great prize of the Presidency justified any means to hold it.

There is no exaggeration in the above assertions. It understates rather than overstates the facts. No more extraordinary example has ever been given of the willingness of personally honest and honorable men to do together for their party, and under the stress of partisan feeling, things that as private individuals they would have shrunk from in horror and in others would have regarded as detestably dishonorable. The situation is well expressed by John Bigelow in his "Life of Samuel J. Tilden." He says:

The Great Tilden-Hayes Contest

Why persons occupying the most exalted positions should have ventured to compromise their reputations by the deliberate consummation of a series of crimes which struck at the very foundation of the republic is a question which still puzzles many of all parties who have no charity for the crimes themselves. I have already referred to the terror and desperation with which the prospect of Tilden's election inspired the great army of office holders at the close of Grant's administration. That army, numerous and formidable as it was, was comparatively limited. There was a much larger and justly influential class who were apprehensive that the return of the Democratic party to power threatened a reactionary policy at Washington, to the undoing of some or all of the important results of the war. These apprehensions were inflamed by the party press until they were confined to no class but more or less pervaded all the Northern States. The Electoral Tribunal, consisting mainly of men appointed to their positions by Republican Presidents or elected from strong Republican States, felt the pressure of this feeling and from motives compounded in more or less varying proportions of dread of the Democrats, personal ambition, zeal for their party, and respect for their constituents, reached the conclusion that the exclusion of Tilden from the White House was an end which justified whatever means were necessary to accomplish it. They regarded it, like the emancipation of the slaves, as a war measure.

No one will ever know the full history of the bargains, deals, and "arrangements" made by both sides in that tremendous struggle that lasted from November 8 until March 2. Corruption and bribery on both sides were charged—and probably both were guilty. There is no use pretending that the partisanship of the Democrats was not just as intense as that of the Republicans, their willingness to win the Presidency regardless of the means just as complete, their determination to take every conceivable advantage just as great. One difference was that they were out of power, the other side was in. They lacked the weight and the weapons to do the unfair and unscrupulous thing; the Republicans had them as well as the will. The Democrats had the will to use force to gain their end; the Republicans had the force. The Democrats undoubtedly were willing, despite the stout denial of the late Henry Watterson in his interesting memoirs, to buy the votes, but the Republicans had the wherewithal to do the buying. That they did openly and without shame buy them is convincingly maintained by Mr. George Ticknor Curtis in his "Constitutional History of the United States," in which he points out that "nearly thirty of those persons who were most active in securing the return of Republican electors in Florida, Louisiana and South Carolina by the returning boards were afterward appointed to offices of trust and profit by the administration which was brought into power by means of their returns." The other difference between the Democrats and the Republicans in this struggle was that the Democrats much more sincerely believed and had far better right to believe their man had won. That conviction, it will be admitted, would justify things done to hold the prize that could not be justified at all in the lack of such conviction. This belief of the Democrats that their side had really won made, it will be conceded, a very great difference. It was a belief shared at the start, and before the Republicans had set out to keep the Presidency anyhow, by Mr. Hayes, the Republican candidate; by General Grant, the Republican President; by Senator Roscoe Conkling, Republican leader of New York; by nearly all the Republican editors and many other prominent party men—according to Mr. Curtis, who supports his statement with a great deal of documentary and convincing evidence. Literally volumes could be written of this four months' struggle, full of intrigue, drama, sordidness, corruption, and passion. It was naturally a period of intense excitement, great public and political turmoil and perturbation. One of the outstanding and remarkable things about the whole business was the peaceful acquiescence in the final decision in face of the fact that the whole Democratic party believed the forms of law had been foully perverted to deprive it of the fruits of a fairly won victory.

It would be hard to find a more striking proof of the strength of the American form of government. Obviously, there is not space here to do more than touch the high spots of this fight, which, in the opinion of most unbiased historians, is the blackest stain on the American political record; but those are certainly essential to this outline sketch of the party history. Setting aside the constitutional question, which leads authorities like Mr. Curtis to declare that "in consequence of the procedure resorted to, although Mr. Hayes became President *de facto,* it can never be said that he became President *de jure*"

—leaving that question aside, the effort here will be to put down the incontrovertible and vital facts about this struggle, without dealing with the technicalities of constitutional and election law. Thirty-eight States took part in the election. On the popular vote Mr. Tilden got a clear majority—even on the Republican count, even after the final adjusted figures. The Democratic total was:

```
Tilden ..................... 4,300,590
Hayes ..................... 4,036,298
    Tilden plurality .......... 264,292
The Republican count gave—
Tilden ..................... 4,285,992
Hayes ..................... 4,033,768
    Tilden plurality .......... 252,224
```

But Presidents are not elected by popular majorities. It is the electoral vote that counts. Its total was 369, which meant 185 was necessary for a choice. On the night of the election the Democrats had 184 certain electoral votes and it was conceded on all sides that the probability was they would have the additional vote necessary for a majority and more. The Republicans could count only 166 sure votes for Hayes and gave up the fight. There is no doubt about that. Their organs conceded defeat, the headquarters were swathed in gloom, the party leaders and workers went away depressed, and the chairman closed up shop and went to his hotel. At the Tilden headquarters there was tremendous enthusiasm, unbounded joy. With 184 votes beyond question, with the other almost sure, with others still in sight, with the Republicans conceding the election, it was a great night.

All over the country the Democracy was thrilled with the return to power; the hordes of Republican job holders who had had the government for sixteen years were in the depths of despair. Colonel Watterson, who was in New York at the time in close touch with the leaders and newspapers, as apt as any man to know the facts, is authority for the following interesting story, which completely checks up as to the main facts with Mr. Curtis and others:

After the early edition of The Times had gone to press certain members of the editorial staff were at supper very much cast down by the returns when a messenger brought a telegram from Senator Barnum, of Connecticut, financial head of the Democratic National Committee, asking for The Times latest news of Oregon, Louisiana, Florida and South Carolina. But for that unlucky telegram, Tilden would probably have been inaugurated President of the United States. The Times people, then intense Republican partisans, at once saw an opportunity. If Barnum did not know why might not a doubt be raised? At once the editorial in the first edition was revised, to take a decisive tone and declare the election of Hayes. One of the editorial council, Mr. John C. Reid, hurried to Republican headquarters in the Fifth Avenue Hotel, which he found deserted, the triumph of Tilden having long before sent everybody to bed. Mr. Reid then sought the room of Senator Zachariah Chandler, chairman of the Republican National Committee. While upon this errand, he encountered in the hotel corridor a small man wearing an enormous pair of goggles, his hat drawn over his ears, a great coat with a heavy military cloak, and carrying a gripsack and newspaper in his hand. The newspaper was the New York Tribune announcing the election of Tilden, the defeat of Hayes. This man was William E. Chandler, even then a very prominent Republican politician in New Hampshire and very much exasperated by what he had read. Mr. Reid had another tale to tell. The two found Mr. Zachariah Chandler, who bade them leave him alone and do whatever they thought best. They did so, sending telegrams to Columbia, Tallahassee and New Orleans, stating to each of the parties addressed that the result of the election depended upon his State. To these was appended the signature of Zachariah Chandler. Later in the day, Senator Chandler, advised of what had been set on foot and its possibilities, issued from national Republican headquarters this laconic message—"Hayes has 185 electoral votes and is elected." Thus began the scheme to confuse the returns and make a disputed count of the vote.

Full credit for initiating the move to contest and reviving the surrendered Republicans is given by Mr. Curtis to W. E. Chandler. To him it was plain that if to the 166 sure Republican votes the nineteen from Florida, South Carolina, and Louisiana could be added, Hayes would have the 185 and the Presidency. He believed those nineteen could be got. There seems no doubt that he was the brains as well as the force of the Hayes fight. There is no doubt that to him more than any one else Hayes owed his seat. As soon as he realized the chance, he put into operation as bold a plan as could be conceived. Its essentials were, first, to deny and contradict the Democratic claim that a majority of Tilden electors had been chosen; second, to secure the nineteen votes from the three States which, fortunately for the

Republican cause, had not yet got wholly out from under the Federal heel.

As told by Colonel Watterson, his first step was to send, in the name of the chairman, telegrams to the Republican governors, leaders, and lieutenants in these three States, impressing upon them that Hayes's success depended upon the result of the counting there. Though these telegrams were dated November 7—the day of the election—Chandler later testified before a congressional committee that they were sent on the eighth. The Chandler strategy was divided into four parts—first, to claim the Hayes election unequivocally and to persist in claiming it through every channel; second, to send agents to Florida, Louisiana, and South Carolina to operate with the returning boards; third, to arrange for enough money for all emergencies; fourth, to bring the full force of the administration to bear on the returning boards and officials in the three States.

The cooperation of the President was essential. Not only would Grant's name have great weight with the party generally, but his sanction and support would give the necessary encouragement to the men in these States who had to "deliver the goods." Some difficulty was experienced in getting General Grant. In the first place, he was convinced Tilden had been elected and Hayes defeated. In the second place, he was with his secretary of war in Philadelphia, attending the Centennial celebration of the Declaration of Independence. Quick action was needed.

Republican leaders, conferring in New York under Chandler, found ways by private wire of getting into personal communication with the President, and putting the situation to him so forcibly that he yielded to their request to send Federal troops into the three States "to protect the Republican canvassers." Late on the night of November 9 the following despatches were sent from Philadelphia to Washington:

To General WILLIAM T. SHERMAN,
    Washington, D. C.

Order four companies of soldiers to Tallahassee, Florida, at once. Take them from the nearest points, not from Louisiana or Mississippi, and direct that they be moved with as little delay as possible.

                                    J. D. CAMERON,
                                    Secretary of War.

To General W. T. SHERMAN,
    Washington, D. C.

In addition to the four companies ordered to Tallahassee order all troops in Florida to the same point and if you haven't more than the companies named draw from Alabama and South Carolina. Advise me of receipt of this and your action.

                                    J. D. CAMERON,
                                    Secretary of War.

To General W. T. SHERMAN,
    Washington, D. C.

Telegraph General Ruger to proceed at once to Tallahassee, Florida, and upon his arrival there to communicate with Governor Stearns. Say to him to leave affairs in South Carolina in the hands of an entirely discreet and reliable officer.

                                    J. D. CAMERON,
                                    Secretary of War.

These telegrams were not made public. They went out on November 9 and the troop movement started immediately. On November 10 the President telegraphed General Sherman:

To General W. T. SHERMAN,
  Washington, D. C.

Instruct General Augur in Louisiana and General Ruger in Florida to be vigilant with the force at their command to preserve peace and good order and to see that the proper and legal boards of canvassers are unmolested in the performance of their duties. Should there be any grounds of suspicion or fraudulent counting on either side it shall be reported and denounced at once. No man worthy of the office of President would be willing to hold the office if counted in, placed there by fraud; either party can afford to be disappointed in the result but the country cannot afford to have the result tainted by the suspicion of illegal or false returns.

U. S. GRANT.

Plainly this order to General Sherman was intended for the public, and it was at once given to the press. In the sending of these troops into these States at the request of Republican party leaders it is contended General Grant acted absolutely without constitutional authority and that nothing could have been more irregular, improper, or unlawful than this interference from without, whether by the President of the United States or by a private citizen of some other State.

Says Mr. Curtis on this subject:

If there was reason to fear that popular violence in these States would prevent the returning boards from peacefully performing their duties, nothing could justify the sending of United States troops into the States in anticipation of such violence unless the application should be made in due form to the President of the United States by the Governor of the State if the legislature were not in session, asking for aid to protect the State authorities against domestic violence. The only despatch asking for troops came from Governor Stearns of Florida on November 9, which said: "We shall need an army to protect us." This was not such an application as was authorized and required by the Constitution of the United States. To act upon it as President Grant did was to act outside of the Constitution and not within it. Consequently all the troops sent into the three States were sent there unlawfully. The President of the United States is not authorized to employ military force for the purpose of preserving order within a State unless he acts strictly within the Federal Constitution.

As a matter of fact, no violence occurred or was anticipated. The request for troops came from the party leaders, not from the constituted authorities of the States. Their purpose there was to encourage the Republican boards of canvassers to certify to the election of Hayes electors, which they did, and to overawe and intimidate the Democrats, which they did. Actually, Chandler (W. E.) was the boss all along the line. It was he who mapped out the strategy, directed the forces, put the whole administration at work to swing Florida, South Carolina, and Louisiana into line. It was he who outlined to the members of the National Committee who gathered at headquarters the desperate measures necessary to bring Mr. Hayes in, and it was he, with an ample credit opened for him at the Centennial Bank of

Philadelphia, who personally went to Florida to take charge of things in the field. That was Wednesday night. On Thursday Thomas J. Brady, with a force of special agents of the Post-Office Department, followed Mr. Chandler, carrying with him considerable money for immediate use. The Department of Justice ordered its available detectives to report to Chandler in Tallahassee at the earliest possible moment. At Chandler's suggestion, William A. Cook of Washington went to Columbia, South Carolina, to take charge there, and both men and money, also at his suggestion, were despatched to New Orleans. All of this activity was "under cover." The telegraphing and letter-writing between W. E. Chandler and Zachariah Chandler were in code and the whole business conducted as surreptitiously and secretly as possible. The only publicity—also at W. E. Chandler's suggestion—was the persistent and insistent claim from Republican headquarters in New York that "Hayes has 185 votes and is elected." In the midst of all this, Mr. Hayes himself gave out an interview carried in the Cincinnati papers Thursday morning, in which he said: "I think we are defeated in spite of recent good news. I am of the opinion that the Democrats have carried the country and elected Tilden, as it now seems necessary for the Republicans to carry all the States now set down as doubtful to secure even a majority of one. I don't think encouraging despatches ought to be given to the public now because they might mislead enthusiastic friends to bet on the election and lose their money. I do heartily deprecate these despatches."

When this statement from the candidate on Thursday is considered, and when the statement of George W. Childs as to Grant's belief that Tilden was elected and his acquiescence in the request to send troops only after strong representation of the necessity from party leaders is added, the things done to swing those three Southern States away from the Democratic candidate, for whom they would naturally have voted, are all the more remarkable. It is reasonable to assume that, left to himself Hayes would have accepted the result and made no contest. It is equally fair on the known facts to believe that let alone General Grant would have sent no troops into these States. The force back of the fight was neither the Republican candidate for President nor the Republican President. The real force was the solid phalanx of Republican politicians and party leaders, office-holders and office brokers, who had been in power for sixteen years and were unable to tolerate the idea of giving up. Chief among these was W. E. Chandler—the man who turned the trick.

In the meantime, while Chandler and other party leaders and administration military and civil authority were arranging for Republican electors from the Republican returning boards in South Carolina, Florida, and Louisiana, and while the Democrats to offset this were arranging for separate returns from these States certifying to the Tilden electors, the battle in Congress over the method and means of counting the vote and determining the disputed questions waged fiercely. The Senate being controlled by the Republicans and the House by the Democrats, it was obvious from the start that one would nullify the other if operated under the regular procedure laid down for the count, and that an indefinite and hopeless deadlock would prevail. The net result was the passage of an act by Congress, proposed by the Republicans and acquiesced in by the Democrats, creating an Electoral Commission or Tribunal to decide disputed questions.

There is not space to give the details of this act, except to say that the commission was composed of five members chosen by the Senate, five by the House, four justices of the Supreme Court designated in the bill, and the fifteenth member selected by the four justices thus named. The Senate selected Senators George F. Edmunds, Oliver P. Morton, and Frederick T. Frelinghuysen, Republicans, and Allen G. Thurman and Thomas F. Bayard, Democrats; the House chose Henry B. Payne, Eppa Hunton, and Josiah G. Abbott, Democrats, and James A. Garfield and George F. Hoar, Republicans. The four justices of the Supreme Court were Justices William Strong, Samuel F. Miller, Republicans, Nathan Clifford and Stephen J. Field, Democrats. These selected Justice Joseph P. Bradley, a Republican, as the fifteenth member. This made the commission Republican—eight Republicans, seven Democrats.

259

It is not worth while here to go into the details of the Florida, South Carolina, and Louisiana cases as they came before the tribunal. It will suffice to say that in each State the Republican returning boards returned Republican electors, regardless of the fact that in two of them the popular vote had been clearly for Tilden, and that in all three the Democrats vigorously contested, claimed the vote, submitted evidence of fraud, irregularity, and gross disregard of the law. It is an astonishing thing, significant of the great power of partisanship over the individual, that these fifteen men, every one of whom was apparently a man of high standing, honor, and intelligence, should have on every test vote day after day divided exactly on party lines. The eight Republicans unvaryingly, and with not even momentary hesitation, on every ballot voted solidly in favor of the Republican electors; with equal regularity and determination the seven Democratic members voted for the Democratic electors.

It was a marvelous exhibition of the extent to which partisanship goes. It was the sort of thing that would naturally be expected of politicians in Congress but hardly of five justices of the Supreme Bench. If only one justice on one vote throughout the whole long procedure had broken away from party lines and indicated a trace of independence, or even a feeble desire to seat the elected man rather than his party's man, it would have raised the place of this commission in history. But there was not a single such occurrence on either side and it goes down in the record as perhaps the most unashamed, unfair, completely and contemptibly partisan body to which was ever committed a high duty calling for non-partisanship, complete fearlessness, and rigid fairness. Of course, what this sort of commission meant was the election of the Republican candidate. The Democrats realized this as soon as the complete and unshakable solidarity of the eight Republican members became apparent, but it was then too late. There was a lot of rough talk about resisting, but it came to nothing. Having joined in creating the commission and voluntarily put their cause in its hands, protest now was futile.

The point is made that this commission was plainly unconstitutional, and wonder has often been expressed that the Democratic leaders should have consented to such a process for determining the result. It is alleged that the chief reason for their yielding was the fear of civil war unless some method of deciding the contest were found that would be generally agreed upon. Colonel Watterson, who was then in the House, and in a way personal representative of Mr. Tilden, protested but was overruled. The loyalty of the Democratic leaders who acquiesced in the commission plan is not questioned, but their judgment has been. They voted for the commission with the idea that the fifteenth member at least would be a man so wholly free from partisan ties that they would at least get an even break. The natural choice of the four justices would have been their associate, Justice David Davis, and he would probably have shown—or so it was maintained—an independence no other member did. But five days before the commission was named Justice Davis was elected Senator from Illinois and regarded it as improper for him to sit. The choice then fell on Justice Bradley, who, while able and honest, was an intense Republican partisan.

It was a bold game Mr. Chandler and his party associates played, but they won. They were pretty well smeared up so far as their reputations went before it was over, but they kept their party in power. On March 2, in the House, the Electoral Commission having completed its work and submitted its report, Hayes and Wheeler were given 185 votes, Tilden and Hendricks 184, and the Republican ticket declared elected. In the Republican 185 were the nineteen from Florida, South Carolina, Louisiana. It had taken the whole power of the administration, the influence and pressure of a considerable part of the army, and the humiliation of the Supreme Court to get those nineteen, but they finally got them. "It was," says Mr. Curtis in his history of the period, "an undertaking from which timid men would have shrunk with fear and honorable men contemplated with horror."

That seems a pretty dreadful indictment but there is no denying it was a desperate fight made by desperate men.

Chapter XIX

THE REVIVAL AFTER THE TILDEN LOSS

Democrats Gain Senate as Well as House in 1878—Lose
Again in 1880—Unable to Make Moral Issue of
Fraud in Face of General Prosperity—Republicans
and the Business Interests

To say that the Democrats were discouraged by the
loss of the Presidency under such circumstances as
they lost it in 1876 is to express it inadequately. For
a while the life just left the party. To have been outside the breastworks for sixteen years, to win a great
fight, and then have the victory snatched away by
superior force, was about the limit. At no time in its
history has the party been flatter, its leadership more
dismayed, its rank and file more disordered and un-
disciplined. There was, of course, burning indignation over the "crime," tremendous threats to avenge
the outrage, but there was also deep despondency
and a dreadful let down. It took most of a year before the party began to get back its fighting spirit,
to lift up its bowed head and crushed heart.

The 1878 congressional elections had a revivify-
ing effect and gave the Democrats control of the
Senate as well as the House. They had forty-two out
of seventy-six members of the Senate, 149 out of
293 in the House. This was some consolation for the

loss of the Presidency but not much, and the country was literally full of heartbroken Democrats. Mr. Tilden himself took his loss with philosophic calm. In some ways he was different from any man the Democrats had ever run for President. Born in 1814, in New York, his father was a close friend of Martin Van Buren and he naturally became a Van Buren man as soon as he was old enough to take an active interest in politics. He was elected to the legislature in 1845 and in 1848 joined whole-heartedly with Van Buren in the Free Soil movement, helped write the platform of that short-lived party, and supported Van Buren for President against Cass. That Free Soil platform showed his attitude on the slavery question to be in all respects the same as that occupied by the Republican party in its 1856 and 1860 platforms.

Throughout the war he was strongly pro-Union, though he was opposed to the unconstitutional methods adopted in its prosecution and to the outrageous abuses of power in the South during the reconstruction period. He was, however, because of his record on the slavery question before the war and his unswerving loyalty during the war, wholly free from the charge of "copperheadism" which the Republicans leveled against the Democratic party and with which they kept many dissatisfied voters in line. Having failed with McClellan, Greeley, and Seymour, the party was turning toward such men as Chase, Davis, and Field—called Republicans by the rock-ribbed Democrats of the Watterson type—when the election of Mr. Tilden as governor of New York in 1874, and his record there, pushed him forward as the logical 1876 nominee. His had been the directing mind in the exposure of the Tweed gang in New York, and it was his examination of the bank accounts of its leaders that formed the basis of the civil and criminal proceedings against them.

By 1868 he had become the recognized State leader in his own party and had made a reputation by the determination and power with which he fought graft inside and outside of party lines. His message as governor, denouncing the extravagance and dishonesty in the canal system, had a ring that attracted attention in the country generally. His nomination for President was inevitable after the movement started, notwithstanding the opposition of Tammany, with which organization he was never popular. But the South wanted him—and the West. To them he seemed a winner, and the point had been reached where that was what above all else they desired. At the time of his selection Mr. Tilden was over sixty, a recognized leader at the bar, with an immense and extremely lucrative law practice, and what—for those days—was a great fortune. It is probable he was the wealthiest man ever nominated for the Presidency by any party. His estate was valued at more than five million dollars, and from 1850 on he had a larger corporate practice than any other New York lawyer. He was in fact a singularly successful, very rich railroad attorney—a curious and unprecedented type for a Presidential candidate; so far as can be found, the only one of his kind who was ever nominated.

It has been the rule of political parties to regard as unavailable for the Presidency men whose connection with the great transportation companies was as close and intimate as was that of Mr. Tilden, who represented more of them than any other individual, who had for years drawn up their financial and reorganization plans, who was their principal legal adviser. Yet his railroad and corporate connections and his wealth were not issues in the campaign, nor much urged as arguments against him. A bachelor, a scholar, a dreamer with a genius for business, a philosopher with a talent for organization, a lover of books, music, art, horses, dogs, good food and good drink, Mr. Tilden was certainly unique among Presidential candidates. In the hour of his defeat he maintained his poise and dignity, and during the terrific struggle that followed the election, while there were plenty of stories of discreditable Democratic attempts to induce a Republican elector to vote for Tilden, there seems no justification for believing that Mr. Tilden knew of them.

I directly know [wrote Colonel Watterson] that the Presidency was offered him for a price and that he refused it; and I indirectly know and believe that two other offers came to him, which he also declined. The accusation that he was willing to buy, and through cipher dispatches and other ways tried to buy, rests upon appearances supporting mistaken surmises. Mr. Tilden knew nothing of the cipher dispatches until they appeared in the New York Tribune. Neither did George W. Smith, his private secretary and, later, one of the trustees of his will. It should be sufficient to say that so far as they involved No. 15 Gramercy Park, they were the work solely of Colonel Pelton acting on his own responsibility and, as Mr. Tilden's nephew, exceeding his authority to act; that it later developed that Colonel Pelton had not been in his perfect mind but was at least semi-irresponsible and that on two occasions when the vote or votes sought seemed within reach Mr. Tilden interposed to forbid. Directly and personally I know this to be true.

Logically, of course, Mr. Tilden was the Democratic nominee for 1880, and he probably would have been had he really wanted to be, in spite of the violent opposition of Tammany to his candidacy and the open threat of John Kelly, the then Tammany leader, that his organization would not support Tilden if nominated. But Mr. Tilden was nearly sixty-five, was not in robust health, and just as the convention met sent a letter to his friends declining to be a candidate, asking that his name be not presented and he be allowed to retire. It is true that like some who have followed him, he left a loophole by which he might be "drafted," but the convention decided to take him at his word and the movement for him was dropped. It is conceded, however, that he could have got the nomination had he chosen to try, and that there would have been more force in seeking to revenge the "Crime of '76" with him than with any one else.

Whether he or any one else could have won then, however, is open to question. The Republicans had in 1880, as they have had various times since, the advantage of a prosperity that absorbs all criticism and is accompanied by a political inertia and indifference to change among the people impossible to shake. Prosperity was made the keynote of the Republican campaign, and the big financial business interests of the country lined up behind the Republican ticket of Garfield and Arthur with an impressive solidity that has since gotten to be more or less a confirmed habit with them. In this day of their dominance it has become the one great asset of the Republican party, the support of which the Republican managers almost always make sure of before selecting their candidates or adopting their platforms. Since the Garfield days, there has been only one Republican candidate of whom this was not true —Theodore Roosevelt. Him they did not want but had to take. Every other Republican ticket and platform has been completely acceptable to the so-called "interests," though it is not true that they have dictated them all—not, for example, that of Mr. Hughes in 1916.

This backing of the Republican ticket by the business interests is not pointed to by way of criticism either of the Republican party or of the business interests. The prosperity and welfare of the people and the fate of the nation depend very largely on the business interests. That their natural tendency has grown more and more to be strongly Republican in national campaigns, even when the Democratic candidate is concededly the superior man, is an unfortunate thing for the party, due partly to hard luck, partly to rotten leadership, partly to the superior skill of Republican politicians, partly to the potency of the Republican propaganda, and the increasing Republican control over the channels of publicity.

In the Garfield campaign the business forces were lined up behind the Republican ticket more solidly than before. The Republican campaign was splendidly financed, well organized, and the country unquestionably was well off. It is also true that there was no enthusiasm or color about the Democratic campaign. The convention held at Cincinnati in June adopted a platform largely written by Colonel Watterson, which, while rather disjointed and paragraphic, was in consonance with the party's principles. It is necessary to present here only the first seven planks, the rest being devoted to denunciation of the Hayes administration, eulogy of Mr. Tilden, and praise of the Democratic majority in Congress for its "honesty and thrift" in reducing public expenditures. The first part of the platform was as follows:

The Democrats of the United States, in convention assembled, declare—

1. We pledge ourselves anew to the constitutional doctrines and traditions of the Democratic party, as illustrated by the

teachings and example of a long line of Democratic states-men and patriots, and embodied in the platform of the last national convention of the party.

2. Opposition to centralizationism and to that dangerous spirit of encroachment which tends to consolidate the powers of all the departments in one, and thus to create, whatever be the form of government, a real despotism. No sumptuary laws; separation of church and state for the good of each; common schools fostered and protected.

3. Home rule, honest money, consisting of gold and silver, and paper convertible into coin on demand; the strict main-tenance of the public faith, state and national; and a tariff for revenue only.

4. The subordination of the miltary to the civil power, and a general and thorough reform of the civil service.

5. The right to a free ballot is the right preservative of all rights, and must and shall be maintained in every part of the United States.

6. The existing administration is the representative of con-spiracy only, and its claim of right to surround the ballot-boxes with troops and deputy marshals, to intimidate and obstruct the electors, and the unprecedented use of the veto to maintain its corrupt and despotic power, insult the people and imperil their institutions.

7. The great fraud of 1876-77, by which, upon a false count of the electoral votes of two States, the candidate defeated at the polls was declared to be President, and, for the first time in American history, the will of the people was set aside under a threat of military violence, struck a deadly blow at our system of representative government; the Democratic party, to preserve the country from civil war, submitted for a time in firm and patriotic faith that the people would punish this crime in 1880. This issue precedes and dwarfs every other; it imposes a more sacred duty upon the people of the Union than ever addressed the conscience of a nation of freemen.

There was certainly nothing in this platform to

alienate the business interests, nor in the character of the candidates selected to stand on it—Winfield S. Hancock of Pennsylvania and William H. English of Indiana. They were unexciting enough, personally, and were at no time able to get the people excited over the "fraud of 1876," which had been declared the overshadowing issue. The whole Democratic trouble was prosperity. No headway could be made against it. It was proved then and has been conclusively proved since that moral issues are unavailing in the face of general prosperity.

The Democratic convention of 1880 was far more harmonious than was usual. There were a number of aspirants for the Presidential nomination—Thomas F. Bayard of Delaware; Henry B. Payne, Ohio; Allen G. Thurman, Ohio; Stephen J. Field, California; William R. Morrison, Illinois; Thomas A. Hendricks, Indiana; Horatio Seymour, New York; and Samuel J. Randall, Pennsylvania, but General Hancock led them all on the first ballot and was nominated on the third by a practically unanimous vote. The one feature of the convention was the exclusion of the Tammany delegation headed by Kelly. They had come out with a threat of bolting if Tilden were chosen and in the end were themselves thrown out.

Three things marked the campaign—first, the virulent but ineffective attacks on the character of Garfield, not by the Democratic candidates, but by their supporters; second, the inability of the Democrats to effectively present their side of the tariff issue when in the last stage of the campaign the Republicans made a violent and concentrated attack on the tariff for revenue plank as aimed at American industry and as essentially free trade. No one really thought General Hancock a free trader, but he was inept in his reply, and the Democratic representatives were uneducated on the tariff as a national policy. The utterly feeble way in which they met the attack aided in solidifying the business interests on the other side; third, the scandals connected with the large contributions to the Republican campaign fund from railroad and other sources.

The people, however, were no more excited over those charges than they were over the revenge for the fraud of 1876 idea. They were getting along too well to be resentful over the moral lapses of politicians and political parties. In spite of all this, however, and in spite of the fact that Garfield and Arthur got 214 electoral votes to 155 for Hancock and English, the Republican popular plurality was extraordinarily small—12,464 out of a total vote of nearly nine million. It showed clearly that any lack of harmony in the Republican camp would put them out of power; that with the South now solidly Democratic, a swing of comparatively few votes in certain pivotal States, notably New York, would give the Democrats an electoral majority; that the long tenure of power was creating rifts in the ranks that made the Republican hold a precarious one. Be-

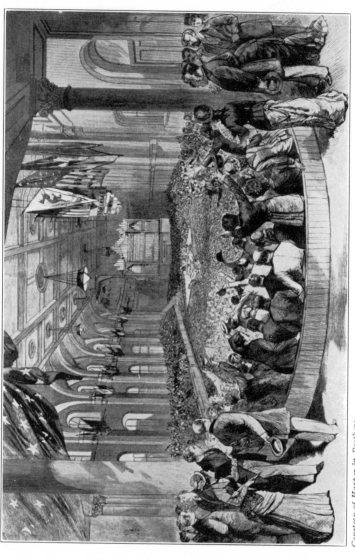

Courtesy of Harper & Brothers

THE DEMOCRATIC CONVENTION AT CINCINNATI, 1880

fore closing this chapter the significant fact ought to be noted that the three Southern States—Florida, South Carolina, and Louisiana—which under pressure from the Federal Government had returned the nineteen Republican electors that saved Hayes and defeated Tilden—with the pressure removed went Democratic by overwhelming majorities. But that loss was more than made up by the Republican victory in New York.

Chapter XX

Cleveland's Character—Tammany Opposition in the Convention—The Rum, Romanism and Rebellion Incident—Closeness of the Result

THE life of the Democratic party, so far, breaks naturally into five great divisions—the Jefferson era, the Jackson era, the Cleveland era, the Bryan era, the Wilson era. The five men thus named, all save one of whom was President twice, and he three times an unsuccessful candidate, are the great outstanding personalities of the party, the five towering figures around whom its history is largely draped, the group of Democrats who, for good or bad, have most affected the party's and the country's history. With no idea at this time of comparing the character, qualities, and statesmanship of these men, and with absolutely no intent to regard them all as on the same intellectual or spiritual plane, or of equal merit as men, it is still impossible to deny that so far as the potency of their party influence is concerned they stand apart from the rest, clearly in a class of their own.

In the present work the Cleveland era has now

been reached. From whatever angle this time—from 1884 to 1896—is viewed, it sticks out as unsurpassed, except for war periods, in the eventful nature of the years it covered, the extraordinary bitterness and ferocity of the struggles that tore the party and the nation, the gravity and greatness of the problems that confronted the President. And from whatever angle he is viewed, no detached person capable of a real judgment these days withholds admiration from Grover Cleveland as a man and as a President, or disputes the greatness of his services to his country and to his party.

Though at the close of his second term he left the White House under a storm of abuse, cursed and reviled as few Presidents have been, it was not long before party as well as popular recognition of the real nobility of the Cleveland character, his unflinching devotion to duty, the clear-headed soundness of his course, his extraordinary courage, and the utter sincerity of his public service, was general throughout the nation, and he died appreciated, respected, honored, loved. In history his place is secure not only as a great Democrat but as a great President. No stancher, truer, braver man than Grover Cleveland has ever been in the White House, none whose rugged honesty was more unshakable, not one whose love of principle was deeper or whose conception of public service was higher.

When long before he became President he declared that "Public office is a public trust," he sounded the keynote of his career. That idea had been expressed by some before Cleveland, and it has been in one form or another mouthed by many since— but he lived up to it. Not a brilliant man, not a genius, not eloquent as a speaker, nor graceful as a writer, neither a diplomat nor a demagogue, not highly intellectual or scholarly profound, singularly lacking in the ingratiating, conciliatory qualities of a politician, there is an immense inspiration in the steadfastness and strength of Mr. Cleveland, his solidity and courage, his uncompromising willingness at all times to sacrifice himself and his chances for his principles, in the big, broad, rugged truth and straightness of the man.

It is true that his two administrations were extraordinarily barren of legislative achievements, that he did not put through Congress—or even propose— any great constructive legislative program, that no particular policy or law or creed bears his name, that he originated no new ideas of government or politics, that he initiated no forward looking measures, took no progressive steps. All that is true, yet it does not in the least alter the fact of Mr. Cleveland's splendid battles for the fundamental principles of his party, his struggles to establish a standard of political morality in party government, his fight against dishonesty and fraud in the appropriation of public money, and his implacable, immovable, invincible opposition to the economic heresy that threatened the financial foundation of the nation—an opposition that rose high above party expediency and resisted all forms of political and personal pressure. These things were of infinitely greater value to the country as a whole than anything else he could have done, constitute a far finer record, meant more in the long run.

Probably the most enduring monument to him is the memory of his magnificent fight for sound money, against free silver, for the gold standard. It was he who made that fight, bore the burden of it, and won it. If there were nothing else in the whole Cleveland career, the tremendous part he played in preventing the free silver forces from gaining control of the government and putting into effect their devastating financial theories would in itself be sufficient to place the nation forever in his debt. That, perhaps, was his finest fight—certainly it was made at the greatest personal cost, calling down on his head a terrific storm of resentment, deluging him with accusations and abuse of unprecedented violence and virulence, sending him into retirement practically repudiated by his party.

Next to that was his great battle for tariff reform in which he swung his party behind him on the great basic Democratic principle and made the most gallant assault on the high protective citadel in all American political history. Convinced, after long and careful study, of the injustice and iniquity of the protective system, of the soundness of the tariff for revenue doctrine, Mr. Cleveland made the first real tariff fight. He made the issue a living one and would have splendidly succeeded but for the treachery of certain Democratic senators, chief among them Arthur P. Gorman of Maryland, whom he later blistered with the charge of "party perfidy and dishonor."

Two other great fights of the Cleveland era stand out—one the grim and determined way in which he blocked the pension frauds and through the unprecedented use of the veto power killed hundreds of utterly dishonest, wholly indefensible bills designed to rob the Treasury. Up to this time no politician of either party had dared incur the unpopularity of opposing pensions for the Civil War veterans. For the first Democratic President since the Civil War to do it required courage of a kind so rare as to be almost non-existent. It subjected him, as he knew it would, to the grossest sort of misrepresentation, the vilest kind of slander. Yet, it was no more possible for Mr. Cleveland to fail to oppose these barefaced steals with all the vigor and strength he had than it was possible for him to steal himself.

To have failed in that would have been to discard the ruling principle of his whole political life—that "Public office is a public trust." There is no known instance—even a trivial one—in which he did discard that principle. The other fight involved even more unpopularity but was just as worth while making. It was the effort to get away from the spoils system, which had been uniformly followed by every President since Jackson, and to strengthen the civil-service principle in the matter of patronage. By the practical requirements of the situation he was prevented from going nearly as far as the reformers wanted, and was equally unable to satisfy the hungry party, twenty-four years out of power, behind him. He did what he thought right, with the inevitable result that he pleased neither side and became the target for both.

It was said of Mr. Cleveland that the people loved him for the enemies he had made. It is certainly true that the crooks and the fools in both parties were almost solidly his enthusiastic foes. The character of his assailants and the reasons for their hatred contribute perhaps the greatest tribute to the man. As his record is reviewed, the most impressive things of all about it are the unshakable convictions of the man and his unconquerable courage in living up to them. Once he said, when in 1889 he was told that if he insisted on making the tariff an issue he would be defeated, "What's the use of being elected or re-elected unless you stand for something?" Stout hearted, clear headed, big, blunt, and broad, Grover Cleveland "stood for something" all the time.

He was a President to be proud of. His rise in politics was almost unparalleled. One term as district attorney of Buffalo, one term as sheriff, one term as mayor—and then nominated and elected governor of New York in 1882 by a great majority. That, of course, made him a Presidential possibility. The governor of New York, like the governor of Ohio, is always a Presidential possibility. The positions are natural spring-boards for the nomination. Usually the incumbent is a candidate for the Presidency the day after his election as governor. This was not the case with Mr. Cleveland. He had not been a spectacular district attorney, sheriff, or mayor. He had been in all these places an efficient, plodding, non-political, rigidly upright official, as utterly intolerant of corruption and graft in his own party as in the other, as unflinchingly devoted to doing the right as he saw it. He was exactly that sort of governor and had no idea of the Presidency in his head.

He had, in fact, been a reform governor, as he had been a reform mayor, and was correspondingly unpopular with the politicians, cordially disliked by Tammany, then headed by John Kelly, but greatly respected by the thinking people of the State. The situation in the country, however, was such that this very unpopularity with the politicians and the political machine was a far greater asset than it had been in any previous campaign. The Republican party faced the Presidential year of 1884 with an accumulation of burdens due in large part to its long and unbroken tenure of power. For twenty-four years they had held the Government, largely as a result of the war. For twelve of those years through the Federal power back of the military state governments the South had been held as Republican territory, but after 1876 the solidity of its adherence to the Democratic party had made the Republican situation less secure. In every campaign they had consistently "waved the bloody shirt," insisted upon regarding the Democrats as a mere faction born for failure and defeat, disregarded the fact that not since the war had the Republicans in any election carried House and Senate majorities in with their Presidential candidate.

They were full of pride and heedlessness, and there was abroad a pretty general feeling that the Republican politicians had become too arrogant and the machine too powerful. The scandals of the Grant administration had been followed by others, and though President Arthur was an efficient executive and a man of the highest personal character, his administration was not free from them. Altogether the people were restive and resentful. They were bored by the reiteration of the charge that the Democrats were responsible for the rebellion, and by the general Republican attitude that because they had "saved" the Union in 1860 they owned it, therefore, in perpetuity. The years of the Arthur administration, following the assassination of Garfield, were not exciting. There were no vital issues, no great congressional battles. Party lines were less sharply drawn than at any previous stage, and there was no particular happening to cause a revolt against the party in power. The President was fairly popular and generally respected. Yet in 1882 the congressional elections went heavily against the Republicans. The

Democrats greatly increased their membership in the House, and gained governors in Pennsylvania and New York—Mr. Cleveland getting the then unprecedented majority of 190,000.

The political publicists of the day read into these results a clear warning to the politicians that unless a first-class ticket, free from machine taint, were put up they could not hope to win in the coming Presidential contest. In the face of these facts, in spite of the rumblings of revolt among independent Republicans and the springing up of two new parties—the Anti-Monopoly party and the National or Greenback party—notwithstanding the logical right of Arthur to the nomination, the Republicans in convention at Chicago nominated James G. Blaine, able, brilliant, but steeped in partisan politics, a leader of the organization who as speaker of the House had been charged with participation in some more or less shady transactions, who had tried for the nomination in 1876 and again in 1880, who had been secretary of state and chief political adviser under Garfield, who had many strong party friends in all sections—but who was not at all the type for which the demand had been made by the reform element. Almost immediately the bolt began. Some of the most important party organs refused their support. Committees were organized and meetings held in New York, Boston, and other cities with the idea of rallying Republican opposition to the Blaine-Logan ticket.

The Cleveland Era

All of this was tremendously encouraging to the Democrats, it clearly being to them that the Republican dissatisfied element looked for an acceptable candidate and platform. The sentiment for Mr. Cleveland was stronger than for any other man. During the year and more during which his name had been urged as the Presidential candidate of his party he had not only not made a single overt gesture indicating his candidacy, but had not made nor permitted to be made for him a single conciliatory move toward Tammany, whose hostility was open and undisguised. When the convention met, his friend Daniel Manning, chairman of the New York State Committee, went out to Chicago as his representative. But he had up to that time made no declaration of candidacy and no one had the least idea of his views on any national issue of the day. The sentiment for him was based on his record in his various New York offices and the size of his 1882 majority.

On the first day of the convention he was not sure of a majority of the New York delegation, and only the most strenuous efforts of Manning got the necessary votes to make the majority. Under the unit rule, this sewed up the Tammany opposition unless some way could be found to break that rule. A violent attempt was made to do this and the Tammany leader fought fiercely for freedom. The convention, outside of New York, however, was strongly pro-Cleveland and by a vote of 463 to 329 refused to permit Tammany to violate the unit rule instructions under which it had come to the convention. Daniel Lockwood in presenting Cleveland's name to the convention simply and accurately described the reasons for his nomination.

A little more than three years ago [he said] I had the honor at the city of Buffalo to present the name of this same gentleman for the office of mayor of that city. It was presented then for the same reason, and from the same causes, that we present it now. It was because the government of that city had become corrupt, had become debauched, and political integrity sat not in high places. The people looked for a man who would represent honest government, and without hesitation they named Grover Cleveland.

The result of that election and of his holding that office was, that in less than nine months the State of New York found herself in a position to want just such a candidate and for just such a purpose. At the State Convention of 1882 his name was placed in nomination for the office of Governor of the State of New York. The same people, the same class of people, knew that that meant honest government, it meant pure government, it meant Democratic government, and it was ratified; and, gentlemen, now, after eighteen months of service there the Democracy of the State of New York comes to you and ask you to go to the country, to go to the independent and Democratic voters of the country, to go to the young men of the country, the new blood of the country, and present the name of Grover Cleveland as your standard bearer.

At once Tammany, through Thomas F. Grady, launched its attack, but the tide was too strong. Cleveland was nominated on the second ballot and with him for Vice-President Thomas A. Hendricks of Indiana. The whole vote of New York was cast for him, Tammany was rolled in the dust, and the

284

convention adjourned with the cry, originated by Governor Edward S. Bragg of Wisconsin, "We love him for the enemies he has made," ringing through the hall—and it rang through the campaign that followed. It was a remarkable victory—for a man without money, without organization, without effort, without even expressing his views on national questions, without an issue or an asset save his own rugged and powerful personality. Up in Albany, at his office, he sat with his secretary, Daniel Lamont, at work on routine matters. "The telephone rang," writes his best biographer, Dr. Robert McElroy of Princeton, "and a voice said: Tell the Governor he has been nominated on the second ballot." Lamont repeated the words.

"Is that so, Dan?" said the governor, as his face brightened for the first time. "By jove, that is something, isn't it?" The platform upon which Mr. Cleveland ran was adopted before his nomination was made and he had nothing to do with its preparation. Nevertheless, it was a strong document, well written, and with a real ring to it. The author was John Prentiss Poe of Maryland, close friend of Senator Arthur P. Gorman, and one of the ablest lawyers the State has produced. It contained the most withering and blasting indictment of the Republican party yet framed, and it was on this indictment that the campaign was made. Outside of it the platform was chiefly remarkable for its length. It was the first of the long platforms. From that year on both parties appeared to find it necessary to state their case in not less than 3000 words. Prior to that they had rarely needed more than 500 or 600. Neither the money plank nor the tariff plank in this platform was clean cut or definite, but the generalities glittered beautifully and the Republican sins were exhibited as never before. There was, however, one brief plank that it is important to give in full. It follows:

"We oppose sumptuary laws which vex the citizens and interfere with individual liberty."

The reason that is important and interesting is because it is a Democratic declaration against prohibition, made in harmony with the great Democratic principle of personal liberty. All doubt that by the words "sumptuary laws" was meant prohibition is removed by the plank adopted by the Prohibition party, held a week later, which, after lambasting the Republicans, said:

The fact that the Democratic party has, in its national deliverances of party policy, arrayed itself on the side of the drink makers and sellers, by declaring against the policy of prohibition of such traffic under the false name of "sumptuary laws," and, when in power in some of the states, in refusing remedial legislation, and, in Congress, of refusing to permit the creation of a board of inquiry to investigate and report upon the effects of this traffic, proves that the Democratic party should not be intrusted with power or place.

This reference to "sumptuary laws," so far as can be found, is the first declaration of the party on this subject. In view of the wide departure from this stand of the party later and the present deep and deadly division in its ranks on this question, this plank is not without interest. It rather sustains the contention that the real trouble with the Democratic party is due to its frequent failures to consistently apply its basic principles.

To return to the Cleveland-Blaine fight: it was a bitter campaign and a dirty one. There were no real issues, save the indictment and defense of the two parties and the personalities of the candidates. Old charges were raked up against Mr. Blaine and some scandalous stories were spread about Mr. Cleveland. The Mugwumps, as the bolting Republicans were called, got behind Cleveland, and the Republicans lost ground in New England and New York. They had, however, as usual, plenty of money, and it was plain the contest would be close. Mr. Blaine was offsetting the defection of independent Republicans by Irish support that came to him because his mother was a Catholic, and Mr. Cleveland was depicted as a narrow Presbyterian with an anti-Catholic bias. It was at the most critical period of the campaign that the justly famous Burchard incident occurred. It has always been claimed that the Burchard incident decided the election, and it must be admitted there seem sound grounds for thinking so. New York with its thirty-six electoral votes was the essential State. Without it neither side could win. Cleveland carried it by the amazingly small majority of 1149 out of a total of 1,125,159 votes. The almost complete disappearance of the 190,000 majority by which he had won his Governorship fight two years before was unquestionably due to Tammany treachery, and to the concentration of the Republican money, organization, and effort in the State.

What happened was this. Late in October, after a strenuous trip through the West, Mr. Blaine reached New York. At the time it was conceded his chance in New York depended upon his personal strength with the Irish and the ability of Tammany to "deliver" against the Democratic candidate. He went to his headquarters in the old Fifth Avenue Hotel and there received a delegation of clergymen who, while belonging to the reform element of the party, had refused to follow the Mugwumps into the Cleveland camp. One of these clergymen, Dr. Samuel Burchard, had in his system a lot of pent-up words which he proceeded to unloose on Mr. Blaine in a speech, the concluding words of which were these:

"We are Republicans and don't propose to leave our party and identify ourselves with the party whose antecedents have been Rum, Romanism and Rebellion." The dynamite in that alliterative phrase ought to have been apparent to even the dullest political mind. To such an astute and experienced warhorse of politics as James G. Blaine its potentiality for harm should have certainly been grasped. The belief is that Mr. Blaine, tired from his trip, bored by the delegation, and particularly by the Rev. Dr.

GROVER CLEVELAND

President 1885-1889, 1893-1897

Burchard, did not listen with his mind to that eloquent and earnest gentleman.

The result was that when the "Rum, Romanism and Rebellion" part of that speech appeared in print, the Democrats were given an opportunity of which they took full and complete advantage. The unfortunate Dr. Burchard was denounced from one end of the country to the other. Mr. Blaine was indicted for listening without rebuke while members of the Catholic church, to which his mother belonged, were thus insultingly coupled with "Rum and Rebellion." There was no way out for Mr. Blaine. There was little he could do. Denials and explanations only served to give additional publicity to the phrase. Beyond doubt it swung back to Mr. Cleveland more than 600 votes of Irish Catholics who had intended to vote for Mr. Blaine. That many would have given the Republican ticket New York and the Presidency. "The Burchard accident," writes John Devoy in his pamphlet, "Cleveland and the Irish," occurring at the last moment, turned back just enough of the Irish seceders to give New York by a miserably meager majority to the Mugwumps. It is probable, too, Dr. McElroy points out, that the result was affected by the anger of Senator Roscoe Conkling of New York, who had cherished a natural hatred of Mr. Blaine since that gentleman in a speech eighteen years before had characterized him as a "grandiloquent swell with a turkey gobbler strut." It was a curious election, almost incredibly close. It is, perhaps, as good an illustration as American politics affords of how overwhelming issues are decided by the most trivial happenings, history made by the merest accident. It was ten days after the election before the Republicans finally conceded defeat. As in the Tilden campaign, they started out with the flat declaration from the Republican National Committee that "there is no ground for doubt that the honest vote of this State has been given to the Republican candidate." The situation was extremely tense. Democratic leaders were fearful that another attempt to take the election through the Federal Government was about to be made, and were determined that it should not be done. There was wild talk of violence and some menacing demonstrations. Cleveland kept his head. Up at Albany he worked at his job as governor without saying a word, but when, on the tenth day, news was brought to him the Republicans had given up, he— according to Dr. McElroy—looked up and remarked, "I am glad of it, very glad. There will now be no trouble. If they had not, I should have felt it my duty to take my seat anyhow."

Chapter XXI

BACK IN POWER AFTER TWENTY-FOUR YEARS

Cleveland's Troubles With the Office-Holders—His Insistence on Making Tariff the 1888 Issue—The Sackville-West Incident—Anti-Prohibition Stand in Platform

THERE is not room here to dwell upon the first Cleveland administration, except to say that the pressure
from the job hunters probably exceeded that applied
to any former incumbent of the White House. For
twenty-four years the Democrats had been out of
power. With the election of this first President since
the Civil War they hungrily, eagerly, confidently
rushed forward from every State in the country. It
was a horrible shock when they found Mr. Cleveland
would not go the limit with them, that a clean sweep
was not to be made of the Republicans, and that a
man had to be something more than a "deserving
Democrat" to land a job. As a result they turned
violently against the President.

At the same time, by refusing to go to extremes
with the reformers, he lost their support and got
cursed by both sides. In the matter of patronage, he
thought his duty lay between the spoilsmen and the

reformers. In adhering to that line, as has been pointed out, he incurred the enmity of both. Personally, he hated the whole business. At times it nearly drove him to distraction. It prevented him from working on the things he knew to be important; it clogged up the whole scheme of things. To his friend and former law partner, Bissell, he wrote: "The damned everlasting clatter for office continues. It makes me feel like resigning and hell is to pay generally."

Naturally, Mr. Cleveland made a lot of mistaken appointments; naturally, he was misled by both sides; naturally, he was harassed and in hot water most of the time; but he hewed to the line nevertheless and gave to his party what recognition he could without violating his obligations to the civil service reformers and his own convictions. No wonder he pleased but few. His successful struggle with the Republican Senate to secure a restoration of the power and dignity of the President, sapped by the Tenure of Office Act passed during the Johnson days; his flint-like opposition to fraudulent pension bills, which resulted in his exercise of the veto power 301 times in four years, whereas all the Presidents preceding him had used it but 109 times; and the courage and vigor with which he faced the violent labor outbreaks, notably the Pullman strike in Chicago—these were the outstanding features of those first years in the White House of the first Democratic President since 1860.

With a Republican Senate and a Democratic

House there was little chance for the enactment of an administrative program, had there been one. The fact is there was none. The 1884 platform had made no specific legislative pledges. Its principal promise had been for an honest administration, and that was being carried out, under considerable difficulties it is true, but to the finish just the same. It was not until just before the opening of the 1888 campaign that Mr. Cleveland developed his tariff-reform plan and took the first step toward its inauguration. When he went into office he knew practically nothing about the tariff—and so informed Carl Schurz when asked what he was going to do on the subject. But he knew a lot about it before he sent in that famous tariff message. He knew because he made it his business to inform himself by hard study and much reading.

And the more he studied the subject, the stronger became his conviction that the protective tariff was a wicked and indefensible thing, that a tariff for revenue only was the only tariff that could be justified by the Constitution or by the facts, and that the Republican tariff created a favored class which, in return for their protection from foreign competition, increased prices to the domestic consumer. His political advisers and close friends, while agreeing with Mr. Cleveland's tariff views and in sympathy with his aim, strongly urged him not to make the subject the dominant issue in the 1888 campaign. At that time his renomination, notwithstanding the opposition of David Bennett Hill in New York, and the continued hostility of the Tammany leaders, was conceded. It was pointed out that his chances of election, notwithstanding the enemies he had made, were extremely good unless some false political step were taken; that the Republicans were not united and had no strong candidate in sight. It was further urged that if he made tariff for revenue only the issue, it would open the door for the other side to accuse him of being in favor of free trade, to charge him with being pro-British, and would likely result in the solidifying of the big business interests back of the Republican ticket with a large campaign fund.

Mr. Cleveland listened to all this, weighed it, conceded it. Yet he went ahead with the remark heretofore quoted, "What's the use of being elected or re-elected unless you stand for something." So, in the face of advice from his own most disinterested friends that it was political suicide to raise the issue at that time, Mr. Cleveland on December 6, 1887, sent a message to Congress which dealt exclusively with the tariff, more directly and specifically and unequivocally than it had ever been dealt with before by any President. He was no middle-ground man, this President, and he took no middle ground on this subject. It was hailed throughout the country with mingled curses and congratulations. The Republicans were jubilant. Blaine, then in France, cabled to "The New York Tribune," denouncing it as "free trade," and the whole country started on a tariff debate such as had never occurred before.

In the House, under the leadership of Roger Q. Mills, the Democrats put through a bill providing for a reduction of more than $50,000,000. It was, however, conceived in a partisan spirit and was by no means in harmony with the reform for which the President had pleaded in his message. Of course, the Republican Senate, led by Aldrich and Allison, responded to the Mills bill by the passage of a substitute just as extreme from the other point of view. Naturally, both bills were blocked; the tariff question remained up in the air and was swept into the campaign as the dominant issue. What Mr. Cleveland did in that message was to force the two great political parties for the first time to take clear-cut positions on the tariff question. They had not done so before. They did then, and that line between high protection and tariff for revenue only has twice been the chief and often the only dividing line between the two since. It is, in spite of the fact that the Democrats seem to have swung around to a certain amount of protection, the only real difference between the two to-day.

It was Mr. Cleveland who drew that line, who swung his party back to its original tariff position, to which, despite modifications and compromises, it still measurably adheres. At the time it greatly intensified the opposition to Cleveland and it certainly did, as was predicted, array every protected industry in the country solidly behind the Republicans. As a matter of fact, Mr. Cleveland had no personal desire to be a candidate. The Presidency had been a tremendous burden. He bore a heavier load than any other save the war Presidents—Lincoln and Wilson. He was ready, glad to quit—but he could not do it. For one thing, strong as was the sentiment against him, there was an equally strong party current for him. For another, he could not make the issue and then run away from it. Therefore, when the year 1888 opened, his close friends knew that he would make the fight it nominated, but would be personally relieved if some one else were named. Here is the way he expressed himself in a private letter to his friend James Shannahan:

My position is this—I should personally like better than anything else to be let alone and let out; but although I often get quite discouraged and feel like insisting on following my inclinations, I shall neither go counter to the wishes of the party I love and which has honored me, nor shall I desert my friends.

Under these conditions, the renomination of Cleveland was inevitable, regardless of the opposition of Tammany and the growing Presidential ambitions of Governor David B. Hill. To have failed to renominate him would have been an unthinkable repudiation by the Democratic party of their only President since Buchanan, a fatal admission of failure in the first Democratic administration in a generation. The thing was so sure that Cleveland himself planned every detail of the convention, wrote the platform, selected the presiding officers, planned the nomination speech. The New York opposition distributed during the convention some scurrilous anti-Cleveland literature and there was a strong undercurrent of resentment, but the Cleveland strength was so overwhelming that no ballot was taken at all and he was nominated by acclamation, the first time such a thing had occurred in a national convention since Van Buren was named by resolution in 1840. The platform was personally given by Mr. Cleveland to Senator A. P. Gorman of Maryland, with whom he was then on friendly political terms but whom later he was to brand as guilty of "party perfidy and dishonor." It was taken by Gorman to St. Louis and there adopted without material change. Largely it was devoted to tariff reform and an indorsement of the Cleveland administration. "Unnecessary taxation is unjust taxation" was its keynote and a reduction of the tariff to a revenue basis was pledged.

On the Republican side, the issue was met by a flat declaration in favor of the protective system. This was the dominant thought in the Republican platform, though of course it did not fail to eulogize the Republican war heroes, denounce the Democrats for the "criminal nullification of the Constitution" in the South, and indict the Cleveland administration for cowardice, weakness, and general incompetency. Mr. Blaine having withdrawn, the Republicans nominated Benjamin Harrison of Indiana, with Levi P. Morton of New York.

Aside from the tariff planks and the straddle on

the monetary question, there was one other small feature of the Republican platform that year that deserves particular notice for the same reason that the short Democratic plank on "sumptuary laws" was singled out. The present sharp division of sentiment in both parties on prohibition makes the original slant of each on that question of special interest. In the Republican platform of 1888 are to be found these words: "The first concern of all good government is the virtue and sobriety of the people and the purity of their homes. The Republican party cordially sympathizes with all wise and well directed efforts for the promotion of temperance and morality." Compare that plank with the Democratic declaration against sumptuary laws and in favor of the highest degree of personal liberty consistent with the public welfare, and it is easy to see that here was as natural and fundamental a division between the two parties as on the tariff. The natural and logical Democratic position was to oppose Federal prohibition as inconsistent with the rights of the States and the liberty of the individual. The equally natural tendency of the Republican party was toward Federal regulation. The issue could not have been more clearly made than in those short statements of 1888.

The Democratic plank was written, as has been said, by Grover Cleveland himself. He was opposed to "sumptuary laws," under which head he classed Federal prohibition, and it is interesting to note that on this issue his views were in exact accord with those of Woodrow Wilson. It is curious that so much of the present difficulties of the party should be concededly due to its swing away from the position on this great question of the only two Presidents it has elected since the Civil War. The difficulty in making the States' rights principles and the Jeffersonian doctrine of personal liberty harmonize with the prohibition amendment are obvious.

But in 1888 the prohibition issue was of small interest. It did not figure in the fight, and the planks above referred to were not regarded as important or significant. There is this to be said of them, however: the Democratic declaration was plainly one of conviction; the Republican plank was with the view of making dry support of their ticket easy without going far enough to alienate wet support. It is a typical party difference. The Democrats in such matters are invariably less politic, expedient, discreet, and adept, more outspoken, injudicious, and careless of consequences than the Republicans. That's what makes them Democrats.

The whole of the 1888 campaign was a tariff debate. In his letter of acceptance, Cleveland strongly reasserted his views and scornfully repudiated the Republican charge that he was a "free trade idealist." From the start the fight was lost. While the Democrats did not lack money, the weight of financial and business support was heavily against them. Harrison was a cold, colorless candidate, but he had no enemies, and Cleveland had made literally thousands. Again the personal attacks on him were brutally vile, and the most dreadful stories, utterly without foundation, were circulated the country over. Hill, who was no friend of Cleveland's, was a candidate for governor in New York, and there will always be the feeling that he betrayed the national ticket. Those who knew the facts best, however, were convinced that such was not the case, and that the Cleveland defeat in the State was due to other causes.

As the Burchard "Rum, Romanism and Rebellion" incident was described as one of the vote-changing influences of the 1884 fight, so the Sackville-West incident of 1888 is equally essential on this account. Sir Lionel Sackville-West was the British ambassador at Washington. He was adroitly used in a Republican "frame-up" to give color to the charge that Cleveland was a "British tool" and that his tariff views were in line with the desires of England. The idea was to further alienate from him the Irish vote in New York. On September 4 a letter from Pomona, California, signed Charles F. Murchison, was addressed to Sir Lionel, in which "Mr. Murchison," representing himself as a loyal Britisher, though a naturalized American, asked the ambassador's advice how best to serve England's interests by his vote. With almost incredible stupidity Sackville-West swallowed the bait, and, replying to his supposed compatriot, declared that on the whole he thought the Democratic party more favorably disposed to England. The Republicans held the reply until two weeks before the election and then sprang it.

At once there was a tremendous commotion. The Republicans were jubilant, the Democrats filled with consternation, the Irish mad as could be. Mr. Cleveland was mad too. He called the attention of Lord Salisbury to the impropriety of an ambassador of a friendly power giving advice as to an election and suggested that Sackville-West be recalled. When no notice was taken of this, he curtly dismissed the unfortunate Sir Lionel, thereby offending the British Government, which refused to name another representative until after Mr. Cleveland went out of office. There is no more question that this incident cost Cleveland some votes than that the Burchard incident cost Blaine votes, but that it decided the election is not so easily maintained.

Again New York was the pivotal State, and had the Democrats carried it Cleveland would have been elected. But in 1888 there was a Republican majority of 12,000 instead of a Democratic majority of 1200. The Sackville-West incident may have turned 6000 votes in New York, but it is doubtful. There seems no escape from the deduction that Cleveland lost on the tariff issue. The view of those closest to him was that he had "thrown away the Presidency" by forcing that issue. Their feeling and his feeling are graphically described by Dr. McElroy, who, writing of a visit paid the defeated President in the White

House a few days after election by William B. Hornblower, quotes that gentleman.

> I was asked into his private reception room [writes Mr. Hornblower] and found him sitting at his desk alone. After a few words of greeting, he spoke of his tariff message, which seemed to be on his mind. He said; "My friends all advised me not to send it in. They told me it would hurt the party; that without it, I was sure to be re-elected, but that if I sent in that message to Congress, it would in all probability defeat me; that I could wait till after election and then raise the tariff question. I felt, however, that this would not be fair to the country. The situation as it existed was to my mind intolerable and immediate action was necessary. Besides, I did not wish to be re-elected without having the people understand just where I stood on the tariff question and then spring the question on them after my re-election." He paused a moment and then added, as if speaking to himself: "Perhaps I made a mistake from the party standpoint; but damn it, it was right," and he brought his fist down on his desk; "I have at least that satisfaction."
> "Yes," said I, "Mr. President, it was right, and I want to say to you, that not only was it right, but that the young men of the country are with you, and four years from now we mean to put you back in the White House."

There was, of course, tremendous Democratic disappointment over the defeat, and mighty little consolation was derived from the fact that the party polled a clear plurality of more than 100,000 of the popular vote and that the change of one State—New York—would have retained the Presidency. That was all very well, but the fact remained that after having come back into power after a lapse of twenty-four years, they had lost control again at the very next opportunity. The Republican jubilation was correspondingly great, and the party leaders smugly assured themselves that "if we behave ourselves well we will hold the government for another twenty years."

Chapter XXII

Democrats in Complete Control for First Time Since
War—Cleveland's Defiance of Tammany Leaders—
The Tariff Again the Issue

THE immediate political developments following the
1888 defeat showed how it is possible for the most
astute of political judges to be completely wrong, how
quickly turns the popular tide, how unsafe it is to
regard a party like the Democratic party as "down
and out." Mr. Harrison was an unexciting President, a man with more ability and more character
than he is generally credited with, but utterly lacking
in the fighting force, the ponderous, unshakable adherence to his convictions of his predecessor. He
aroused no violent antagonisms and inspired no
strong enthusiasms. Not to him or to anything he did
or did not do is to be attributed the shift.

The two things that had most to do with it were
the McKinley Tariff Bill, which was passed and became a law, and the Force Bill, to establish Federal
control over national elections, beaten after a desperate fight in the Senate by the Democrats under the
leadership of Gorman of Maryland. The former

aroused the intense hostility of the Democrats and was denounced as a clear violation of the Republican pledge of tariff revision. Actually, the bill increased duties all along the line. It was clearly dictated by the protected manufacturers, and some of the Republican leaders themselves—Blaine among them—feared it went too far.

The Force Bill created the most extraordinary feeling in the South. It appeared to be a Republican effort to return to the reconstruction days, to saddle the South with negro government, and thus Republicanize it again. The fight failed, but it had the effect of uniting and enthusing Democrats generally, putting them in a fighting frame of mind. The net result of the combination of the enactment of the McKinley bill and the failure of the Force Bill was to lose the 1890 congressional elections for the Republicans. The Democrats gained control of the House, elected governors in a number of Republican States and threw the Republican national leaders into more or less of a panic about 1892. All their smug complacency about "holding power for twenty years" had vanished.

In the meantime, Grover Cleveland had retired to New York, was living quietly there with his family, practising a little law, laboriously replying to the letters written him by Democrats all over the country, and occasionally—very occasionally—making a speech at some notable gathering. On these occasions he made it clear that he was permanently enlisted in the fight for tariff reform, ballot reform, civil-service reform. In an interview just before the 1890 elections he spoke of "the positive distress daily threatening our people's homes under the operation of a new and iniquitous tariff law and other reckless enactments that stifle the results of the people's suffrage," and then declared that "the party that knew no discouragement in 1888 will not waver nor falter in 1890," which was a pretty clear indication that Mr. Cleveland himself would not "waver nor falter" if asked to lead his party again in 1892.

As a matter of fact, the popular party sentiment was as overwhelmingly strong for him as the Hill-Gorman brand of party leader was emphatically, bitterly, determinedly against him. Both Hill and Gorman were candidates for the nomination. Hill, hating Cleveland at all times, had carried New York for governor in 1888 by 19,000, while Cleveland had lost the State by 14,000, and he was in control of the State organization. Gorman, who had been the Cleveland leader in the 1888 convention, had turned against him and, on the strength of his Force Bill record and his powerful New York connections, felt that if Cleveland could be sidetracked he might get away with the prize. And there were others who, foreseeing party victory, had their Presidential aspirations and hopes.

Under the circumstances, the success of Cleveland, without power or organization, in securing the nomination was a tremendous tribute to the personality of the man and to his hold on the rank and file of the party. And of course his election was an utterly unprecedented restoration, putting him in a class by himself as the only man in the country's history to serve once as President, to be defeated for reelection, and to be then triumphantly put back in the White House. It was an amazing and unparalleled performance, made the more remarkable by the fact that once again he met head-on an issue his friends urged him to avoid and which he was told made his nomination impossible.

This was the free coinage of silver issue, which was just then taking deep hold on the party West and South, and which was beginning to acquire the proportions of a popular wave. Yet in February, 1891, Mr. Cleveland wrote a letter to a friend in which he said:

It surely cannot be necessary for me to make a formal expression of my agreement with those who believe that the greatest peril would be invited by the adoption of the scheme, embraced in the measure now pending in Congress, for the unlimited coinage of silver at our mints.

If we have developed an unexpected capacity for the assimilation of a largely increased volume of this currency, and even if we have demonstrated the usefulness of such an increase, these conditions fall far short of insuring us against disaster if, in the present situation, we enter upon the dangerous and reckless experiment of free, unlimited, and independent silver coinage.

At once the cry went up from the politicians in all sections, "That's the end of Grover." Indignation was particularly pronounced in the South, and while from the business men of the East his declaration was hailed as courageous and sound, denunciation was far more marked than praise. This was particularly gratifying to the eminent politicians in the party who were plotting to sidetrack him for the nomination, and who, by arousing his pugnacity and creating resentment among his friends, did more to put him in the fight than keep him out. Particularly was this true in New York, where the Hill-Croker-Murphy combination called the state convention at an absurdly early date in February in order to select delegates to the national convention free of Cleveland instructions. This so-called "snap" convention created intense indignation in the Cleveland following and resulted in the coming out by Mr. Cleveland in March as a candidate for the nomination, in the sense of being willing to fight if his party wanted him. His friends were, of course, at work not only in New York but in every other State, but his enemies were virulent and active and the Hill campaign for the nomination had strong political support.

A combination of anti-Cleveland senators, chief among them Gorman, was secretly behind the Hill movement, and when the national convention met, Mr. Cleveland was without support from his own State. By this time, however, it was clear that his nomination could not be stopped, that the Hill campaign, the snap convention, and the Tammany fight were all doomed to collapse. Gorman, who had been,

under cover, a serious candidate himself, was among
the first of the Hill leaders to grasp the facts and
promptly deserted the combination. William C.
Whitney, in charge of the Cleveland fight, had in
hand over 600 votes before the convention came to
order. They were for Cleveland because Cleveland
was the outstanding and towering party figure, the
logical and strongest man, the most powerful personality in the party. They were for Cleveland because
he was Cleveland, and the Tammany-Hill-New York
opposition made them more determinedly for him
than ever. There was but one ballot. The Cleveland
leaders listened for two hours to the great Tammany
orator, Bourke Cockran, while he eloquently attacked
Cleveland and lauded Hill. The reply to Mr. Cockran
was a demand to vote, and when the vote was taken
Cleveland had been named. The lone ballot was as
follows—

Whole number of votes.................909½
Number necessary for 2/3 majority......607
Grover Cleveland of New York..........617½
David B. Hill of New York.............114
Horace Boies of Iowa..................103
Arthur P. Gorman of Maryland........ 36½
Adlai E. Stevenson of Illinois........... 16½
John G. Carlisle of Kentucky............ 14
William R. Morrison of Illinois.......... 3
James E. Campbell of Ohio.............. 2
William C. Whitney of New York........ 1
William E. Russell of Massachusetts..... 1
Robert E. Pattison of Pennsylvania....... 1

It is interesting to note that, not having a single delegate from his own State, Mr. Cleveland had to be put in nomination by Governor Leon Abbett of New Jersey, not because of any enthusiasm upon his part for Cleveland—at heart he was a Hill man— but because his whole delegation was under Cleveland instructions. Adlai E. Stevenson of Illinois was named as the Vice-Presidential candidate, and the platform was long and comprehensive. An effort of the protection senators of the Gorman type to put into it a tariff plank vague and general in tone, with a half promise to continue a certain amount of protection, was the occasion of a violent debate on the floor, and the compromise was defeated by a vote of 564 to 342. The tariff plank as finally framed was clean cut and unequivocal, really reflecting the Cleveland attitude. It read:

We denounce the Republican protection as a fraud, a robbery of the great majority of the American people for the benefit of the few. We declare it to be a fundamental principle of the Democratic party that the federal government has no constitutional power to impose and collect tariff duties, except for the purposes of revenue only, and we demand that the collection of such taxes shall be limited to the necessities of the government when honestly and economically administered.

We denounce the McKinley tariff law enacted by the Fifty-first Congress as the culminating atrocity of class legislation; we indorse the efforts made by the Democrats of the present Congress to modify its most oppressive features in the direction of free raw materials and cheaper manufactured goods that enter into general consumption, and we promise its repeal as one of the beneficent results that will follow the action of the people in intrusting power to the Democratic party. Since the McKinley tariff went into operation, there have been ten reductions of the wages of laboring men to one increase. We deny that there has been any increase of prosperity to the country since that tariff went into operation, and we point to the dullness and distress, the wage reductions and strikes in the iron trade, as the best possible evidence that no such prosperity has resulted from the McKinley Act.

Once more the "sumptuary laws" were denounced as undemocratic; the Republican administration and the Republican convention, made up largely of Federal office-holders, were flayed, and a stand taken on a variety of specific measures, but the keynote was tariff reform. It had to be with Cleveland as a candidate. There is not space here to dwell much on the campaign, which was not particularly eventful. On the defensive from the start, the Republicans concentrated their hopes, their money, and their efforts largely on New York, which had held the balance of power in 1884 and 1888 and which it was reasonable to assume, with its thirty-six electoral votes, would again. They counted heavily on the Democratic split, the known hostility of Tammany to the Democratic ticket, the lukewarmness of the Irish vote, the disappointment of Governor Hill and his friends, and the financial support of the tariff-protected interests, whose fear of Cleveland was great.

At Mr. Cleveland's request, William C. Whitney, who had managed his convention fight, took charge of his campaign. From the start Mr. Whitney, a keen, clear-headed politician, bent his efforts upon conciliating Tammany, getting its leaders into line. Time and again he urged upon Mr. Cleveland the necessity of some friendly gesture toward them on his part, and was upset and even irritated at the reluctance of Mr. Cleveland to make such a gesture. He really despised them. Finally, after much persuasion, Mr. Cleveland consented to meet Croker, Sheehan (Blue-Eyed Billy), and Murphy. It took a good deal of pressure from all sides to get him to go to a private "reconciliation" dinner to meet these men at the old Victoria Hotel, but he went. It was a dramatic business, the sort of thing that happens in political fiction, but very, very seldom in real political life. Dr. McElroy tells the story in his book "Grover Cleveland—the Man and the Statesman."

When the dinner ended and the hour for discussion arrived, he turned to the expectant machine men and said, "Well, gentleman, what do you want?"

"We want pledges from you," replied Mr. Sheehan. "We want to know what you are going to do if you are elected. We want you to give us promises that will satisfy us that the organization will be properly recognized if you become President again."

Mr. Cleveland doubled up his huge fist and smote the table.

"Gentlemen," he said, speaking slowly and with almost painful distinctness, "I will not go into the White House pledged to you or to anyone else. I will make no secret promises. I'll be damned if I will."

Again the fist whacked the table.

"What are you going to do then?" inquired Mr. Sheehan cynically.

"I'll tell you what I'm going to do," said Mr. Cleveland as he rose to his feet. "I intend to address a letter to the public in which I shall withdraw from the ticket. I intend to explain my situation and to report what you have said to me here. I will tell the voters of the country that I cannot give any secret pledges, and that unless I do you will not support the Democratic ticket. I will tell the voters that I do not want to stand in the way of a Democratic victory. That is what I shall do. Then, gentlemen, you can pick out a candidate to suit you, and if he is a proper man and the candidate of the party I will vote for him."

There was a pause.

"But I'll tell you one thing, Mr. Sheehan," added Mr. Cleveland, as he turned to the now breathless lieutenant-governor, "in my opinion public indignation will snow you and your organization out of sight before the end of a week."

Mr. Croker leaped to his feet at this point, exclaiming: "This must stop, Mr. Sheehan; I agree with Mr. Cleveland. He cannot make any pledges and it is not right to ask him."

"Thus," says Dr. McElroy, "did Mr. Whitney's policy of conciliation conciliate by conquering, and Grover Cleveland again faced the election a free man." Even at this late day there is a thrill in merely reading about the sturdy honesty and courage of him as illustrated in this incident, the authenticity of which is beyond question. There have been so few, so amazingly few, who had that sort of courage under that sort of condition.

He won a perfectly astonishing victory. He carried every doubtful State and would have won this time if he had lost New York, which, however, he carried by more than 45,000 plurality. His total electoral vote was 277 against 145 for Harrison; his total popular vote 5,556,543, against 5,175,582. With him went in not only a Democratic House but a

Democratic Senate. For the first time in thirty-two years the Democratic party was in full control of the Government, with not only the President but a clear working majority in both branches of Congress. It was as complete a victory as could be won. It was one of the high moments in the life of the party. That the ensuing four years were to be more economically and politically tempestuous and turbulent than any since the Civil War, and that they should end in another crushing defeat—preceded by a party split that was second only to the slavery split in its disastrous effects, keeping the party out of power for sixteen solid years—could of course not be foreseen, and for a while Democrats everywhere gave themselves up to rejoicing.

So far as the party is concerned, the four years following the great 1892 Cleveland victory were beyond doubt the most pregnant and important in the whole party history, save only the war periods. Packed with events of far-reaching public and political significance, they stand out as in a class by themselves, and immediately preceded the second great Democratic smash-up. In 1860 it was the slavery rock upon which the party split; in 1896 it was the free-silver issue that wrecked it. The first smash drove it out of power and kept it out for a generation. The second opened wide a jagged wound that was sixteen years healing sufficiently to permit the election of another Democratic President. And while the party has been twice successful since, while it has been responsible for two of the most remarkable and constructive administrations in the whole history of the country, administrations filled with events to which Democrats can properly "point with pride" —in spite of this, it has not yet fully recovered from that second historic smash. Certain highly deleterious effects persist to this day.

One of these is its disposition to continue sectionally divided, South and West against East, to view issues from different angles. Another, as a result of its long adherence to the free-silver heresy, is the banking tendency to regard the party as "unsafe" from the business standpoint. Notwithstanding the economic soundness and sanity of the Wilson administration, the stain on the party's financial record of those free-silver years is still recalled, and the natural inclination of the big business interests to regard the Republican party as their own was undoubtedly strengthened. Those years—from 1892 to 1896—marked the beginning of the great struggle between the free-silver and sound-money forces, in which the real leaders were William Jennings Bryan and Grover Cleveland, the real fight made by Democrats, the real and only political beneficiary the Republicans. Once again the Democrats beat themselves, but once again it was the Democratic party that really grappled with the issue and forced it to a conclusion. It was typical of their difference in emotional capacity and of the better discipline of the Republicans that the great silver movement, which

315

operated in both parties, should have split widest the Democrats, and through the courageous resistance of a Democratic President, whose record as an advocate of the gold standard was consistent and clean cut, should have resulted in the election of a Republican President—William McKinley—who had been on both sides of the questions and whose convictions, like those of his party, were more a matter of political expediency than of deep belief.

Chapter XXIII

CLEVELAND'S SOUND MONEY FIGHT

The Tariff Battle and the Gorman Treachery—The
Smash of the Party on the Free Silver Rock—Cleve-
land Retires Under Unprecedented Abuse but
Undismayed

BUT to pick up again the thread: when Mr. Cleveland took hold after his second election he found the
country on the verge of financial panic. The storm
broke soon after he was inaugurated, and from then
until the last of 1893 the business depression and
general economic distress were as intense as at any
period in the past, and have not been greater at any
period since. Failures of banks and business houses
occurred by the scores in all sections and there was a
general crash in values. Soup kitchens and charity
organizations did their best to relieve the situation,
but the widespread unemployment was accompanied
by acute suffering among the poor and there was
general discontent.

Affairs became very much worse by an extraordinary outbreak of labor-capital clashes in various
States. There were during the four years approximately two hundred strikes of one sort or another.

The chief of these was the Pullman strike in Chicago, which was accompanied by great violence, and which was quelled by the sending of Federal troops to the scene regardless of the protest of Altgeld, the Illinois governor. Mr. Cleveland acted in that case with characteristic courage. He was a strong advocate of arbitration, but when the strikers interfered with the United States mails he acted quickly and effectively. At least that was the pretext on which he sent the troops. Actually, it was a situation which bordered on anarchy, and but for his decisive and swift steps might have got terribly out of hand.

But Chicago was only the center of a disease that seemed to have spread to all sections. The whole country seethed with trouble, and there has been no peace-time period in which the problems of the executive were as harassing and heavy. It has been the custom of Republican partisans, both writers of history and players of politics, to attribute all the turbulency of the Cleveland administration, the disasters that befell the business of the country, the unemployment and the labor difficulties, to the Democratic party. In the following campaign all of these things were laid at the Democratic door, and the chief plea of the Republican politicians was that the election of their ticket meant a return of prosperity, that Democratic administrations are accompanied by "hard times," that all the suffering and trouble of the past four years were due to the dreadful mistake of having elected a Democrat in 1892. And there is no question that in that campaign, as in others, they impressed the people with this view and swung a lot of votes.

One reason they were able to do so was, of course, the tendency of the public to blame the party in power for whatever unpleasant conditions occur while it is in the saddle, without having either the desire or the intellectual capacity to go back to the "real responsibles." The other was the fact, then as now, that the control of the Republicans over the channels of publicity was greater than that of the Democrats, and their propaganda far more elaborate and skilfully planted and developed. The truth, of course, was that the Republican party had sown the wind and the Democratic party reaped the whirlwind. The basic causes for the general economic upheaval in the second Cleveland administration, it is pretty generally agreed by thinking persons, were three in number, for all of which the Republican party, in power almost continuously for thirty-two years, was responsible.

The chief of these was the disordered condition of the currency, which for a long time had threatened collapse, and to the straightening of which no real thought had been given. Another was unquestionably the free-silver legislation enacted by the Republicans in order to placate the militant free-silver sentiment in their party, and as a result of the characteristic straddles on monetary issues made in their platforms. The passage of the Sherman Silver

Purchase Law was a piece of economic unsoundness that was bound to result disastrously. It was done deliberately by the Republican party in response to the demand that "something ought to be done for silver" and for reasons of pure political expediency. Every clear-headed economist in the country regarded it with abhorrence.

Still another reason was the McKinley Tariff Law, which had jacked rates up to an unprecedented height and which beyond question added greatly to the cost of living. The panic began before Mr. Cleveland had got fairly settled in the White House, before he or his party had had so much as a chance to initiate a policy or propose a reform. When retiring from office at the end of his first term, Mr. Cleveland turned over to Harrison a cash balance of $281,000,000, of which $196,689,614 was in gold. When he came back four years later Harrison turned over to him only $112,450,577, of which $103,500,000 was in gold, and this gold reserve would certainly have been below the $100,000,000 mark, fixed by the act of July 12, 1882, as the danger point, had not the Harrison secretary of the treasury obtained several million dollars in gold from greenbacks sold to New York banks for the sole purpose of keeping the gold reserve above the $100,000,000 limit.

Doubt of the stability of the Government had begun to be felt in the last days of the Harrison administration, and Mr. Cleveland clearly saw that the deluge was bound to come unless some way could be found to change the direction of the financial forces. At once the pressure upon him to call an extra session of Congress began, but Cleveland, to the great vexation of the eastern bankers, did not act hastily. Their feeling was well expressed by a circular issued by one firm, which said: "The actual intrinsic value of our present silver dollar is but fifty-three cents and growing less each day. Still this great American nation is obliged to calmly face inevitable ruin— the sweeping away of far more wealth than was involved in the great war between the North and the South, simply because its representatives are not called together, in accordance with the authority vested in its Chief Executive, and forced to remove from the Statute Books the law which is eating away the vitals of American honesty."

In his own time—August, 1893—Mr. Cleveland called Congress into session and made the repeal of the Sherman law the first item in his program for currency reform. His message, composed under great difficulties following his recovery from an operation to remove a malignant growth on the roof of his mouth which threatened his life, and all knowledge of which was kept from the public for fear of its effect on the situation, had in it the real Cleveland ring. It was the first gun in the fight for sound money and against free silver. It charged that the unfortunate financial plight of the country was directly and principally chargeable to congressional legislation touching the purchase and coinage of silver by the general Government, and it flatly demanded the prompt repeal of the Sherman act of 1890. It said in part:

> Our government cannot make its fiat equivalent to intrinsic value, nor keep inferior money on a parity with superior money. . . .
> The people of the United States are entitled to a sound and stable currency, and to money recognized as such on every exchange and in every market of the world. Their government has no right to injure them by financial experiments opposed to the policy and practice of other civilized states.

This message, which was hailed with joy by the business interests in the East and denounced unstintedly by the free-silver forces in the South and West, is significant not only because with it started a great fight that ultimately divided the Democratic party into two bitterly hostile camps, but it also made plain for the first time that the real leaders of the opposing sides in this fight were Mr. Cleveland against free silver and Mr. Bryan for it. The latter was at the time a member of the House of Representatives from Nebraska. He had been elected as a Democrat and was at all times willing and ready to defend the position that free silver was in entire harmony with the fundamental principles of the party.

On the other side, Mr. Cleveland believed that free silver was an economic heresy that directly clashed with the Democratic doctrine of sound money, and he did not regard the men who advocated free silver as Democrats. He regarded Mr. Bryan not as a Democrat but as a Populist. He was willing to concede his personal honesty but not his Democracy, and, as he expressed it, "Patriotism is no substitute for a sound currency."

Mr. Bryan on his side, after this message, felt that Mr. Cleveland was a "tool of Wall Street," a "creature of the British Government," who had betrayed his party. He had been in favor of Mr. Cleveland's nomination in 1884 and 1888, but opposed him in the 1892 convention because of the utterly uncompromising hostility of Mr. Cleveland to the free-silver idea. From the delivery of the message on, Cleveland and Bryan were as wide apart as the poles. To either one the other was the reverse of a Democrat, and, as the months passed, it became manifestly absurd for the same party to harbor both.

With his eloquence, magnetism, and force, Bryan easily took his place as one of the free-silver leaders in Congress, and his speeches in the House during this fight made him a hero to the silverites all over the country, gave him a status and standing that put him in position for the 1896 national convention by which the "stampede" to him was made possible. Though the odds were against him in both House and Senate, Mr. Cleveland won his fight to stem the silver tide, but to do so he had to use every ounce of weight in the Federal administration.

It was an even more bitter contest in the Senate

than in the House, and in both the free-silver advocates were in an actual majority. Party lines broke down under the impact of the forces, and when it was over and the law repealed it was clear that a greater struggle lay ahead in which a good many political bones would be broken. The party significance of the repeal fight is best summarized by Woodrow Wilson, then a professor at Princeton, who, writing in the "Atlantic Monthly" four years later, said:

It was the President's victory that the law was at last repealed and everyone knew it. He had forced the consideration of the question; he had told Senators plainly, almost passionately, when they approached him, that he would accept no compromise,—that he would veto anything less than absolute repeal, and let them face the country as best they might afterwards. Until he came on the stage, both parties had dallied and coquetted with the advocates of silver. Now he had brought both to a parting of the ways. The silver men were forced to separate themselves and look their situation in the face, choose which party they should plan to bring under their will and policy, if they could, and no longer camp in the tents of both.

Such a stroke settled what the course of Congressional politics should be throughout the four years of Mr. Cleveland's term, and made it certain that at the end of that term he should either have won his party to himself or lost it altogether. It was evident that any party that rejected the gold standard for the currency must look upon him as its opponent.

The result, of course, as Mr. Wilson knew when he wrote the above, was that the Cleveland victory only temporarily halted the free-silver movement;

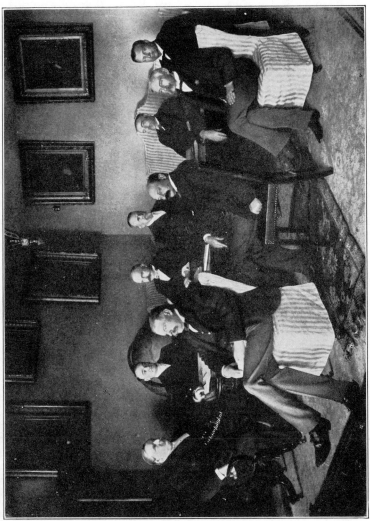

GROVER CLEVELAND'S CABINET—1893-1897

that the free-silver forces, led by Bryan, concentrated on the Democratic party, bent it to their will, and controlled it; that Mr. Cleveland, regarding Mr. Bryan as a Populist and being regarded by Mr. Bryan as a devil, was repudiated by the Bryan-Silver party in 1896, and went out of office execrated and denounced by those who had seized party control and their followers. One of the most interesting things in party history is that sixteen years later this same Woodrow Wilson, who was in complete accord with the Cleveland financial policy and who hated the free-silver theory too, should have been nominated for President—and elected—with the help of Bryan, who later entered the Wilson cabinet as secretary of state. Sixteen years is not a long time in politics, but no one on earth in 1896 could have dreamed of those happenings in 1912.

While there were much more spectacular things in the two Cleveland administrations than this currency fight, there was none so important and far-reaching in the effect on the party—or on the nation. It is certainly at least probable that if it had not been for Mr. Cleveland the country would have embarked on the free-silver experiment, with what disastrous results it is not pleasant even now to contemplate. The Cleveland fight, while it proved only a temporary check to the movement, did two big things—first, it made it impossible for his own party to win the election after it had been taken over by the free-silver Mr. Bryan and committed to an extraordinary economic heresy; second, it made it politically expedient for the Republican party, which dealt with this question as with most others largely from the standpoint of political expediency, to declare flatly and firmly for the gold standard instead of trimming, pussy-footing, hiding, and hedging as it had been doing on this issue for nearly twenty years.

That was, beyond all doubt, the greatest of the Cleveland fights, the climax of his public service. It would, however, be unforgivable to close the account of Mr. Cleveland's administration without touching upon two other of its outstanding features, both of which are important not only to national history but to party history. One of these is, of course, the Venezuelan incident, in which Mr. Cleveland, a Democratic President, expounded and applied the Monroe Doctrine—laid down by one of his Democratic predecessors and generally accepted as the bedrock American policy in foreign affairs—more dramatically, boldly, and effectively than it has ever been expounded and applied. Monroe and Jefferson created the policy; Cleveland used it. It is of course impossible here to give the details of the Venezuelan affair, which are, besides, too well known. All that is necessary to say is that the Cleveland message on the subject, which is his most famous state paper, was due to the idea that to settle the century-old boundary dispute between Venezuela and Great Britain, the latter was about to seize the disputed territory in order to establish the British contention.

The keynote of the message is found in these words, which are bound to be treasured by those interested in the story of the Democratic party, because few Presidential utterances have had a bolder ring, or a more electrical effect upon the nation:

The answer of the British Government . . . claims that . . . a new and strange extension and development of this [the Monroe] doctrine is insisted on by the United States; . . . that the reasons justifying an appeal to the doctrine . . . are inapplicable. . . .

If a European power by an extension of its boundaries takes possession of the territory of one of our neighboring republics against its will and in derogation of its rights . . . this is the precise action which President Monroe declared to be "dangerous to our peace and safety," and it can make no difference whether the European system is extended by an advance of frontier or otherwise. . . .

The dispute has reached such a stage as to make it now incumbent on the United States to take measures to determine . . . the true division line between the Republic of Venezuela and British Guiana. . . . When such report is made . . . it will . . . be the duty of the United States to resist by every means in its power . . . the appropriation by Great Britain of any lands . . . which after investigation we have determined of right belong to Venezuela.

In making these recommendations I am fully alive to the responsibility incurred and keenly realize all the consequences that may follow. . . There is no calamity which a great nation can invite which equals that which follows a supine submission to wrong.

The unmistakable meaning of this, the unequivocal words, the startling lack of the soft verbiage of diplomatic usage, its complete finality and utterly implacable character, created a most tremendous sensation at home and abroad. It might have meant war, and everybody realized it—best of all, of course, Cleveland. In the end he achieved what is perhaps our greatest diplomatic victory. The conduct of the English Government and the English people in a particularly delicate and trying situation was dignified, admirable, fine; but it is none the less true that they yielded in the face of that unbending, uncompromising, unshakable, heroic old fellow in the White House. Whatever else may be said of him, he was certainly all man. Nobody bossed him and nobody bluffed him.

The other feature of his last administration above referred to was the fight over the Wilson-Gorman Tariff Law. Immediately after the repeal of the Sherman act, Mr. Cleveland plunged into the fight to redeem his tariff-reform pledge. There was a certain amount of party opposition in the House, but the Wilson bill, embodying the Cleveland ideas, repealing the McKinley law, reducing rates all along the line, putting wool, iron ore, and sugar on the free list, aroused resentment, and the fight was not easy. Still, it went through that body by a vote of 180 to 106, the Tammany Congressmen, strange to relate, under orders from Croker, supporting the President's policy and voting with him. It was in the Senate that the bill hit the rock upon which it was wrecked.

Cleveland's Sound Money Fight

There the interests stood intrenched. There the senators who represented these interests were able to make themselves felt. There, under Gorman of Maryland, a small group of Southern Democrats opposed the Cleveland-Wilson bill, and rendered nonexistent an administrative majority. In New York, Alabama, West Virginia, Louisiana, Pennsylvania, Delaware, and elsewhere there were powerful business interests that demanded special consideration. In order to get what they wanted for their own States, senators were willing to give other senators what they wanted for theirs. It was easy for Gorman, a protectionist at heart, and who was on terms of close personal and political friendship with the great financial figures back of the McKinley tariff, to cluster around him enough Democrats in the Senate to hold the balance of power.

Seeing clearly his game from the start, Cleveland hated and despised him. Though Gorman had practically managed one of his campaigns and had represented him in one national convention, Mr. Cleveland had had no use for him personally or politically since about 1888. There were now no relations of any sort between them. In the end the Gorman group and the Republicans so emasculated the Wilson bill that it was literally unrecognizable. The special interests did not get all they wanted. They did not dare try, but they got enough to make the bill a farce so far as being a real and a full redemption of the Democratic platform pledge was concerned. Branded by the President as guilty of "party perfidy and dishonor," the Gorman group refused to give an inch, forced the House in conference to take the emasculated bill or get nothing, defeated Cleveland and repudiated the platform pledge, dealt their party a blow below the belt. The bill became a law without Mr. Cleveland's signature. He was so disgusted with it that he would not give it sanction by signing, yet he could not veto without depriving the country of the relatively small reductions of the McKinley tariff it contained.

As 1896 approached, Mr. Cleveland determined that his own public career would end when he went out of office. Realizing the strength of the party drift toward free silver, convinced of the dreadful consequences to the party and to the country in the free-coinage-sixteen-to-one theory, he unquestionably felt that the most imperative duty that remained for him was to combat the silver movement both within and without the party. Accordingly he lost no opportunity to sound his warning. In letters to his friends and in his public pronouncements he pointed out that to permit the free-silver element to control the party was to wreck it. One of the strongest of these, quoted in Dr. McElroy's book, was to Governor Stone of Mississippi, written on April 26, 1895, and turned out to be an absolutely accurate analysis of the political situation. In it he said:

If we, who profess fealty to the Democratic party, are sincere in our devotion to its principles, and if we are right

330

in believing that the ascendancy of those principles is a guarantee of personal liberty, universal care for the rights of all, non-sectional, American brotherhood and manly trust in American citizenship in any part of our land, we should study the effects upon our party and consequently upon our country of a committal of the national democracy to this silver aberration.

If there are Democrats who suppose that our party can succeed upon a platform embodying such a doctrine, either through its affirmative strength or through the perplexity of our opponents upon the same proposition, or if there are Democrats who are willing to turn their backs upon their party associations in the hope that free, unlimited and independent coinage of silver can win a victory without the aid of either party organization, they should deceive themselves no longer, nor longer refuse to look in the face the results that will follow the defeat, if not the disintegration of the Democratic party upon the issue which tempts them from their allegiance. If we should be forced away from our traditional doctrine of sound and safe money, our old antagonists will take the field on the platform which we abandon, and neither the votes of reckless Democrats nor reckless Republicans will avail to stay their easy march to power.

That tells the story better than anything else. From that point on the struggle between the factions in the party grew more bitter every day. Cleveland clung to the hope that the 1896 convention might after all be controlled by the sound money forces, but it was a slender hope and not well founded. For twenty years this free-silver craze had been in both parties. For twenty years it had been, as Mr. Wilson pointed out, trifled with by both parties. For twenty years the Republicans in Congress and in their platforms had straddled and ducked it, compromised in legislation and faced both ways in campaigns. It was the unifying bond of the more or less new Populist party that had arisen, and which was now represented in Congress by several senators and a considerable group of representatives—all of them full-fledged free-silver men.

It was Cleveland who took the free-silver theory by the throat and forced a show-down. It was his flat-footed, uncompromising opposition to it, his indictment of it as a dangerous and degrading fallacy, and his declaration that it was abhorrent to the sound-money principles of the Democratic party, that split that party and made it safe for the cautious and convictionless Republican leaders to swing their party to the sound-money side. There isn't any possible doubt that Cleveland, more than any other man, won the sound-money fight, avoided the danger of the free-silver experiment. And, no matter what his course did to his party, it certainly served the country. There is no doubt, either, that he believed his fight not only for the good of the country but of the party as well. "We can," he wrote, "survive as a party without immediate success at the polls, but I do not think we can survive if we have fastened upon us as an authoritative declaration of party policy the free coinage of silver."

He was wrong about that. The party survived both of those things and came back; but he was right in his conviction that it would split it wide open in the 1896 campaign and that the Republicans

"BEFORE THE CRIME OF '73
THIS IS THE ONLY KIND OF MONEY LITTLE WILLIE BRYAN
EVER SAW IN 'THE GOOD OLD FREE COINAGE DAYS'"

This was one of the numerous anti-Bryan cartoons of the 1896
campaign

would take advantage of the split. That Mr. Cleveland's attitude and views were extremely influential in molding the Republican policy on the financial issue is attested by an abundance of evidence. It is, for example, contended by Dr. McElroy, who cites some convincing facts, that the communication of Cleveland's political and financial views, and the certainty that a sound-money policy would gain for the Republicans the support of the Cleveland Democrats, colored the whole Republican convention, and had not a little to do with switching William McKinley from soft money to hard money. Mr. Cleveland literally left nothing undone to stem the tide, but it was a hopeless fight and he recognized it long before the convention met.

The party was in the hands of its new leaders, chief among them the eloquent and earnest Bryan, who vibrated with a holy zeal for the free-silver theory, and who, in Congress and out, assailed the gold standard as an English policy which Wall Street sought to fasten on the people, and of whom Mr. Cleveland was the pliant tool. South and West the country seemed ablaze with free-silver enthusiasm, and plainly there was no checking the advance. In the face of the most extraordinary abuse, Mr. Cleveland kept up the fight to the very day of the convention. To his friend Don M. Dickinson he wrote, on June 10:

I believe I am by nature an undismayed and persistent fighter and I do not believe in giving an inch until we are obliged to; and yet it is hard to call on friends to maintain a struggle which seems so hopeless. It does not seem to me that there should be any relaxation in the effort to prevent our party from entering upon a course which means its retirement for many years to come. If we cannot succeed in checking the desperate rush, perhaps a demonstration can be made which will indicate that a large section of the party is not infected. I don't know how this can best be done, but I very much desire that we shall not all have to hang our heads when our party is accused of free silverism. Of course I have never seen anything like this craze before, but my faith in the American people is so great that I cannot believe they will cast themselves over the precipice. But there is our old party with its glorious traditions and all its achievements in the way of safe and conservative policies, and its exhibitions of indestructibility. Is it to founder on the rocks? Will not sanity return before we reach the final plunge? While I am not completely discouraged, I confess the way looks dark.

It was this sort of appeal, backed by the weight of the President, that made the silver forces hate him above all other men, and when the convention met in Chicago, on July 7, the bitterness toward Mr. Cleveland was terrific. Controlled completely by the free-silver leaders, entirely in the grip of the craze, the convention practically read Mr. Cleveland out of his party. It adopted a platform demanding the free and unlimited coinage of both silver and gold at the ratio of sixteen to one, without waiting for the consent of any other nation; it refused to commend the Cleveland administration, rejecting a resolution offered by David B. Hill, who knew perfectly well it would be rejected; it nominated William Jennings Bryan, who held Mr. Cleveland a traitor and a "servant of the interests" and whom Mr. Cleveland regarded as a gifted but misguided Populist with no claim whatever to be called a Democrat.

No President was ever so completely repudiated by the party that elected him, not even Tyler by the Whigs nor Johnson by the Republicans. The abuse was astonishing. During the campaign that followed the Democratic convention and the nomination of Mr. Bryan, Mr. Cleveland took no part. His heart was with the sound-money Democrats, who held their convention in Indianapolis, nominated Palmer and Buckner, declared for the gold standard, denounced the free-silver "aberration," indorsed the Cleveland policies, highly praised Cleveland the man and the President. His heart was with these sound-money Democrats, but he was far too clear headed and practical to think the Palmer-Buckner ticket had any chance of winning. Though debarred by his sense of the dignity of his office and his position as the party President from making a public pronouncement, there is no doubt that he wanted McKinley elected, great as was his distrust of the Republican party and his hatred of its other policies. To him this question of sound money was greater than party, and when the Bryan defeat came he unquestionably rejoiced.

Four months later he went out of the White House, respected, loved, and admired by those who knew him best and appreciated the courage and character of the man, but denounced and derided by the

Democratic press and politicians with unprecedented violence. One orator declared him to have "the ignominious distinction of being the only American President to accumulate millions during his term of office." "The Atlanta Constitution" editorially said: "Grover Cleveland will go out under a greater burden of popular contempt than has ever been excited by a public man since the foundation of the Government." Said "The Kansas City Times": "The Democratic party, which he deceived, betrayed and humiliated, long ago stamped him as a political leper and cast him out as unclean."

Another paper declared "the reproaches and contumely of the entire American people accompany him into retirement." But neither the abuse, which he felt keenly, nor his repudiation by the party under control of the Bryan wing, changed Mr. Cleveland's conviction as to the righteousness of his course. The fight was one he had to make and there can be no doubt that the victory was his.

In the end it has come to be that the thing for which he was most fiercely hated at the time is the thing that now stands out as his most enduring monument. The unsuccessful fight he made within his party to keep it away from the free-silver heresy was the noblest fight of his eight years as party leader and President, every one of which was a fighting year. Long before he died, the party swung back, and would in all probability have nominated him again in 1904 had he not decisively checked the movement in words that could not be misunderstood and allowed of but one interpretation. Time so completely vindicated Grover Cleveland, both as a Democrat and as a President, and his place in history is so high and secure as both, that the violence of the fulminations against him in 1896—and 1900 too— seem at this distance absurd and exaggerated. But they were neither at the time.

Chapter XXIV

His Remarkable Domination of the Party—Character
and Caliber of the Man—His Responsibility for the
Democratic Reputation of Economic Unsoundness

IN some ways William Jennings Bryan's is the most singular figure in the whole singular Democratic story. In some ways the part he played in party history was the most extraordinary of any individual who has been called or who ever called himself a Democrat. In some ways his party dominance and its effect on his times were more unusual and extensive than that of any other. In some ways he was absolutely unique in American politics. No other man ever approached his political power as a private citizen.

He never led his party in a successful battle; he split it into two utterly irreconcilable factions; he was three times overwhelmingly beaten as a candidate for the Presidency; he never reached his personal goal, or held, except for his brief career as secretary of state, high official place; he was without financial, journalistic, or organization support. Yet, not more than three others in the whole party history wielded so potent an influence in its affairs for as long a time, had as large or as blindly devoted a party following, remained a factor in so many of its national conventions, flavored with their views more of its platforms.

For thirty years—from 1894 to 1924—he was a force to be reckoned with, for nearly half of that time a dominant and controlling force; during all of it an influence that heavily counted; for two thirds of it the most powerful unofficial individual in the United States in his ability to influence public opinion and sway the masses. He was an amazing man. Not really able nor even clear headed, lacking capacity either as a thinker or as an executive, not broad or big and with none of the qualities of a statesman, he was none the less without parallel in the power of his personal appeal to the people. By nature an evangelist and a crusader, with a great, musical, vibrant voice wonderfully fashioned for political purposes, a powerful and impressive physique, a great gift for simple and graphic expression, an almost matchless eloquence, an inner fire that burned and blazed, and a courage that did not falter, his political convictions were religious in their depth and intensity and his political attitude toward the toiling masses of his fellow-men was that of a Messiah.

Fiercely denounced as a humbug and fraud, a mountebank, a demagogue, a faker, and a fool, the truth about Mr. Bryan seems to be that he was a fundamentally and deeply religious man, with great natural gifts, a powerful and magnetic personality, but a somewhat cloudy mind, whose undoubted sincerity was marked by occasional selfish political lapses, who would have willingly died rather than sacrifice his principles—or at least thought that he would—almost but not quite noble, unquestionably narrow, just as unquestionably moral, but with a clearer conception, a closer kinship, and a surer knowledge of the common people, of whom he was certainly one, than any other man in politics in a hundred years.

They did not—the people—for a good many reasons elect him to office, but they gave him his power, and they made it possible for him not only to direct the destinies of the Democratic party over a long period of years, but helped to force into the Constitution of his country amendments that have not only vastly altered political conditions but actually changed the conditions of life itself within the nation. For example, whether they would have been eventually adopted or not, it is generally conceded that Mr. Bryan's was the strongest individual force behind the income tax amendment, the direct election of senators amendment, the woman suffrage amendment, and the prohibition amendment. All four of these might have been ratified without him. On the other hand, one or more of them might have failed. It is impossible to tell about that but it is equally impossible to deny that the Bryan voice and the Bryan crusade did more to put them over than any other single agency. In the course of his life—

up to the development of the radio—Mr. Bryan personally addressed more people and more came directly under the spell of his voice than any other man in the country not only of his generation but of any generation. He was the greatest talker of all time.

As to the character of his influence and leadership on the Democratic party no man in all its history, save only the little group that smashed it up on the slavery rock, has done it so much damage, swung it so far away from its moorings, divided it so deeply and disastrously. Prior to 1860 it was the slavery question that caused that most deadly of all divisions in a political party—along geographical lines on a moral issue. It took some sixteen years for the party to regain its health after 1860, but in the Tilden campaign it once more assumed the proportions of a really national party, whose members in all sections were agreed on basic economic issues.

It remained that sort of party, with two victories to its credit, until 1896. It was Mr. Bryan who then divided it, again along geographical lines, on the silver issue, which, though economic at base, he made, as he made all issues, moral in effect. In his subsequent campaigns he widened and deepened this sectional division between South and West on the one hand and East on the other. He clung to his silver issue long after it was dead, and when it completely disappeared turned to others equally sectional in their appeal. Under his guidance the party held New

York and the East as the "enemy's country." His anti-trust and government ownership of railroads campaigns were aimed against this section, designed to be popular in South and West.

Aside from the economic weaknesses of his issues, the political fallacy was in the idea of winning without New York and the small group of pivotal States that swing with it. A Democratic electoral majority is almost impossible without them. Such a majority has been obtained only twice since the war, once by the veriest fluke, not likely to be duplicated. Of course, in prohibition, to which he devoted himself in his later years with flaming enthusiasm, Mr. Bryan found an issue even more sectional in its appeal than that of free silver. Just as it was his influence and leadership in 1896 and 1900 that swung the party away from its fundamental principle of sound money, so it was his influence and leadership that divided it geographically on prohibition, utterly abandoning its basic tenets of States' rights, personal liberty, and opposition to "sumptuary laws."

It seems to be true that it was Mr. Bryan more than any one else who turned the Democratic party definitely into a minority party. Up to 1896 it could not be so classed. Even immediately after the war, when the situation in the South was such as to utterly preclude any chance of an electoral majority, the Democrats polled from 42 to 48 per cent. of the popular vote, and, beginning with the Tilden-Hayes election in 1876, they consistently polled a majority.

Tilden had a clear popular majority, and Cleveland had the best of the popular vote in all three of his fights. Even in 1880 Hancock was less than 10,000 votes short of a majority in a total of 9,000,000. In not a single one of the eight Presidential elections held since 1896 has the party had a majority of the popular vote; in only two has it had a plurality— the 1912 and 1916 Wilson elections. It has, since the free-silver split, been definitely the minority party, forced to depend for success on a schism in the opposition coinciding with party unity in itself. Twice only in thirty-two years have those conditions prevailed.

When in 1896 Mr. Bryan seized the party leadership and swung it away on the free-silver fallacy, he drove into the Republican party a vast number of northern and eastern men who were real Democrats at heart, who hated the protective-tariff policy of the Republicans, who distrusted and disliked the Republican party, but who felt that the Democratic party under false leaders had abandoned its sound foundations and could not under existing conditions be trusted to administer the Government. By his continued dominance of the party situation and by the persistency with which he held to and pushed his economic theories, Mr. Bryan increased the number of these deserting Democrats and made it impossible for them to come back.

Sixteen years of this sort of experience confirmed the habit of these former Democrats of voting the

Republican ticket in national elections. In state and off-year congressional elections they voted—and still do—Democratic, but in the Presidential years a large proportion of them have become confirmed Republicans. The Bryan era left the Democratic party with a reputation of being economically unsound. It increased the tendency of the big business interests to support the Republicans. It increased the number of Republican and decreased the number of Democratic newspapers. It threw the weight of the great banks and railroads and money in the scales against it. It gave the other side unparalleled material and facilities for effective propaganda. It has made the Republicans clearly the majority party and enabled them to control the Government for thirty-two years, with the exception of the eight Wilson years, in which a stronger personality than Mr. Bryan's overshadowed his figure and gave to the party new virility, character, color, substance, and stamina.

But with the passing of Wilson the party became again afflicted with the Bryan blight. Bryan was no longer a dominant figure or a controlling influence, but he was a convention factor in 1920 and 1924. He still had a following in the South and West. He still had the ear of a lot of Democrats in the small towns. He was still a hero and an idol in the Daytons. He still had enough force left to flavor the platform in the last national convention and to get his brother on the ticket for Vice-President with the Presidential candidate he had unsuccessfully opposed. And, though dead these two years, the sectional lines he drew and the sectional animosities he created still exist in the party. Nor have the Democrats he drove out come back.

A good many years ago a noted writer defined a political party as "a body of men joined together for the purpose of protecting by their joint endeavor the national interest upon some particular principle on which they are all agreed." Largely due to the direction in which Mr. Bryan led it, the Democratic party is no longer a party in this sense. It not only has no unifying issue on which all Democrats agree, but upon the one vital and vibrant issue of the day —prohibition—it is sectionally cleft and without visible hope of harmony. But for the extraordinary record of the party in achieving victory when victory seems most remote; but for the strength of the Democratic state organizations and their remarkable off-year and local successes; but for the ever-present possibility of another Cleveland or Wilson rising to restore its national power and prestige; but for the inevitable crack that comes in the dominant party through too long tenure of office—but for these things, the Democrats would indeed be in a hopeless plight.

As it is, they have gone into every campaign since 1896 with the odds against them, and will undoubtedly do so in 1928. Twice they have won against odds through a combination of candidate and conditions. They are reasonably sure to win again soon or late, but that hopeful belief does not lessen appreciation of the damage done by Bryan, nor alter the fact that for the sectional division and lack of unifying principles which handicap it to-day he is largely responsible.

It is true the Republicans are also sectionally divided over the same issue, though not so deeply nor with such rancor. Always the conservative party takes these controversial questions less seriously than the liberal party. In addition, a division is not necessarily as deadly to election prospects in the majority as in the minority party. Finally, the regularity, frequency, and force with which Democratic national tickets have been defeated since the Civil War have had the effect of compelling Democratic politicians and political machines to look to state and city patronage for nourishment rather than to the Federal Government. The natural tendency is to make them regard local success in their individual States for their local tickets as more vital than success in the country for the national ticket. Playing politics from this angle has encouraged Democrats to fight in their national conventions and among themselves with a far more complete disregard of the effect on the national election than would be the case if their chances of victory in the Electoral College were greater.

As things are to-day, the professional Democratic politician is more interested in electing his state than his national ticket. The Republicans, who have had

the Federal patronage for forty-two of the last
sixty-eight years and whose state machines are
largely built on the Federal offices, are always more
concerned about the success of the national ticket
than the local ticket. The one party insists on sub-
ordinating national issues to local interests, the other
subordinates local issues in the interests of the national ticket. It is a curious state of affairs. It makes
of the Republicans a pussy-footing but successful
national party, and it gives to the Democrats state
governors, state legislatures and a representation in
Congress altogether out of proportion to their electoral vote. It makes, as has been pointed out, national
success for the Democrats hinge upon the development of an unusual leader, capable of polling Republican votes in the New York group of States,
aided by a rift in the Republican ranks—two things
that may happen when least expected. It makes impossible Democratic victory with an average man
under average conditions. And it is impossible to
study the political life of Mr. Bryan, and the party
record of his period, without reaching the conclusion that for the remarkable state of the Democratic
party to-day, for its present status of a sectionally
split minority party, the principal blame must rest
on this extraordinary man who so completely believed in himself, who was so sure that he and none
other was the savior of the Democracy, and who
regarded those who differed with him as sinister and
malign.

Chapter XXV

Repudiation of Cleveland—Bolt of the Sound-Money
Democrats—Bryan's Hold on Party Undisputed
After Election—His Insistence on Reaffirming Free
Silver Plank at Kansas City in 1900—Beaten Again

BUT to take up the thread: the strength of the free-
silver movement can be grasped when it is pointed
out that notwithstanding Mr. Cleveland's determined and insistent opposition and in spite of the
vigor with which the great metropolitan journals
and business interests of the East denounced it,
thirty Democratic state conventions in the spring of
1896 declared in favor of free coinage in the most
emphatic terms. Only fourteen were with the administration and for the gold standard. The sectional
division caused by the issue is shown by the fact
that the anti-silver States were New Hampshire,
Vermont, Maine, Massachusetts, Rhode Island, Connecticut, New York, New Jersey, Pennsylvania,
Delaware, Maryland, with Michigan, Wisconsin,
and Minnesota. The entire South and West was
silver; New England and the Middle Atlantic States
were opposed. Long before the convention met it was
clear the free-silver forces would control, but Mr.

348

Cleveland and the party leaders in the East hoped to the last that the free silverites would be restrained from going the limit and a flat free-silver declaration would be avoided.

It was a vain hope. The free-silver people were not only filled with belief in the righteousness and soundness of their cause, but they were also convinced that it was the one way to win the election. Their conviction was that the gold-standard attitude of the Republican party would alienate so many silver Republicans in the West that these normally Republican States would certainly be carried by a free-silver Democrat, more than compensating for any loss sustained in the East. It was a sad miscalculation, but when the 1896 convention assembled in Chicago it seemed logical enough. Moreover, there was at the time real ground for such belief. The Republican convention had already been held and, led by Senator Henry Teller of Colorado, the silver Republicans had bolted. Thirty-four delegates, including four senators and two members of Congress, with Senator Teller at their head, withdrew from the convention. No secret was made that they were headed toward the Democratic party if that party declared for free coinage of silver. Even before this, the issue had split the Prohibition party, one wing of which had gone over to the silver side, and it was perfectly well known that the Populist party and the National Silver party, postponing their conventions until after the Democrats, would accept the Democratic ticket as their own if the platform was a free-silver platform.

Take it all in all, it did look as if politically there was a real chance for victory on the silver issue. It was a delusion but it was strong enough to steamroller the gold-standard men in the convention, and the platform as adopted was unequivocally and emphatically in favor of free coinage of silver at the ratio of sixteen to one. The gold standard was denounced and the monetary issue was declared the paramount one. There was no straddling or hedging. They went the limit. The feature of the debate over the platform was the remarkable "cross of gold and crown of thorns" speech by Mr. Bryan, which aroused an unparalleled enthusiasm and undoubtedly brought about his nomination, though as he points out in his "Memoirs," he had considerable strength before the convention met, and had always believed he stood an excellent chance for the nomination. For over two years he had been working steadily toward it, and his name had been mentioned in that connection fairly widely in the southern and western press, though not in the East. There is no question about the greatness of the speech, and no question but that it nominated him. It was not, however, as he points out, spontaneous eloquence, but a very carefully planned and perfectly staged effort.

It is probable that if a ballot had been taken at the close of his speech he would have been nominated by a stampede, so extraordinary was its effect. The nominations were not made, however, until the following day, and on the first ballot the leading candidate was Richard P. Bland of Missouri, recognized in Congress—and by Mr. Bryan—as the real silver leader. He had 235 votes, Mr. Bryan 119. Some fifteen others received votes ranging from one to ninety-five. It was not until the fourth ballot that Bryan forged ahead and on the fifth that he was nominated. Arthur Sewall of Maine was made Vice-President and the deed was done. The Democratic party had changed hands, changed principles, changed leaders. It went farther than that—it repudiated its old leaders; it repudiated the Democratic administrations of Cleveland, it voted down a resolution of indorsement of the Democratic President. It kicked him and his friends and their principles out of the party. In the hall 178 sound-money Cleveland Democrats sat still and refused to vote either for the platform or for the candidate. Before they acted, the gold-standard forces under David Bennett Hill made a strong but unavailing protest. The vote by which they were overwhelmed, by which the minority report and the Cleveland resolution were rejected, was 628 to 301.

That shows the extent of the domination. As had been expected, the Populists and the National Silver parties met and accepted Mr. Bryan as their candidate, indorsed the platform, which, by the way, he had as a member of the Resolutions Committee largely written. On the other side, the Democratic convention had no sooner adjourned than a movement started among gold-standard Democrats to organize into a party and hold a convention. There were in the country thousands of Democrats who would not accept the Chicago platform and candidates, and who would not vote for a Republican. Many conferences occurred, and on September 2, in Indianapolis, the convention of the National Democratic party was held, a gold-standard platform adopted, the Cleveland administrations strongly indorsed, Mr. Bryan and the free-silver declaration at Chicago repudiated, and John M. Palmer of Illinois and Simon B. Buckner of Kentucky nominated for President and Vice-President.

In the meantime, Mr. Cleveland, preserving an ominous silence in the White House, lent what encouragement he could to the Palmer and Buckner movement, and the members of his cabinet, except Hoke Smith of Georgia, came out more or less openly against Mr. Bryan. It was an astonishing campaign. No such candidate as Mr. Bryan had ever appeared before the people. Young, of tremendous physical vigor and endurance, he traveled from end to end of the country, spoke at hundreds of meetings big and little, appealed to the people with an eloquence and power no other man had used, subjected himself to a strain few men could have borne without breaking. The people turned out to see and hear him in unprecedented numbers and with incredible enthusiasm.

WILLIAM JENNINGS BRYAN
TAKEN IN 1900

Early in the fight it seemed as if the chances favored Mr. Bryan. The silver forces had effected an almost perfect fusion, the popular excitement was intense, and the alarm in the East was great. It was not until October that the tide turned. By that time the Republicans had collected and were distributing in the pivotal States a campaign fund far in excess of any previous one in history. They literally had unlimited money, whereas the Democratic headquarters were impoverished and in debt. The weight of the business forces, the effectiveness of the campaign fund, and the power of the press, which was strongly anti-Bryan, began to tell about four weeks before the election. By the end of the month the betting was two to one against Bryan. It was plain he would get a great vote, but to the practical politicians it was also plain he could not get a majority in the Electoral College.

Mr. Bryan made one of the most gallant single-handed fights ever made by a Presidential candidate, but after October 1 it was up-hill all the way. Toward the close, the sound-money Democrats mostly swung to the McKinley ticket as the surest way of beating Mr. Bryan, and the Palmer and Buckner ticket got only 222,583 votes in the country, not carrying, of course, any State and not even being the balance of power in any. When the showdown came, the Republicans had a plurality of more than 500,000 and 271 electoral votes to 176. Mr. Bryan carried most of the Western States—Washington, Utah, Nevada, South Dakota, Wyoming, Montana, Idaho, Nebraska, Colorado, and Kansas, and got one vote from California, but the only other States he carried were in the South, which left him 53 short of a majority and seems to prove that it just cannot be done without New York, the only exception since merely proving the rule.

No Northern State east of the Missouri River gave Mr. Bryan a single electoral vote. The sectional line was sharply drawn. In the hour of his defeat he said, "I have borne the sins of Grover Cleveland," but that was not true. It was not the sins of Mr. Cleveland that had weighed him down but the fundamental financial heresy to which he had pledged himself and his party. That was not Cleveland's sin, but it got for him the unswerving and tremendously effective Cleveland opposition. It was the Cleveland opposition and the grim, silent but eloquent Cleveland fight against free silver that threw hundreds of thousands of Democrats in the pivotal Eastern States into the Republican camp. The situation was well summed up the day after the 1896 election by a Baltimore newspaper editorial, which said:

When the history of the present time comes to be seriously written, the name of the hero of this campaign will be that of a man who was not a candidate, not a manager, not an orator. The fight which has just been won was made possible by the noble service of one steadfast and heroic citizen, and the victory which was achieved yesterday must be set down as the crowning achievement of his great record. . . . It is impossible to overestimate the value of the service Grover Cleveland has done through his twelve years of unswerving fidelity to the cause of honest money.

That tells the story. But—and this is one of the most remarkable things about the career of Mr. Bryan—his crushing defeat, so far from killing him politically, appeared to make him stronger, both in the country and in the party. His party leadership was as completely established as if he had won instead of losing the fight, and there was never a day between the election in 1896 and the meeting of the convention in 1900 on which his renomination was in doubt. No other defeated candidate had ever assumed or been conceded such complete party authority—not even Van Buren. There was literally no one to dispute his party leadership, no one with a tithe of his popular following. Democratic congressmen and senators from South and West looked to him for counsel and advice—which he freely gave. Through his newspaper, the "Commoner," and by speeches in various parts of the country, and by letters, Mr. Bryan kept in constant touch with the people and retained his hold.

When the convention met in Kansas City, though he remained at his home in Lincoln, he was in supreme command. The Cleveland Democrats were by no means reconciled, but the bitterness had to some extent disappeared. The gold standard had been established and a great many Democrats, unable to swallow Mr. Bryan and his free-silver platform in 1896, but disgusted with the character of the Republican party under Mark Hanna, and thoroughly opposed to the tariff and foreign policies of the McKinley administration, were anxious to find a way back to their own party. The taking over of the Philippines and the establishment of a protectorate over Cuba following the Spanish War had given rise to the issue of imperialism, and Mr. Bryan was strongly urged to concentrate the fight on that and eliminate from the platform all reference to free silver. It was pointed out that the increased production of gold had greatly reduced the importance of the question, that imperialism and the trusts were more vital and more interesting questions, that the wise political course would be to ignore free silver and get the gold-standard Democrats back in line.

But Mr. Bryan did not see it that way. He resisted the appeals of friends and the overtures of former foes. David Bennett Hill went out to Lincoln to reason with him. So did a lot of others. It did no good. Mr. Bryan in his "Memoirs" explains:

I insisted upon the restatement of the free silver plank because I thought a refusal to restate it would, under the circumstances, be considered a repudiation of that plank and, while I recognized the force of the arguments made by some of our friends, I was not willing to run upon a platform which either ignored the question or put me in the attitude of pretending to endorse it when the endorsement was not genuine. I considered the matter very fully and nothing ever distressed me more than being compelled to differ from so many of my trusted friends. I told them that I could afford to lose the nomination, that it was not necessary to my happiness, but that I could not afford to lose the confidence that all voters had in my honesty and that I would decline to be a candidate if the convention saw fit to write the platform as then proposed.

Mr. Bryan being in control, his wishes prevailed. While imperialism was, with his consent, made the paramount issue, the Chicago free-silver plank was restated and reaffirmed. There was a real fight on it in the Resolutions Committee, where the Bryan forces finally had their way by a majority of a single vote. According to Mr. Bryan's autobiography, he had the support of his silver views in this convention of Richard Croker, the Tammany leader, who, he asserts, had been converted by reading his book and was his sincere supporter. It was the Croker influence, he maintained, that prevented Hill from submitting a minority report and enabled the platform to be adopted without a floor fight. It was one of the longest of all Democratic platforms, vehemently indicting the McKinley administration for its conduct of the Spanish War, denouncing the Republican policy toward the Philippines and Cuba as militaristic imperialism that imperiled our most cherished institutions, assailing the trusts and monopolies, urging the direct election of United States senators, condemning the Dingley Tariff Law, recommending an increase in power of the Interstate Commerce Commission, opposing "government by injunction" and favoring the creation of a Department of Labor. It was a progressive platform, but there was nothing in it to seriously alarm the business interests and offend the gold Democrats except the money plank. But that was enough. That said:

> We reaffirm and endorse the principles of the National Democratic platform adopted at Chicago in 1896 and we reiterate the demand of that platform for an American financial system made by the American people for themselves, which shall restore and maintain a bimetallic price level, and as part of such system the immediate restoration of the free and unlimited coinage of silver and gold at the present legal ratio of 16 to 1, without waiting for the aid or consent of any other nation.

That effectually drew the same lines that had been drawn in the 1896 campaign. Again the Silver party and the Populists accepted Mr. Bryan as their candidate and again the great eastern newspapers and business interests froze solidly against him. In the campaign that followed his nomination at Kansas City, with Adlai E. Stevenson of Illinois as his running-mate, Mr. Bryan, though declaring imperialism to be the paramount issue, found a more popular and appealing subject to be the trusts and the unjust burdens of the laboring classes. To these he devoted the major part of the six hundred and more speeches he made in all parts of the country, touching lightly on the silver issue and finding the imperialistic argument not one capable of deeply stirring the people.

The Republicans, however, made the free-silver plank their principal object of attack. They pointed out Mr. Bryan's insistence on its repetition in his platform, declared his election would endanger the gold standard, and tear the props from under the prosperity of the country. Though McKinley had of course been renominated, the real fight was between Mr. Bryan and Mr. Roosevelt. The latter had been nominated for Vice-President at the Republican convention in Philadelphia and "swung around the circle," making almost as many speeches as Mr. Bryan. As in 1896, the odds were strongly against the Democrats. They had almost no money, little newspaper support, and the almost solid opposition of the business and banking interests. The result of the election was a defeat even more decisive both as to popular and electoral vote than in 1896. The Democrats carried only seventeen States instead of twenty-four, got 155 electoral votes instead of 176, and lost by 860,000 instead of 600,000 in the popular vote. It is characteristic of Mr. Bryan that in his "Memoirs" he should assert his belief that the friends who told him his insistence on the free-silver plank was responsible for his defeat were wrong, and that if he had not done so he would have been even worse beaten. It is hard to see how, as in 1904 the Democrats carried literally nothing outside of the solid South and four politically insignificant Western States—Colorado, Montana, Idaho, Nevada —with a total of thirteen electoral votes.

Chapter XXVI

THE PARKER NOMINATION AND DEFEAT

The Conservative Wing in Control of 1904 Convention—
Bryan Regains Leadership After the Election and Is
for Third Time Nominated and Beaten

THE plight of the party after the 1900 election was
naturally pretty bad, and there was tremendous discouragement about the future. Mr. Bryan, of course,
came in for vast abuse as the wrecker of the party,
as the millstone around its neck, as the Old Man of
the Sea. Soon after the election he announced that
he would not be a candidate for the 1908 nomination, that he thought it best another standard-bearer
be named, but that he proposed to continue to battle
for progressive principles and to wage unrelenting
warfare against the reactionary interests.

The temporary relaxing of the Bryan grip encouraged certain conservative Democrats of the East
to attempt a reorganization of the party and the development of a candidate, strong in the East, who
could command the confidence of the gold Democrats
who left the party in 1896 and had not returned. It
was considered important to pick a New York man,
and it was conceded that he had to be a Democrat

who, in spite of his sound-money views, had not bolted the party but in both 1896 and 1900 had supported Mr. Bryan. Hill was interested in the movement; so was Gorman of Maryland, Clarence W. Watson of West Virginia, Thomas Fortune Ryan, and August Belmont.

The man picked was Judge Alton B. Parker. He was put out as a "safe and sane" candidate, took well in the East, and the old-time machine Democratic leaders in various sections began to line up behind him. Almost from the start it was plain that, with Mr. Bryan out of the field, the forces behind Judge Parker were strong enough to put him over in convention; but from the start, almost from the first mention of his name, Mr. Bryan opposed him with all his power. Nor did he let up until after his nomination. In a speech in April, 1904, he assailed the so-called "reorganizers" of the party and their candidate, concluding his attack with these words: "I am sanguine to believe that I can prove to every unbiased mind that Judge Parker is not a fit man to be nominated either by the Democratic party or by any other party that stands for honest and fair dealing in politics."

To still further complicate matters, William Randolph Hearst, owner and publisher of a string of newspapers covering the country from coast to coast, militant radical, vastly rich and resourceful, became an avowed candidate for the Democratic nomination. He had been a member of Congress from New York city in 1902, and both as a congressman and an editor—but mainly as an editor—his attacks on corporate wealth, monopolies, and trusts were of extreme violence and vigor, equaled only by his championship of the "rights of labor" and the "downtrodden masses." At first the Hearst candidacy seemed to the practical politicians back of the Parker movement more or less a joke. It was not long, however, before they became genuinely alarmed. Mr. Hearst with his money and newspaper power created a personal but very real organization, and it became plain that he would show up in the convention with a considerable number of votes. As soon as this was realized steps were taken to tighten the organization in the important State, to block the Hearst progress, and assure control against a stampede.

A tremendous amount of under-cover work was done in the pre-convention campaign. Those who had inspired the Parker boom were determined to put the party back on a conservative basis and relegate Mr. Bryan to the rear. They left no stone unturned, and when the convention met in Chicago on July 6, 1904, at least a third of the delegates were instructed for Parker. With additional alliances that had been made, the Parker people were in sufficient control of the convention to effect its organization and to steam-roller Mr. Hearst in the Credentials Committee. Up to the day of the convention, while Mr. Bryan had continued his opposition to Parker and the men back of Parker, he did not declare him-

self in favor of any one else and serenely resisted
the efforts to line him up behind Mr. Hearst. In
his paper, the "Commoner," and in speeches he had
suggested a list of names, any one of whom he urged
would be "available" as candidates, and Mr. Hearst
was included in his list. His main purpose, open and
declared, was to prevent the nomination of Parker
on the ground that while he had personally supported the ticket in 1896 and 1900, the men behind
him were responsible for its defeat in those years,
had led the bolt of the gold Democrats, and were "in
league with Wall Street."

As a delegate from Nebraska, he was a member
of the Committee on Resolutions, and at a session
of this committee lasting all night he made a tremendous fight for his platform ideas. The Parker
forces were under the command of David B. Hill,
who also represented New York on the Resolutions
Committee. While he had control of the convention,
Mr. Hill's control of the committee was by no means
complete, and Mr. Bryan was able to prevent the
incorporation of a gold plank and to force a modification of the tariff plank, which he charged was
framed to please the protectionists and "to betray
the Democratic party."

In the end the platform as reported by the committee was molded more by Bryan than by Hill. The
declaration on tariff and the denunciation of trusts
and monopolies were both written by him. The gold
plank was knocked out, direct election of United

States senators favored, and the monetary question ignored. While Mr. Bryan was able to prevent a gold-standard indorsement, he was not able to again write in the 1896 and 1900 free-silver planks. But when the platform was completed Mr. Bryan accepted it, and insisted that he had won a great victory by preventing the conservatives from utterly making over the party principles of 1896 and 1900.

As a matter of fact, it was when completed one of the weakest platforms the party has ever adopted. It contained literally nothing upon which a fight could be made. It did not present a single issue. The party had been beaten on the tariff issue, the free-silver issue, and the imperialism issue. It was in 1904 out of issues. It had nothing to present, little on which to appeal. The conservatives back of Parker were more concerned in keeping the radical wing from inserting into their platform something that would again alienate the business interests of the East and in putting over their candidate than in finding a new issue. Mr. Bryan finally seconded the nomination of Senator Francis M. Cockrell of Missouri, thrilling the convention with an oratorical effort second only to his 1896 "Cross of gold and crown of thorns" speech, in which he defended himself and his course and scathingly denounced the Parker movement and the men behind it. The keynote of this speech was "I have kept the Faith" and it was undoubtedly one of the best he ever made, but it was unavailing. The Parker forces, under Governor Hill, steam-rollered him, and Parker was nominated on the first ballot. Mr. Hearst got 200 votes, Parker 658, Cockrell 42, and 97 votes were scattered among ten others. The two thirds necessary to nominate was 667, and before the result of the first ballot was announced enough had changed to give Parker 689 and the nomination.

Back in New York the big fellows who were to finance the Parker campaign—Ryan, Belmont, Watson, and others—were terribly upset over Hill's failure to get the gold plank into the platform. It was clear that without it the real purpose of the movement—to rid the party once for all and completely of the free-silver heresy—was lost. The wires were hot with telephonic and telegraphic exchanges between St. Louis and New York. Finally Parker sent to one of the New York delegates the following telegram:

I regard the gold standard as firmly and irrevocably established, and shall act accordingly if the action of the convention today shall be ratified by the people. As the platform is silent on the subject, my view should be made known to the convention, and if it is proved to be unsatisfactory to the majority, I request you to decline the nomination for me at once, so that another may be nominated before adjournment.

When this was sprung on the convention there was consternation for a while. A hot debate ensued in which Mr. Bryan opposed the sending of any acquiescent reply to Mr. Parker, and insisted that if the party was to accept the gold standard it should do so in its platform, and not allow the candidate to go beyond the platform. But he was voted down by an overwhelming majority and the answer was sent as follows:

The platform adopted by this convention is silent on the question of a monetary standard because it is not regarded by us as a possible issue in this campaign, and only campaign issues were mentioned in the platform. Therefore, there is nothing in the views expressed by you in the telegram just received, which would preclude a man entertaining them from accepting a nomination on said platform.

The convention then proceeded to select as Judge Parker's running-mate Henry Gassaway Davis of West Virginia, over eighty years old and with nothing to recommend him as a candidate except his ability to make a large campaign contribution—which incidentally he did not do. His selection was entirely due to Senator A. P. Gorman.

Thus the party went into the campaign with a conservative candidate, a platform that was neither one thing nor the other, an octogenarian for second place, and the radical wing as disgruntled and disaffected as the conservative wing had been before. The gold Democrats voted for Parker, but they were about all who did. He made a lifeless, colorless campaign. He was ponderous and heavy and uninspiring. On the Republican ticket the colorful Roosevelt had a tremendous personal following. In addition, he was much more "progressive" than Parker, though the candidate of the supposedly conservative party.

The Parker Nomination and Defeat

Neither party had a program. The Democratic campaign denounced the Republicans and the Republican orators denounced the Democrats, but there were few ideas and no issues. The Democrats had the weaker candidates and a split party. Mr. Bryan gave nominal support to the ticket, but he did more harm than good. Right after the convention he declared that Parker's nomination "nullified the anti-trust plank," that the labor plank was a "meaningless straddle," that the party was now "under the domination of Wall Street." That the bulk of the Bryan following did not support the ticket is shown not only by the decreased Democratic vote but by the increase in the vote of the Populist and Socialist parties, each of whom had a ticket in the field. The net result was a crushing defeat. Roosevelt was elected by a popular plurality of more than two and a half million. He had 336 electoral votes to 140 for Parker. The Democrats lost Missouri, carried only the thirteen States of the South, nothing in the East, not a single State west of the Mississippi. It was a defeat more complete than any that had been suffered since the reconstruction period immediately following the Civil War. Again both branches of Congress were heavily Republican, and the Democratic party was reduced nationally to a state of almost complete impotency.

It is an interesting and significant fact that these three defeats and the one that followed in 1908 did not in any way weaken the Democratic organizations in the individual States. In the off years the party regained many seats in the House and elected senators and governors and legislatures in States that had gone overwhelmingly Republican in the national elections. It was split wide open as a national party, but the state units stayed strong and virile. No defeat since has seemed to weaken them, which fact is the soundest argument as to the indestructibility of the party. So long as the state machines continue strong in state elections, there is always the chance of an issue, a leader, and a division in the Republican ranks uniting them again into a formidable and successful national party. Cleveland did it twice and Wilson twice. There is no reason to think it will not happen again.

The 1904 disaster so flattened out the Parker group of leaders that they did not have enough vitality left to hold the control they had gained in the convention. Cleveland, who had supported Parker because he felt that his candidacy at least brought the party back to a sound economic basis, but was not at all enthusiastic about him as a man, was in retirement. Hill was pretty thoroughly discredited. Gorman, though always a secret aspirant for the Presidency, was not a popular figure and most vulnerable. Literally, there was no one in the conservative Eastern Democracy who stood out. Inevitably the party leadership swung back to Mr. Bryan, the one man in the party with a large and idolatrous personal following, who was increasingly active in

JUDGE ALTON B. PARKER

Taken with William Jennings Bryan and his cousin,
Governor William S. Jennings of Florida in 1904

politics. Beyond doubt it was a tribute to the power of the man, a remarkable demonstration of his hold on a multitude of people, that after crushing defeats in two campaigns, followed by the rejection of his leadership in a third, he should have been able without a struggle to reestablish his ascendancy over a great national party for a fourth fight, to stand out as its inevitable and logical candidate.

Yet that is what happened. It was an unprecedented performance. Defeated in 1896 and 1900, discredited and despised in 1904, in 1908 he came back stronger than he had been at any time in his career. If he had made just one successful fight it would not have been so amazing, but in spite of the fact that he never led his party anywhere except into the ditch, he maintained the leadership of a large part of it for twelve years, and clear to the day of his death he had a following that made him a factor.

Soon after the Parker defeat Mr. Bryan proclaimed the necessity of reorganizing the party along "progressive" lines, taking it out of the hands of the "money changers in Wall Street." He sounded a trumpet call to his followers in the "Commoner," and in a series of speeches laid the foundation for another fight against the "interests." However, the free-silver ghost had been finally laid and there was unquestionably a disposition among Eastern Democrats who had opposed him in his two first campaigns to be with him this time on the ground

369

that time had mellowed his judgment and modified his radicalism. Unquestionably this trend toward him was heightened by the extraordinary ovations given him in European countries which he visited in 1906.

It was in 1905 that he started with Mrs. Bryan on a trip around the world, and the enthusiasm with which he, as a private citizen, was greeted by the people, and the respect paid him by the rulers abroad, unquestionably enhanced his prestige at home. When, in August, 1906, he returned to New York, a great reception was given him in that city. Democrats from all over the country gathered to greet him. Every State sent its delegation, and in Madison Square Garden he made a great speech outlining his political ideas.

Great hopes had been entertained in the East that he would refrain from again striking a radical note that would alarm business, and prior to the meeting various leaders begged Mr. Bryan to eliminate from his speech a part advocating governmental owner- ship of railroads as an ultimate solution of the trans- portation problem. It was pointed out to him that the hostility in the East toward him had abated, and if only he would give it a chance the conservative wing would accept his nomination in 1908 and give him a support he had never before had. The appeals were fervent and earnest but they had no effect on Mr. Bryan. He kept the government ownership part of his speech intact and was next morning denounced as "the same dangerous old demagogue" by the Eastern Democratic press.

This, however, did not alter Mr. Bryan's course nor diminish the strength of his reestablished leadership. There were some bitter protests and much talk of a fight against him, but there was no one to make it. The Parker leaders had been too completely crushed to inspire any following, and the Bryan sentiment was a concrete political fact that caused most of the Democrats in Congress to accept his leadership without question. Among certain conservative senators a movement started looking to the rejection of Mr. Bryan as a candidate, and it was proposed to call on him in the interests of the party to remove himself from the field. But the movement got nowhere, the call was never made. When Mr. Bryan made a visit to Washington this tentative opposition collapsed and there was, from the beginning of 1907, no doubt at all about his nomination. The conservative element was helpless, but did not yield without a struggle. Various booms were launched—by Governor John Johnson of Minnesota, Judson Harmon of Ohio, Judge George Gray of Delaware, and others—but they did not last long or get far. When the convention met in Denver the Bryan control was complete. He did not have a two thirds majority of instructed delegates, but his nomination was recognized as inevitable, and from his home at Lincoln he wrote the platform and dictated the organization of the convention and the candidate for Vice-President—John W. Kern of Indiana. There was a prolonged and bitter fight in the Committee on Resolutions over some of the planks, but the platform went through largely as Mr. Bryan had written it, and the conservatives were rolled under by the Bryan steam roller. Judge Gray and Governor Johnson were put in nomination but on the first and only ballot Bryan got 888½ votes out of a total of 994.

It was as complete a demonstration of power over a national party by an unofficial individual as has ever been given. The platform was thoroughly "progressive," and the dominant issue was declared to be, "Shall the people rule?" Carrying out this idea, the Republican party was denounced as dominated, controlled, and financed by the great corporations which used it to exploit the people and enrich themselves. Regulation of the rates of telegraph and telephone companies were demanded, and while Mr. Bryan refrained from inserting a government ownership plank, the increase of the regulatory power of the Interstate Commerce Commission over the railroads was strongly urged. Publicity for campaign contributions was demanded, and the Republican promise to revise the tariff downward declared insincere. The direct election of senators and a Federal income tax were favored. Trusts, monopolies, and the Roosevelt administration were flayed.

It was a long platform but in the main sound, and promulgated no particular principle abhorrent to the

Photograph by Brown Brothers

DEMOCRATIC BANNER DISPLAYED IN NEW YORK IN THE 1908 CAMPAIGN

gold Democrats of the East, such as was the case in
1896 and 1900. Many more of them supported Mr.
Bryan this time than in either of his other campaigns, but there were still thousands who refused to
accept him. A good many of these by this time had
formed the habit of voting the Republican ticket in
national elections—a habit which still holds a lot of
them. They regularly vote the Democratic ticket in
off years and state elections, consider, call themselves, and register as Democrats, but almost invariably support the Republican candidate for President. There is no doubt that Mr. Bryan gave them
this habit.

Taft was the Republican candidate in 1908, and
the platform on which he ran definitely promised
tariff revision downward, which practically eliminated that issue. There really was no issue, except
that Mr. Bryan made himself the champion of the
masses and attacked Mr. Taft as the hand-picked
candidate of Mr. Roosevelt, thoroughly acceptable
to the great corporate interests of the East. Both
candidates started out with the declared purpose of
not taking the stump, but Mr. Bryan broke away
first, and before the end had covered the country
from coast to coast. While, as usual, the Republicans
were infinitely better financed and the great weight
of the business and banking interests were behind
their ticket, Mr. Bryan proved a stronger candidate
this time than in either of his previous campaigns.
He aroused more enthusiasm and had more support

in the East. Up to a few weeks before the election it seemed as though his chances of success were good, but the odds were too heavy. Despite his marvelous personal magnetism, the wild enthusiasm with which his followers were filled, and the fight he gave the Republicans on election day, he could not get his vote to the polls. His campaign from headquarters was loosely managed, poorly financed, and lacked heart. The Republicans had a vastly superior machine, three fourths of the press support, three times as much money.

Though Mr. Bryan got 1,323,000 more votes than Parker, there was a popular majority against him of 1,270,000. In the Electoral College Taft had 321, Bryan 162 votes. He, however, carried seventeen States to Parker's thirteen, and got twenty-two more electoral votes. All this only proved that Bryan, the radical Democrat for whom the conservatives in the East would not vote, could poll a slightly larger vote than a conservative Democrat, whom the radical wing would not support. It showed that neither wing could carry the pivotal States with the heavy electoral votes—New York, New Jersey, Indiana, Ohio—without which success was impossible. It showed that the split in 1896 had not healed, that after four consecutive defeats the party was still in two widely separated sections. It showed that success could come only in two ways—first, the rise of a new leader from the conservative East, who would eclipse Mr. Bryan and yet gain his real support—not the sort of sup-

374

port he gave Parker, but genuine and hearty; second, a division in the ranks of the Republicans.

Disheartened, dismayed, divided, defeated for the fourth consecutive time, in debt and distress, without patronage, power, prestige, or issues, it is doubtful whether the Democratic party even after the Civil War was in a more hopeless condition than immediately following this last Bryan defeat. Triumphant, united, harmonious, the Republicans seemed in an invincible and impregnable position. It is one of the most remarkable happenings of political history that at this period, when the party pulse beat alarmingly low and the party spirit was almost gone, the new leader should arise, the split in the opposite camp simultaneously occur, and the Democrats swing back into full control of the Government after a lapse of sixteen years, during which it had been derided and despised by the opposition and deserted by vast numbers of its adherents. The disposition had grown among political writers and analysts to regard it as a local party, strong in the States and to be reckoned with during the off years, but not really formidable in a Presidential election. Its return to power was a dramatic and spectacular one, the remembrance of which has kept a certain apprehension in the breasts of the Republican managers in the times of their greatest subsequent triumphs, and a corresponding hope in Democratic hearts through a period of what has seemed hopeless disunion. It was an amazing performance.

Chapter XXVII

THE WILSON ERA

The Two Views of Him as a Man and a Statesman—
His Entrance Into New Jersey Politics and Active
Presidential Candidacy While Governor of That
State

So long as the generation to which Woodrow Wilson belonged survives there will be no agreement as to his place in history. To vast numbers he will stand out clearly as the greatest American of his time, a shining and heroic figure, an indomitable and inspiring leader, a President unsurpassed in patriotism, understanding, courage, character, and achievement. To others he will appear an intolerant egotist, an impracticable dreamer, a man cold, selfish, dictatorial, and overwhelmingly ambitious, who tragically failed through the weakness of his judgment and his inherent inability to take advice or tolerate opposition.

There cannot, however, be any disagreement over the fact that he played a larger part in world affairs than any other American who ever lived, and that his two administrations were the most eventful in the nation's history: that in the domestic as in the foreign field he more deeply affected the course of the country than any of his predecessors; that in the Democratic party only the figure of Jefferson towers above him—none other is as high. There is no place in this book for a review of the Wilson career or a discussion either of the extraordinary record of constructive legislation that marked his first term, or of the conduct of the great war that marked the second. Difficult as it is to do, this account will be confined to Wilson's part in the Democratic story. The great controversial question of the League of Nations and the war itself, save as they bear on the Democratic story, will be avoided and no effort made to depart from the political aspects of the extraordinary career of this great party figure.

It is, however, an essential part of that story to point out that the two Wilson administrations are in a class by themselves, and despite the extraordinary hostility engendered by Mr. Wilson, a hostility that pursued him, stricken and ill, long after he had left the White House, no President ever accomplished so much in so short a time. And while it is true no President ever had more bitter and unrelenting enemies, certainly no Democrat ever had so vast a number of his fellow-citizens to devotedly admire him, completely believe in him, and unvaryingly support him. The Wilson era in Democratic history in many ways is unmatched in interest and importance not only because of the vibrant personality of the man but because of the amazing legislative record, which, notwithstanding differences of opinion as to the man, dislike of his methods, and hatred of his policies, few fair-minded persons attempt to minimize. The truth is that no Democrat since the foundation of the party—not even Jefferson or Jackson—was more completely the leader of his party than Wilson during the eight years between his nomination at Baltimore in 1912 and his physical collapse early in 1919. Even after he left the White House his influence was dominant. Sick and out of power as he was, he remained, curiously, the undisputed leader of his party until his death, though he was unable to exercise his leadership or even to see his friends with frequency. But his ideas and his policies dominated the party, and the 1920 candidate, James M. Cox of Ohio, made his fight almost completely on the Wilson policies and stood four-square on a Wilson platform, adopted by a convention in which the Wilson influence, had he chosen to exert it, could have dominated in every detail.

In those eight active years of his leadership the effectiveness and efficiency of Wilson as the boss of his party is attested by his extraordinary success in getting through Congress what he wanted. His great tragic failure to secure the Senate ratification of the peace treaty and the League of Nations covenant does not alter the fact that no party ever secured greater legislative results or redeemed more completely its platform pledges than did the Democratic party in those first four years under Wilson.

The Wilson Era

As to his second administration, whatever the feeling about the League of Nations, whatever the opinion of the man, it must be conceded that the institution of the selective draft in an unprepared country, the enrolling of an army of four million men, the training and transportation in eighteen months of two million and them three thousand miles across a submarine infested ocean, the conduct of the war on the fighting front abroad and the financial front at home, the almost complete absence of scandal or graft in the expenditure of billions of dollars—these things will stand out to the everlasting credit of the Democratic party and the great Democratic leader who was in the White House during the war.

It is possible, of course, to indict Mr. Wilson for this, that, and the other, to denounce him for failing to go in soon enough or for going in at all. It is possible to assail his policies, to arraign the members of his cabinet, to pick out blunders here and there—and there were of course plenty of them —to dwell on the inevitable waste, the inescapable injustices, and the maddening mistakes incidental to war, but in the end the attack on Wilson's conduct of the war falls to the ground in the face of the big facts of the raising of that army, the sending it over, the bringing it back—the doing of these things in a way and in a time that caused them to be unfeignedly regarded by our allies and our enemies alike as little short of miraculous. Beyond doubt there was ample justification for fault-finding, but the great outstanding achievements so notably free from the political plundering inseparable in the past from war seems to absorb all minor criticism.

While to Thomas Jefferson it owes its origin, and while the magnificent battles of Jackson against nullification and Cleveland against free silver stand out conspicuously in its history, take it all in all and it is difficult to deny that there is in the administrations of Woodrow Wilson more to which the Democratic party has a right to "point with pride" than in any other. Wholly aside from the war and wholly apart from the League of Nations, founded by this Democratic President, the record of the party in the domestic field during the Wilson period is a remarkable one. The list of laws for which the Democrats under Wilson leadership were responsible includes:

The Federal Reserve Act, which is generally conceded to be the soundest piece of financial legislation in the nation's history, without which the war could not have been won, and which has practically removed the menace of recurring panic in the country;

An income tax amendment to the Constitution followed by an income tax law that measurably equalizes the burden of taxation;

Amendment to the Constitution providing for the popular election of United States senators;

A Tariff Law reducing the import duties all along the line and claimed by Democrats to have been the best tariff law in fifty years, closely adhering to the

ELECTIONEERING TORCHLIGHT PARADE TAKEN ON FOURTEENTH STREET,
NEW YORK CITY—1908

Democratic principle of "tariff for revenue only";

A Rural Credits Law which it is claimed renders it easy for the farmer to borrow money at approximately what it is worth in the money market;

A law creating a Federal Trade Commission, the theory of which is not to interfere with legitimate business but to prevent abuses;

A companion Anti-Trust Law, declaring a private monopoly to be indefensible and intolerable;

A Shipping Law creating a government-owned merchant marine;

A Child Labor Law;

An Eight Hour Day Law;

An Anti-Injunction Law, recognizing the right of trial by jury when the alleged contempt is not committed in the presence of the court;

The Philippine law giving to the Filipinos the promise of ultimate independence.

These constitute only a partial list of the Democratic domestic legislation under Wilson, but as it stands it presents an unparalleled record. One of the reasons why, following the Wilson era, there came a period of vast political inertia and indifference during which people took little interest in politics, and the vote fell off all over the country, was that Wilson had left in the domestic field little to arouse interest. He had practically cleaned the country up. All the reform measures that for years had been pending, promised by both parties but never enacted, were put through by Wilson with such speed and completeness that it left the so-called progressives nothing much to fight for, certainly nothing for which there was a widespread popular demand. Income tax, currency reform, Child Labor Law, eight hour day, direct election of senators, woman suffrage—all these questions, agitated for years, were taken up by the man with whom the Democrats returned to power after four successive defeats, and placed on the statute books in concrete and enduring form. There is room to criticize the wisdom or the desirability of some of these measures, but there is no room to question the effectiveness and efficiency with which Wilson put through his program. He conceived that his election as President carried with it the leadership of his party, and his idea of the duty of a leader was to lead. Whatever else may be said of him, it cannot be denied that he led.

Though it will be denied, it is certainly probable that because of the tremendous and widespread dissatisfaction with the Taft administration, the deep resentment of the progressive Republicans over the iniquities of the Aldrich-Payne Tariff Law, the Ballinger scandal, the apparently dominating influence at the White House of the reactionary Republican leaders, and other causes—it is probable that by reason of these conditions the Democrats, with Wilson as their candidate, could have won the 1912 election even had there been no open Republican split. The time was ripe. Harmony had really been restored.

Bryan was sincerely with Wilson in a way very different from the way he had been with Parker. The vigor and force of Wilson as a speaker, his great gift for clear and impressive utterance, his record as governor of New Jersey, his high character, fighting spirit, and "progressive" views all contributed to make him an ideal candidate for the period.

As has been said, he would probably have beaten Mr. Taft if there had been no split. But of course he and his party would never have achieved the sweeping and tremendous triumph that gave Mr. Wilson more electoral votes than any other Presidential candidate ever received, carried for the Democrats forty of the forty-eight States, and placed the party in complete control of both branches of the Congress, in which position it had been but once since the Civil War; nothing like that would have been possible but for the break between Roosevelt and Taft which ripped the Republican party from stem to stern in the first and only really disastrous split in all its well-disciplined history.

This book is no place for the story of that dramatic and historic break between friends. It is the one big drama of the whole Republican story. All that need be said of it here is that the hint of it was in the air long before the Democratic convention of 1912 met in Baltimore, the signs of the smash were unmistakable. Democratic leaders in all sections, seeing the bitterness and sensing the public unrest, were convinced that victory was in store for them if only a way could be found to consolidate behind the right man the Bryan following in the South and West with the sound-money Democrats of the East—in other words, if in the face of the inevitable Republican break they could refrain from repeating the stupidity of former conventions. The congressional elections of 1910 more than anything else encouraged the Democrats and correspondingly depressed the Republicans. While the Democrats gained in the Senate, the Republicans still held a majority of ten; but in the House there was a complete upset. The Republican majority of forty was wiped out. The Democrats elected 223 members, the Republicans 168—giving the Democrats a majority of fifty-five, a most amazing and significant turnover.

It was in this year that Mr. Wilson was elected governor of New Jersey, and there is not the least doubt that he was a candidate for President before ever he entered his New Jersey campaign. He had been first mentioned in that connection by Colonel George Harvey in his "Weekly," and those close to him knew before he was elected governor that the White House was his goal. As governor the eyes of the party and the country were on him. His spectacular and victorious fight with the Jersey bosses, Smith and Nugent; his singular success in compelling a reluctant Jersey legislature to pass the measures he wanted and reject those he did not want; the force, clarity, and polish of his messages and speeches—all combined to make him within a year the most conspicuous figure in the Democratic party; and before 1911 closed, quite a number of political analysts and publicists in various parts of the country were reechoing Colonel Harvey's slogan of "Wilson for President."

There developed a very real sentiment for him. A number of Democratic and independent newspapers strongly urged his nomination, and Wilson himself, while still governor of New Jersey, left Trenton and made a speech-making tour of the country clear to the Pacific coast, an unprecedented but nevertheless an exceedingly effective thing to do. Accompanied by a secretary and one or two newspaper men, Governor Wilson spoke a great many times and aroused a great deal of enthusiasm. He was a singularly charming and effective speaker, vastly different from the regulation campaign orator, and wherever he spoke he created a profoundly favorable impression and made friends. Incidentally, in addition to making speeches on this tour, care was taken that Mr. Wilson should meet personally the controlling Democrats in each state organization. To these he made himself agreeable and did what could be done to remove the impression that he was a highbrow schoolmaster who could not bear practical politics, who hated politicians and was at heart a reformer— which of course he was. Altogether the tour was a great success in spite of the criticism to which he was subjected for leaving the job to which he had been elected in order to race over the country after another. He returned to Trenton a full-fledged, recognized, open candidate for the nomination, with more sentiment for him than for any one else and more newspaper support.

In the meantime, other candidacies had developed —that of Champ Clark of Missouri, speaker of the House; Oscar Underwood of Alabama, Democratic leader of the House; Governor Judson Harmon of Ohio. Of these Clark was easily the most formidable. In the first place, he had the strong support of William Randolph Hearst and his string of newspapers and periodicals. In the second place, he had undercover connections with the Tammany crowd that were counted on to swing the New York delegation at the proper time. In the third place, he had been a popular figure in Congress for years and had the friendship of a great many politically influential Democratic congressmen and ex-congressmen with whom he had served. In the fourth place, he was preferred by the practical politicians to Mr. Wilson, had much more in common with them. There were a number of more or less dark horses, including Thomas R. Marshall, then governor of Indiana; Eugene N. Foss, governor of Massachusetts; Simeon E. Baldwin, governor of Connecticut, and a number of others.

The struggle in the Democratic party as in the Republican party at this period was between the "progressives" and the "reactionaries." As a rule the "progressives" were those out of office, the reactionaries were the ones in office. The words "progressive" and "reactionary" were on every tongue. Nearly all the newspapers were "progressive." All anti-organization politicians were "progressive" and all the machine leaders were reactionary. There was little talk about concrete ideas or issues in the Democratic pre-convention canvass. All the interest was centered on whether the reactionary or the progressive elements would control, Tammany and the New York group being regarded generally as the very essence of reaction, just as Mr. Bryan was generally accepted as the very acme of progressivism, or liberalism, or radicalism. A great many of the orators in both parties who mouthed the words reactionary and progressive at this time could not to save their souls have told what the two words meant or what they meant by them. It was a day when it was popular to be progressive, unpopular to be reactionary. It was not so much a matter of ideas as it was a matter of the crowd you trained with and the tag placed on you by the papers. Accused of being a reactionary by "The Baltimore Sun," the late John Walter Smith, then senator from Maryland, exasperatedly exclaimed: "Hell, what do they want me to do to qualify as a progressive? I have thrown away the long drawers I have been used to all my life and have taken to wearing these little short running pants. What more can a man do? I don't know what they mean."

Chapter XXVIII

The Baltimore Convention and Bryan—His Indictment
of Ryan, Belmont, and Murphy—The Temporary
Chairmanship the Real Turning Point in the Fight

OF course, the real dividing line in the party was machine and anti-machine. Those in control of the organizations, particularly in the East, were satisfied with things as they were, wanted as little change as possible, favored promising only enough to win. The progressives were earnestly determined to "curb the trusts," reduce the tariff, and "restore the Government to the people," principally by adopting income tax and direct election of senators amendments and enacting child labor and other humanitarian legislation. The most flaming advocate of these measures and the most insistent upon the nomination of a progressive candidate and the adoption of a progressive platform was of course Bryan, who after his third defeat had for the second time declared he would not be a candidate for the nomination but would "continue to fight in the ranks for the progressive cause." He began by declaring absolutely against Mr. Underwood and Governor Har-

mon, branding both as "reactionaries," but having
nothing to say as between Wilson and Clark.

By the time the convention met, Wilson sentiment
among the people generally was far stronger than
for all the other aspirants combined. In most of the
States Wilson clubs had been organized, and in the
East the more influential of the Democratic and
independent papers were vigorously urging his selection. He was of course much stronger with the people than with the politicians. The old-line leaders
resented his attitude toward the organization in New
Jersey and distrusted him as too pronouncedly progressive and too denunciatory of bosses and
machines. There was, however, a considerable number of practical workers enlisted in the Wilson pre-
convention campaign, and some of the more astute
leaders of the party, feeling no personal warmth
toward the man, nevertheless realized that the
chances of Democratic victory with him were infinitely greater than with any other. The Princeton
alumni all over the country were among his most
earnest advocates and were responsible for no small
part of the enthusiasm for him in different sections,
though as president of Princeton University he had
made some bitter enemies there.

From January 12, when the National Committee
issued the call for the convention, until June 25,
when it assembled in Baltimore, the pre-convention
campaign was a warm one, with Wilson making the
pace, producing most of the news, getting much the

best of the publicity. Two things at this time were used with considerable effect against him. One was a letter he had written to a friend some years before expressing the wish to see Bryan "knocked into a cocked hat." The other was a letter to Colonel Harvey, who was the original Wilson man, expressing the belief that Harvey's advocacy of him in his "Weekly" was doing him more harm than good. The basis of this feeling was that Colonel Harvey's friendship with the "interests" would tend to cause any candidate urged by him to be suspected by progressive Democrats. The first letter was used by his enemies in the hope of discouraging Mr. Bryan from his support. The second was cited to show that he was a cold and selfish man, ungrateful for services and not loyal to his friends. Neither had much effect, though widely printed.

It was one of the most dramatic and thrilling conventions in the history of the party. The fight for the nomination was a tremendous and bitter one, in which feeling was aroused to fever pitch and at times the whole gathering seemed on the verge of a riot. However deep may be the resentment over Mr. Bryan's blighting effect on the party between 1896 and 1912, and however much he may be blamed for the sort of leadership that alienated the business interests and gave the other side the chance to brand the Democrats as economically dangerous, a brand which they have not yet succeeded in fully wearing off, still it was difficult to watch Mr. Bryan in this

convention without yielding to him full admiration
and respect, without conceding him to be splendidly
courageous, resourceful, determined, a magnificent
fighter, more than a match in such a gathering for
his enemies, an unshakable, indomitable man.

It really was a Bryan convention. From start to
finish he was its central figure. The whole show re-
volved around him. Single handed, he made his attack on his enemies and to their faces, amid the wildest turmoil and excitement—arraigned, indicted,
and denounced them. The great bulk of the convention delegates were anti-Bryan. Most of the leaders
were hostile to him. His own Nebraska delegation
was not unitedly with him. His three defeats were
enough to have buried politically any other man in
the country. Yet the utter fearlessness, fire, and
force of the man swung and swayed that convention,
compelled it partly through fear, partly because of
inability to cope with him, to yield point after point.
At one time it looked as if he would be subjected to
physical violence. Curses and threats were hurled at
him. In the end he came forth the victor. Beyond all
question it was he who defeated Clark after he had
received a majority of the convention on the tenth
ballot. It was he who nominated Wilson and it was
he who wrote the platform almost as completely as
he had the platforms in the three previous conventions in which he was himself the nominee.

None who saw Mr. Bryan in that convention will
ever forget him. He was far more admirable in this

party gathering than in those of 1896, 1900, 1904, and 1908, the four conventions immediately preceding the first Wilson convention, or in those of 1916, 1920, and 1924 that followed, though in every one of these eight national conventions he was a conspicuous figure. His influence in most of them was a dominant one, in all of them a thing that had to be reckoned with—even in the Parker convention of 1908 and in the John W. Davis convention of 1924, which was his last appearance in the national arena of politics. But beyond question he shone more brightly in the 1912 convention than in any other. Nothing more dramatic ever occurred in a national convention than his denunciation to their faces of Charles F. Murphy, August Belmont, and Thomas F. Ryan, who sat as delegates close to him while he spoke. In that convention Mr. Bryan aroused unbounded hatred, but he also compelled enormous respect.

Early in the winter he had undoubtedly leaned to the support of Champ Clark as against Wilson, though he made no declaration and maintained strict neutrality in the Nebraska primaries which resulted after a bitter fight in the delegation from that State, including himself, being instructed for Clark, though a majority was personally friendly to Wilson. It was clear by this time that while Clark and Wilson would each have over 300 votes in the convention, neither would start off with a majority, and that Clark was in the lead. The Bryan idea was that the "Wall

Street interests" were behind Harmon, and that the thing of vital importance was to secure the election of a "progressive" temporary chairman in order to keep the convention out of the hands of the reactionaries. Accordingly, a few weeks before the convention he started his fight. He wrote to Governor Wilson urging his support in the subcommittee on organization of the National Committee of Senator Ollie James of Kentucky for temporary chairman. James at the time was favored by Clark. Wilson replied that he preferred Senator James O'Gorman of New York. When the subcommittee met neither the Clark nor the Wilson forces had control and a compromise was effected on Judge Alton B. Parker, the defeated candidate of 1904. At once Bryan went into action. He denounced the selection of Parker as calculated to stamp the convention reactionary from the start. He wrote a strong appeal to Wilson to join him in the fight to prevent his choice and promptly got back a reply, agreeing that he was right and assuring him that he was in sympathy with his stand. From Clark, to whom he had also written, Bryan received the following evasive reply:

Have consulted with committee having my interests in charge and agree with them that the supreme consideration should be to prevent any discord in the convention. Friends of mine on the sub-committee of arrangements have already presented the name of Ollie James to the sub-committee. I believe that if all join in the interest of harmony in an appeal to the entire national committee to avoid controversies in matters of organization that the committee will so arrange

393

as to leave the platform and nomination of candidates as the only real issues on which delegates need divide.

The Wilson letter was as follows:

You are right. Before hearing of your message I clearly stated my position in answer to a question from the Baltimore Evening Sun. The Baltimore convention is to be the convention of progressives—the men who are progressive in principle and by conviction. It must, if it is not to be put in a wrong light before the country, express its convictions in its organization and its choice of the men who are to speak for it. You are to be a member of the convention and are entirely within your rights in doing everything within your power to bring that result about. No one will doubt where my sympathies lie, and you will, I am sure, find my friends in the convention acting upon a clear conviction and always in the people's cause. I am happy in the confidence that they need no suggestion from me.

There has been much discussion as to the turning point in this convention. Many inside stories have been related as to the influences that swung this delegation or that delegation, and of the various little things that affected the result. In reviewing the history of the whole fight it seems plain at this distance to a detached mind that these two letters written by the two leading candidates before the convention met had more to do with the result than anything else. Because unquestionably it was these letters that started the swing of Bryan, an instructed Clark delegate, away from Clark and to Wilson. They convinced him of the undoubted fact that Clark was ready to compromise with Wall Street and Tammany, to gain the nomination with their support, and Wilson was not. From that moment the weight of his influence was against Clark and it grew heavier every day.

It has always been charged that Bryan, despite his announcement that he would not be a candidate, hoped all through this fight that the convention would deadlock and turn to him. Perhaps he did, though there is certainly no evidence to show it. But even if that were so, it seems clear that his real fight was to prevent the candidate being named or the platform written by the New York and eastern leaders who had so consistently opposed him in three campaigns, and whom he regarded as representing all that was evil and sinister in the politics of the country. On the day the convention assembled, Mr. Bryan met Judge Parker in the convention hall and told him personally he intended to fight him because he was not in sympathy with the reforms essential to the success of the party. As soon as Parker's name was put in nomination for temporary chairman Mr. Bryan rose, and a tremendous uproar composed partly of cheers and partly of hisses, cat-calls, epithets, and curses ensued. He mounted the platform and with an unshakable calm waited for the turmoil to subside. It took many minutes, but with his extraordinary experience in the handling of crowds and the personal magnetism of the man, he eventually dominated the assemblage and made it listen.

His speech against Parker he always considered

one of his greatest efforts. Certainly he never made
one under more dramatic circumstances. It was a
terrific indictment he made of the forces back of
Judge Parker and an extraordinary appeal he made
for his defeat, concluding with the nomination of
John W. Kern of Indiana, who had been his running-
mate in 1908. After quiet had again been restored,
Mr. Kern came to the platform and appealed to
Judge Parker to withdraw with him in the interest
of harmony. There was complete silence in the great
hall while he waited for his answer, but Judge
Parker remained mute in his seat. Then Mr. Kern
appealed to Charles F. Murphy, leader of Tammany
Hall, to use his influence with Parker to get him to
withdraw. Murphy sat and glared, while, led by the
New York delegates, the anti-Bryan, Clark, Underwood, and Harmon delegates nearly went wild with
anger and the galleries, which were overwhelmingly
pro-Wilson, rocked with applause. Finally Mr. Kern
declared that if a fight was inevitable, as it seemed
to be, then Mr. Bryan and not himself was the man
to lead the progressive group, and he placed him in
nomination for temporary chairman.

Again pandemonium reigned, and again when the
vote, amid intense excitement, was announced as:
Parker 579, Bryan 508. Parker was supported by
the Harmon, Underwood, and most of the Clark
delegates, and the result seemed to indicate Clark's
selection, as the Underwood-Harmon group were
anti-Wilson. The victory, however, did not arouse

the enthusiasm that might have been expected. The shadow of the vote darkened the convention, made the Clark leaders shiver with apprehension at a nomination obtained with such flaming opposition and under such devastating fire. But that was not all. The Clark-Harmon-Underwood leaders had control of the convention, but the fight by which they won was followed by one of the most extraordinary demonstrations of public sentiment ever seen in the country. From all sections telegrams began to pour in upon the delegates. The "folks back home" evinced an interest in this convention which has no parallel either before or since. From almost every State telegraphic denunciation of the reactionary element flowed in a stream that grew as the convention proceeded.

This was inspired not by Bryan sentiment but by Wilson sentiment. Friends of the New Jersey governor saw in the initial victory danger to his candidacy. They knew the Tammany group—and they knew that the elder Democratic machine leaders, such as Roger Sullivan of Illinois and Taggart of Indiana, played the game with Murphy, and that at heart these were against Wilson and the Wilson type. The rank and file of the party everywhere wanted Wilson and they made themselves vocal in a remarkable way. Mr. Bryan stated at the time that he personally had received 1182 telegrams signed by an average of three names, each commending him for his fight against Parker. The total number of telegrams received from the country by delegates was incredible. No such avalanche had ever occurred before. Unquestionably it had been planned to a certain extent by the astute Wilson managers in the field, but it did not need much planning. The sentiment was there and the spontaneity and genuineness of the bulk of the telegrams were apparent. Alarmed by the situation, on the night following the afternoon of the Parker selection the Clark managers called on Bryan at the Belvidere Hotel and offered him the permanent chairmanship of the convention, which he declined with the statement that "those who owned the ship should furnish the crew." He also declined the chairmanship of the Committee on Resolutions but agreed to serve on the subcommittee. Kern was chosen chairman of the Resolutions Committee.

There was much confusion and no little consternation in the Clark camp and every effort to placate Mr. Bryan was made. Ollie James was chosen permanent chairman, and all sorts of arguments were made to persuade Mr. Bryan out of his idea that Clark was tied in with the reactionaries. It was about this time that Thomas Fortune Ryan, one of the men of vast wealth whom the progressives regarded with particular abhorrence but who was a delegate from Virginia, arrived in Baltimore at night. The following morning "The Baltimore Sun" printed his picture on its first page with an interview. The psychological effect of this was to still further inflame progressive sentiment and stimulate the flood of telegrams. But the climax came the following day when, without warning, Mr. Bryan, who had been quietly at work with the subcommittee drafting the platform, obtained recognition from Chairman James, went to the platform, and offered the following resolution:

> Resolved, That in this crisis in our party's career and in our country's history this convention sends greetings to the people of the United States, and assures them that the party of Jefferson and of Jackson is still the champion of popular government and equality before the law. As proof of our fidelity to the people, we hereby declare ourselves opposed to the nomination of any candidate for President who is the representative of or under obligation to J. Pierpont Morgan, Thomas F. Ryan, August Belmont, or any other member of the privilege-hunting and favor-seeking class.
>
> Be it further resolved, That we demand the withdrawal from this convention of any delegate or delegates constituting or representing the above-named interests.

It is impossible to exaggerate the sensation of this "bombshell." There in their delegations sat Murphy, Belmont, and Ryan. Their friends and supporters were in a white heat of anger. The whole convention was in the wildest turmoil. Calm, unruffled, and unafraid there stood Bryan on the platform. In the end he again obtained quiet because of the obvious fact that he could not be howled down. What he demanded was a roll-call, and after he had been assailed, denounced, cursed, and almost physically assaulted, he got it. He withdrew the final sentence of his resolution, but no one heard that and the convention voted on it as a whole. The Bryan idea was that if it was passed it would automatically make the nomination of any candidate favored by Ryan, Belmont, and Murphy impossible, and if they voted it down the rebuke from the country would make it equally impossible for the New York delegation to name the nominee. The tumult was at its height while the roll was being called. Delegation after delegation was polled. Fights broke out all over the hall. In the end the impossibility of defeating the resolution was realized and it was adopted by a vote of more than four and a half to one. Even New York voted for it. During the vote Murphy turned to Belmont, seated next to him, and said: "August, listen and hear yourself voted out of the convention."

The effect of the Morgan-Belmont-Ryan resolution was enormous. The enthusiasm of the Wilson Democrats all over the country was stirred and the flood of telegrams given increased impetus. It seemed to stamp the convention as progressive and to make it impossible for Tammany to name the ticket. The balloting began the day after its adoption. Forty-six ballots were taken before the Wilson nomination was made, and during their course some of the most strenuous wire-pulling, delegate hauling, and intriguing ever seen at a national convention occurred. The first ballot showed—

Wilson of New Jersey....................324
Clark of Missouri.....................440½
Underwood of Alabama.................117½

The New York delegation voted solidly for Harmon, but it was recognized the Belmont-Morgan-Ryan resolution had made his nomination impossible and that the delegation was being held together to await developments. Bryan, tied by his instructions, with the other Nebraska delegates voted for Champ Clark. On the tenth ballot New York went over to Clark and he received 556 votes, more than a majority of the convention. Only once before—Van Buren in 1844—had a candidate for the Presidential nomination received a majority of the convention and failed to get the two thirds necessary under the rules to win. When the majority line was crossed the wildest enthusiasm prevailed among the Clark delegates and a great demonstration occurred. It seemed as if the selection of their man was assured. The fighting spirit of the Wilson line-up was strengthened, however, rather than weakened by this, and the determination of Mr. Bryan to prevent a Tammany nomination increased. Again the flood of telegrams poured in on the delegates, and the many delegates friendly to Wilson but bound by instructions for other candidates began to get out of hand.

It is a curious and interesting fact that from this tenth ballot, when Clark received his majority, his vote on every succeeding ballot steadily decreased while that for Wilson just as steadily grew. It was

on the fourteenth ballot that Mr. Bryan broke away
from his Clark instructions and cast his vote for
Wilson. This too caused a great sensation and tremendous feeling, but Mr. Bryan made it effective by
expressing his conviction that if the New York delegation supported Clark instead of Wilson it was because they knew Clark to be more conservative than
Wilson, adding that despite his instructions he would
continue to vote for Wilson as long as New York
supported Clark. Again the excitement was intense
and again a storm of abuse was heaped on the un-
caring Mr. Bryan, but the balloting went steadily on.

Not until the forty-third did Wilson get a majority. On that ballot his vote was 602, while Clark's
had shrunk to 329, Underwood's to 99, Harmon to
28, Foss of Massachusetts to 27. There were a few
scattering ballots, but the fight was now recognized
as over, and Wilson on the forty-sixth ballot got
990, Clark 84, Harmon 12. On motion of Senator
Stone of Missouri, the Clark manager, the nomination was made unanimous and this ended one of the
most dramatic and stirring of all convention fights.

The balance of the proceedings were relatively
tame. Governor Thomas R. Marshall of Indiana was
unanimously nominated for Vice-President on the
second ballot, and the platform was unanimously
adopted without discussion. It denounced the trusts
and the Republican tariff, declared it to be a fundamental principle of the party that the Federal Government under the Constitution has no right or

power to impose or collect tariff duties except for the purpose of revenue, and promised an immediate revision downward of the existing rates. It promised legislation providing full publicity for campaign contributions and a law prohibiting corporations from contributing. It promised currency reform, rural credits, anti-trust legislation, the establishment of a parcel-post system, and the regulation and control of private monopolies. It was a voluminous document, decidedly "progressive" in tone, and, as has been stated, very considerably molded by Mr. Bryan, who was from start to finish easily the most potent and conspicuous figure in the seven days the convention lasted. It was of course the pressure of the sentiment behind Wilson that ultimately crushed down the opposition to him, but it was Mr. Bryan who made it possible for that sentiment to be effectively used.

The enthusiasm engendered throughout the country by the Wilson nomination is hard to exaggerate. There was of course intense soreness among the Clark following, but their resentment was directed almost entirely toward Mr. Bryan, upon whom they placed, and rightly so, the responsibility for preventing Clark from receiving the nomination after he had got a majority of the convention. In part, too, they blamed Roger Sullivan, who was then Democratic boss of Illinois and who swung his delegation from Clark to Wilson at a moment when W. L. McCombs, the Wilson manager, had practically given up hope of putting his candidate over and was preparing to release the Wilson delegates. He had actually telephoned Governor Wilson to that effect, and Wilson, according to Joseph P. Tumulty, his secretary, was on the point of telegraphing congratulations to Clark. It was Sullivan who stopped McCombs from giving up the fight. After it was over, the Clark people realized that the Illinois boss had at heart been for Wilson all the time and had merely been waiting for the right moment to break. They were exceedingly bitter toward him, but it was Bryan upon whom their most fervent curses were heaped.

Their disappointment, however, was completely lost sight of in the general Democratic rejoicing. It was not only the caliber of the candidate and the existence of a very genuine and very strong sentiment among all classes and in all sections for him that united the Democratic party in a way it had not been united for twenty years, but more effective than this was the almost certain prospect of victory. From the start it was apparent that Democratic success was assured. The Republican split at Chicago was deep and wide. Far more absorbingly engaged with fighting each other than the Democrats, one Republican faction made its attack on the other with the slogan "Thou shalt not steal," to which the reply of the Taft wing was, "Thou shalt not bear false witness." After the Roosevelt nomination and the launching of the Progressive or Bull Moose party, while some of the adherents in each of the Repub-

WOODROW WILSON WITH HIS SECRETARY, JOSEPH P. TUMULTY

lican camps had a certain measure of confidence, no detached and posted person had any doubt of the result.

Wilson made a brilliant campaign. His speeches were concededly the best that had been heard in a Presidential campaign in many years. Clear, forceful, graphic, and thoughtful, they took hold and made votes. Full advantage of the Republican split was taken by the candidate and by the Democratic management. Before the middle of October, Democrats all over the land sensed the coming victory and the party was harmonious, united, and enthusiastic. Tammany had swung early into line, and the Democratic campaign, well financed and well managed, was the only real one it had made since 1892. Mr. Bryan went on the stump and in more than twenty States made a series of particularly effective speeches. In marked contrast to the support he gave Parker, there was in the 1912 campaign literally nothing he left undone. Champ Clark, too, though bruised, sore, and bitter to the day of his death, outwardly did his part, supported the ticket, spoke for it. There was not a break in the line anywhere and the net result was an overwhelming and smashing victory. No man before or since received such a majority in the Electoral College. It broke all records. Wilson got 435 electoral votes, Roosevelt 88, Taft 8. While it is true the Wilson popular vote did not equal by more than a million the combined vote of Roosevelt and Taft, yet his plurality over Roosevelt was 2,173,510 and over Taft 2,808,061, and he carried forty of the forty-eight States. Michigan, Minnesota, Pennsylvania, South Dakota, Washington, and California were carried by Roosevelt; Utah and Vermont by Taft. Everything else went Democratic, and the Democrats even got two of the thirteen votes from California.

With Wilson the Democrats won control over both Senate and House. For the first time in eighteen years they had full charge of the Government. For the first time since Cleveland left the White House in 1896 the Democrats had a chance at the offices. A party that had been counted down and out by some of the most astute and experienced political analysts in the country had come back with one of the most complete political victories in history, leaving the opposition, so long dominant in the country, more hopelessly split and more deeply depressed than the Democrats had been at any time except immediately following the Civil War. Moreover, with the election of its ticket the Democratic party found itself supplied with a real leader as well as a real President.

Chapter XXIX

His First Term Accomplishment—His Freedom and
Fearlessness—The Tremendous Bitterness Created
by His Uncompromising Course—His Enemies in
and Out of the Party—The 1916 Renomination and
Campaign

THE Wilson idea was that in nominating him for
the Presidency the party had also nominated him as
its leader. From that day until his physical collapse,
near the end of his second term, he was its undisputed and accepted boss, dominating the organization and National Committee, molding its policies in
every respect. The party became a Wilson party far
more completely than it had been a Cleveland party
—almost as completely as it was a Jackson party
from 1828 to 1836. As to the efficiency of the Wilson
leadership it is best attested by the extraordinary
legislative achievements of his first term. These have
already been cited and need not be again, but they
do stand almost unrivaled as a record of achievement and seem to be the completest possible answer
to the silly idea so earnestly and persistently propa-
gandized by the Republican machine that the Demo-

crats lack the capacity for running the Government and that a Democratic administration is bad for business. The Wilson administration in sheer executive efficiency has no superior in the whole history of American Presidents. As to its effect on business, it is generally conceded that the Federal Reserve Act, passed by the Wilson administration, has done more to stabilize business conditions and, as has been previously pointed out, to make practically impossible such panics as occurred in earlier days, than any other single piece of legislation.

As to the war, conceding the inescapable waste, the inevitable injustices done, and most of the mistakes of judgment and execution charged by the critics, it is again worth while to point out the great outstanding facts—the raising of the army, its equipment, training, transportation, the successful performance abroad, and its return home, with the unprecedented problems of finance involved and the tremendous difficulties that had to be overcome; when to these things is added the almost complete absence of thievery or graft in the prosecution of the greatest war in history, it is impossible to deny that the achievement was an extraordinary one. Certainly not a great many unprejudiced persons will dispute that the two Wilson administrations, in both the domestic and the foreign field, constitute the most splendid chapter in the whole party history.

It is true that few Presidents aroused more intense hostility inside his party as well as outside, created fiercer antagonisms, made more violent, unforgiving, and wholehearted enemies than Wilson. It is true too that no President ever had a larger or a more devoted following or inspired more passionate admiration among the people. With each of his legislative fights he made a host of enemies; every policy he advocated met with opposition. His program had to be forced through a more or less reluctant Congress, relentlessly dominated by his will, forced to acquiesce in his leadership and accept his views. With Wilson came into power a new set of Democratic national leaders and in a number of States men who had not before been conspicuous in Democratic councils but who had been active in the pre-convention Wilson campaign, and considerable party friction was the result.

Mr. Bryan, who had still a large following in the country and a considerable influence in Congress, was made secretary of state and was undoubtedly of great help in putting through the Wilson program in his first term. The Bryan appointment was dictated partly from gratitude for what Mr. Bryan had done in the convention to nominate Wilson and partly because it was unquestionably good politics to name him. Mr. Bryan was greatly gratified at being given this the highest cabinet post and accepted immediately. Many of the enemies of Mr. Wilson were undoubtedly his own fault. He tied up with the wrong men, made a considerable number of very poor appointments, and had some very poor advisers, but unquestionably the great bulk of his enmities were unavoidably due to the fighting character of his leadership and his aggressive determination as President to fulfil in letter and spirit every platform pledge—in other words to the fact that he was a strong man. No man could have used the fire and force necessary to secure the enactment of the laws he advocated without offending large and influential interests and a great many more or less important persons.

The very character of his program aroused opposition. Its scope touched almost every class and gave a chance for the awakening of many sorts of prejudice. Any President who had really put the full weight of his power and personality behind such a program as Wilson's would have made enemies, and been sure to leave in his wake many discomfited and pained persons. Wilson made more than a good many others might by the utterly uncompromising spirit with which he conducted his fights. Unbendable in his determination, completely convinced of the soundness and righteousness of his cause, he refused to compromise with expediency, to yield an inch in the face of threats, to give way at any point to insure the gain of any other, once he had thought his plan through and reached his conclusion. Mostly he got his way because he had the power, but he undoubtedly left a lot of bruised and bitter spirits along his triumphant trail.

Of course, there was the inevitable horde of disappointed office-seekers and unsuccessful favor-hunters, larger perhaps under Wilson than under any other President except Cleveland. One reason for this was that the Democrats, out of power for sixteen years, were extraordinarily hungry for patronage. The other was because there were so few strings that could be pulled to influence Mr. Wilson. No President was ever less amenable to outside influence. No administration was ever freer from either political or financial domination. The big business interests had the same standing as any one else, but very little more, the net result of which was that long before his first term ended, most of the representatives of these interests were deeply resentful of Mr. Wilson, attributing to him all sorts of crimes and misdemeanors and apparently willing to believe almost any discreditable story about him. For neither his nomination nor his election had it been necessary for Mr. Wilson to incur any obligations that weighed on him. No President was more free from promises direct or implied than he; none in better position to go fearlessly ahead to put through the reforms for which he stood, and none ever did more fearlessly go ahead. Wilson had his faults and his weaknesses, but lack of courage was not one of them.

The 1924 congressional elections considerably reduced the Democratic majorities in Congress, leaving the party with a margin of six in the Senate and thirty-five in the House, small but sufficient to get results under the Wilson leadership. By the close of his first term the record of the administration, which was also the record of the party, was officially and with a fair degree of accuracy summed up for platform purposes as follows:

We challenge comparison of our record, our keeping of pledges and our constructive legislation, with those of any party of any time.

We found our country hampered by special privilege, a vicious tariff, obsolete banking laws, and inelastic currency. Our foreign affairs were dominated by commercial interests for their selfish ends. The Republican party despite repeated pledges, was impotent to correct abuses which it had fostered. Under our administration, under a leadership which has never faltered, these abuses have been corrected, and our people have been freed therefrom.

Our archaic banking and currency system, prolific of panic and disaster under Republican administrations, long the refuge of the Money Trust, has been supplanted by the Federal Reserve Act, a true democracy of credit under Government control already proved a financial bulwark in a world's crisis, mobilizing our resources, placing abundant credit at the disposal of legitimate industry, and making a currency panic impossible.

We have created a Federal Trade Commission to accommodate the perplexing questions arising under the anti-trust laws so that monopoly may be strangled at its birth and legitimate industry encouraged. Fair competition in business is now assured.

We have effected an adjustment of the tariff, adequate for revenue under peace conditions, and fair to the consumer and to the producer. We have adjusted the burdens of taxation so that swollen incomes bear their equitable share. Our revenues have been sufficient in times of world stress and will largely exceed the expenditures for the current fiscal year.

We have lifted human labor from the category of com-

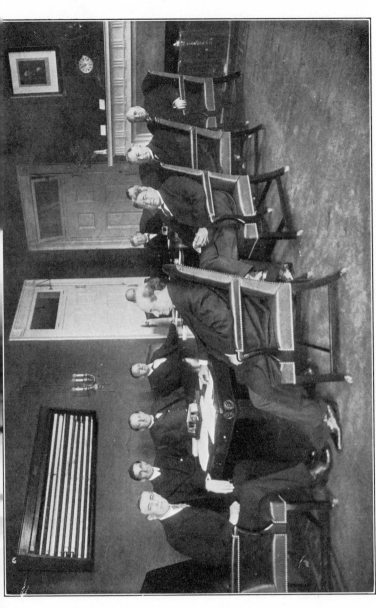

© Brown Brothers.

PRESIDENT WOODROW WILSON AND HIS CABINET—1913

modities and have secured to the working man the right of voluntary association for his protection and welfare. We have protected the rights of the laborer against the unwarranted issuance of writs of injunction, and have guaranteed to him the right of trial by jury in cases of alleged contempt committed outside the presence of the court.

We have advanced the parcel post to genuine efficiency, enlarged the postal savings system, added 10,000 rural delivery routes and extensions, thus reaching two and one-half millions additional people, improved the postal service in every branch, and for the first time in our history placed the post-office system on a self-supporting basis, with actual surplus in 1913, 1914 and 1916.

The reforms which were most obviously needed to clear away privilege, prevent unfair discrimination and release the energies of men of all ranks and advantages have been effected by recent legislation. We must now remove, so far as possible, every remaining element of unrest and uncertainty from the path of the business men of America and secure for them a continued period of equal, satisfied and confident prosperity.

It is easy to appreciate that no such record as this could have been made without lacerating the feelings of a good many figures in the political and financial world, trampling on the toes of a lot of people who for one reason or another were not in accord with the progressive views of the President. Some of these were in the Senate, some in the House, some in the various state organizations, and some wholly outside of the political field. Lumped together they made a considerable total long before the end of his first term. Disliked when inaugurated, he had the bitter enmity of the business men who dominate opinion in New England and the Eastern

413

States. They accused him of truckling to labor, and scoffed at what they called his "idealism." They were particularly bitter about his handling of the Mexican crisis which arose in 1916, and by the series of notes with which he held the country neutral for the four years from 1914 to 1917, in which latter year we finally entered the World War. As you look back, there seems considerable justification for the self-restraint of Wilson during a period of great turmoil and excitement and under a terrific pounding from his political foes and a hostile press. He waited until he had such a complete case for the entrance of this country on the side of the allies that it could not be disputed. To have gone in sooner would have been to go in before the whole country was ready and unitedly behind him. It is true that in the East the Wilson self-restraint during the early years of the war was construed as timidity, and the most intense resentment was felt over his course, which was greatly heightened by the use of, for him, the exceedingly unfortunate expression in a speech that "there is such a thing as being too proud to fight."

By 1915 the Republicans were beginning to center sentiment around Justice Charles E. Hughes of the Supreme Court, and former governor of New York, as their candidate. It was believed that with Mr. Hughes the party could again be united and returned to power. The Republican press, particularly in the East, opened its heavy guns against Mr. Wilson early in 1916, and from then on the attack on his foreign policy both in Europe and in Mexico was violent, sustained, and determined. Through most of 1916, and at the very time of the convention the Mexican situation was exceedingly acute, a state of war almost actually existing. It did not, however, remain critical long and was not a major issue in the campaign.

It was in the handling of the submarine situation, however, that the most intense feeling against him was aroused. Every sinking of an American ship brought from Wilson vigorous protests in the shape of notes, which were highly unsatisfactory to the belligerent press of the East, the political opponents of the President, and those in the business world who instinctively disliked his type of man. In spite of the difficulties of the situation, with the increased hostility toward him in the East adding enemies to the rather fair accumulation he had as a result of his battles as president of Princeton and governor of New Jersey, there seemed relatively little diminution in his popularity with the masses of the people, and certainly no weakening of his grip on the party.

As the time for the 1916 convention approached it was clear not only that Wilson would be renominated by acclamation, and that no other name would be mentioned there in connection with the Presidency, but that nothing would be done there except as desired by him. When the delegates assembled in St. Louis on June 12 the World War had been in progress two years and the Mexican blaze had died down only to blaze up again as soon as the convention was over. William F. McCombs, who had been chairman of the National Committee since 1912, called the convention to order and ex-Governor Martin H. Glynn of New York was temporary chairman. A few days before, some opposition to the renomination of Vice-President Marshall led by Henry Morgenthau developed and for a while threatened to attain serious proportions. It collapsed completely, however, upon the arrival in St. Louis of Secretary of War Newton D. Baker, bringing with him a copy of the platform as written by Mr. Wilson, together with direct word from him that he wanted Marshall renominated. That ended it. From that moment on the harmony was unmarred by so much as a ripple. All the Vice-Presidential booms that had been brought to St. Louis wilted and disappeared. Mr. Glynn made the keynote speech paying such eloquent and beautiful tribute to Mr. Wilson that Mr. Bryan, not a delegate but with a seat in the press section, wept from emotion. Later Mr. Bryan by request ascended the rostrum, was given a good ovation, and aroused tremendous enthusiasm by his opening words: "We are here to begin the fight of 1916, a united party in every State of the Union, ready for battle."

It was the first convention since 1896 in which Mr. Bryan had not either dominated the proceedings or made a lot of trouble for those who did. In this one he was harmonious from start to finish, with

WOODROW WILSON

President 1913-1921

neither platform nor candidatorial suggestion and
no official voice in the assemblage. Senator Ollie
James of Kentucky, who had presided in 1912, was
the permanent chairman, and both he and Mr. Bryan
delivered speeches eulogistic of Mr. Wilson that
aroused the crowd to a fever pitch of enthusiasm.
Wilson and Marshall were nominated by acclamation and an extraordinary demonstration lasting
more than an hour followed the mention of Wilson's
name by John W. Westcott, attorney-general of New
Jersey, who had nominated him in 1912. The platform was adopted practically as written by Mr. Wilson, the only struggle in the committee being over
the woman suffrage plank. To this there was bitter
opposition, but Wilson was for a clear-cut declaration in its favor, more definite than the Republicans
had made, and in the end he had his way. The fight
was all in committee. On the floor the whole platform was adopted without a dissenting voice. It was
a long and ably written document, reciting in detail
the party record of the past four years, containing
a strong neutrality plank, denouncing the intrigues
and plots carried on in the interests of foreign Governments on American soil, insisting upon the determination of this administration to maintain the
honor of the nation and to protect the interests,
rights, and lives of its citizens, wherever they might
be. It was pointed out that this was a critical hour
in the world's history and that the aim of this country should be to keep the friendship of all others

while at the same time upholding our honor and our rights. Disturbers of these conditions were denounced, and there was also this paragraph, which was more significant and effective as far as the campaign was concerned than any other:

"In particular we commend to the American people the splendid diplomatic victories of our great President, who has preserved the vital interests of our government and its citizens and kept us out of war."

Those last five words were extremely effective in the fight that followed. They were never actually used by Wilson himself, but Democratic orators and local candidates did use them with great effect, not only pointing out that Wilson had "kept us out of war" but asserting that he would keep us out if reelected. There is no doubt that many votes particularly in the middle and far West were swung to him by that pregnant phrase.

The Republican convention was held a week before the Democratic. Hughes had been nominated by the Republicans and the party united behind him through the refusal of Roosevelt to accept renomination from the Progressive party which he had brought into being in 1912, and which wholly hinged on him. When he went back into the regular Republican fold his party went completely out of existence and the split that had proved so fatal in 1912 was closed. Mr. Hughes sent his resignation from the Supreme Bench to President Wilson in a

418

singularly curt note, with none of the courtesy that could reasonably have been expected from a man of his type. He wrote:

June 10, 1916.

To the President:—

I hereby resign the office of Associate Justice of the Supreme Court of the United States.

I am, sir

Respectfully yours,

CHARLES E. HUGHES.

When it is recalled that there existed a personal feeling of friendship toward Mr. Hughes upon the part of the whole Wilson family, and that the personal relations between him and the President were close, this note appears singularly ungracious and harsh. Joseph P. Tumulty, Wilson's secretary, is authority for the statement that Wilson was hurt by the tone of the letter and was urged by Senator Ollie James of Kentucky, to whom it was shown, not to dignify it with a reply. To this Wilson replied: "No, I must reply. The President of the United States must always be a gentleman." What he wrote was this:

June 10, 1916.

Dear Mr. Justice Hughes,

I am in receipt of your letter of resignation and feel constrained to yield to your desire. I therefore accept your res-

419

ignation as Justice of the Supreme Court of the United States to take effect at once.

Sincerely yours,

WOODROW WILSON.

The Republican platform had ferociously assailed the Wilson administration and particularly denounced and condemned Wilson's handling of foreign affairs, both as to the European war and Mexico. It attacked the Democratic tariff, slurred at the Federal Reserve Act and the other achievements of the administration, but it was on the Wilson foreign policy the real emphasis was laid. Apparently Mr. Hughes, cordially supported by Colonel Roosevelt, had behind him a thoroughly reunited party determined to regain control of the Government. The big business interests of the East, hostile to Wilson, were determined to check his power, and the Republicans were able to finance their campaign up to the hilt. With Hughes as the candidate and the progressives in line behind him, they had every expectation of winning.

Colonel Roosevelt took the stump and made a series of savage attacks on Wilson, declaring that after the Lusitania sinking he had "chosen the course of dishonor," accusing him of "mean timidity," declaring that "instead of speaking softly and carrying a Big Stick, Wilson spoke bombastically and carried a dish rag." Mr. Hughes, too, started out along this line, but before many weeks modified his attack, lost his stride, and never struck it again. His campaign was a disappointment to his friends and a surprise to his foes. It had been anticipated that he would prove an exceedingly effective campaign speaker. It did not turn out so, and while when the campaign ended the Republicans were still full of confidence, it was conceded that the Hughes western tour to the California coast had not been a success and there was some danger in the situation. At the close of the fight, though Colonel Roosevelt kept pounding Mr. Wilson on his "mean timidity" in foreign affairs, and Mr. Hughes insisted we should have broken with Germany after the Lusitania incident, the Republican candidate was talking tariff and "protection for the American working man" almost exclusively.

On the Democratic side the campaign was largely conducted by Wilson from Shadow Lawn, the summer White House on the Jersey coast. He made only one speech away from there—in Chicago; but in a series of devastating statements and neighborhood speeches, spaced about a week apart, he dealt with the attacks on him and made a few of his own from his front porch at Shadow Lawn to visiting delegations and friends. "The real issue," he declared, "is whether the government shall be run for the people or for the Special Interests. The mask is off. The men in control of the Republican party form one of the most sinister combinations American politics ever saw."

On both sides there were a few clear headed men who saw that American entrance into the war was inevitable within a short time. The Republican leaders who grasped this wanted their party to conduct the war. They felt that there was more at stake in this campaign than in any other since the Civil War, and they left nothing undone to win it. While Wilson did not himself promise to keep the country out of war, members of his cabinet on the stump, Democratic orators, and propagandists generally undoubtedly did, and there is no question that he received thousands of votes because of the belief that this was so. Particularly was this true in the West, where there was little feeling about the war at the time save a desire to keep out of it. Vance C. McCormick of Pennsylvania had succeeded McCombs as chairman of the National Committee, and though short of money, as all Democratic campaigns invariably are, under his direction a special drive was made to enlist the sympathy and support of the women voters who were participating for the first time in a Presidential election. One of the small but effective incidents of the campaign was caused by an Irish agitator named O'Leary, who was endeavoring to organize the Irish vote and wrote Wilson an offensive letter, calling attention to the Maine September election results and predicting his defeat in November. Mr. Wilson made the following reply to O'Leary:

I would feel deeply mortified to have you or anybody like you vote for me. Since you have access to many disloyal

Americans and I have not, I will ask you to convey this message to them.

The discovery that O'Leary had been conferring at Republican headquarters, the character of his activities, and the character of his letter made the Wilson rejoinder exceedingly popular, and put new zest into the Democratic campaign. With both sides apparently genuinely confident and the betting odds about even, the fight ended, with Wilson still at Shadow Lawn and Hughes at his home in New York.

Early on the night of the election the returns from the Eastern States were so overwhelmingly Republican that the stanchest Wilson newspapers—"The New York World," "The New York Times," "The Baltimore Sun," and many others—conceded the election of Hughes, and about nine o'clock most of them issued extras conceding the Democratic defeat. New York, New Jersey, Connecticut, Rhode Island, Delaware, and Indiana had gone Republican. It seem incredible that Wilson could be saved. Yet the little band of Democrats around Tumulty at the White House and Vance McCormick in New York refused to concede it, insisting that the losses in the East would be made up by gains in the West. Before dawn Wednesday morning their faith was justified. By that time enough had been heard from the West to show that there had been an amazing turn-over in apparently impregnably Republican States, that Nebraska, Kansas, Idaho, Nevada, Washington, Wyoming had gone for Wilson, that California and Minnesota trembled in the balance. By Wednesday afternoon it was clear Wilson had won, though the margin was close. It was not until Sunday morning that the completed returns were all in and the remarkable Wilson victory established beyond all doubt and recall—with 277 electoral votes to 254 for Hughes. On the popular vote Wilson had a plurality of 403,312. He got 8,563,713 votes to 8,160,401 for Hughes. The Democrats lost the House by a small margin, but retained control of the Senate.

Probably no one except Tilden was ever so close to the Presidency and missed it as Mr. Hughes. It must have been a terrific blow, particularly as there was no hint of fraud to take away from the mortification of the failure. On the contrary, the loss of the great State of California was generally held due to the failure of Mr. Hughes while in the hotel at San Francisco to meet and speak to Senator Hiram Johnson of that State, who was in the same hotel. In fairness to Mr. Hughes, it should be said that this was not his fault, but was due to the stupidity and smallness of the local committee which had him in charge. Hughes did not know Johnson was in the hotel. When he found it out it was too late. The failure of the Presidential candidate to meet the Senator, however, was printed in such a way as to make it seem an intentional slight, and it greatly angered the Johnson following all over California. The political writers agreed that this Hughes-Johnson incident lost the State to the Republicans. It lost more than that—its thirteen electoral votes lost the Presidency for them as well.

Chapter XXX

WILSON AND THE WAR

His Appointment of Republicans as a Reply to Republican
Drive for a Coalition Cabinet—The Great Mistake
of 1918 in Appealing for a Democratic Congress—
His European Experience

BEYOND doubt Wilson was largely elected in 1916 on
the Democratic slogan "He kept us out of war," but
it was not long after his second election that it became clear to him and to every one else close enough
to have a real knowledge of the facts that the time
when America could be kept out of war was rapidly
passing, that the course of Germany in fact was
inevitably driving it into war. Volumes could be
and volumes have been written around these four
years between 1916 and 1920. In many ways they
formed the most dramatic, stirring, and momentous
period in the whole history of the country. The tremendous story of America in the greatest of all wars
was followed by the almost equally tremendous story
of the part played by the American President in the
most remarkable peace and that by a Senate battle of
almost unprecedented ferocity over the League of

Nations, climaxing in the rejection of the treaty and the tragic physical collapse of Wilson at the very height of his magnificent fight.

It was a time of great emotional disturbance. The whole range of human feelings, from the purest form of patriotism to the most malignant and despicable type of personal hate, was covered by those who played conspicuous public parts in these four years. It is probably accurate to say that this second administration of Woodrow Wilson was more vibrant and eventful than any other since the republic was founded. So far as this book is concerned, however, the only thing to do is hold hard to the thread of the Democratic narrative and resist every temptation to digress into a discussion of the great problems of the war and the peace, the way in which they were met, and the results.

Almost immediately after the declaration of a state of war between the United States and Germany, made by Congress on April 6, 1917, the drive by the Republicans for a coalition cabinet began. The idea that now war had come it was to be conducted by a Democratic President with Democrats at the head of every department was an intolerable one to a certain type of Republican, and for a while a tremendous clamor for a bipartisan super-cabinet or coalition cabinet was kept up. To this Wilson was unalterably opposed. He announced there would be no politics in the conduct of the war, no political generals chosen, no partisanship tolerated, but that there was no necessity for a super-cabinet or a change in department heads.

After awhile this attempt of the Republicans to "wedge in" on the conduct of the war was abandoned, and Wilson in his own way proceeded to demonstrate his utter and complete disregard of politics by naming Republicans to the bulk of the key positions in the great war machine that had to be built with such extraordinary speed. Though it was recognized that the soldier in command of the American troops in France might easily develop into a Presidential possibility, this post was given to General John J. Pershing, a lifelong Republican and a son-in-law of Senator Francis Warren of Wyoming, one of the Republican Old Guard. Admiral William S. Sims, another strong Republican, was placed in charge of the American naval forces abroad. Howard E. Coffin, a Republican, was made head of the Aircraft Board, with Colonel Edward A. Deeds, another Republican of great regularity and vigor, as his assistant. When failure and corruption were charged against this board, Wilson appointed Charles E. Hughes, his opponent in 1916, to conduct the investigation, which came to nothing, as did all subsequent charges and investigations by Republicans into the conduct of the war, both during the war when the Democrats were in charge and after the war when their own party gained complete control.

The Emergency Fleet Corporation was in charge

of Charles M. Schwab and Charles Piez, both Republicans. The three assistant secretaries of war named by Secretary of War Newton D. Baker were all Republicans—Benedict Crowell, F. E. Keppel, and Emmet J. Scott. So was the special assistant secretary—E. R. Stettinius of the J. P. Morgan firm, who was placed in charge of supplies. Samuel McRoberts, president of the National City Bank, one of the strongest Republicans in the country, was made chief of the procurement section of the ordnance division. The provost marshal-general was E. H. Crowder, a regular Republican, who named Charles Beecher Warren, a member of the Republican National Committee, to a position of great power and importance. Henry P. Davison, a Republican, was in supreme authority in the Red Cross, and on the Red Cross war council were William Howard Taft, Charles B. Norton, and Cornelius N. Bliss, all active and conspicuous Republicans. Frank A. Vanderlip was in charge of the War Savings Stamps campaign, Herbert Hoover was food controller, Harry A. Garfield was fuel administrator, and on the Council of National Defense the only real Democrat was Bernard M. Baruch, afterward Chief of the War Industries Board, where his energy, ability, and devotion were of incalculable service. All the others on that council were Republicans—Daniel Willard, Howard E. Coffin, Julius Rosenwald, Dr. Hallis Godfrey, Dr. Franklin Martin, Walter S. Gifford. There was one independent—Samuel Gompers.

These names are cited to show that while Wilson rejected the effort of the Republicans to force a coalition cabinet on him, so far as the conduct of the war was concerned he really did adhere as closely as any man could to the rule he laid down right after his historic speech in Congress on April 2, 1917, which was, "the best man for every place regardless of his politics." Not his most virulent enemy charged that Wilson let political considerations enter into his calculations so far as the building and operation of the great war machine was concerned, unless his refusal to permit the Republicans to force either the coalition or super-cabinet scheme on him is construed as political. Perhaps it was, but it was certainly plain that the Republican drive for the coalition cabinet was entirely political, plainly inspired by the idea that a successful war would redound to the credit of the party in power, and that a coalition cabinet would give them a share of the credit. The straightforward, utterly non-partisan policy of the administration from the day we entered the war was unquestionably recognized and approved in the country generally.

There was a strong undercurrent of criticism of Wilson personally, sharp disagreement over policies, soreness and resentment in many quarters over the multitudinous war-time activities and decisions, but there was no charge of partisanship or politics until October, 1918, immediately preceding the congressional elections of that year. At that time, acting upon the advice of men in whom he had confidence and who were close to him, he made an appeal to the country for the election of a Democratic Congress. His reasons for making the appeal were certainly not purely partisan, although of course some of those who urged him most strongly did so from personal political motives.

He believed, and he had reason to believe, that a Republican Congress would not cooperate with him, that its main purpose would be to discredit him, to interfere and block him so far as it could without laying itself open to the charge of lack of patriotism or actually endangering the cause for which we were fighting. Without reflecting upon the patriotism of the Republicans, there is no question that Wilson believed the successful conduct of the war depended upon having a Congress in sympathetic accord with him—not one which would endeavor to control rather than follow him. So after considering the question a long while, conferring with various Democratic leaders and friends, Wilson finally wrote personally the following appeal to the country:

My Fellow Countrymen: The Congressional elections are at hand. They occur in the most critical period our country has ever faced or is likely to face in our time. If you have approved of my leadership and wish me to continue to be your unembarrassed spokesman in affairs at home and abroad, I earnestly beg that you will express yourself unmistakably to that effect by returning a Democratic majority to both the Senate and the House of Representatives. I am your servant and will accept your judgment without cavil, but my power to administer the great trust assigned me by the Constitution would be seriously impaired should your judgment be adverse, and I must frankly tell you so because so many critical issues depend upon your verdict. No scruple of taste must in grim times like these be allowed to stand in the way of speaking the plain truth.

I have no thought of suggesting that any political party is paramount in matters of patriotism. I feel too keenly the sacrifices which have been made in this war by all our citizens, irrespective of party affiliations, to harbor such an idea. I mean only that the difficulties and delicacies of our present task are of a sort that makes it imperatively necessary that the nation should give its undivided support to the Government under a unified leadership, and that a Republican Congress would divide the leadership.

The leaders of the minority in the present Congress have unquestionably been pro-war, but they have been anti-Administration. At almost every turn since we entered the war, they have sought to take the choice of policy and the conduct of the war out of my hands and put it under the control of instrumentalities of their own choosing. This is no time either for divided counsel or for divided leadership. Unity of command is as necessary now in civil action as it is upon the field of battle. If the control of the House and Senate should be taken away from the party now in power, an opposing majority could assume control of legislation and oblige all action to be taken amidst contest and obstruction.

The return of a Republican majority to either House of the Congress would, moreover, certainly be interpreted on the other side of the water as a repudiation of my leadership. Spokesmen of the Republican party are urging you to elect a Republican Congress in order to back up and support the President, but even if they should in this way impose upon some credulous voters on this side of the water, they would impose on no one on the other side. It is well understood there as well as here that the Republican leaders desire not so much to support the President as to control him. The

432

PRESIDENT WOODROW WILSON TAKING THE OATH OF OFFICE—MARCH 4, 1913

peoples of the Allied countries with whom we are associated against Germany are quite familiar with the significance of elections. They would find it very difficult to believe that the voters of the United States had chosen to support their President by electing to the Congress a majority controlled by those who are not in fact in sympathy with the attitude and action of the Administration.

I need not tell you, my fellow countrymen, that I am asking your support not for my own sake or for the sake of a political party, but for the sake of the nation itself, in order that its outward unity of purpose may be evident to all the world. In ordinary times I would not feel at liberty to make such an appeal to you. In ordinary times divided counsels can be endured without permanent hurt to the country. But these are not ordinary times. If in these critical days it is your wish to sustain me with undivided minds, I beg that you will say so in a way which it will not be possible to misunderstand either here at home or among our associates on the other side of the sea. I submit my difficulties and my hopes to you.

It was a great mistake, regardless of the purity of his purpose and his freedom from small political motives. At once there was an extraordinary country-wide protest. The Democratic appeal gave to the host of Wilson enemies, large enough in all conscience at the close of his first administration but vastly augmented since his second election, their great opportunity. Up to this point the patriotic necessity of supporting the President in the non-partisan conduct of the war had kept them quiet. But when Wilson made what could be construed as a partisan appeal, with the war still on, it gave them their chance, and there was a roar of anger from coast to coast. An avalanche of denunciation in the press followed and the reaction against the Democrats was too clear to be mistaken.

It is probable the party would have lost control anyhow, because the anti-Democratic tide had already set in, but there is not the least doubt the Wilson appeal cost many thousands of votes and added to the size of the defeat. When the election was over, the Republicans had control of both Senate and House by wide margins. Then came the armistice on November 11, the decision of Wilson to attend the peace conference, his departure for Europe, his amazing reception on the other side, his great struggle with the European politicians over the League of Nations, the sniping at him while abroad, his return to the United States with the League incorporated in the treaty, the long and bitter Senate battle against it led by his personal enemy Henry Cabot Lodge, his direct appeal to the people on a trip West in September, 1919, the tremendous enthusiasm aroused by his speeches, the stroke of paralysis that laid him low at Pueblo, Colorado, and brought him back to Washington a crippled, broken man, who though he served to the end of his term never regained his health or strength; the final rejection of the treaty by the Senate; and then the extraordinary malevolence with which his enemies pursued him even after he had been stricken. The story of these things—or most of them—belongs in a history of the great war, or a history of the peace, or a history of the United States, rather than in a history of the Democratic

party. They will therefore, in this volume, be merely
mentioned in order to keep the Democratic story coherent and consecutive.

Chapter XXXI

THE 1920 SAN FRANCISCO CONVENTION

McAdoo's First Fight—Wilson's Complete Neutrality
as to Candidates—Cox and Palmer—Prohibition and
the League of Nations—Smith, Davis, and Ritchie
Figure in Convention

As the 1920 national convention approached, the
position and the prospects of the Democratic party
were anything but encouraging. With House and
Senate in possession of the Republicans; with its
President and its leader ill, broken, and hopelessly in-
capacitated in the White House; with no figure in the
party even approaching his tall stature; with the vast
accumulated resentment from eight long years of
control; with the inevitable hostility and jealousy
aroused by the complete dominance, amounting to a
real dictatorship during the war, of such a man as
Wilson, fearless, determined, unbendable, with fire,
force, and fighting spirit, equipped both with ideals
and power; with the terrific feeling engendered by
prohibition unreasonably laid to Wilson; and the
general backwash of the war, which illogically
enough seemed to hurt Wilson and the party rather
than redound to their credit—with all these things,
and some others, as June approached, Democratic

436

leaders generally were dispirited, discouraged, and at sea.

Ill though he was, Wilson was still the party leader, and it was recognized that this convention would nominate a ticket of his choice and adopt a platform that met his views. At this time few persons other than Mrs. Wilson, his secretary, Joseph P. Tumulty, and his physician and friend Admiral Cary T. Grayson saw much of him, though in February, 1920, the Democratic National Committee, headed by Homer Cummings of Connecticut, who had succeeded to the chairmanship, called on him at the White House. To them he made an extended and never published speech in which he insisted that the League of Nations be made the paramount issue in the Democratic campaign, urged that everything else was of relatively minor importance, but advised against making it appear a partisan issue, as it was much too big and far too vital for that. It was a long and impassioned and not always clear speech he made. The members of the committee went away from the White House saddened by the sight of his drawn face but profoundly touched by the indomitable spirit of the man.

So far as candidates were concerned, though a word from Wilson would have nominated any one of the aspirants, he outlined early in the year a policy of strict neutrality from which he at no time and in no way departed. A good many leaders sought some hint of his preference but in vain, and when the

Democratic delegates assembled in San Francisco in June no one knew how he felt toward any one of the half dozen and more men mentioned in connection with the nomination. There was even a feeling that he would have been glad, sick as he was, to have the convention nominate him, and there were moments at San Francisco when there was a chance that that would be done, notwithstanding the general knowledge of his pathetic physical condition.

Bryan was there as a delegate. He had resigned as secretary of state in 1915, long before our entrance into the war, not because of any diminution of his admiration for Wilson but because of the strength of his pacifism and his belief that the tone and tendency of the Wilson notes to Germany would inevitably bring the break that meant war. In this of course he was right. His withdrawal from the cabinet was a relief to him and to his colleagues. Though he had the affection and respect of them all, he had been there long enough to clearly demonstrate that any sort of an executive job was not the thing for which he was fitted. The cause closest to his heart these days was prohibition. More than any other single individual in the country he had contributed to the ratification of the Eighteenth Amendment to the Constitution which was adopted while the country was still at war. The Democratic party was in power, but the Democratic President and party leader, though he hated the thought of putting this police power in the Constitution, took no public position on the amendment, and neither party can be properly praised or blamed for it. They were about equally responsible. As a matter of fact, more normally Republican States voted for its ratification than Democratic. The two party organizations were coerced in an extraordinary way by the Anti-Saloon League, representing the prohibition forces. The ratification of the amendment is the best example in history of what can be done by a compact, organized, and directed force operating between the two major parties as a balance of power. It forced both to do its bidding, and ratification by state legislatures was secured even in States like New York and Maryland, where public sentiment was strongly against prohibition.

While local option is of course a fundamental Democratic principle, prohibition by the Federal Constitution was in conflict with the basic party doctrines of States' rights and personal liberty. Nothing could be clearer than that. Yet the strongest Democratic section of the country—the South—was solidly in favor of Federal prohibition, and the Southern States were among the first to ratify. There is clear evidence that Wilson was personally opposed to putting prohibition into the Constitution, that he thought it an unwise and an unnecessary thing to do. The Democratic party had more than once taken firm ground against "sumptuary legislation," but between the war, which absorbed his every thought, the impetus of the prohibition movement in

South and West, the amazing skill with which the Anti-Saloon League played one party against the other, and the fact that the fight was in the state legislatures and not in Congress, there was no road open to him to interfere and the movement could not be headed. Prohibition went into effect January 16, 1920.

Mr. Wilson vetoed the Volstead Enforcement Act, passed by Congress to give the amendment effect, on the ground that it was too rigid, that it was unenforceable, and was not in the spirit of the amendment. It was promptly passed over his veto by a Republican Congress, in which both Democrats and Republicans were about equally dominated by the Anti-Saloon League. Almost immediately the reaction began. The 1920 convention was the first to follow the ratification of the amendment, and already a sentiment had developed that once again split the party sectionally over a moral issue. Mr. Bryan went to San Francisco not in the interests of any candidate but to combat the wet element of the East, which clamored for a modification of the Volstead act that would permit the manufacture of light wines and beers. His interest was to oppose the selection of any moist candidate and to force the adoption of a bone-dry plank.

That was what he went to the convention to do, and though he was defeated in both respects—his plank was rejected and the candidate he opposed nominated—still he made a great fight, a fight so strong and so determined that the wet plank was rejected along with the dry, and the candidate favored by the wet interests declared himself strongly in favor of law enforcement in order not to alienate the drys. It was a thrilling battle between the two sides, which was carried from the Committee on Resolutions to the floor of the convention. Congressman Bourke Cockran of New York, eloquent, brilliant, and witty, led the assault on prohibition, and Mr. Bryan was of course the champion of the drys.

The net result was that the platform avoided mention of the subject of prohibition, just as the Republicans had avoided it, though more than any other it was the issue with which the people were most deeply concerned. The fight clearly marked the sectional division in the party—agricultural South and West against the industrial East—which on this question has grown more pronounced and more bitter with each passing year. Recognizing the impossibility of reconciling the two factions, and appreciating fully the political dangers of taking a decided stand on either side of a question that aroused such strong feeling, the tendency of politicians in both parties was in 1920, and has been ever since, to "soft pedal" on the issue, to say as little as possible on the subject, to completely ignore the controversy, to avoid offending either side, to hold that the whole business had been settled and was no longer a proper topic for a political platform.

In other words, the Democratic party adopted toward the prohibition issue almost exactly the same course it adopted toward the slavery issue, and if an analysis is made of the sectional divisions created by the two issues the parallel becomes more impressive. The extraordinary fear of the politicians of coming to grips with the subject was strikingly shown in this 1920 convention, when Mr. Bryan's bone-dry plank was voted down by 925½ to 155½ and almost immediately afterward Mr. Cockran's wet plank was defeated by a vote of 726½ to 356½. After both these planks had been rejected the platform, with no mention of prohibition at all, was adopted by acclamation. Instead of subsiding, each time the conventions of the two parties have ignored the situation created by the revolt against the Volstead act, the sentiment has apparently increased until the point has been reached in 1928 where both drys and wets agree it is the one issue which really interests the people generally and about which any one really cares. Yet the fear of the political managers on both sides of dealing with it is greater, the desire to dodge it as an issue stronger. In the end, of course, it will have to be met and fought out, just as every other real issue has been. Up to date the Republicans have been more successful than have the Democrats in smothering it in their party gatherings, this success being largely due to the fundamental differences between the parties, which always make Democrats more willing to grapple with a controversial question than the Republicans.

But to return to the 1920 convention: with the prohibition planks all kicked out, the only important section of the platform was that dealing with the League of Nations. There had been opposition to the straight-out declaration in favor of it. Mr. Bryan did not think it should be the paramount issue, and some of the old-line organization leaders were out of tune with the League idea and feared its effect on their local tickets. But the Wilson administration forces were in control. Homer S. Cummings as temporary chairman had in the keynote speech created tremendous enthusiasm by his reference to Wilson and the League. The portrait of the sick President displayed at the psychological moment caused a tremendous demonstration lasting more than an hour. Eloquent tributes were paid him by Bryan and Cockran, and four members of his cabinet—Colby, Meredith, Daniels, and Burleson—were on hand to see that his wishes so far as the League was concerned were carried out.

And they were. The first plank in the platform, reported by Senator Carter Glass of Virginia, chairman of the Committee on Resolutions, was a straight-out, clean-cut declaration in favor of the League and a pledge to put the United States in if the party were successful. This made the issue, which was what Wilson wanted, because the Republican platform had, without mentioning the League directly by name, to all intents and purposes declared against it. The rest of the platform was of minor importance and no other issue was created. So sharply was the line drawn on the League that it amounted to a referendum. So much for the platform. As to candidates, when the convention met there were a dozen men mentioned in connection with the nomination, but in the absence of any indication of a preference from Mr. Wilson, his friends were divided and no one had anything approaching a majority. For a good many months William Gibbs McAdoo, son-in-law of the President, who had been secretary of the treasury during the war, was most conspicuously mentioned. Mr. McAdoo, a vigorous, able, forceful man, had many friends and quite a few enemies. After the war he had resigned from the cabinet in order, as he said, to "rehabilitate" his fortunes and "for the sake of my family." By many he was regarded as the administration candidate, but not by Woodrow Wilson, who never at any time or to any one indicated that he was for him.

On the contrary, Attorney-General A. Mitchell Palmer of Pennsylvania, anxious himself for the nomination, had gone personally to Mr. Wilson to find if he had a choice or would have one, and if he was free to go in. If the President had a choice Palmer would not be a candidate but would support whomever the administration or Wilson wanted. He was told that the position of the President was and would be one of strict neutrality as between candidates and that he was entirely free to enter the

444

field. There is not the slightest evidence that Mr. Wilson ever deviated from this attitude. His only pre-convention public expression was made on June 18, through the medium of Louis Seibold, then a reporter for "The New York World" and an old friend. In a remarkable interview given to Mr. Seibold in the White House, Wilson expressed his confidence that the Democratic party would back his stand on the League, and denounced the Republican platform as "the very apotheosis of reaction," but said no word as to candidates.

Three weeks before the convention met, Mr. McAdoo was undoubtedly far in the lead of all others. Governor James M. Cox of Ohio had the support of his State and the friendship of certain leaders. Palmer had the big Pennsylvania delegation and some outside support. There were several "favorite sons," including Alfred Emanuel Smith of New York, then serving his first term as governor, but notwithstanding Wilson's impenetrable silence on the subject, most of the members of his cabinet and most of his friends were behind Mr. McAdoo, who was being bitterly assailed in the Republican and anti-Wilson press as the crown prince, and who had aroused the intense antagonism of the railroad and banking interests, though he undoubtedly had strong support among the railroad workers and the good-will of organized labor.

It was on June 19, just when his candidacy seemed most promising, that Mr. McAdoo in New

York made public a letter emphatically saying "no" to his supporters. He declared that he would not accept the nomination, asserted that his decision was irrevocable, said that he could not himself afford to make the campaign if nominated, and that he would not permit his friends to furnish the money. He had resigned from the cabinet he said in order to "rehabilitate" his family and could not at the same time make the sacrifices the nomination would call for.

If he had not made this statement there is small doubt Mr. McAdoo would have been nominated, notwithstanding the opposition to him and regardless of Wilson's silence. At that time he was too far in the lead to be stopped, and the ticket forecast by the most experienced political observers was McAdoo and Meredith (Edward T. Meredith of Iowa, secretary of agriculture). At once the McAdoo declaration threw the field wide open and candidates began to multiply. Had Mr. McAdoo been an avowed candidate, Mr. Palmer would probably not have gone ahead with his candidacy and most of his support would have gone to the former secretary of the treasury. With Mr. McAdoo professedly not a candidate, Palmer plunged ahead in real earnest.

It developed, however, that Mr. McAdoo's friends refused to accept his declination. Senator Glass of Virginia declared he was still for McAdoo and believed he would be nominated, and other McAdoo supporters followed suit. Instead of weakening the

McAdoo line-up, his statement appeared to strengthen it, and a deadlock was forecast at San Francisco that would "force him to yield." "He is not a candidate," said his friends, "but we will draft him and he will not refuse." The net result was that when the delegates and managers assembled in San Francisco, there was considerable confusion and general bewilderment. There were a dozen or more candidates and dark horses galore, but while the administration forces were in control of the organization of the convention it had by no means strength to make a nomination with the Palmer candidacy splitting their ranks and no word from Wilson.

It is interesting to note that in this convention, besides Mr. McAdoo, three other Democratic figures destined to play much larger parts in party affairs in later years made their first appearance in the national field. One of these was Governor Smith of New York, who was put forward merely as a "favorite son" by his State and without any expectation or desire of being a bona fide candidate. He had not at that time made the record and acquired the strength that made him in later years the outstanding Democrat of the country.

Another was John W. Davis of West Virginia, who was at the time ambassador to Great Britain. Mr. Davis had many real admirers scattered over the country, and the movement behind him, while it never in 1920 promised success, was seriously proposed. It was believed by Clarence W. Watson, who had the Davis boom in charge, that in the event of a deadlock that made impossible the selection of any one of the three leaders—McAdoo, Cox, or Palmer, —Davis offered the strongest and best compromise material, which was undoubtedly true.

The third figure was that of Albert Cabell Ritchie, then serving his first term as governor of Maryland. Governor Ritchie was not put forward with the "favorite sons," but was the chairman of his delegation, represented Maryland on the Resolutions Committee, and strongly took the side of the modificationists in the fight over the liquor plank in the committee and on the floor. He made a fine impression. Four years later all three of these men played a much more conspicuous part. One of them—Mr. Davis—became the compromise candidate after another—Governor Smith—had engaged in one of the most spectacular convention duels in the party's history.

JAMES M. COX

Democratic Presidential nominee in 1920

Chapter XXXII

COX'S NOMINATION AND DEFEAT

The San Francisco Deadlock Between McAdoo-Palmer-
Cox — Cox's Gallant but Hopeless Fight — The
League the Issue—Republicans on Both Sides—
James A. Reed at San Francisco

It is also interesting to note that at the 1920 convention another Democratic leader—Senator James
A. Reed of Missouri—was refused a seat and his
claims scornfully rejected by the convention. Senator Reed had joined the Lodge forces in the Senate
in the fight against the treaty. He was one of the
bitterest opponents of the League of Nations, had
assailed Wilson on the floor of the Senate, and in
turn been denounced by Wilson as a "marplot." The
Democratic press had denounced him as a traitor,
and in Missouri the party organization turned violently against him, and, branding him as disloyal,
called on him to resign. Undaunted, Senator Reed
refused to yield an inch, and fought back at his
foes with extraordinary ferocity and courage. He
was defeated in the effort to go to the convention as
a delegate from Missouri, but went to San Francisco
anyhow to contest the seats of the victors and claim

his own. He was "thrown out," and it was pretty generally felt that he had been eliminated from politics in his State. His successful fight for renomination and reelection to the Senate, followed in 1924 by another primary defeat that sent an anti-Reed delegation to the national convention and kept him home, and finally the complete recovery of his political power and prestige, make one of the most remarkable stories in American politics. By every rule of the game Senator Reed, beaten and discredited, should have politically expired at the close of his Senate term in 1922. Instead, he survived, took two years later another defeat, and then, through the power of his personality and the distinguished nature of his services in the Senate, rose to a position of dominance in his State which he had not enjoyed before, and has become one of the recognized and outstanding Presidential possibilities of 1928.

To return again to San Francisco: it was made apparent before the convention came to order that old-line political bosses—Charles F. Murphy of Tammany, George Brennan of Illinois, Thomas Taggart of Indiana—were strongly opposed to McAdoo, almost equally opposed to Palmer, and inclined toward Cox as the logical man around whom to center. It was further recognized that Governor Cox was by no means as dry in his political feeling as either McAdoo or Palmer, and the wet forces favored him in spite of a statement given out by him at Columbus, Ohio, standing for law enforcement.

The Cox campaign was managed by the late Edward Moore of Ohio, one of the shrewdest and most astute of politicians, and a personal friend of the Murphy-Brennan-Taggart group. Though his supporters had gone ahead with renewed energy, declaring that Mr. McAdoo would not refuse the nomination in spite of his declaration, no further word came from Mr. McAdoo and he made no effort to stop them. On the contrary, Dr. Burris A. Jenkins of Kansas City, who placed him in nomination—it being impossible to get a New York delegate to do it—gave the convention his word that if "drafted" Mr. McAdoo would accept. There ensued a big McAdoo demonstration, and it was recognized that he was in effect just as much a candidate as any of the rest of them. The withdrawal from and return to the field of Mr. McAdoo inflamed Mr. Palmer and his friends against him, and hope of getting the attorney-general out in the interest of the McAdoo nomination was abandoned. Sixteen candidates were voted on at one time or another, as follows:

William G. McAdoo, New York.	Edward I. Edwards, New Jersey.
A. Mitchell Palmer, Pennsylvania.	John W. Davis, West Virginia.
Gilbert M. Hitchcock, Nebraska.	Carter Glass, Virginia.
Robert L. Owen, Oklahoma.	Furnifold M. Simmons, South Carolina.
Alfred E. Smith, New York.	Champ Clark, Missouri.
Homer E. Cummings, Connecticut.	William J. Bryan, Nebraska.
James W. Gerard, New York.	Oscar W. Underwood, Alabama.
Edward T. Meredith, Iowa.	Francis Burton Harrison, New York.

Of the list only McAdoo, Palmer and Cox had real strength and the thing soon settled down to a three cornered fight, with nearly every state delegation splitting its vote and immense opportunities for dealing, dickering, and intrigue. On the first ballot the vote was:

McAdoo	266	Smith	109	Clark	9
Palmer	256	Davis	32	Bryan	1
Cox	134	Meredith	27	Underwood	½

The second ballot gave McAdoo 289, Palmer 265, Cox 159, with New York still voting for Smith, Indiana for Marshall, and Illinois giving Palmer 9, McAdoo 9, Cox 25. About the tenth ballot New York dropped Smith and swung solidly to Cox. So did Indiana and New Jersey. On the twenty-second ballot McAdoo had 372½, Palmer 166½, Cox 430. Cox had steadily gained from the first ballot to the nineteenth, then slipped off from 468 to 430. When the convention recessed on Saturday night there seemed no prospect of breaking the deadlock. Sunday was July 4. All day the politicians fought and struggled, pulled and hauled, conferred and cursed in the hotels without result. When the convention reassembled Monday morning ostensibly the situation was the same. Actually, however, a change had come. Palmer, realizing the hopelessness of his cause, decided to withdraw and release his delegates. This he did after the thirty-eighth ballot, and on the thirty-ninth ballot the vote stood—

McAdoo....440   Cox....468½   Davis....71½

From that moment on the Cox victory was assured. With Palmer out, the bulk of the convention preferred him to McAdoo. Also, he had the more adroit managers and was better liked by the Palmer leaders, who felt a sense of personal grievance against McAdoo they did not feel toward Cox. The big argument in favor of the latter was that he could carry Ohio, a pivotal State necessary to success. The Republican candidate having been picked from there, it seemed essential to name a man who could beat him in that State. "Here is the man," said Cox's friends. "He has carried the State for governor twice and can do it again." The McAdoo vote began to crumble after the fortieth ballot, and the Cox nomination came with a whoop on the forty-fourth, taken at 1:40 o'clock in the morning after the convention had been in continuous session for eighteen hours.

The nomination of Franklin D. Roosevelt of New York for Vice-President was made by acclamation. One reason for picking him was the necessity of having the Wilson administration represented on the ticket, and Mr. Roosevelt, as assistant secretary of the navy, had been a conspicuous member of the administration. Another reason was that though he was from New York he was not a Tammany man nor so regarded, but was known as an independent progressive Democrat and a friend of Wilson. Yet in spite of this he was on personally friendly terms

453

with the Tammany leaders and liked by the Tammany delegates.

In many ways it was one of the most interesting conventions the party ever held. For one thing, it was the first in which women sat as delegates, and it was the first in which a division over what is called a moral issue had arisen since 1856. Mr. Cox at the time of his nomination was not a flaming advocate of the League of Nations. He was for it of course, but he did not start out with any particular degree of enthusiasm for it. That came later. On his way back from San Francisco Mr. Roosevelt stopped off at Dayton and conferred with Governor Cox, suggesting that they both go to Washington and see Wilson.

They did. The shattered leader received them sitting on the south portico of the White House, congratulated them, wished them success, and talked about the League. From that moment there was no lack of ardor about Cox's championship of the League cause. The appearance of the President and his words tremendously touched him and he came away from that conference determined that whatever happened to him in the election, he would not disappoint that gallant and indomitable spirit that still lived in the broken body of Woodrow Wilson. He was, of course, terribly beaten. Both the popular majority and the electoral majority against him were unprecedented, but no unprejudiced and disinterested person who knew the facts and the factors of that campaign will deny that Governor Cox not only made the better fight but was the better man.

He never had a chance. From the start the odds were overwhelmingly against him. If Wilson had been a colorless and commonplace President, if he had made a policy of inaction instead of action, as did some of his successors, if he had lacked force and fire and character and courage, he might have ended his second term pretty generally popular with the great bulk of the people. Certainly if he had been a mediocre man, an executive who took advice instead of giving advice, who followed instead of led, who was dominated instead of dominating, who was inert instead of vibrant, who lacked convictions and principles and vision—if he had been that sort of man and that sort of President, he would certainly have had infinitely fewer enemies in the country and vastly more general popularity. But if he had been that sort of President no such tribute would have been paid him as the simultaneous holding of more than seven hundred Wilson banquets in all sections of the country on his birthday six years after his death.

He had in his first term put in force and effect more needed reforms and more sound and constructive legislation than any preceding President. In his second term he had led the country into the greatest of all wars, conducted it to a successful conclusion without scandal or graft, played a potent part in the peace, founded the League of Nations, which, no matter whether you believe in it or not, and regardless of its failures and flaws, its imperfections and weakness, must be recognized as the only instrumentality in the world that holds out hope of peaceful international cooperation. It at least makes war more difficult.

Not only no better or even as good an idea looking toward the ending of war and the promotion of international cooperation has been offered, but no idea of any sort has been suggested. The League may not be practical. It may not work; but it happens to be the only hopeful international experiment in the world to-day, and it is useless to deny the fact that it has in ten years scored more successes than failures, that while it has disappointed in some respects it has measured splendidly up in others, that no clear-headed man any longer holds the view that the League is not here to stay. Not many would care to contemplate a Europe without the League. In Geneva, where the meetings of the League are held, in the center of the wall surrounding the secretariat is an oblong stone on which is the following inscription:

"The League of Nations—Founded by Woodrow Wilson, President of the United States of America"

With such a record of achievement it should have been reasonable to expect Wilson to have wound up his eight-year tenure of office more or less of a popular hero. Such was distinctly not the case. It is true that in every section of the country there were thousands of men and women who literally worshiped him, who believed him to be the greatest man of his generation and the greatest of all Presidents. It is also true that in every section there were thousands who hated and despised him, who could or would see no good in him, who were opposed to everything and anything for which he stood. Particularly was this true of the bigger banking and business figures. Not even his illness seemed to soften the malignancy with which his foes in Congress and out regarded him. No weak man could ever have aroused such amazing hatred and hostility. Perhaps, too, the Wilson speeches, messages, policies, and performances were all on too high a plane to be comfortable for the common people. It was a strain to live up to him.

In the beginning he was to them an appealing and engaging figure and they thrilled to the campaign he made in 1912. By the close of his first term the hostility of the elements offended by the energy with which he put over his program, and the dominant, determined, utterly uncompromising nature of the man, had begun to swing sentiment against him, and he was saved in the 1916 election by the "He kept us out of war" slogan and some lucky breaks such as the Hughes mistakes in California. During the war he again became a shining and heroic figure, but with the peace the reaction began. The forces against him were numerous and powerful. The channels of publicity were to a large extent poisoned against him. The Senate battle over the treaty was waged so as to distort the perspective and confuse the minds of the people. Before he had his stroke the tide had already turned against him, and when the convention met in San Francisco it was running strongly against the Democrats.

Eight years of such strenuous leadership as Wilson's was inevitably followed by a let-down. The accumulated resentment from a dozen different directions piled up. It is perfectly clear that no one the party could have nominated in 1920 would have won. Cox probably made as good a showing as any one. In addition to the handicaps already mentioned, the Democrats found it terribly hard to get money. No campaign except the three Bryan campaigns of 1896, 1900, and 1908 was so poorly financed as the Cox campaign. The national chairman, George White of Ohio, found it impossible to keep out of debt. There never was enough money to pay the headquarters bills, and the deficit with which the party wound up the fight was a large one.

On the other hand, the Republican campaign fund broke all records. The money available for the Harding-Coolidge campaign was literally without limit. It has been conservatively estimated that more than seven million dollars was raised and expended in the interests of the ticket. Certainly no chairman of any political committee before or since had the money to spend or spent it with such a lavish and reckless extravagance as Mr. Will Hays of Indiana, head of the Republican National Committee, did in this campaign. The country was literally drenched with money, and records for waste and prodigality were established that will probably not soon be equaled.

It is not likely, however, that even if the situation had been reversed and the Democrats had the Republican money they could have won. The anti-Democratic tide was too strong, the Republican party too united. The split of 1912 had wholly healed and every element and faction was behind the Harding-Coolidge ticket, in spite of the fact that Senator Harding was obviously a fifth-rate senator and the Ohio crowd with whom he played politics an odoriferous and unscrupulous set. While on the surface the fight was decent enough, underneath it was one of the dirtiest that ever was waged. Particularly was this true in Ohio, where the "whisper campaign" was developed to an extraordinary extent and stories of the most unprintable and almost unthinkable nature were spread—and widely believed—about both candidates.

Governor Cox began his campaign mildly enough, but about the middle of October his speeches were full of fire and his appeal for the League impassioned and earnest. From the start he took the offensive and riddled the pretenses of the Republican platform and the pussy-footing of the Republican candidates. The fact was that the Republicans played both the pro-League and the anti-League game. On the one side were such bitter anti-Leaguers as Senators William E. Borah of Idaho, Hiram Johnson of California, Henry Cabot Lodge of Massachusetts. On the other hand, Republicans such as Elihu Root, William Howard Taft, and Charles Evans Hughes strongly inclined toward the League. Illogical as it seems, Harding had the support of both. The anti-League leaders urged that the election of Harding meant the end of the League so far as America was concerned. The pro-League Republicans professed to believe that the election of Harding meant the entrance of America into the League with "proper reservations."

Mr. Harding inclined both ways, trimmed, soft-pedaled the issue, avoided it as far as he could. It seems incredible after reading the respective platforms and reviewing the speeches of the two candidates on the subject that any friend of the League should have voted the Republican ticket in that campaign. Yet many thousands of them undoubtedly did. By the end of October the drift against the Democrats was too clear to mistake. Cox's meetings were well attended and enthusiastic, but Cox was too practical a politician not to see the facts clearly. He knew he was beaten, but it is to his credit that this knowledge did not in the least detract from the vigor of his campaign, and he finished with a gallantry and gameness that made him better thought of when it was over than he had been before it began. The odds were all against him, but he made a good fight.

It is true he was not a first-grade man. He was a great let-down from Wilson; but so would have been any of the other aspirants for the nomination. No detached and informed person ever doubted that Cox was a better man from every angle than his Republican opponent, or that he made as good a showing as any other Democrat would have made, regardless of the testimony of the election figures.

The result was a smashing Democratic defeat. The Republicans were swept back into power after an absence of eight years by a popular plurality of unprecedented size—seven million, or to be officially exact, 6,996,476. Harding had 404 electoral votes to 127 for Cox. Except for the little State of Delaware, the Democrats carried literally nothing outside of the South—eleven States in all. They lost again such normally Democratic stronghold States as Maryland, Missouri, and Tennessee. They were snowed under in every Eastern State and carried nothing west of the Mississippi except Arkansas. In addition, of course, the Republicans greatly increased their majorities in both House and Senate.

It was about as complete as it well could be. In debt, defeated, discouraged, leaderless, with neither issue nor man around whom it could rally, the party was once more flat on its back, apparently not even formidable as opposition. The fact that the Republican victory had been won with a candidate of the type of Warren G. Harding, with as little personal popular appeal and as commonplace a record, made the verdict against the Democrats the more crushing. It was fully two years before hope began to revive among party people in any section—and it was not until January, 1924, that the developments occurred which sent a thrill through the Democrats all over the country, stirred dormant aspirants for the next nomination into real activity, made it seem as if a victory were in sight for 1924 that would wipe out the deep humiliation of that 1920 defeat.

It turned out to be a delusion, but it certainly seemed a justifiable notion at the time. Among politicians generally it had always been counted as axiomatic that any party in city, state, or nation, exposed as corrupt, would be driven from power by the people at the next election. It seemed incredible that open and wholesale thievery and crookedness in government should not arouse deep popular resentment and react upon the party responsible. Probably it would have in this case but for the sudden death of Mr. Harding before the disclosures concerning his administration came. The accession to the Presidency of Vice-President Calvin Coolidge, to whom attached no personal responsibility for any part of the most shameful chapter in the history of any political party, coupled with the extraordinary political inertia induced in the people by the unprecedented prosperity that began in 1921 and with slight recession has continued over a period of six years, formed the combination that kept the Republicans from the punishment that should—and in all probability would—have been theirs. It was a tough break for the Democrats—to catch the other party red-handed in crime, and then have it saved by an act of God and the workings of great economic laws.

Chapter XXXIII

The Rise of Smith in National Prestige and Power—
His Defiance of Murphy at Syracuse—"If He's On,
I'm Off; if I'm On, He's Off," His Ultimatum as to
Hearst

BUT to tell the story in order: Long before the exposures of Republican corruption, Mr. McAdoo was
out in the open as a candidate for the 1924 nomination. Soon after the 1920 defeat he had moved from
New York to Los Angeles and there plunged both
into politics and business. Back in New York he
had two devoted and extremely wealthy friends—
Bernard M. Baruch and Thomas L. Chadbourne. In
almost every State there were Democrats who had
held office under him as secretary of the treasury,
men whom he had helped personally or politically,
party workers who were attached to him in one way
or another. In addition, he was as popular with the
railroad brotherhoods, embracing the conductors, en-
gineers, and employees generally, as he was unpopular with the railroad executives, stock- and
bond-holders. This time Mr. McAdoo went after the

WILLIAM GIBBS MCADOO
Secretary of the Treasury under Wilson

nomination tooth and toenail, with neither coyness nor concealment. A declared dry, a foe of "reaction" and "special privilege," with press agents, paid campaign managers, a large publicity machine and expensive headquarters, he was from the start the leading and most aggressive candidate, entering the Presidential primaries in every State he could, corralling delegates, organizing his friends, speaking, conferring, campaigning with the tremendous vigor and energy characteristic of the man. Undoubtedly he had his fight planned before he went to California, and he was in active pursuit of the nomination at least two years ahead of the convention. He had a big start over every other contender.

Tall, virile, and magnetic, McAdoo's first appearance in politics was in 1912 when he became interested and active in the effort to nominate Wilson. After the Democratic victory of that year he entered the Wilson cabinet as secretary of the treasury. He was a potent factor in the Federal Reserve fight, and during the war no man in the country except Wilson himself played a more important rôle. In addition to conducting the Liberty Loan campaigns and handling the great problems of war finance, when the Government took over the operation of the railroads McAdoo became their director-general. It was a huge responsibility he shouldered and a tremendous power he wielded. While he earned the everlasting hostility of the railroad executives, accumulated many bitter enemies among the bankers, and of course made many blunders, it is impossible to deny that he had an enormous job and did it well. During Wilson's first term McAdoo married one of the President's daughters, and no doubt the fact that he was Wilson's son-in-law was a handicap to him in 1920. The crown prince idea was effectively used against him, and unquestionably the relationship was embarrassing, particularly as Wilson at no time and in no way gave the remotest indication of a desire to be succeeded by his son-in-law.

In 1924 there was no such embarrassment. A Republican President was in the White House and Wilson was dead. There was nothing to prevent McAdoo from making his supreme effort for the great prize, and make it he did. Probably, too, he would have been successful, so far as the 1924 nomination was concerned, had it not been for one man —Alfred Emanuel Smith, governor of New York. While almost any governor of New York is regarded as available Presidential material by his party, because of the pivotal nature of the State and the size of its electoral vote, Smith in 1920 was only a single-term governor and, while he figured in the San Francisco convention as New York's favorite son, was not a serious contender. Following the convention he was again nominated for governor and, though defeated, ran more than a million votes ahead of Cox in the State, an amazing and unprecedented exhibition of popular strength that, coupled with the really fine record he has made in his first term, at once marked him as a rare political figure. In 1922 renominated, he was triumphantly and overwhelmingly elected.

There is no space here to go into the details of the Smith record, but before this second gubernatorial term was half over he had demonstrated both as a political leader and as an executive a capacity and character that awoke admiration all over the country, compelled respect from his political foes in New York, and brought tributes to his honesty, courage, and force from the Republican press of New York of a sort they had paid no other Democrat who can be recalled. On the political side Smith had become the real leader of Tammany, too strong within the party and without for any one to dispute his influence, the greatest Democratic vote-getter of his generation in New York.

His achievements in the face of hostile Republican legislatures were due primarily to three things—first, the remarkable knowledge he had acquired of the State's business, which gave him an advantage in every fight; second, his extraordinary gift for trenchant expression, his power to clearly and graphically present his case; third, his deep understanding of the common people of New York, of whom he was one.

There is no more stirring incident in the whole political career of this remarkable man than his defiance of the Tammany boss—Charles F. Murphy —at the 1920 state convention in Syracuse, when he was nominated for the second time. William Randolph Hearst, still cherishing political ambitions, after for years having violently assailed Murphy in his newspapers, cartooning him in the garb of a convict, and editorially roasting him as a plundering boss, had patched up a peace, and Murphy went to Syracuse pledged to nominate him for the United States Senate and determined to do it. Smith was slated for the gubernatorial nomination, and the organization control seemed complete. But that was before Smith heard about the proposed Hearst nomination. In his first campaign Hearst had attacked Smith as a creature of the boss, said things that aroused his deep resentment, caused him to hit back hard.

When at Syracuse Smith met Murphy and heard that he had surrendered to the Hearst demand, made peace, and was prepared to present his arch enemy with the senatorial nomination, he shouted "No" in no uncertain tone, and served notice on the boss in effect as follows: "Top or bottom I will not run on any ticket with him. If Hearst is on, I'm off; if I'm on, he's off." Moreover, boiling mad, he made it plain that if the Hearst plan was pushed he would not only refuse the nomination for governor with him, but he would go on the floor of the convention and fight the Tammany ticket with every ounce of force he had in him. There was no way to placate him, bring him into line, and the boss "caved in." Hearst was "ditched." Smith was nominated and from that moment on there has never been any question as to who was the real leader of the Democratic organization in New York—city and State—no doubt in whose hands was lodged the real power.

With such a public and political record it was logical and inevitable that in 1924 this three times nominated, twice elected governor of the greatest State in the Union should be a Presidential aspirant. He was, but not in the way McAdoo was. He stuck strictly to his job as governor, made no speeches, went on no campaigning tours, engaged in no delegate hunting, and did not enter the Presidential primaries in the different States. In the last two months preceding the convention there was a Smith headquarters in New York and Franklin D. Roosevelt headed a Smith-for-President Committee, but the fact was that the Smith candidacy was more with the view of heading McAdoo off than nominating Smith. The prime purpose of the forces behind Smith in this fight was to beat McAdoo. There is no doubt about that. The nomination of Smith was incidental, and Smith himself, while glad to have his chance at the Presidency, felt that his own nomination was much more improbable than McAdoo's.

The elements of the party which opposed McAdoo and supported Cox in the San Francisco convention centered behind Smith as the one hope to prevent the former secretary of the treasury from running away with the nomination in 1924. The great business interests of the East—the banks, the railroads, the newspapers, and the large industrialists—what Mr. McAdoo, adopting the terms used by Mr. Bryan for twenty-five years, called the "predatory interests," the "forces of reaction," and "Wall Street" —were opposed to him even more violently in 1924 than in 1920, possibly because he seemed much stronger than had been supposed. In these circles hostility to him was intense, and there was an exaggerated fear of his radicalism.

But there was much more to the McAdoo opposition than that. There was the inherent and instinctive dislike of the Democratic machine bosses in the large cities for a man who denounced bosses and machines, and there were the wets. Probably as much as anything else wet sentiment in the East contributed to solidifying the anti-McAdoo forces. As has been stated, McAdoo was an avowed and emphatic dry, an ardent upholder of the prohibition amendment and the Volstead act. In the four years between the 1920 and 1924 conventions the anti-Volstead sentiment in the East had tremendously increased. The obvious breakdown of prohibition enforcement, the legions of bootleggers with whom the country swarmed, the apparent impossibility of making the law effective, all contributed to a state of unrest and revolt in the great cities, but particularly in the Eastern States. The Anti-Saloon League was as dominant as ever in both branches of Congress, and the South and West were undoubtedly dry in sentiment.

It was in these sections that McAdoo had his strength.

Everywhere the dry forces were with him. Undoubtedly at that time the great majority of the States were politically dry, and if united behind any one candidate could control the convention. It was that fact that gave the McAdoo movement its real strength South and West, garnered him most of his delegates, gave him and his managers their confidence in the result. There were of course a number of "favorite sons" in the field, but besides Smith the only other aspirant whose candidacy had a national flavor and who had friends in every section was Oscar W. Underwood of Alabama.

Mr. Underwood was one of the outstanding Democrats of the country. He had served for many terms in the House, had been the Democratic leader there, been elected to the Senate, become the Democratic leader there, made a great national reputation, rendered really fine service to his party and his country, and had thousands of friends who admired him for his sanity, judgment, character, and ability. He was strongly against prohibition, had voted against the Volstead act. Besides the prohibition amendment he had vigorously opposed the suffrage amendment. A distinguished and able man, he was recognized as a pronounced conservative, and was as cordially disliked by the so-called "progressives," for so many years led by Mr. Bryan and in 1924 taken over by Mr. McAdoo, as he was highly regarded by the big business interests of the East.

The wetness of both Underwood and Smith naturally threw Mr. Bryan, still a power in the party and with a diminished but recognizable personal following, into the McAdoo camp. It is again worth while to point out with what curious readiness the Democratic party divides, as in this campaign, on a so-called moral issue, while the Republicans, in whose ranks the same sectional sentiment on the same issue existed, were able to prevent a split, avoid a fight before their convention as well as in it. But, as if it were not enough to divide over prohibition, which as a controversial question has proved itself capable of generating more bitterness than almost any other (except slavery) that has arisen in American politics from the beginning—as if that were not enough, the Democrats in this campaign had to raise among themselves, for the first time in a serious way, the religious issue, which in blighting and destructive effect upon the party unity surpasses all others.

It was a curious and unprecedented combination that injected it. The first factor was of course the Ku-Klux Klan. Using the name of the organization that flourished in the South in the years immediately following the Civil War, a new Klan had sprung up with headquarters in Atlanta, and, though thoroughly sordid in the purpose back of its conception, was cleverly contrived to capitalize the racial and

DEMOCRATIC NATIONAL CONVENTION IN NEW YORK—1924

religious prejudices of the people. It was anti-negro, anti-Jew, anti-foreign born, and anti-Catholic—particularly and specially anti-Catholic. Though time and again the evil character and mercenary motives of the men back of the movement were exposed, it apparently had no effect upon its astounding growth. By 1922, when Mr. McAdoo began his active campaign, while the Klan was strongest in South and West, there was scarcely a State in which it was not organized. It was claimed at the time that close to a million well meaning but muddy minded and misguided men had enrolled in this secret order, with its silly regalia, ridiculous oaths, and other absurdities. It had entered politics in all of them, and in some had attained actual dominance, electing governors, controlling legislatures, mayors, and United States senators. Led by fifth-rate men, with its ranks recruited from the ignorant, bigoted, and prejudiced, it had become almost a national menace, unquestionably a power in national politics. Its numerical strength at the polls filled politicians and candidates of both parties with fear, compelled them to yield to its demands, induced some to secretly join the order, others to form alliances with the Klan leaders, still others to keep discreetly silent while the poisons of religious intolerance and racial hate were distilled under their noses. Apparently it thrived on opposition. Denunciation merely strengthened the belief of the deluded thousands, taken in by the Atlanta selling force, that they were performing a high and patriotic service by adhering politically to Klan policies as mapped out by the dragons, kleagles, wizards, and other such absurd humbugs.

To resume the narrative: it was Senator Underwood who, as a candidate for the Democratic Presidential nomination early in 1924, challenged the Klan and denounced it. In a speech made in Texas he arraigned and indicted it as no other public man had done, declared its existence in America was an affront to every decent man and woman, declared war on it to the finish. Inasmuch as Senator Underwood's own State was a Klan stronghold, as all through the South its grip was strong, as it was necessary for him to run in the Presidential primaries where the Klan could get a chance at him, his denunciation was a particularly courageous performance. It had the immediate effect of throwing the Klan back of Mr. McAdoo in every Southern State—in fact, all over the country. He became the Klan candidate. In justice to Mr. McAdoo it should be stated that he did not seek Klan support, that he unquestionably had no sympathy with the Klan ideas, did not share Klan religious or racial prejudices, and had no Klan alliances or affiliations. None the less, he indulged in no Klan denunciations, repudiated no Klan support, and swept every Southern and Western State in which he entered. The only State Senator Underwood carried at all was his own State of Alabama, and there the combination of the

Klan, Mr. Bryan, and organized labor gave him a real battle, almost succeeded in defeating him.

In December, 1923, through the influence of Herbert Bayard Swope, executive editor of "The New York World," and against both its judgment and desire, the National Committee meeting in Washington decided to hold the convention in New York. At that time McAdoo was so far in the lead that it did not seem to make much difference. He had got such headway that there was apparently no stopping him, though then the primaries had not been held. It was about six weeks later—to be exact on January 24, 1924—that the first of a series of developments occurred, which, while they thrilled Democrats generally with hope that had not previously existed, also dealt the McAdoo candidacy a deadly blow.

Chapter XXXIV

THE OIL SCANDALS

Exposure of Fraud and Corruption in the Harding Administration Thrills Democrats With Hope—His Connection With Doheny a Blow to McAdoo's Candidacy—His Gallant Recovery and Spectacular Campaign—The Klan and the Catholics

IT was on that day—January 24, 1924—that Edward L. Doheny frankly admitted before the Senate investigation committee of which Senator Thomas J. Walsh, Democrat, of Montana, was chairman, that he had secretly sent $100,000 in bills in a little black satchel to Albert B. Fall, secretary of the interior under Harding, during the negotiations for the naval reserve oil leases in California. These leases—that for Elk Hills (California) and Teapot Dome (Wyoming)—had been made in April, 1922, to Edward L. Doheny and Harry F. Sinclair respectively. From the beginning there had been suspicious circumstances connected with the transfer and there had come to the late Senator Robert M. La Follette of Wisconsin, leader of the "insurgent" Republicans, information that inspired him to ask for a Senate investigation.

The administration forces blocked the resolution

as far as they could, but after a year's delay, on January 16, 1923, it was passed by a combination of independent Republican and Democratic votes. In the interim between the making of the leases and the passage of the resolution President Harding had died, been succeeded by Vice-President Calvin Coolidge, and Secretary Fall, who had negotiated both the Elk Hills and Teapot Dome leases, had left the cabinet. For more than a year after the inquiry was ordered Senator Walsh probed and pried into the whole business. Firmly convinced with Senator La Follette and others that there was corruption and fraud at the bottom of both transactions, he found himself balked and blocked, frustrated and hampered in an extraordinary way by political, social, and financial influences in the Republican party interested in keeping the lid on and fearful of exposure.

The story of how, when at the end of his resources, after following up every lead and exhausting every effort, discouraged, almost defeated, but still convinced of the sinister nature of the transfers, luck finally played into Senator Walsh's hands and the clue was given that ultimately uncovered the whole black business, is an extremely fascinating and dramatic one. This is not the place to tell it except as it bears on the Democratic campaign of 1924. It is enough to say that the Doheny admission of January 24, 1924, opened things up, and once opened there was no closing them. Simultaneously with the oil investigations, another Senate probe, directed by Senator Wheeler, Democrat, also of Montana, was being made into the conduct of the Department of Justice under Attorney-General Harry L. Daugherty; criminal prosecution was ordered of Charles Forbes, head of the Veterans' Bureau and an intimate personal friend of the late President, charged with outrageous misuse of public funds. Later, frauds developed under the custodian of alien property, Colonel Thomas R. Miller, another Republican prominent in administration circles, who with Forbes was later convicted. Forbes served a term in the Federal penitentiary.

Between January 23, when Mr. Doheny made his admission about the little black satchel, and the date of the conventions enough wholesale and retail thievery, fraud, and conspiracy had been revealed to utterly damn the Harding administration and make of its brief two and a half years probably the most shameless of any administration in the nation's history. Doheny, Fall, and Sinclair had been indicted for conspiracy and bribery. Slightly in advance of a Senate resolution directing him to do so, Mr. Coolidge named special counsel for the Government to seek annulment of the leases. Daugherty was driven from the cabinet in disgrace; Edwin Denby, secretary of the navy, generally acquitted of any corrupt connivance but just as generally regarded as negligent in permitting the leases to be taken out of his hands by Fall, resigned in the face of a pending resolution requesting him to do so.

The Oil Scandals

There is reason to believe that the full story of the corruption in the Government under Mr. Harding never has come out—and probably never will now; but enough did at this time to fill Republican leaders in all sections with alarm and inject a confidence among the Democrats that the situation prior to the disclosures had not seemed to justify.

Here, on the eve of a Presidential election, was the administration of the party in power caught red-handed in as evil a mess as had marked any administration since the beginning of the Government. The trail of corruption ran not only through the Department of the Interior, the Veterans' Bureau, and the alien property department, but through the Department of Justice practically to the door of the White House itself. Daugherty, Fall, and Forbes—but particularly Daugherty— were personal intimates and boon companions as well as political advisers and supporters of Harding, who, though suspicion of his personal integrity was not voiced even by the Democrats, undoubtedly had an amazing lot of crooked friends. It was perhaps the most sinister and unsavory gang that ever ran the Government, and it did seem that when exposed a popular reaction against the party responsible for these fellows would be inevitable and strong. Both Democrats and Republicans thought so, notwithstanding the fact that Harding had died and Coolidge, his successor, not only was wholly clear of any responsibility for what had gone on under Harding

479

but had not the least personal touch with the Harding circle. He was, so far as it was concerned, a complete outsider, regarded as so insignificant and unimportant that just prior to his death, Harding's political friends seriously contemplated sidetracking him for renomination as Vice-President in 1924, in order to get a stronger and more colorful man to fill out their ticket. Regardless of the Coolidge lack of responsibility, the corruption in the administration unquestionably presented the Democrats not only with an issue but what, according to all the rules of politics and logic, ought to have been a winning issue. It seemed incredible that the American people would not revolt in the face of such an exposé, that the party in power should not pay the penalty.

But to get back to Mr. McAdoo. At the time Mr. Doheny made his historic black satchel admission —January 24—the McAdoo campaign was in full swing and McAdoo was unquestionably the leading candidate. It seemed pretty well impossible to head him off, and his enemies in the East were not happy. A few days after the Doheny admission, information came to Senator James A. Reed of Missouri and others that Mr. McAdoo had had professional relations with Mr. Doheny. That gentleman was recalled by the committee and in reply to questions casually testified that he had employed Mr. McAdoo after he left the Wilson cabinet at an annual retainer of $50,000 a year for five years. He particularly stressed the fact that he had engaged Mr. McAdoo for work in Washington during the Wilson administration. It was a bombshell.

Here was the Democratic party, presented with what seemed a winning issue in the corruption of the other side, more eager and confident than it had been in eight years. Suddenly its leading candidate for the Presidential nomination, who has been campaigning as the champion of the people and the foe of the "interests," is revealed as the highly paid attorney of the chief corruptionist. It was a stunning blow to the McAdoo machine and it was promptly seized upon by his opponents as eliminating him from the field. He was branded by "The New York World," "Baltimore Sun," and other independent Democratic journals of the East as unavailable. It was pointed out as clearly impossible for the Democrats to avail themselves of the corruption issue if they named Doheny's attorney as their standard-bearer, even though he had with the first hint of wrong-doing severed his connection with Doheny, returned one year's retainer, and rendered absolutely no service in connection with the oil leases. The first reaction to the disclosure of the Doheny-McAdoo connection was that McAdoo was through. But those who jumped to that conclusion did not know Mr. McAdoo.

A less resourceful and courageous man, no matter how consciously righteous, would have been dismayed at the unexpectedness of the blow and the loudness of the outcry—but not Mr. McAdoo. Mr. McAdoo met the attack head-on, demanded the privilege of appearing before the committee, did appear, and right gallantly acquitted himself. He made it clear that he not only had not rendered Mr. Doheny any legal services in connection with the Elk Hills oil lease but had known nothing about these leases. As soon as it had appeared that the breath of suspicion touched these leases he had severed the legal tie that bound him to Doheny and refunded the fee for that year. At no time had he ever had any relations with Mr. Doheny that were not clear and aboveboard, or which in any way reflected on him as a lawyer or as a man. It was a clear-cut, manly, convincing statement he made, but it did not in the least diminish the clamor nor lessen the vigor with which he was denounced as "Doheny's attorney." Following talks with his friends in Washington, Mr. McAdoo on February 12 announced that he would leave it to his supporters to decide whether or not he should stay in the field. He indignantly repudiated the attacks of his foes, proclaimed the purity of his soul, expressed his abhorrence of Doheny's method of obtaining the Elk Hills lease, and asked that his friends meet in Chicago on February 18, "consider in a cold blooded way" the whole case, and render a verdict.

They met. They unanimously and enthusiastically adopted resolutions declaring that no odium attached to the fees received by him from Mr. Doheny, and by acclamation urged him to continue in the fight. Mr. McAdoo, happening to be in Chicago, was called before the convention, given a great ovation, promised to continue his fight against the "predatory interests," asserting that the attack on him came from those who feared an honest and incorruptible administration at Washington. So, instead of dropping out of the fight, Mr. McAdoo plunged ahead with new vigor and a desperate determination hard to exaggerate. The difference was that now instead of being on the offensive, Mr. McAdoo was distinctly on the defensive. It was not only the Doheny connection which had to be explained, but allegations that he had after his retirement from the cabinet frequently appeared in taxation reduction cases, for which he received large fees as an attorney before his own Treasury appointees, had to be met and combated.

But Mr. McAdoo met these allegations as he did the Doheny charge, head-on, fiercely hurling the charges back in the face of his foes, denouncing Wall Street and the wets, insisting that the whole business was a slimy attack planned by the sinister financial interests that desired to defame him and destroy him. With unstinted money, organization, publicity, and hurrah, he went after the delegates in the Presidential primaries, and in the South and West, supported by the Klan, was singularly successful. But the East was solidly against him, and as the convention drew near it became more and more apparent that the religious issue could not be kept out of the convention. In the States east of the Mississippi and north of Virginia the Democratic party organization was almost exclusively run by Catholics—Illinois, Indiana, Pennsylvania, Maryland, New Jersey, New York, Massachusetts. In each of these States the Democratic boss was a Catholic and the Democratic machine naturally anti-McAdoo, made vastly more so by the support of his candidacy by the Klan in the South and West.

The failure of Underwood in the Southern States compelled the whole anti-McAdoo opposition to center around Governor Smith, himself a Catholic. In the end the fight settled down to a tremendous duel between McAdoo and Smith, with every Ku-Klux delegate from the South and West tenaciously behind the former and every Catholic delegate from the East behind the latter. Both had support that was neither Klan nor Catholic, but there was enough of each in the gathering to make it more or less of a religious battle-field, and turn the convention into the most prolonged, tempestuous, bitter, dramatic, and disastrous since 1860. The deadlock that ensued was the tightest in all political history; the life of the convention—sixteen days—longer than any other; the ballots necessary to nominate—103—an unprecedented number.

It was the first national convention since the development of the radio to the stage where proceedings of such gatherings could be broadcast. The result was that millions of people in all sections of the country listened in on the terrific din of a battle that lasted over two weeks, and that exhibited the

Democratic party as lacking in dignity, discretion, and restraint, that showed the rawness of its wounds, and created an impression of division even deeper than the actuality, which made things more difficult later on. Of the depth of the religious feeling in the convention there was not the least doubt, though in the main it was submerged. But it was there and everybody knew it, felt it, discussed it. It saturated the atmosphere, raised the temperature, caused an extraordinary tenseness and bitterness. It was not alone the presence of the Klan delegates that enraged the Catholics; but the fact that for the first time in the history of the country a Catholic was a serious contender for a Presidential nomination inflamed the forces of bigotry and intolerance not only in the convention but outside.

Another phase that marked this 1924 convention as unique was the presence on the ground of the leading candidates for President, in personal charge of their own campaigns, directing their forces, rallying their delegates, right down in the arena, almost at grips with each other. In the past there had been a sort of tradition that the office of President was one which required a certain amount of aloofness and dignity from aspirants, that candidates for Presidential nominations left the active direction of their convention forces to their managers, and themselves maintained an attitude of at least surface inactivity.

At this convention all such pretenses were cast

aside. Mr. McAdoo came on from Los Angeles a week ahead of the convention, rented an entire floor in the Vanderbilt Hotel, took additional headquarters in a building opposite Madison Square Garden, placed himself at the head of his battalion. Speeches, statements, interviews, flowed in a steady stream from the McAdoo publicity bureau, and his paid managers and agents cluttered up the place. Governor Smith, also in New York, was in command of his own fight, which, as has been stated, was far more for the purpose of beating McAdoo than of nominating himself.

Hence, while he was the rallying post for the opposition, there was far less of the spectacular about his campaign than that of his rival. Claiming 600 votes before the convention met, the McAdoo strategy was to put on such steam and speed, to arouse such enthusiasm and confidence, that the convention would be swept off its feet and the opposition crushed. The policy of the anti-McAdoo leaders, centered back of Smith, was first to keep sufficient "favorite sons" in the field to insure against any change in the two thirds rule, and second to insure the unshakable and everlasting resistance of more than one third of the delegates to the McAdoo nomination. The convention met on June 24, with the McAdoo forces supremely confident that they had control of a majority of the convention and would win after a few ballots had shaken out the "favorite sons." The Smith forces were equally sure that

486

whatever happened in the convention, McAdoo could not be nominated.

By this time the feeling between the factions was intensely bitter. Mr. McAdoo fiercely assailed the bosses and the "predatory interests" opposing him and in return was violently attacked as "Doheny's attorney," cartooned and lambasted in "The New York World" and other Eastern Democratic papers. The character of his campaign was denounced and he was indicted for his acquiescence in Klan support and as "smeared with oil." Both sides were completely unrestrained in their assaults, and the pre-convention campaign was violent and fierce. No one in the party's history had ever gone after a Presidential nomination in quite the way of Mr. McAdoo, and the spectacle of candidates at the convention itself in charge of their own forces had not been seen before.

A very real source of strength to Mr. McAdoo was Mr. Bryan, who in 1924 made his last convention appearance. He had moved his residence from Nebraska to Florida and become financially independent through his fortunate Florida real estate investments, but this had not changed his political feelings. He had early declared for McAdoo and been elected a delegate from Florida. He had also taken part in the Alabama primaries against Underwood, and had exerted his influence for McAdoo in other Southern States to the limit.

487

Chapter XXXV

THE DAVIS NOMINATION

Thrilling Struggle between Klan and Catholics—The
Baker Speech and the League of Nations—"Charlie"
Bryan's Selection for Second Place Chills the East
—"Prosperity Absorbs All Criticism"—A Seven
Million Majority Defeat

THE convention was called to order on June 24 by
Congressman Cordell Hull, chairman of the National Committee, and ended on July 9. It was the
longest, wildest, most turbulent political gathering
in the history of the country. It was also the only
one in which the religious issue was openly raised,
fought out on the floor, debated with unpent fury
and bitterness.

It would require a volume by itself to tell the full
story of that convention, to recount the extraordinary currents that swept the delegates, the plots and
intrigues, the deals and combinations, the violence
of the clashes in conference and committees, the
utter disregard by both factions of the effect of their
fight on the party prospects. Senator Pat Harrison of Mississippi was the temporary chairman
and in his keynote address stressed the corruption of the Harding *régime* as the great issue,

and caused a twenty-minute demonstration with the mention of the name of Woodrow Wilson. The permanent chairman, Senator Thomas J. Walsh of Montana, who more than any other man was responsible for uncovering the scandal of the Fall-Doheny-Sinclair oil lease transactions, was accorded a tremendous reception and hit the same note in his speech.

Under normal circumstances the picture of the other party caught red-handed in corruption would have thrilled such a gathering with confidence and enthusiasm about the campaign. In this case the pending clash between the "Klucks and the Turks" as the Klan and the Catholics were described in the political slang of the day, together with the determination of the eastern bosses, most of whom were Catholic, too, not to let the Klan-supported leading candidate run away with the nomination, overshadowed and obscured the future and concentrated attention on the convention fight. Not only were McAdoo and Smith, the two leading candidates, present in person and in active charge of their respective campaigns, but nearly every one of the dark horses and favorite-son candidates was himself a delegate, sitting in the convention. Of them all the only absentee candidate, the only one who preserved the traditional dignified aloofness, was John W. Davis of West Virginia, and even he was in New York at the home of his friend Frank L. Polk and in constant touch with his managers.

There were so many candidates for the Presidential nomination—seventeen in all—that in order to save time the nominating speeches were made prior to the adoption of the platform, though the balloting was held later. There is no space here to speak of the demonstrations that followed the mention of the more prominent names, except to say that the McAdoo demonstration was marred by the unified shout from the Smith-packed galleries of "Oil! Oil! Oil!" The Smith demonstration was so noisy and prolonged and the Smith adherents so vociferous in the galleries that at one time a serious effort was made to bring the convention to an end and adjourn to some other city. The uproar was deafening, and for more than an hour after Smith's name was presented bedlam reigned. While the nominating speeches were being made the Committee on Resolutions, of which Homer Cummings of Connecticut was chairman, and of which as usual Mr. Bryan was a member, wrestled in long hot night sessions over the platform.

The struggle there was over the plank proposed by Edward H. Moore of Ohio and backed by George Brennan of Illinois, and the Smith forces, denouncing the Klan by name, and the plank proposed by Newton D. Baker of Ohio, secretary of war in the Wilson cabinet, declaring flat-footedly for the League of Nations. On all other issues the committee was able to agree. On the wording of the anti-Klan plank and the League plank they could not agree.

These two it was compelled to take to the floor of the convention. Not many who witnessed the fight over the anti-Klan plank will forget it. Early in the day it became known the committee could not agree and that the decision would be with the convention. Feeling was tense and usually cold-blooded politicians were in a real state of excitement. The battle began at night. Mr. Bryan opposed the plank, and Bainbridge Colby of New York, secretary of state under Wilson, spoke for it. During the vote the convention was in an uproar. Half a dozen state delegations had to be polled, and the thing was so close that it was nearly half an hour before an accurate and complete tabulation could be made and the result finally announced—542 3-20 against denouncing the Klan by name, 541 3-20 in favor.

No more dramatic and certainly no closer vote was ever taken in any political assemblage in this country. Catholics and Kluxers glared and shouted at each other, and the galleries stormed and yelled. There was in the beginning fear among many of a free-for-all fight, and extra policemen were on hand to suppress any outbreak. In spite of the intense bitterness and excitement and the amazing closeness of the vote, when the result finally was announced the convention adjourned peaceably enough, and the delegates, exhausted by the heat and the battle, dispiritedly returned to their hotels. The McAdoo forces saved the Klan from being denounced, but they did not thereby improve McAdoo's position.

On the contrary, their victory strengthened the determination of the group of leaders—Smith, Brennan, Hague of New Jersey, Walsh of Massachusetts, all of them Catholics—to die in the ditch before they would permit him to win.

The League of Nations fight was dramatic but nothing like so close. It was chiefly remarkable for the magnificent speech made by Mr. Baker favoring a ringing out-and-out declaration for it. It was a moving and impassioned appeal, into which he put all there was in him of heart and mind and strength. The convention was deeply stirred, but when it came to vote turned down the clear-cut declaration and adopted a shifty and meaningless plank favoring a referendum on the subject. The vote was 742½ to 353½. For the rest, the platform sidestepped the prohibition issue, declared for "law enforcement," and was chiefly built around denunciation of the oil lease and other scandals of the Harding administration. The Republican party was arraigned for its misdeeds, and corruption in government declared to be the paramount issue of the campaign.

The first ballot for President was taken on June 30, after four days of hot nominating speeches and fierce fighting over the platform. It was as follows:

Oscar W. Underwood.................... 42½
Joseph T. Robinson..................... 21
William Gibbs McAdoo........... ......431½
Alfred E. Smith................... 241
Willard Saulsbury 7

Samuel M. Ralston...................... 30
Jonathan M. Davis..................... 20
Albert Cabell Ritchie................... 22½
Woodbridge N. Ferris.................. 30
James M. Cox......................... 59
Charles W. Bryan..................... 18
Fred H. Brown........................ 17
George S. Silzer...................... 38
Carter Glass.......................... 25
John W. Davis........................ 31
William E. Sweet...................... 12
Pat Harrison.......................... 43½
Houston Thompson..................... 1
John B. Kendrick...................... 6

The total number of votes in the convention was 1098. Under the two thirds rule 732 was necessary for a choice; 550 constituted a majority. In two days thirty ballots were taken at the end of which McAdoo had 415½, Smith 323½, John W. Davis 126½, and the rest scattered about among the numerous favorite sons. It was by now apparent that the deadlock between McAdoo and Smith was an unbreakable one, that neither could be nominated, that a compromise candidate was inevitable. Smith from the start had realized that he could not be named and was ready to withdraw if McAdoo would, but the McAdoo leaders, still believing that they could achieve a majority, refused all such overtures and renewed their drive to break down the favorite sons, and particularly to swing the Virginia delegation over from Senator Glass.

If they could have done that they could have got

their majority, and firmly believed that then the nomination could not be refused. It is doubtful, however, that this would have been the result, as more than a third of the convention was apparently determined to hold out until the end. The influence of Governor Harry Flood Byrd and John Stewart Bryan, however, held the Virginia delegation away from McAdoo, and though on the sixty-ninth ballot he reached 530 votes, he never got beyond that point and from then on steadily dwindled, though keeping his lead until the eighty-seventh. Smith never got above 368; but the "favorite sons," each of whom had his hopes, held among them the balance. After the fiftieth ballot Smith sent for Senator Underwood and told him that if he could get two more States from the South besides his own, the Smith strength would be swung to him and he could be nominated. Senator Underwood asked twenty-four hours to work in, but at the end of that time his friends reported their inability to get even one State, and the deadlock continued.

After the eightieth ballot the hopelessness of the situation as to either McAdoo or Smith brought about a conference at the Waldorf Hotel of representatives of all the candidates in an effort to find some way out of an intolerable situation that seemed to many to threaten the very life of the party. At this conference it was made plain that while Smith was ready to retire, he could not do so unless McAdoo did. Still full of hope, the McAdoo people repelled the suggestion. In fact, the day before they had in the convention voted down a motion to have Smith appear before the convention to speak. Later, McAdoo himself requested that the consent be given, but it was then too late and Smith refused.

At the conference futile efforts to agree on the abolition of the two thirds and unit rules were made, but finally a plan was acquiesced in that eventually broke the deadlock and brought about the solution. It was conceived by a Maryland man—B. Howell Griswold, Jr., not a member of the convention but present as a friend of Governor Ritchie—and was offered in the conference by another Marylander, Howard Bruce, representing Ritchie, who after an hour of argument secured acquiescence in the idea, which was the very simple one of releasing the delegates from the instructions given by their States. This was proposed next day in the convention, adopted, and the McAdoo strength began to crumble from that time on. His friends realized their mistake when States like Missouri and Oklahoma, bound by instructions for McAdoo, began to switch to other candidates, but it was too late. On the eighty-seventh ballot McAdoo was driven down to 333½ and for the first time Smith took the lead with 368. On the one hundredth ballot the end came: California, Tennessee, and Washington, which had unwaveringly stood by him, broke. He dropped to 190. Smith held steady at 351½ and John W. Davis had 203½. On July 8, after that one hundredth ballot, McAdoo

495

withdrew, released his delegates, indicated his first choice as Edward T. Meredith of Iowa, his second Thomas J. Walsh of Montana. It was then the rush to John W. Davis began. With McAdoo out, there was no thought of nominating Smith either on his part or the convention's, and on the one hundred and first ballot his vote jumped above Smith's. On the one hundred and second the Smith delegations swung in for him, and on the one hundred and third he was unanimously nominated, the "favorite sons" holding out to the last.

The story of Mr. Davis's candidacy is an interesting one. Mr. Davis had had a distinguished career. Born in West Virginia of fine old Democratic stock, he had been congressman from that State, solicitor-general of the United States, and ambassador to Great Britain. Recognized as one of the great lawyers of the country, he was also conceded to be an unflinching and regular Democrat. A man of extraordinary personal charm, of the highest character, unblemished reputation, and great ability, he had thousands of friends and admirers in all parts of the country. His candidacy was a purely receptive one, entirely uninspired by himself. A few of his friends in West Virginia, without consulting him, but knowing there was an underlying sentiment for him, determined to present his name. A week before the convention they engaged a room for headquarters at the Waldorf, had a handsome picture of Mr. Davis in the lobby and launched his boom. There was

Photograph from Brown Brothers

JOHN W. DAVIS

Democratic Presidential nominee in 1924

no hurrah or literature or propaganda and no money. True, many newspapers had urged Mr. Davis as the ideal candidate, but all he had behind him in the way of delegates were the sixteen votes from his State. His headquarters were in charge of Clem Shaver of West Virginia, a singularly quiet person but a politician of unusual shrewdness and a man of substance and character. Equally interested were his friends Clarence W. Watson, president of the Consolidation Coal Company and a former senator from West Virginia, Frank L. Polk, and Norman Davis, both of whom had been conspicuous in the Wilson administration.

That was about all, except that in pretty nearly every Smith and McAdoo delegation Davis was the second choice. From the start of the convention the Davis sentiment among the delegates had been apparent and the Davis strength recognized. One of his political handicaps was that after he came back from Great Britain he had engaged in the practice of law in New York, where his talents and ability made him an outstanding member of his profession and gained for him many big corporate clients. Among these was the great banking firm of J. P. Morgan & Company. In the eyes of Mr. Bryan and his followers this stamped him as a representative of "Wall Street" and the candidate of "the interests," and Mr. Bryan early in the convention, realizing the undercurrent toward him, made a speech attacking his candidacy along those lines. Mr. Davis's character and standing were so high, however, that the attack was futile, and when his nomination finally came a thrill of enthusiasm was sent through Democrats in every part of the country.

It seemed to them that after nearly two weeks of insanity the Democratic party had returned to sanity, that out of the wildest conflict in party history there had come the best possible nomination, that the party had picked not only its best qualified and equipped man for the Presidency, one wholly free from any of the religious bitterness that had so torn the convention, but one who could win.

So it seemed for a few hours; but it did not last long. Mr. Davis, who was at Mr. Polk's house in New York, was brought before the convention, given a tremendous reception, and made a graceful speech. Governor Smith appeared, pledged his support, and was enthusiastically received, but Mr. McAdoo did not appear. And then, while Democrats generally in the East were rejoicing over the selection of such a man as their Presidential candidate, the blow fell. Charles W. Bryan, governor of Nebraska and brother of William Jennings Bryan, was nominated for Vice-President. At once a chill succeeded the thrill. To the Democrats in the East, in the great pivotal States needed to insure election, the name of Bryan was abhorrent. Though Governor Bryan was a worthy man and had made a good governor, he seemed—and was—a reflection of his famous brother who had so often led the party to defeat, and the combination of Davis and Bryan seemed so obviously incongruous that the shouts of the jubilant Democrats died in their throats, and opportunity was afforded the Republicans to picture the party as facing both ways, to play on the old Bryan string, to alarm the business interests over the prospect of a Bryan, through death, becoming President.

That Mr. Davis could have won with any other running-mate is extremely doubtful, but it does seem sure he could have made a better showing. He has been criticized unjustly for making the Bryan selection. It could not have been helped. The facts are that as strongly as possible he personally urged Senator Thomas J. Walsh to take the nomination. He urged Newton D. Baker to take it, and Edward T. Meredith, and others. When with a number of leaders the final conference was held in a room at the Manhattan Club, just across from Madison Square Garden, no candidate was in sight, the convention was in a high state of excitement, demanding action. It was reported—and truthfully —that unless a decision was reached as to whom Mr. Davis wanted, the convention could not be held, would get out of hand. The delegates, after two weeks of sweating and fighting, loss of sleep, and desire to get home, had just about reached the end of their rope. It was reported that Walsh, undoubtedly the choice of the convention, would refuse if named, as he certainly would have.

The suggestion of Bryan first came from George Brennan, the Chicago boss. It was pointed out that the field had been combed, the desirable men could not be induced to run, it was necessary to pick a man West of the Alleghanies. Governor Bryan might carry his own State, and anyhow it would placate his brother, which it did. Mr. Davis acquiesced but not with enthusiasm. There seemed nothing else to do. Word was passed down the line for Charles Bryan and he was nominated with a whoop, while his brother beamed with delight and apparently sloughed off all of his prejudice against Mr. Davis as a representative of the "Morgan interests." From that time on he did all he could for the election of the ticket and spoke many times in the Western States. Governor Smith's support was equally hearty and he did all that he personally could for Mr. Davis. Mr. McAdoo, on the other hand, called on Mr. Davis in New York, made later a perfunctory and unenthusiastic declaration for the ticket, and three days after the convention got on a boat and went to Europe. When he returned he did merely enough in the way of support to maintain his regularity as a party man.

After the convention the troubles of Mr. Davis multiplied rapidly—and he had no luck. Every "break" in the campaign was against him. He had unusual difficulties in effecting his organization, in getting the men he wanted into his headquarters. Mr. Shaver, who did not want the job, was forced to take the chairmanship of the National Committee. The Democratic publicity bureau was poorly manned, and the effort to raise an adequate campaign fund never did succeed. Mr. Davis's speech of acceptance and his other speeches throughout the campaign, with a few exceptions, were of a statesmanlike quality, and personally he played his part as well as a man could. But back of him there was neither effective organization nor solid support. After the election one of his close friends said, "He was the finest race horse that ever started on a political track, and he got the worst ride."

That about describes it. Looking back, however, it is hard to believe that, no matter how efficiently the Davis campaign had been organized nor how well financed, the result would have been changed. He might have carried more States; he certainly would have got more votes; but that he or any other Democrat could have won seems most improbable. It was not only that the fearful war in the party had opened wounds that would not heal, that the Bryan nomination was a handicap, and the bedlam of the convention transmitted to millions over the radio had created an unfavorable popular reaction; there was much more to it than that. More than anything else the Republican victory was due to the unprecedented and undreamed of prosperity with which the country was drenched, a prosperity greater than had existed in any other country at any other time, a prosperity due to great economic laws, to our position after the war, and not at all to the Republican party, which however assumed all and got much of the credit.

It was the sort of prosperity that absorbed all criticism and made the attacks of the Democrats on Republican corruption utterly futile. The fact that the Republican candidate—Calvin Coolidge— had succeeded to the Presidency by death, was in no way responsible for the corrupt appointees, or practices, though Vice-President at the time, and that he was personally honest and free from taint, seemed a complete answer to the charges. With money plentiful, work for everybody, and no great problems or issues of an emotional nature, the people could not be stirred over the scandals, outrageous and indefensible as they were.

The utter absence of genuine popular indignation over them was and will continue to be a difficult thing to explain adequately about the American people, but the fact remains that they did not get indignant. Democrats contend that it was because they were drugged with prosperity and the propaganda of the Republican party, which, so far as it could be done, minimized and ignored corruption, the subject being one that every Republican, from their Presidential candidate down, avoided as he would the plague. The Republican contention was that the people had confidence in Mr. Coolidge, knew that he was not responsible, felt sure he would "clear the rascals out." The fact remains that they did not flame, and the issue of corruption which the Democrats had so counted on as a winning one signally failed.

Perhaps as much as any the attitude of the big business and banking interests contributed to the result. Primarily interested in the continuance of prosperity, they were uniformly opposed to a change. As secretary of the treasury, there had been put into office by Harding, and continued by Coolidge, Andrew W. Mellon of Pittsburgh, the richest man who ever held public office in America, controlling vast and varied industries, banks, and corporations, with an influence that extended into many States. The financial world felt him to be the ideal man for the post, and he brought the administration a greater business and newspaper support than any other administration had had. Though, as he himself said, what he did was to continue the financial policies of debt and tax reduction inaugurated by his Democratic predecessors, he was proclaimed by the Republican press and publicity agencies as "the greatest Secretary of the Treasury since Alexander Hamilton," and the bankers, regardless of politics, were almost solidly behind him. What the great business interests wanted was a continuation of the Mellon *régime* in the Treasury, and a President who would not do anything to disturb conditions. In other words, the ideal President in such a period was an inactive one. In Mr. Coolidge, who had, as one nonpartisan publicist wrote, made a major policy of inaction, they had their ideal President.

In any event, they froze solidly behind him. When to that support is added the success with which the unprecedented propaganda created the impression that tax reduction was due to "Coolidge economy" and debt reduction to "Mellon genius," and when to that is added the fact that the country had become normally heavily Republican in national elections, and the great bulk of the newspapers and publicity channels were in Republican hands, the defeat of the handicapped Democratic ticket is not to be wondered at. Though the presence in the field of a third ticket headed by Senator Robert M. La Follette of Wisconsin buoyed the Democrats with hope that at least for the first time in a hundred years the election would be thrown into the House of Representatives, the more clear headed among them saw the inevitable result weeks before the end.

But even to these the overwhelming and crushing nature of the defeat came as a shock. The popular plurality of the Republicans was approximately seven million—to be exact, 6,988,473, within a few thousand of the unprecedented plurality against Cox in 1920. Both the Republican and Democratic total votes were slightly reduced from 1920 by the La Follette vote, which, while dominant in but one State —Wisconsin—totaled 4,667,312. The Republican vote was 15,749,030 as compared to 16,152,200, the Democratic vote 8,760,557 as compared to 9,147,363 in 1920. The plurality of Mr. Coolidge in the Electoral College was 246. He had 382 votes, Davis 136,

La Follette 13. But Davis received nine more electoral votes than Cox, due to the fact that while he lost Kentucky with thirteen votes, he carried Oklahoma with ten and Tennessee with twelve, both of which Cox had lost. Though their candidate carried no State outside the solid South and Oklahoma, nothing at all in the West, and lost every border State except Tennessee, it was not quite so bad either in electoral or popular vote as 1920, though more depressing because of the undeniable personal superiority of the Democratic Presidential candidate, plus the fact that the indictment against the party in power was never more complete. Up to the last there was hope on one side and fear on the other that there would be manifested at the polls a popular resentment against the evil record of the Harding administration and the natural disposition to punish the party responsible for corrupt government. To repeat, its failure to materialize put into the creed of the politicians a new basic principle, to wit— "prosperity absorbs all criticism."

Chapter XXXVI

THE 1928 OUTLOOK

Conditions Essential to Democratic Success—Smith the
Outstanding Party Figure and Probable Nominee—
His Handicaps—Wet, Tammany, and Catholic—Uncovering Corruption the Great Party Achievement
of the Past Four Years

SINCE the 1924 election, so far as the Democratic
party is concerned, certain concrete facts have become so clear that most—though not all—Democratic leaders now appear to grasp them. Certainly
all detached observers do. Chief of these is that
though it has twenty-two of the forty-eight governors, 194 of the 435 members of the House, and
forty-seven of the ninety-six senators, and while it
is silly to talk of its disappearance as a national
party, in a Presidential year it has become definitely
the minority party.

There are for purposes of Presidential election
many more Republicans than Democrats. The extraordinary industrial development of the country,
the enormous influence on public opinion of the great
corporate business and banking interests, the completeness with which the Republicans since the war

have devoted themselves to those interests, the degree to which they have assumed credit for prosperity, the preponderance of Republican newpapers and periodicals, plus the dissensions, divisions, and mistakes of the Democrats, are sufficient to account for the situation, though much more could be written in analysis of it. It is plain that however virile the party may be in state and off-year congressional elections, the odds are against it even when united in the Presidential year, and its chances of victory are contingent on conditions quite off the normal. Either through abuse of power, long tenure of office, or cessation of prosperity, there must come a popular reaction against the Republicans; or there must occur a factional split in Republican ranks comparable to that of 1912; or there must be found by the Democrats a popular, powerful, and unifying issue; or there must develop within their party a leader of exceptional personal strength, capable of holding the South and swinging the great group of States in the East—New York, New Jersey, Connecticut, Massachusetts—without which the 266 votes necessary for choice in the Electoral College are not possible.

Any one of these conditions can develop with surprising suddenness, or several of them can, but without at least one there is small hope. Without one the Republicans can again defeat any first rate Democrat with a second or even third rate man of their own. While it is true that to some extent prosperity has diminished, it is not likely there will be a sufficient business depression before November, 1928, to take it away from the Republicans as an issue and an asset. Nor does there seem any real likelihood of a formidable split in the dominant party, notwithstanding the disaffected farmers in the great Republican strongholds of the West. Those two contingencies therefore can be pretty well ruled out. What is left for the Democrats then is hope of developing a unifying issue of their own, and the presentation of the exceptional candidate.

As for the first, it may as well be admitted that there is at this time but one real issue in the country —prohibition. It is the one topic uppermost in the minds of people in every section and both parties. There is no other question capable of emotionally disturbing the voters. Prosperity absorbs not only all criticism but nearly all issues as well. The obvious inability of the Government to enforce the Eighteenth Amendment has in every State created a condition of lawlessness that is apparently growing worse and not better and which has created the most intense feeling between the opponents and the advocates of the prohibition experiment. Both parties are split on the issue and both have consistently in their national platforms evaded and avoided recognition of conditions, sidestepped definite recommendations.

As usual, Republican discipline has up to now been reasonably successful in smothering feeling and keeping either wet or dry faction from becoming too belligerent, but in the Democratic ranks, also as usual on a moral issue, the flame blazes high. On this question the minority party is unquestionably more deeply and bitterly divided than the other, which at once does away with the idea of a unifying issue for the Democrats in the next campaign. There is no other. No one thinks it possible under existing conditions to make a successful national appeal on the tariff, on taxation, on agriculture, or foreign policy—even if there were among the Democrats any clear-cut and whole-hearted and unifying convictions on these matters, which there are not. Corruption in government, tried last time, should have been a winning issue but was not. It cannot be made again, because while the Harding administration reeked with fraud, that has not been so under Mr. Coolidge. As to the rest they are unusable. Prosperity has blurred them all; and the people, except on prohibition, are in an unprecedented state of political inertia. Thus, all that is left in the way of hope for the Democrats in 1928 is the development of the man—and here a curious and interesting situation exists.

Since Mr. Davis's defeat the one real hopeful development in the party has been the extraordinary growth as a party figure of Governor Alfred E. Smith of New York. In him a man has arisen of whom the Republicans are unquestionably somewhat apprehensive, despite his handicaps. They think they can beat Smith if he is nominated in 1928, but there is enough uncertainty about it to instill an alarm not felt regarding any other possible Democratic choice. Quite naturally Smith's extraordinary and unprecedented victories in New York, where he has been four times elected governor, where he has been chiefly responsible for the election of two Democratic United States senators, and for the undoubted demoralization of the Republican organization, make him the outstanding Democrat of the party, its leading and logical candidate for the 1928 nomination. This position is accentuated by the withdrawal from the field of Mr. McAdoo and the failure so far of the elements represented by McAdoo to find a figure around whom to rally.

It seems pretty generally agreed—by Republicans as well as Democrats—that Smith is an exceptional man, with character, capacity, courage, a vibrant personality, a rare talent for politics, and a wide popular appeal. Based on his record, it is not extravagant to say that he would stand a better chance of carrying the indispensable New York group of States than any other Democrat. Few dispute that. It is, however, his and his party's hard luck that along with his undeniable assets as a candidate he should have certain liabilities that, while they have not weighed against him at all in New York, in the event of his nomination for President unquestionably do create a real doubt not only as to the border States of Kentucky, Tennessee, and Missouri, but actually as to the solid South itself.

The 1928 Outlook

The chief trouble about the Smith candidacy is his religion. He happens to be the first Catholic who has ever been within reach of a Presidential nomination in any political party in the whole history of the country. The existence of an anti-Catholic sentiment in every section is an acknowledged fact. The best evidence of this is the rise and spread of the Ku-Klux Klan. In the South the people are overwhelmingly Protestant and overwhelmingly dry, and it is in this section that the opposition to the wet, Tammany, Catholic Smith is strongest. Most political judges early in 1928 believed that Smith would be nominated notwithstanding the feeling in the South and the two thirds rule. They point to the fact that he is apparently assured now of a majority of the delegates to the convention and has no formidable rival, both Ritchie of Maryland and Reed of Missouri being on his side of the prohibition fence and not unfriendly to his selection.

There are some, however, who believe that one of two things will happen—either Smith will himself decide not to make the fight, or the dry forces will form a block that will prevent him from getting two thirds of the convention and force another choice. Either of those things may easily happen. Among the names mentioned in this connection are those of Newton D. Baker of Ohio, Owen D. Young of New York, Senator Thomas J. Walsh of Montana, Edwin T. Meredith of Iowa, Governor Victor Donahey of Ohio, Evans Woolen of Indiana, Atlee B.

Pomerene of Ohio, Senator Joseph T. Robinson of Arkansas, Governor Harry Flood Byrd of Virginia, Governor Albert C. Ritchie of Maryland, Senator James A. Reed of Missouri.

It is a curious and interesting thing that any one of these men—including Ritchie and Reed, who are wet, or Walsh, who is a Catholic but dry—in the judgment of practically every present-day political observer and politician would more surely hold the South and the border States than Smith. Whereas not one of them would have Smith's chance of carrying New York, New Jersey, Connecticut, and Massachusetts.

It is rather a tragic situation for the party. The most hopeful feature is the uneasiness among Republicans over the Smith nomination, which they at least consider fairly well assured—an uneasiness accounted for by his past impregnability in New York. Very few Presidents have been elected without New York.

But to get away from personalities and back to principles: the Democratic party after a continuous history of 136 years, though it has not elected a President since 1916 and has become definitely the minority party, is in 1928 still full of energy and vigor and promise. Whether it wins or loses its next fight, no one need be concerned as to the permanence of the party. It is still young. It may be divided and it may be defeated, but it is far too virile and vital a force in the individual States of which the nation is

ALFRED EMANUEL SMITH

Four times governor of New York and candidate for Presidential
nomination in 1928

composed to make the suggestions of its impending doom and disappearance other than ridiculous. Thoughtful men with a clear view of the politics of the country, and a real comprehension of its political history, regard such notions as altogether half baked, wholly without foundation. Such men are as sure that, whether it be in 1928 or 1932 or 1936 or some other four-year period, soon or late the Democrats will sweep back into national power, as they are that the present period of Republican ascendancy is temporary.

When, as it inevitably will, prosperity ebbs and the national problems, becoming more social than industrial, require something beyond a material conservatism for a solution, the people will turn to the party with the more liberal tendency and the more progressive tradition. The history of the past fifty years has been sufficient to show that it is the only one from which action along those lines can be expected. About once every decade or so such action becomes imperative, and it can be supplied only by an inherently progressive party. Perhaps the nation needs the conservative party in power most of the time in order that the reforms taken through the progressives may be consolidated and made workable. But part of the time its need of the progressive party is overwhelming.

The Democratic party is that party, and it will continue to be that party, regardless of splits, setbacks, and stupidity. No clear-headed person doubts that. It can be proved in too many ways. The extraordinary developments of the last four years alone have been enough to convince any unbiased person of the national need of the Democratic party, of its national use even out of power. Though it may be true as has been so frequently said that "Prosperity absorbs all criticism," it does seem that the reflecting few at least would realize that the party in power is not a party that can be trusted with too much power too long. Probably that is true of any party, but to those who think that uncovering corruption in politics and government is a real public service, who consider the moral welfare of a people as important as their material welfare, it must seem that, out of office though it has been, the Democratic party has not been out of power or without its uses in the last four years. For example, if it had not been for a Democrat—Senator James A. Reed of Missouri— the two most sensational political scandals that have occurred in a generation, those connected with the nomination and election of Mr. William S. Vare in Pennsylvania and Mr. Frank L. Smith in Illinois, would totally have escaped national notice, and these two men would have taken their seats in the Senate without a critical or unkind word, instead of being denounced from one end of the country to the other as unfit to sit in that body and refused admission. It is also true that but for Senator Reed the nation would not have known that Mr. Samuel Insull, a multi-millionaire public-utility magnate, had contributed a quarter of a million dollars to the senatorial campaign of Mr. Smith, who until after his election was chairman of the State Utility Commission, with rate-making powers over Mr. Insull's corporations. But for a Democrat, Mr. Insull's methods in these matters would not have been disclosed and he would to-day bear an unblemished reputation instead of a very badly spotted one.

But an even greater service to the nation than that of exposing Mr. Vare and Mr. Smith and Mr. Insull was performed by another Democrat. If it had not been for Senator Thomas J. Walsh of Montana, Mr. Fall, the Republican secretary of the interior under Harding, and Mr. Doheny, and Mr. Harry F. Sinclair would have succeeded in stealing the naval oil reserves of the nation at Elk Hills and Teapot Dome, and would all three of them to-day be living among us as honorable and respectable men, utterly free of that indelible Supreme Court brand that marks them as infamous, stamps them as guilty of "fraud, conspiracy and corruption." It was Senator Walsh, blocked and thwarted at every turn by the Republican organization, without sympathy or help from the Republican administration, and in the face of a barrage of criticism from Republican organs and spokesmen that he was playing politics, seeking publicity, making a mountain out of a molehill, who kept at his job until he brought the amazing facts to light.

When the results of his work are considered, it

does seem that even in such a material age as this something more of national appreciation and gratitude should go to him. The nation has recovered its great oil reserves. The men who conspired to take them away, disgraced and denounced by the highest court, have been compelled to return to the Government more than thirteen million dollars. The Supreme Court in two burning decisions has unanimously upheld the Walsh contentions, and in denouncing Fall, Sinclair, and Doheny employed scalding words that, in the 1924 campaign when used in the Democratic platform and by Democratic spokesmen, were called partisan and demagogic.

If these two senators have not rendered a national service it is hard to think of any who have. Glorious though it is to be prosperous, magnificent as it may be to reduce taxes when revenues are vastly in excess of expenditures, splendid though it is to preach economy and protect business, still, the uncovering and frustration of such a gigantic governmental conspiracy and such flagrant political corruption would seem to the fair mind as at least worthy of comparison with the material achievements of the party in power. It is worth noting that in the exposures here mentioned no regular Republican played any part, lent the least help. On the contrary, the regular Republican activity was concentrated in the effort first to prevent the facts from coming out, second to minimize and ignore them after they had come out.

The 1928 Outlook

It is further worth noting that neither Senator Reed nor Senator Walsh could have succeeded in their fights had they not had their party solidly behind them. After all, the disclosures of these black chapters in political government, the revealing of the sinister set of men who dominated the Harding administration, and the cleaning out of as unscrupulous a lot as ever infested Washington—these things constitute a real Democratic achievement. When it is considered that the Democrats were out of office, that they were in control of neither the Department of Justice, nor either branch of Congress, the size of the achievement can be better appreciated. It will stand comparison with any of the Republican party in the last fifty years. If there were nothing else in its long and eventful history, that alone would justify its existence and its continuation.

BIBLIOGRAPHY

"Encyclopedia of Politics."

Stanwood's "History of the Presidency."

Bowers's "Jefferson and Hamilton" and "Party Battles of the Jackson Period."

McElroy's "Life of Grover Cleveland."

Gray's "Biography of James Madison."

Shephard's "Biography of Martin Van Buren."

Von Holst's "Biography of John C. Calhoun."

Hirst's "Life and Letters of Thomas Jefferson."

James Kerney's "Political Education of Woodrow Wilson."

"Memoirs of William Jennings Bryan."

"Memoirs of Henry Watterson."

Macy's "Political Parties in the United States."

Morse's "Parties and Party Leaders."

McCormac's "Biography of James K. Polk."

"The Democratic Machine from 1850 to 1854," by Roy Franklin Nichols.

Robinson's "The Evolution of American Political Parties."

Schlesinger's "New Viewpoints in American History."

Woodburn's "Political Parties and Party Problems."

Ostrogorski's "Democracy and the Party System."

Ray's "Political Parties and Practical Politics."

Brooks's "Political Parties and Electoral Problems."

Benton's "Thirty Years' View."

APPENDIX

DEMOCRATIC NATIONAL COMMITTEE

1928

CLEM W. SHAVER, *Chairman*

State	National Committeemen	National Committeewomen
ALABAMA	Walter Moore	Mrs. Charles J. Sharp
ARIZONA	W. L. Barnum	M r s. Theodora Marsh

Appendix

State	National Committeemen	National Committeewomen
ARKANSAS	Vincent M. Miles	Miss Alice Cordell
CALIFORNIA	Isidore B. Dockweiler	Mrs. Charles L. Donohoe
COLORADO	John T. Barnett	Mrs. Gertrude A. Lee
CONNECTICUT	Thomas J. Spellacy	Mrs. Lillian S. Abbott
DELAWARE	Andrew C. Gray	Mrs. John R. Eskridge
FLORIDA	J. T. G. Crawford	Mrs. Lois K. Mayes
GEORGIA	John S. Cohen	Mrs. Edgar Alexander
IDAHO	Robert H. Elder	Mrs. Teresa M. Graham
ILLINOIS	George E. Brennan	Mrs. Kellogg Fairbank
INDIANA	Charles A. Greathouse	Mrs. Bessie L. Riggs
IOWA	Clyde L. Herring	Mrs. Madge O'Neill
KANSAS	Dudley Doolittle	Mrs. Florence G. Farley
KENTUCKY	Urey Woodson	Mrs. J. C. Cantrill
LOUISIANA	Lee Emmett Thomas	Mrs. Genevieve Clark Thomson
MAINE	D. J. McGillicuddy	Mrs. William R. Pattangall
MARYLAND	Howard Bruce	Mrs. S. Johnson Poe
MASSACHUSETTS	Edward W. Quinn	Mrs. Nellie M. Sullivan
MICHIGAN	William A. Comstock	Mrs. Etta C. Boltwood

Appendix

State	National Committeemen	National Committeewomen
MINNESOTA	Joseph Wolf	Miss Jessie Scott
MISSISSIPPI	Henry Minor	Mrs. Daisy McL. Stevens
MISSOURI	W. T. Kemper	Mrs. Emily Newell Blair
MONTANA	J. Bruce Kremer	Mrs. J. S. M. Neill
NEBRASKA	Arthur F. Mullen	Dr. Jennie Callfas
NEVADA	Samuel M. Pickett	Mrs. Frances Friedhoff
NEW HAMPSHIRE	Robert C. Murchie	Mrs. Dorothy B. Jackson
NEW JERSEY	Frank Hague	Mrs. James J. Billington
NEW MEXICO	Arthur Seligman	Mrs. Jennie Martin Kirby
NEW YORK	Norman E. Mack	Miss Elisabeth Marbury
NORTH CAROLINA	F. M. Simmons	Miss Mary O. Graham
NORTH DAKOTA	R. B. Murphy	Mrs. Esther S. Johnson
OHIO	W. A. Julian	Mrs. Bernice Pyke
OKLAHOMA	Scott Ferris	Mrs. D. A. McDougal
OREGON	Will R. King	Mrs. Irene E. Stuart
PENNSYLVANIA	Joseph F. Guffey	Mrs. Lillian D. Bergey
RHODE ISLAND	Patrick H. Quinn	Mrs. Jane A. Newton
SOUTH CAROLINA	John Gary Evans	Mrs. Leroy Springs

Appendix

State	National Committeemen	National Committeewomen
SOUTH DAKOTA	W. W. Howes	Mrs. H. C. Snodgrass
TENNESSEE	Cordell Hull	Mrs. Benton McMillin
TEXAS	Jed Adams	Mrs. J. T. Bloodworth
UTAH	James H. Moyle	Mrs. Weston Vernon
VERMONT	Frank H. Duffy	Miss Alice D. Sullivan
VIRGINIA	Carter Glass	Mrs. Beverly B. Munford
WASHINGTON	George F. Christensen	Mrs. E. D. Christian
WEST VIRGINIA	C. W. Osenton	Mrs. Frank Mann
WISCONSIN	John M. Callahan	Mrs. Gertrude Bowler
WYOMING	Patrick J. Quealy	Mrs. Burke H. Sinclair
ALASKA	T. J. Donohoe	Mrs. John W. Troy
DISTRICT OF COLUMBIA	John F. Costello	Mrs. J. Borden Harriman
HAWAII	John H. Wilson	Mrs. L. L. McCandless
PHILIPPINE ISLANDS	Robert E. Manley	Grace E. Westerhouse
PORTO RICO	Henry W. Dooley	Mrs. Isabel Locke Horton
CANAL ZONE	Frank T. Hamlin	Mrs. L. O. Keen

Appendix

1832......*Andrew Jackson, Tennessee.

1836......*Martin Van Buren, New York.

1840......Martin Van Buren, New York.

1844......*James K. Polk, Tennessee.
Martin Van Buren, New York.
Lewis Cass, Michigan.

1848......Lewis Cass, Michigan.
James Buchanan, Pennsylvania.
Levi Woodbury, New Hampshire.
George M. Dallas, Pennsylvania.
W. J. Worth, Tennessee.
John C. Calhoun, South Carolina.
W. O. Butler, Kentucky.

1852......*Franklin Pierce, New Hampshire.
James Buchanan, Pennsylvania.
William L. Marcy, New York.
Samuel Houston, Texas.
Stephen A. Douglas, Illinois.
Joseph Lane, Oregon.

1856......*James Buchanan, Pennsylvania.
Thomas Benton, Tennessee.
Stephen A. Douglas, Illinois.
Franklin Pierce, New Hampshire.

1860......John C. Breckinridge, Kentucky.
Stephen A. Douglas, Illinois.

1864......George B. McClellan, New Jersey.
Thomas H. Seymour, Connecticut.
Horatio Seymour, New York.
Charles O'Conor, New York.

1868......Horatio Seymour, New York.
George H. Pendleton, Ohio.
*Elected.

Andrew Johnson, Tennessee.
Winfield S. Hancock, Pennsylvania.
Samuel E. Church, New York.
Asa Packer, Pennsylvania.
Joel Parker, New Jersey.
James E. English, Connecticut.
James R. Doolittle, Wisconsin.
Thomas A. Hendricks, Indiana.
Salmon P. Chase, Ohio.

1872......Horace Greeley, New York.
Jeremiah S. Black, Pennsylvania.
Thomas F. Bayard, Delaware.
William S. Groesbeck, Ohio.
Thomas A. Hendricks, Indiana.

1876......Samuel J. Tilden, New York.
Thomas A. Hendricks, Indiana.
Winfield S. Hancock, Pennsylvania.
William Allen, Ohio.
Thomas F. Bayard, Delaware.
Joel Parker, New Jersey.
Allen G. Thurman, Ohio.

1880......Winfield S. Hancock, Pennsylvania.
Thomas F. Bayard, Delaware.
Henry B. Payne, Ohio.
Allen G. Thurman, Ohio.
William R. Morrison, Illinois.
Thomas A. Hendricks, Indiana.
Samuel J. Tilden, New York.
Horatio Seymour, New York.
Samuel J. Randall, Pennsylvania.

1884......*Grover Cleveland, New York.
Thomas F. Bayard, Delaware.
Thomas A. Hendricks, Indiana.

*Elected.

Allen G. Thurman, Ohio.
Samuel J. Randall, Pennsylvania.
James E. McDonald, Indiana.
John G. Carlisle, Kentucky.
Roswell P. Flower, New York.
George Hoadly, Ohio.
Samuel J. Tilden, New York.

1888......Grover Cleveland, New York.

1892......*Grover Cleveland, New York.
David B. Hill, New York.
Horace Boies, Iowa.
Arthur P. Gorman, Maryland.
Adlai E. Stevenson, Illinois.
John G. Carlisle, Kentucky.
William R. Morrison, Illinois.
James E. Campbell, Ohio.
William C. Whitney, New York.
William E. Russell, Massachusetts.
Robert E. Pattison, Pennsylvania.

1896......William J. Bryan, Nebraska.
Richard P. Bland, Missouri.
Robert E. Pattison, Pennsylvania.
Horace Boies, Iowa.
Joseph S. C. Blackburn, Kentucky.
John R. McLean, Ohio.
Claude Matthews, Indiana.
Benjamin F. Tillman, South Carolina.
Sylvester Pennoyer, Oregon.
Henry M. Teller, Colorado.
Adlai E. Stevenson, Illinois.
William E. Russell, Massachusetts.
James E. Campbell, Ohio.
David B. Hill, New York.
David Turpie, Indiana.

*Elected.

527

Appendix

1900......William J. Bryan, Nebraska.

1904......Alton B. Parker, New York.
William R. Hearst, New York.
Francis M. Cockrell, Missouri.
Richard Olney, Massachusetts.
Edward C. Wall, Wisconsin.
George Gray, Delaware.
John S. Williams, Mississippi.
Robert E. Pattison, Pennsylvania.
George B. McClellan, New York.
Nelson A. Miles, Massachusetts.
Charles A. Towne, Minnesota.
Arthur P. Gorman, Maryland.
Bird S. Coler, New York.

1908......William J. Bryan, Nebraska.
George Gray, Delaware.
John A. Johnson, Minnesota.

1912......*Woodrow Wilson, New Jersey.
Champ Clark, Missouri.
Oscar Underwood, Alabama.
Judson Harmon, Ohio.
Thomas R. Marshall, Indiana.
Eugene N. Foss, Massachusetts.
Simeon E. Baldwin, Connecticut.
William Sulzer, New York.
William J. Gaynor, New York.
Ollie M. James, Kentucky.
James H. Lewis, Illinois.
John W. Kern, Indiana.
William J. Bryan, Nebraska.

1916......*Woodrow Wilson, New Jersey.

1920......James Middleton Cox, Ohio.
William G. McAdoo, New York.

*Elected.

Appendix

A. Mitchell Palmer, Pennsylvania.
Alfred E. Smith, New York.
John W. Davis, West Virginia.
Robert L. Owen, Oklahoma.
Carter Glass, Virginia.
Bainbridge Colby, New York.
Edward I. Edwards, New Jersey.
Homer Cummings, Connecticut.
James W. Gerard, New York.
Gilbert M. Hitchcock, Nebraska.
Edwin T. Meredith, Iowa.
Thomas R. Marshall, Indiana.
Josephus Daniels, North Carolina.
Champ Clark, Missouri.
Oscar W. Underwood, Alabama.
Leonard Wood, New Hampshire.
William R. Hearst, New York.
William J. Bryan, Nebraska.
John S. Williams, Mississippi.
Furnifold M. Simmons, North Carolina.
Francis B. Harrison, Philippines.

1924......John W. Davis, West Virginia.
William G. McAdoo, California.
Alfred E. Smith, New York.
Oscar W. Underwood, Alabama.
Albert C. Ritchie, Maryland.
Carter Glass, Virginia.
Joseph A. Robinson, Arkansas.
Jonathan Davis, Kansas.
Willard Saulsbury, Delaware.
George Silzer, New Jersey.
Thomas J. Walsh, Montana.
Charles W. Bryan, Nebraska.
Samuel Ralston, Indiana.
James M. Cox, Ohio.
Pat Harrison, Mississippi.
Houston Thompson, Colorado.

Appendix

1832......*Martin Van Buren, New York.
Philip P. Barbour, Virginia.
Richard M. Johnson, Kentucky.

1836......*Richard M. Johnson, Kentucky.
William C. Reves, Virginia.

1840......Richard M. Johnson, Kentucky.
James K. Polk, Tennessee.
L. W. Tazewell, Virginia.

1844......*George M. Dallas, Pennsylvania.
Silas Wright, New York.
Levi Woodbury, New Hampshire.
John Fairfield, Maine.
Lewis Cass, Michigan.
R. M. Johnson, Kentucky.
William L. Marcy, New York.
Commodore Stewart, Pennsylvania.

1848......General William O. Butler, Kentucky.
John A. Quitman, Mississippi.
John Y. Mason, Virginia.
William R. King, Alabama.
James J. McKay, North Carolina.
Jefferson Davis, Mississippi.

1852......*William R. King, Alabama.
S. U. Downs, Louisiana.
John B. Weller, California.
W. O. Butler, Kentucky.
Gideon J. Pillow, Tennessee.
David R. Atchison, Missouri.
Robert Strange, North Carolina.
T. J. Rusk, Texas.
Jefferson Davis, Mississippi.
Howell Cobb, Georgia.

*Elected.

Appendix

1856......*John C. Breckinridge, Kentucky.
        Linn Boyd, Kentucky.
        John A. Quitman, Mississippi.
        Herschel V. Johnson, Georgia.
        James A. Bayard, Delaware.
        Aaron V. Brown, Tennessee.
        James C. Dobbin, North Carolina.
        Benjamin Fitzpatrick, Alabama.
        Truston Polk, Missouri.
        Thomas J. Rusk, Texas.

1860......Joseph Lane, Oregon.
        Herschel V. Johnson, Georgia.
        Benjamin Fitzpatrick, Alabama.

1864......George H. Pendleton, Ohio.
        James Guthrie, Kentucky.
        Lazarus W. Powell, Kentucky.
        George W. Cass, Pennsylvania.
        Daniel W. Voorhees, Indiana.
        John D. Caton, Illinois.
        Augustus C. Dodge, Iowa.
        John S. Phelps, Missouri.

1868......Francis P. Blair, Jr., Missouri.

1872......B. Gratz Brown, Missouri.
        John W. Stephenson, Kentucky.

1876......Thomas A. Hendricks, Indiana.

1880......William H. English, Indiana.
        Richard M. Bishop, Ohio.

1884......*Thomas A. Hendricks, Indiana.
        John C. Black, Illinois.
        William S. Rosecrans, California.
        George W. Glick, Kansas.

1888......Allen G. Thurman, Ohio.
        Isaac P. Gray, Indiana.
        John C. Black, Illinois.

        *Elected.

1892......*Adlai E. Stevenson, Illinois.
            Isaac P. Gray, Indiana.
            Allen B. Morse, Michigan.
            John L. Mitchell, Wisconsin.
            Henry Watterson, Kentucky.
            Bourke Cockran, New York.
            Lambert Trie, Illinois.
            Horace Boies, Iowa.

1896......Arthur Sewall, Maine.
            Joseph C. Sibley, Pennsylvania.
            John R. McLean, Ohio.
            George F. Williams, Massachusetts.
            Richard P. Bland, Missouri.
            Walter A. Clark, North Carolina.
            John R. Williams, Illinois.
            William F. Harrity, Pennsylvania.
            Horace Boies, Iowa.
            Joseph S. C. Blackburn, Kentucky.
            John W. Daniel, Virginia.
            James H. Lewis, Washington.
            Robert E. Pattison, Pennsylvania.
            Henry M. Teller, Colorado.
            Stephen M. White, California.
            George W. Fithian, Illinois.

1900......Adlai E. Stevenson, Illinois.
            David B. Hill, New York.
            Charles A. Towne, Minnesota.

1904......Henry G. Davis, West Virginia.
            James R. Williams, Illinois.
            George Turner, Washington.
            William A. Harris, Kansas.

1908......John W. Kern, Indiana.
            Charles A. Towne, Minnesota.
            Archibald McNeil, Connecticut.
            Clark Howell, Georgia.

        *Elected.

Appendix

1912......*Thomas R. Marshall, Indiana.
John Burke, North Dakota.
George E. Chamberlain, Oregon.
Elmore W. Hurst, Illinois.
James H. Preston, Maryland.
M. J. Wade, Iowa.
William F. McCombs, New York.
John E. Osborne, Wyoming.
William Sulzer, New York.

1916......*Thomas R. Marshall, Indiana.

1920......Franklin D. Roosevelt, New York.
James Hamilton Lewis, Illinois.
Governor Stewart of Montana.
Ex-Governor Hawley of Idaho.
W. T. Vaughn, Oregon.
L. D. Tyson, Tennessee.
David R. Francis, Missouri.

1924......Charles W. Bryan, Nebraska.
George L. Berry, Tennessee.
Jonathan M. Davis, Kansas.
Mrs. Leroy Springs, South Carolina.
George S. Silzer, New Jersey.
Alvin Owsley, Texas.
John C. Greenway, Arizona.
Bennett Clark, Missouri.
William A. Gaston, Massachusetts.
John F. Hylan, New York.
Edwin T. Meredith, Iowa.
William Smith Flynn, Rhode Island.
James W. Gerard, New York.

*Elected.

Appendix

Year	Party	Candidate	Vote
1828	Dem.	Andrew Jackson	647,231
	Nat. Rep.	J. Q. Adams	509,097
1832	Dem.	Andrew Jackson	687,502
	Nat. Rep.	Henry Clay	530,189
	Anti-Mas.	William Wirt	33,108
		John Floyd	33,108
1836	Dem.	Martin Van Buren	761,549
	Whig	W. H. Harrison	
	Whig	Daniel Webster	736,656
	Whig	Hugh L. White	
	Whig	W. P. Mangum	
1840	Whig	W. H. Harrison	1,275,017
	Dem.	Martin Van Buren	1,128,702
	Liberty	James G. Birney	7,059
1844	Dem.	James K. Polk	1,337,243
	Whig	Henry Clay	1,299,068
	Liberty	James G. Birney	62,300
1848	Whig	Zachary Taylor	1,360,101
	Dem.	Lewis Cass	1,220,544
	Free Soil	Martin Van Buren	291,263
1852	Dem.	Franklin Pierce	1,601,474
	Whig	Winfield Scott	1,380,678
	Free Soil	John P. Hale	156,149
1856	Dem.	James Buchanan	1,838,169
	Rep.	John C. Frémont	1,341,264
	Know Nothing and Whigs	Millard Fillmore	874,534
1860	Rep.	Abraham Lincoln	1,866,352
	Dem.	S. A. Douglas	1,375,157
	Sou. Dem.	J. C. Breckinridge	845,763
	Const. Un.	John Bell	589,581

Appendix

Year	Party	Candidate	Vote
1864—Rep.		Abraham Lincoln	2,216,067
	Dem.	G. B. McClellan	1,808,725
1868—Rep.		Ulysses S. Grant	3,015,071
	Dem.	Horatio Seymour	2,709,613
1872—Rep.		Ulysses S. Grant	3,597,070
	Lib. Rep.	Horace Greeley	2,834,079
	Dem.	Charles O'Conor	29,408
	Pro.	James Black	5,608
1876—Rep.		R. B. Hayes	4,033,950
	Dem.	S. J. Tilden	4,284,885
	Greenback	Peter Cooper	81,740
	Pro.	G. C. Smith	9,552
1880—Rep.		Jas. A. Garfield	4,449,053
	Dem.	W. S. Hancock	4,442,035
	Greenback	James B. Weaver	307,306
	Pro.	Neal Dow	10,487
1884—Dem.		Grover Cleveland	4,911,017
	Rep.	James G. Blaine	4,848,334
	Pro.	J. P. St. John	151,809
	Gr.-Labor	Benjamin F. Butler	133,825
1888—Rep.		Benjamin Harrison	5,444,337
	Dem.	Grover Cleveland	5,540,050
	Pro.	Clinton B. Fisk	250,125
	Union Labor	A. J. Streeter	146,897
	United Labor	Robert H. Cowdrey	2,808
1892—Dem.		Grover Cleveland	5,554,414
	Rep.	Benjamin Harrison,	5,190,802
	Pop.	James B. Weaver	1,027,329
	Pro.	John Bidwell	271,058
	Soc.-Labor	Simon Wing	21,164

Year	Party	Candidate	Vote
1896—Rep.	William McKinley	7,035,638
Dem.	William J. Bryan ⎫	
Pop.	William J. Bryan ⎬	6,467,946
Silver	William J. Bryan ⎭	
Nat. Dem.	J. M. Palmer	131,529
Pro.	J. P. Levering	141,676
Silver-Pro.	C. I. Bentley	13,969
Soc.-Labor	C. H. Matchett	36,454
1900—Rep.	William McKinley	7,219,530
Dem.	William J. Bryan	6,358,071
Pro.	J. G. Woolley	209,166
Soc.-Dem.	E. V. Debs	94,768
Soc.-Labor	Fr. Malloney	32,751
M. R. Pop.	W. Barker	50,232
Un. Ref.	Seth Ellis	5,098
Un. Chr.	J. F. R. Leonard.......	518
1904—Rep.	Theodore Roosevelt	7,628,834
Dem.	A. B. Parker	5,084,491
Pro.	Silas C. Swallow	259,257
Soc.	E. V. Debs	402,460
Soc.-Labor	C. H. Corregan	33,724
M. R. Pop.	T. E. Watson..........	114,753
1908—Rep.	William H. Taft	7,679,006
Dem.	William J. Bryan	6,409,106
Pro.	E. W. Chafin	252,683
Soc.	E. V. Debs	420,820
Soc.-Labor	Aug. Gillhaus	13,825
People's	T. E. Watson	28,131
Ind.	T. L. Hisgen	83,562
1912—Dem.	Woodrow Wilson	6,286,214
Prog.	Theodore Roosevelt	4,126,200
Rep.	William H. Taft	3,483,922
Soc.	E. V. Debs	897,011

Year	Party	Candidate	Vote
	Pro.	E. W. Chafin	208,923
	Soc.-Labor	Arthur Reimer	29,079
1916—Dem	....	Woodrow Wilson	9,129,606
	Rep.	Charles E. Hughes	8,538,221
	Soc.	Allan L. Benson	585,113
	Pro.	J. F. Hanly	220,506
	Soc.-Labor	Arthur E. Reimer	13,403
1920—Rep.		Warren G. Harding.....	16,152,200
	Dem.	James M. Cox	9,147,353
	Soc.	E. V. Debs	919,799
	Farm-Labor	P. P. Christensen	265,411
	Pro.	A. S. Watkins	189,408
	Soc.-Labor	W. W. Cox	31,175
1924—Rep.		Calvin Coolidge	15,725,016
	Dem.	John W. Davis	8,386,503
	Ind. Prog. Soc...	Robert M. La Follette..	4,822,856
	Pro.	Faris	57,520
	Amer.	Nationa	23,967
	Com. Land	Wallace	1,532
	Soc. Labor	Johns	36,428
	Workers	Foster	36,386

ELECTORAL VOTE FOR PRESIDENTIAL CANDIDATES

Year	Party	Candidate	Vote
1800—Dem.-Rep.		Thomas Jefferson	73
	Dem.-Rep.	Aaron Burr	73
	Federalist	John Adams	65
	Federalist	C. C. Pinckney	64
		John Jay	1
1804—Dem.-Rep.		Thomas Jefferson	162
	Federalist	C. C. Pinckney	14
1808—Dem.-Rep.		James Madison	122
	Federalist	C. C. Pinckney	47
	Dem.-Rep.	George Clinton	6

Appendix

Year	Party	Candidate	Vote
1812—Dem.-Rep.		James Madison	128
	Federalist	De Witt Clinton	89
1816—Dem.-Rep.		James Monroe	183
	Federalist	Rufus King	34
1820—Dem.-Rep.		James Monroe	231
	Dem.-Rep.	John Quincy Adams	84
1824—Dem.-Rep.		Andrew Jackson	99
	Coalition	John Quincy Adams	1
	Dem.-Rep.	W. H. Crawford	41
	Dem.-Rep.	Henry Clay	37
1828—Dem.		Andrew Jackson	178
	Nat. Rep.	J. Q. Adams	83
1832—Dem.		Andrew Jackson	219
	Nat. Rep.	Henry Clay	49
	Anti.-Mas.	William Wirt	7
		John Floyd	11
1836—Dem.		Martin Van Buren	170
	Whig	W. H. Harrison	73
	Whig	Daniel Webster	14
	Whig	Hugh L. White	26
	Whig	W. P. Mangum	11
1840—Whig		W. H. Harrison	234
	Dem.	Martin Van Buren	60
	Liberty	James G. Birney	
1844—Dem.		James K. Polk	170
	Whig	Henry Clay	105
	Liberty	J. G. Birney	
1848—Whig		Zachary Taylor	163
	Dem.	Lewis Cass	107
	Free Soil	Martin Van Buren	

Appendix

Year	Party	Candidate	Vote
1852—Dem.		Franklin Pierce	254
	Whig	Winfield Scott	42
	Free Soil	John P. Hale	
1856—Dem.		James Buchanan	174
	Rep.	John C. Frémont	114
	Know Nothings and Whigs	Millard Fillmore	8
1860—Rep.		Abraham Lincoln	180
	Dem.	S. A. Douglas	12
	Sou. Dem.	J. C. Breckinridge	72
	Const. Un.	John Bell	39
1864—Rep.		Abraham Lincoln	216
	Dem.	G. B. McClellan	21
1868—Rep.		Ulysses S. Grant	214
	Dem.	Horatio Seymour	80
1872—Rep.		Ulysses S. Grant	292
	Lib. Rep.	Horace Greeley	
	Dem.	Charles O'Conor	
	Pro.	James Black	
		T. A. Hendricks	42
		B. Gratz Brown	18
		Charles J. Jenkins	2
		David Davis	1
		Not Counted	17
1876—Rep.		R. B. Hayes	185
	Dem.	S. J. Tilden	184
	Greenback	Peter Cooper	
	Pro.	G. C. Smith	
1880—Rep.		James A. Garfield	214
	Dem.	W. S. Hancock	155
	Greenback	James B. Weaver	
	Pro.	Neal Dow	

Appendix

Year	Party	Candidate	Vote
1884—	Dem.	Grover Cleveland	219
	Rep.	James G. Blaine	182
	Pro.	J. P. St. John	
	Gr.-Labor	Benjamin F. Butler	
1888—	Rep.	Benjamin Harrison	233
	Dem.	Grover Cleveland	168
	Pro.	Clinton B. Fisk	
	Union Labor	A. J. Streeter	
	United Labor	Robert H. Cowdrey	
1892—	Dem.	Grover Cleveland	277
	Rep.	Benjamin Harrison	145
	Pop.	James B. Weaver	22
	Pro.	John Bidwell	
	Soc.-Labor	Simon Wing	
1896—	Rep.	William McKinley	276
	Dem.	William J. Bryan ⎫	
	Pop.	William J. Bryan ⎬ 176	
	Silver	William J. Bryan ⎭	
	Nat. Dem.	J. M. Palmer	
	Pro.	J. P. Levering	
	Silver-Pro.	C. I. Bentley	
	Soc.-Labor	C. H. Matchett	
1900—	Rep.	William McKinley	292
	Dem.	William J. Bryan	155
	Pro.	J. G. Woolley	
	Soc.-Dem.	E. V. Debs	
	Soc.-Labor	Fr. Malloney	
	M. R. Pop.	W. Barker	
	Un. Ref.	Seth Ellis	
	Un. Chr.	J. F. R. Leonard	
1904—	Rep.	Theodore Roosevelt	336
	Dem.	A. B. Parker	140
	Pro.	Silas C. Swallow	

Appendix

Year	Party	Candidate	Vote
	Soc.	E. V. Debs	
	Soc.-Labor	C. H. Corregan	
	M. R. Pop.	T. E. Watson	
1908—	Rep.	William H. Taft	321
	Dem.	William J. Bryan	162
	Pro.	E. W. Chafin	
	Soc.	E. V. Debs	
	Soc.-Labor	Aug. Gillhaus	
	People's	T. E. Watson	
	Ind.	T. L. Hisgen	
1912—	Dem.	Woodrow Wilson	435
	Prog.	Theodore Roosevelt	88
	Rep.	William H. Taft	8
	Soc.	E. V. Debs	
	Pro.	E. W. Chafin	
	Soc.-Labor	Arthur Reimer	
1916—	Dem.	Woodrow Wilson	277
	Rep.	Charles E. Hughes	254
	Soc.	Allan L. Benson	
	Pro.	J. Frank Hanly	
	Soc.-Labor	Arthur E. Reimer	
1920—	Rep.	Warren G. Harding	404
	Dem.	J. M. Cox	127
	Soc.	E. V. Debs	
	Farm-Labor	P. P. Christensen	
	Pro.	A. S. Watkins	
	Soc.-Labor	W. W. Cox	
1924—	Rep.	Calvin Coolidge	382
	Dem.	John W. Davis	136
	Ind. Prog.-Soc...	Robert M. La Follette	13

Index

543

Index

Index

546

Index

Index

549

Index

Index

Democratic party—(*Continued*)
Wilson, 378, 407 *et seq.*, 1896 convention, 352, Eighteenth amendment and, 438, 439, electoral commission and, 261, Emancipation Proclamation, 95, 96; finances, 11, 208; first break in, 63; first formal platform adopted, 130 *et seq.*; first national convention, 102; five great divisions of, 274; Force bill and, 305; freedom from corrupt administrations, 240; free-silver issue, 315, 322, 325, 331, 348 *et seq.*; friction under Wilson, 409; fundamental doctrine, 90; full control of government in Cleveland's second administration, 314; germ plasm in constitutional convention of 1787, 15; gold-standard, 352; growing power of, 21 *et seq.*; habits of violent disagreement, 209; handicap of Federal machine, 105; hard times fallacy, 318; Hays-Tilden investigation, 260; hopelessness of 1860 campaign, 198; humiliation of 1836 election, 121; Hunkers, 151 *et seq.*; inability to resist Bryan, 371; indicted by Van Buren, 156; influence under Tyler, 134; intenseness of feeling in 1876 election, 247 *et seq.*; interest in state ticket, 346; importance of Wilson era, 377; impoverished condition of, 353, 458; Jackson's influence on, 88; Jeffersonian identity, 19; lack of leadership in 1856, 180 *et seq.*; lack of unifying issues, 209, 345, 509; liberal nature of, 513; loss of votes through Wilson partisanship, 434; McAdoo nomination battle, 470, 481, 484, 488, *et seq.*; made a minority party through Bryan, 342; majority party until 1896, 342, 343; mass principles, 83, Missouri question, 73, mistake of Wilson's Congress appeal, 433; money plank in 1900, 358, Monroe Doctrine, 50; moral issues in,

509; moral righteousness, 210, 211; name formally adopted, 82, 83, 120; national committeemen, 521 *et seq.*; national committeewomen, 521 *et seq.*; National Democratic wing, 352; near-extinction of, 220; necessity of, 38; negro suffrage (*see* separate item); neutrality plank in 1916, 417; New York victory in 1868, 223; 1904 convention, 362 *et seq.*; 1904 weakness, 366; 1916 Wilson policy, 422; 1924 Congressional elections, 411; 1928 outlook, 506 *et seq.*; nomination tradition broken, 145; odds against since 1896, 345; office-seekers in Wilson administrations, 411; opposed by industrial "interests," 299; opposition to sumptuary laws, 286; origin, 13–26; overwhelming defeat of 1860, 199; platforms (*see* separate item); political mistakes, 507; Polk a "compromise candidate," 144; Polk's accession, 147; popular reaction against, 121; position of Wilson in, 377; power to hold factions, 75; presidential candidates, 525 *et seq.*; pride in Wilson administration, 407; principles, 4, 17 *et seq.*, 21, 38 *et seq.*, 55, 56, 127, 227 *et seq.*, 286, 439; "progressive," 369, 386, 387; prohibition issue, 75, 178, 298, 345, 440, 442; pro-slavery trend, 137; publicity in, 9, 501; "reactionaries," 386, 387; reasons for depleted vitality, 204 *et seq.*; reconstruction criticism, 225; reconstruction dominant in after-war policy, 221; record during Wilson administration, 380, 381; record since the 1860 split, 202 *et seq.*; rejection of Van Buren by, 149; religious issue in 1924, 472; Republican sympathizers in 1896, 349; Republican voters in presidential elections, 215, 343, 373; repudiation of Cleveland, 334 *et seq.*; repudiation of

551

Index

Democratic party—(*Continued*)
principles, 54, 56, 61, 226 *et seq.*,
232, 351; reputation of economic
unsoundness, 344; return of
sound money sympathizers, 356;
reverses of 1839, 126; revival of
economic principles, 238; revived by 1924 exposure of
Republican corruption, 462;
rigid constitutional construc-
tionists, 55; Sackville-West
incident, 300; scope, 6; secession
and, 213, 214, 220; sectional
divisions, 315, 341 *et seq.*; services to nation, 210, 514 *et seq.*;
significance of Monroe administration, 65; slavery and, 65,
71, 74, 123, 139, 147, 164, 178
et seq.; Smith candidacy, 466 *et
seq.*; Smith domination, 510;
Smith-McAdoo candidacy fight
of 1924, 484; "snap" convention
of 1892, 308; Solid South, 10,
231; sound-money faction, 335,
353; sound money issue in 1896
convention, 351; Southern domination, 184; split in 1844, 147;
split in 1860, 192 *et seq.*, 197;
split in 1896, 332; split of 1920,
441; split of 1924, 472; State's
rights doctrine, 51, 227; strength
of latter day organization, 367;
strict construction under Van
Buren, 126; success in Pierce
campaign, 171; sumptuary laws
and, 439; surviving capacity,
3, 237, 368, 512; tariff issue in
1888, 297; tariff policies, 60,
239, 272; Texas annexation a
party issue, 136 *et seq.*; under
Bryan direction, 340; under
Madison, 19 *et seq.*; united in
1912, 404; United States Bank,
and, 56; United States foreign
policy and, 65; unjust defeat of
1876, 262; unsound financial
theories, 207, 315; value of
Harding corruption to, 480;
Van Buren and, 123, 149, 150;
vice-presidential candidates, 530
et seq.; victories (*see* separate
item); weak organization, 211,
374; weakened by growth of
industry, 206 *et seq.*; Wilson's
campaign tour, 385; Wilson
war organization, 379 *et seq.*;
woman suffrage plank of 1916,
417; World war record, 6 *et seq.*;
wrecked by Bryan, 360.

Democratic-Republican party, 14;
and Jacobin-Democrats, 23 *et
seq.*; became known as Democratic party, 81; campaign of
1796, 29; decrease in power
after 1860, 37; feuds of, 44;
forty years of uninterrupted
power, 37; "government by the
people" in theory only, 17;
Jeffersonian conception, 16 *et
seq.*; name officially adopted,
24; relation to anti-Federalist
party, 15; skilful politics, 44.

Denby, Edwin, 478.
Denver, Democratic convention,
of 1908 in, 371.
Denvoy, John, 289.
Dickerson, Daniel S., 195.
Dickinson, Daniel C., 151.
Dickinson, Don M., 333.
Dingley Tariff law, 357.
Direct Election of Senators amend-
ment, 340.
Dix, John A., 151.
Dobbin, of Pierce's cabinet, 173.
Doheny, Edward L., 481, 515, 516;
in oil scandal, 476 *et seq.*;
McAdoo and, 480 *et seq.*
Donahey, Governor Victor, 511.
Donaldson, in Polk campaign, 143.
Doolittle, James R., 224.
Douglas, Stephen A., 168; attitude
toward slavery issue, 173; bal-
lots cast for in 1860, 195, 196,
197; ballots in 1856 convention,
176; candidacy, 164 *et seq.*, 167,
175, 191 *et seq.*; character, 164,
165; debate with Lincoln, 192;
defeat, 199; in the convention
of 1852, 169; nomination, 197;
popular sovereignty doctrine,
192; view of Civil war, 212.
Dred Scott Case, Supreme Court
decision, 186.

Edmunds, George F., 259.
Edwards, Edward I., 451.

552

Index

Eighteenth Amendment, 340, 438, 439, 471, 508.
Eight Hour Day law, 381.
Electoral college, 35; system, 36.
Electoral Commission, 259 *et seq.*; corruption, 260; denunciation, 261; investigation of Hayes-Tilden contest, 260; origin, 259; report, 262; unconstitutionality, 261.
Elk Hills, California, oil lease, 446, 447, 515.
Emancipation Proclamation, 96.
Emergency Fleet Corporation, 429.
England, Buchanan in, 184; relations with Madison, 51; Sackville-West incident, 301; Venezuelan boundary dispute, 326 *et seq.*
English, James E., 224.
English, William H., candidacy, 271; defeat, 272.
"Era of Good Feeling," 59, 70, 71; character of, 63; delusion destroyed, 64.
Everett, Edward, 200.
Exposition, John C. Calhoun, 95.

Fall, Albert B., oil scandal and, 476 *et seq.*, 510, 516.
"Father of the Constitution," 50.
Federalist party, 14, 17, 22, 237; and French Revolution, 23; and Louisiana purchase, 42; campaign of 1796, 29 *et seq.*; causes of defeat, 31 *et seq.*, 56; coalition with Clintonians, 53; fight for power, 25; New York convention, 53; principles of, 16; support of Burr in House, 35; under second Madison administration, 56, 57; wreck of, 31, 34.
Federal Republican party, 59.
Federal Reserve act, 208, 209, 380, 408; McAdoo and, 465.
Federal Trade Commission, 381.
Ferris, Woodbridge N., 493.
Field, Justice Stephen J., 259, 264, 271.
Fifteenth Amendment, 226, 235.
Fillmore, Millard, candidacy in 1856, 182; defeat, 183; succession to Presidency, 163.
Finance, adjustment under Van Buren, 125; attitude of Democrats in regard to Government, 132; disordered condition in Cleveland administrations, 319; Federal Reserve act (*see* separate item); free-silver issue, 321 *et seq.*, 348 *et seq.*; gold and silver issue, 277, 307, 315; gold standard established, 355; McKinley Tariff law, 320; panic of 1837, 125; panic of 1873, 238; panic of 1893, 317, 320; post-Civil war, 225, 226; Sherman Silver Purchase law, 318, 319; World war, 408.
Fitzpatrick, Benjamin, 197.
Flagg, Azariah C., 151.
Forbes, Charles, 478.
Force bill, 304, 305, 306.
Foreign policy, United States, history of, 65 *et seq.*
Foss, Eugene N., 386, 402.
Fourteenth Amendment, 226, 235.
Free-Silver issue, 201, 237, 277, 307, 314, 319, 321 *et seq.*, 348 *et seq.*; Bryan and, 341, 343, 356; Cleveland denounced by sympathizers, 322; Democratic party and, 325, 348 *et seq.*; heresy, 315; importance of, 325; in 1896 campaign, 333, 355; influence on Democratic party, 325, 330; legislation, 315; National Silver party, 349; Populist party and, 349; Prohibition party, 349; refused as issue in 1904; sound money struggle, 315, 321.
Free Soil party, 171, 264; antislavery platform, 154; convention, 156, 157; Democratic convention of 1848 and, 155; deserted by Van Buren element, 164; nomination of Van Buren, 137, 157; origin in Barnburners, 155; platform, 157; slavery stand, 158.
France, relations with Madison, 51.
Frelinghuysen, Frederick T., 259.

553

Index

Frémont, John Charles, candidacy, 182; nomination, 215.
French Revolution, American neutrality, 23.
Freneau, popular leader, 24.

Garfield, James A., 259, 282; assassination, 281; candidacy, 268; character attacked in campaign of 1880, 271; election, 272.
Garfield, Harry A., 429.
Gay, Sydney Howard, 51.
Geneva, League of Nations in, 456.
Gerard, James W., 451.
Germany, war with, 426.
Gifford, Walter S., 429.
Glass, Carter, 451, 493; McAdoo support, 446; on League of Nations, 443.
Globe, Washington, 106.
Glynn, Martin H., 416.
Godfrey, Dr. Hallis, 429.
Gold standard, 320; and silver issue, 277; assailed by Bryan, 333; denounced by Democrats, 348, 350; established, 355; "hard money" basis, 125; Republican party and, 349; struggle for, 316.
Gompers, Samuel, 429.
Gorman, Arthur P., 278, 285, 297, 304, 308, 309, 361, 366, 368; candidacy, 306; Cleveland and fight against Wilson tariff, 329; desertion of Cleveland, 306; firmness of group in opposition to Wilson law, 330.
Government, ability to enforce laws, 51; Alien and Sedition acts, 33; aristocracy of early leaders, 18 *et seq.*; "by the people" in name only, 83; corruption of Harding administration, 478 *et seq.*; corruption of 1924 issue, 492; debates over centralized, 14 *et seq.*; Democratic control of 1912, 406; Democratic idea of Federal, 131; Democratic principles, 61; Democratic-Republican direction of, 17; efficiency of a Republican, 18; ex-presidents, 48, 49; Federalist *vs.* Jeffersonian conception, 16; Federal offices of, 104; finances of Federal, 125; financial instability in Harrison administration, 320; Hamilton-Jefferson feud, 25; inability to enforce prohibition, 508; national convention originated, 108; need for liberal party, 513 *et seq.*; negro amendments, 228 *et seq.*; oil lease annulments, 478; power of Federal, 32, 33, 55, 76; protection of negro suffrage, 222; recovery of oil leases, 516; Republican dominance in, 280, 281; restriction on early national, 22; restrictions on negro suffrage, 230; rights of Federal, in regard to slavery, 139; rights of people in presidential elections, 102; silver coinage, 322; silver forces fight to control, 277; States' rights (*see* separate item); strength proved by Tilden-Hayes contest, 249; territorial, 173, 179; treatment of South after Civil war, 212; under Madison, 50; unequaled record of Jefferson, 48.
Grady, Thomas F., 284.
Grant, Ulysses S., 249; cooperation in Republican strategy of 1876, 253 *et seq.*; election of 1868, 222; letter to General Harry White, 243; nomination, 225; opposed by Liberal Republicans, 234; popularity, 233; reelection, 236; telegram to Sherman, 255; third term movement, 243, 244.
Grant administration, corruption denounced by Democratic party, 240, 241, 242; reconstruction policy, 234; resentment against, 238; scandals of, 281.
Gray, Judge George, 371, 372.
Grayson, Admiral Cary T., 437.
Greeley, Horace, 266; defeat, 236; nominated by Democrats, 235; nomination by Liberal Republicans, 234; spokesman of Liberal Republicans, 234.
Greenback party, 282; free-silver issue, 349.
Griswold, B. Howell, Jr., 495.

554

Index

Index

557

Index

Index

Index

Index

563

Index

Index

Watterson, Colonel, 261; on supposed election of Tilden, 251; on Tilden, 266, 267.

Webster, Daniel, 100; bank issue and, 100; campaign of 1836, 115; support of Clay's slavery resolutions, 163.

Weekly, Harvey's, 384, 390.

Westcott, John W., 417.

Wheeler, Burton K., 478.

Wheeler, William A., election, 262; nomination, 244.

Whig party, 162, 191, 221, 235, 237; campaigns, 133, 171, 182; decay, 171; decline of power under Tyler, 134; hatred of Van Buren, 159; Henry Clay and, 81, 99, 138; lack of organization, 129; opposition tactics, 115, 122; platforms, 147, 188; power under Van Buren, 126; slavery avoided as an issue, 164.

White, George, 458.

White, General Harry, letter from Grant, 242, 243.

White, Hugh L., 115, 116.

Whitney, William C., 309; campaign leader for Cleveland, 311 *et seq.*

Willard, Daniel, 429.

Wilmot, David, 148.

Wilmot Proviso, 147 *et seq.*, Buchanan and, 184; condemned, 156; principle of, 148.

Wilson, Woodrow, 6, 92, 296, 329, 331, 343; accomplishments, 377, 455; attacked by Roosevelt, 420; attitude toward prohibition, 299; Bryan and, 393; Bryan eulogy of, 417; campaign tour, 385; candidacy, 383, 385 *et seq.*; career, 377; character, 409 *et seq.*, 436, 455; collapse in 1919, 378; criticism of, 430, 433; devoted following of, 409, 455, 456; election, 211, 405; enduring influence, 49; enemies of, 455, 456; European tour, 434; fight with Jersey bosses, 384; foreign policy an issue in 1916, 420; free-silver policy, 324, 325; governor of New Jersey, 384; hostility to, 408, 409; Hughes and, 419, 428;

influence on 1920 convention, 437 *et seq.*, 454; leadership, 123, 378, 382, 407 *et seq.*, 437; League of Nations and, 434, 455; letters, 390; McAdoo and, 465; nomination in 1912, 136, 378, 391, 400, 402; opposition to bi-partisan cabinet, 427; opposition to prohibition, 438, 439; party domination by, 378; peace policy, 418, 426; personality, 377 *et seq.*; physical breakdown, 434; politics indicted, 433; politics of, 409; popularity, 403; position in world history, 376 *et seq.*; praised by Glynn, 416; pre-convention campaign of 1912, 389; reaction against, 457; Reed and, 449; renomination, 415 *et seq.*; state clubs, 389; submarine policy, 415; success, 368; uncompromising spirit, 410; unprecedented majority election, 405; veto of Volstead act, 440; victory in 1912, 383; victory in 1916, 424.

Wilson administration, 7, 10, 274, 315, 407 *et seq.*; accomplishments, 412, 413; charges against, 413, 414; control of 1920 convention, 443; denounced by Republicans, 420; effect on business, 408; efficient war organization of, 408; eventful nature of 437, executive efficiency of, 382, 408; failure of League of Nations, 378; Federal Reserve Act, 208, 209; foreign policy, 414; Franklin D. Roosevelt in, 453; freedom from outside domination, 411; legislation during, 380, 381; Mexican crisis, 414; mistaken politics of, 433; nonpartisan policy during war, 430; peace treaty failure, 378; proof of efficiency of Democratic party, 407, 408; reforms during, 381, 382, 455; uniqueness of, 377; World war pacifism, 414 *et seq.*; World war policy, 426 *et seq.*

Wilson-Lodge conflict, 93.

Wilson Tariff law, 328.

567